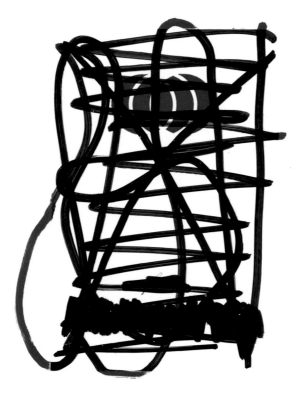

322.440952 B55p
Bix, Herbert P.
Peasant protest in Japan,
1590-1884

DATE	ISSUED TO
21JUL95 NEH Summer Inst./MacWilliam	

322.440952 B55p
Bix, Herbert P.
Peasant protest in Japan,
 1590-1884

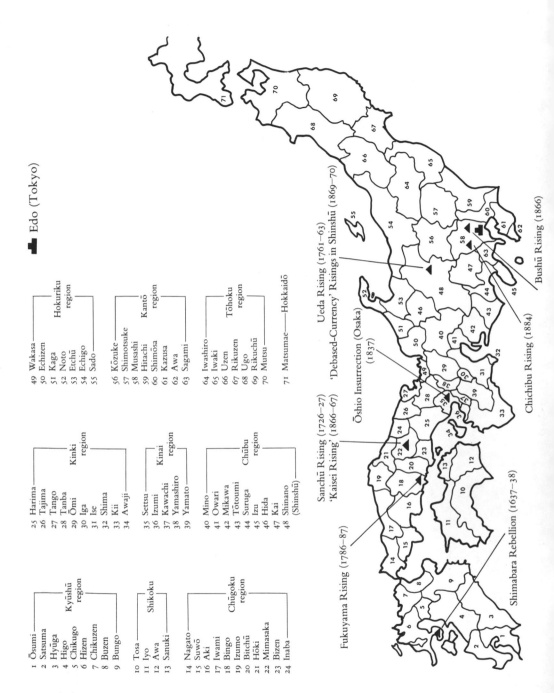

Edo (Tokyo)

1 Ōsumi
2 Satsuma
3 Hyūga
4 Higo } Kyūshū region
5 Chikugo
6 Hizen
7 Chikuzen
8 Buzen
9 Bungo

10 Tosa
11 Iyo } Shikoku
12 Awa
13 Sanuki

14 Nagato
15 Suwō
16 Aki
17 Iwami
18 Bingo } Chūgoku region
19 Izumo
20 Bitchū
21 Hōki
22 Mimasaka
23 Bizen
24 Inaba

25 Harima
26 Tajima
27 Tango
28 Tanba } Kinki region
29 Ōmi
30 Iga
31 Ise
32 Shima
33 Kii
34 Awaji

35 Settsu
36 Izumi
37 Kawachi } Kinai region
38 Yamashiro
39 Yamato

40 Mino
41 Owari
42 Mikawa
43 Tōtoumi
44 Suruga } Chūbu region
45 Izu
46 Hida
47 Kai
48 Shinano (Shinshū)

49 Wakasa
50 Echizen
51 Kaga
52 Noto } Hokuriku region
53 Etchū
54 Echigo
55 Sado

56 Kōzuke
57 Shimotsuke
58 Musashi
59 Hitachi } Kantō region
60 Shimōsa
61 Kazusa
62 Awa
63 Sagami

64 Iwashiro
65 Iwaki
66 Uzen
67 Rikuzen } Tōhoku region
68 Ugo
69 Rikuchū
70 Mutsu

71 Matsumae—Hokkaidō

Fukuyama Rising (1786–87)

Sanchū Rising (1726–27)
'Kaisei Rising' (1866–67)

'Debased-Currency' Risings in Shinshū (1869–70)

Ueda Rising (1761–63)

Ōshio Insurrection (Osaka) (1837)

Chichibu Rising (1884)

Bushū Rising (1866)

Shimabara Rebellion (1637–38)

Peasant Protest in Japan, 1590–1884

HERBERT P. BIX

YALE UNIVERSITY PRESS

New Haven and London

Designed by James J. Johnson
and set in Monophoto Bembo Roman by
Asco Trade Typesetting Ltd. Hong Kong
Printed in the United States of America by
BookCrafters, Inc., Chelsea, Michigan.

Library of Congress Cataloging-in-Publication Data

Bix, Herbert P.
    Peasant protest in Japan, 1590–1884.

    Bibliography: p.
    Includes index.
        1. Peasantry—Japan—Political activity—History.
2. Peasant uprisings—Japan—History.
3. Japan—Social conditions—1600–1868. I. Title.
HD1339.J3B59 1986   322.4′4′0952   85-17889
ISBN 0-300-03485-7 (alk. paper)

10 9 8 7 6 5 4 3 2 1

To Toshie, my in-laws, and my father, for waiting patiently

Contents

List of Illustrations   ix

Acknowledgments   xi

Introduction: Journey into the Past   xiii

Notes on the Text   xxxix

Part I   Defeat: The Onset of Feudal Decline   1

1. Class Structure and Dynamics in Seventeenth-Century Tsuyama   3
2. The Coming Conflict: Taxes, Competition, and Reform   20
3. The Sanchū Rising of 1726–1727   31
4. Epilogue: Tsuyama after 1727   51

Part II   Forward Again: Readjusting the Social Contract   55

5. Historical Setting in Eighteenth-Century Ueda   57
6. A Decade of Polarization, 1751–1761   65
7. Prologue and Periodization of the Ueda Hōreki Rising, 1761–1763   73
8. Results and Aftermath   102

Part III   Reaction: Social Developments of the Late Eighteenth Century   107

9. The Crisis of Tenmei   109
10. The Tenmei Rising in Fukuyama, 1786–1787   114
11. Dealing In the Landlords: The Kansei Reforms and Fukuyama Fief, 1790–1805   127

Part IV   Transition to a New Order: Class Conflicts up to the Late
          Nineteenth Century   135

12. Problems of Interpretation   137
13. Conflict and Social Change, 1800–1873   149
14. The Kaisei Rising in Tsuyama, 1866–1867   174
15. The Debased-Currency Risings in Shinshū, 1869–1870   194
16. Results and Conclusion   215

Notes   229
Era Names   259
Glossary   261
Bibliography   271
Index   285

Illustrations

MAPS

Locations of Major Peasant Uprisings   Frontispiece
1. Outbreaks of Ikki by Province, 1590–1867   xxiv
2. Tsuyama: A 100,000-Koku Fief, Showing the District Boundaries
    of Its District Headmen in 1698   16
3. Ueda: A 53,000-Koku Fief within Shinshū (Shinano)   61
4. Fukuyama: A 100,000-Koku Fief in Bingo Province with Its
    Territorial Boundaries in the 1780s   117

FIGURES

1. Breakdown of 3,001 Peasant Risings between 1590 and 1871 and
    Their Seven Main Forms   xxi
2. Changes in Forms of Peasant Risings (hyakushō ikki) in Different
    Periods   xxii
3. A Simplified Chart of Official Positions: The Matsudaira Family's
    Rural Chain of Command in Tsuyama Fief, 1698–1727   17
4. A Simplified Chart of Official Positions: The Rural Chain of
    Command in Ueda Fief during the 1740s   63

TABLES

1. Rice Tribute Payments in Tsuyama Fief   21
2. Leaders of the Kaisei Rising in Tsuyama   178

3. Class Composition in Terms of Landholdings in the Western
Branch of Yukishige Village, Tōhokujō District   179
4. Holdings and Occupations of People Who Were Arrested after
the First Wave of Rioting Subsided in the Matsushiro Rising,
1870   207–208

Acknowledgments

Both the themes of this book and the research for it were developed over a long period of time. It began in discussions during 1978 with Nakamura Masanori, Sasaki Junnosuke, and Yokoyama Toshio. After launching the project, I visited Ueda City, Nagano. There, for two days, I enjoyed the hospitality of Yokoyama Toshio, who provided me with expert comment on the problems involved in doing research on peasant risings. At a later stage of research, he also arranged for my visit to Yubara, Okayama, where I met many students of local history. My special gratitude is due to those local historians, mentioned individually by name (in the text and in the introductions to the notes) on whose work I drew to reconstruct actual historical events.

Upon completing the first draft of part two, Sasaki Junnosuke gave me criticisms that helped deepen the analysis. During the last stage of preparation, Teodor Shanin read and commented on a chapter of the manuscript. Both he and James C. Scott also allowed me to quote from their own unpublished work. Esther Murata of TBS-Britannica Company typed the entire first draft.

The final text reflects the searching, constructive comments of Frank Baldwin, John W. Dower, James C. Scott, and an anonymous reader for Yale University Press. Each of them contributed to improving the final product in many ways.

Ōkubo Genji showed me the way in Tokugawa history, and my deepest intellectual debt is to him. Despite his own busy schedule, he always gave unstintingly of his time to talk over problems and instruct me in the translation of difficult materials. His advice and moral support over many years saved me from countless errors of fact and analysis. My hope is that this book is worthy of his friendship and instruction.

My wife, to whom this volume is dedicated, prepared the glossary and maps. Much more than that, however, she has always been my greatest source of encouragement and help in whatever projects I have undertaken.

Needless to say, responsibility for any errors or aberrant interpretations that remain in the text is mine alone.

Introduction
Journey into the Past: Class, State and Peasant Revolt

In the period before World War II, scholarly writing by Westerners on Japan centered largely on its great tradition of elite politics and high culture. Interest in the vast majority who were peasants and workers was slow to develop. The first icebreaking study was Hugh Borton's monograph *Peasant Uprisings in Japan of the Tokugawa Period*, which appeared in 1938. It at least furnished some information on peasant protests where little had existed before. But Borton never developed his peasant studies further.[1] In 1940 E. H. Norman published *Japan's Emergence as a Modern State*. By placing peasants in the context of a rich, complex social and political life, Norman became the major Western pioneer of Japanese peasant studies and social history. But although he wrote insightfully and suggested how to view popular struggles, Norman did not delve deeply into any particular incident.

In the decade after Norman's pioneering work, Japan studies in the United States and Britain was reconstituted along cold-war, anti-Marxist lines. In Japan, scholars opened themselves to all currents of thought and continued to search the Tokugawa record, as they had begun to do during the 1920s and 1930s, for the light it could shed on the roots of their own tradition of democratic struggle. The focus of Japanese historians was on conflict and change, and it invariably included critical analysis of the feudal legacy and the fatal flaws in the Meiji Restoration. But in the West the pendulum swung sharply away from such concerns and from the earlier critique of Japan's feudal past and Restoration. It became the task of intellectuals to present the "new Japan" as a success story. In keeping with the new scholarly fashion, the Tokugawa legacy of the period from 1600 to about 1868 was reinterpreted as a positive story of bureaucratic, institutional, and economic success under benevolent samurai rule. This recasting of the Japanese past was conducted in the United States and elsewhere under the banner of "modernization studies," which purported to be "value free." [2] Modernization concepts and assumptions, however, derived in large part from American state ideology, whose construction of the past meshed nicely with the needs of American foreign policy.

In 1959, when modernization studies were at an early stage, Thomas C. Smith published *The Agrarian Origins of Modern Japan*. His book furnished information on the minority population in seventeenth-century villages and tried to account for the emergence of landlord-tenant relations. Smith observed insightfully that "deep beneath the everyday appearance of propriety and friendliness there were in many Japanese villages suppressed hatreds that merely needed some shock, some momentary lapse of customary restraint to send them boiling to the surface." [3] But his history, despite its discussion of "Political Conflict in Villages," was at one with the emerging modernization orthodoxy, for he made the market the main motor of historical change while downplaying the role of tribute exploitation and class conflict.

During the 1960s, a comfortable consensus prevailed among American academics specializing on Japan. They were virtually unanimous in believing that modernization, bureaucratization, the actions of governing elites, and the speed of Japan's post-Restoration transformation should be the main areas of historical concern. What emerged in studies during that decade was a distorted picture of how power worked in the prewar state and an uncritical celebration of productivity growth and political consensus under Tokugawa rule. Inevitably, the recurring conflicts between peasants and lords, later workers and capitalists, were either excluded or treated as mere peripheral phenomena.

In the 1970s the modernization line continued among conservative historians of the Tokugawa period. They steadfastly ignored social history, concentrating instead on issues of demographic change and early modern productivity growth. Other historians, however, sought to supplement such efforts by going beyond modernization in order to account for the human costs, lost opportunities, and paths not taken in Japan's transition to the modern world. They represented a revisionist current in historical studies fertilized eclectically by the anthropology of Clifford Geertz and the historical sociology of E. P. Thompson and the French structuralists.

Within this revisionist current, the contributions to the interpretation of peasant conflict have been registered mainly in such collections of essays as *Japanese Thought in the Tokugawa Period: Methods and Metaphor* (1978) and, most recently, *Conflict in Modern Japanese History: The Neglected Tradition* (1982). These essays tend to place the analytical focus on consciousness and (through an essay by Irwin Scheiner) introduce the notion of the exemplary martyr, or *gimin*, as found in the work of Yokoyama Toshio.[4] But such discussions of conflict in Japanese history seem too preoccupied with consciousness, meaning, discourse, ideas, and their symbolic modes of expression. The historians working in this tradition avoid the problem of class contradiction and invariably consider ideas independently of the material and historical contexts from which they derive their import.

My intention is to move the discussion away from conventional presentations of the Japanese past, in a different direction, and to do so by concentrating more on the actual events and definite historical contexts which are the foundations of any symbolic discourse. By proceeding through a series of case studies of conflict episodes in different periods and regions of Japan, we shall place the struggle process and the distribution side of feudal economic development at the center of the analysis. Once that is done, the development of peasant consciousness—that is, those beliefs that are always a constituent part of collective actions—can be discussed historically, over a time span of centuries, and without falling into the pitfalls of excessive abstractness and idealism that mar the work of the revisionists. Most important, the crucial problem of the beliefs of the ruled can then be discussed in relation to questions of class structure, economic growth, bureaucratic organization, and state power.

This book seeks to explain, then, the causes of Japanese peasant protests, the various ways they were waged, and the ideas of right and justice that underlay them. But its themes and method of approach eschew any narrow parochialism of Japan. The aim throughout is to be of interest to the general reader and to historians and sociologists of other countries and periods. To attain these multiple objectives the stage must be carefully prepared. In what follows, we shall define, very briefly, certain key terms, discuss the characteristic types of protests that occurred, and indicate statistically the broad trends in the main conflict between lords and peasants over the course of the Tokugawa period. Preparation for our particular type of journey into the past also requires an understanding of the power networks in which Japanese peasants were entwined at the state and village levels. We shall accomplish that by identifying the main characteristics of the feudal state and specifying its relationship to the Tokugawa village. Once these steps have been completed, we can introduce a key concept for understanding the problem of peasant consciousness and go on to outline the structure of the book.

KEY TERMS

To sketch the social history of feudal society and the role of conflict in its transformation is to commit oneself to certain claims concerning a number of controversial social science terms. Words like *social class* and *status*, *exploitation*, *tribute*, and *feudalism* appear throughout this book. They are the tools of its construction. Although there will never be complete agreement about them, ideally they should be defined precisely and analyzed at length.[5] Instead, I have chosen to keep the definitions summarily short and relatively unproblematic, despite the terms' difficulty.

The concepts I have found useful for the tasks at hand were developed and refined largely within the Marxist tradition of historiography. The first of them, *class*, refers to relations of economic exploitation and unequal power among different social groups within the social structure. Conceptually, class means exploitation and nonreciprocal social relations. Larger economic, political, and cultural phenomena are its constituent elements and defining characteristics. In addition, a psychological bonding element, arising out of class antagonisms, is involved in setting approximate boundaries for class. (Marx registered this complicated relationship between thought and action in class conflict by distinguishing, in Hegelian fashion, "class in itself" from self-conscious "class for itself.")[6]

To resume: social class is a concept that denotes the relationships among social groups that are definite structural components of—or social formations within—a society. These social formations are hierarchically ordered and dynamic (that is, historical in nature). They are also major agents of change in their own right. At the same time, the class relationship implies the practice of exploitation and the struggle against it.

Generally speaking, the polar classes in any form of class society—the minority who control the appropriation of society's wealth and the vast majority who produce it—can be determined easily enough. In Tokugawa society these were the samurai and the peasants. The samurai were part of a ruling class, which determined the general conditions under which all subordinate classes labored. They established and forced upon peasants and others the mechanisms of surplus labor extraction.

But over time Tokugawa class relationships changed, as did the content of the classes themselves. When the specificity of classes in Tokugawa society is examined carefully, all sorts of differences emerge among peasants, merchants, artisans, and samurai. We shall see numerous instances in the course of this study in which poor and rich peasants, as well as town and rural merchants, found themselves on different sides during protests. We shall also observe the precarious foothold that the top stratum of peasants had within the samurai rural administrative structure. And we shall find very low-ranking samurai, whose level of subsistence was little different from that of poor peasants, sometimes identifying (sympathetically but passively) with them during protests. However, issues of class location, stratification, and classification enter into our narrative only when they are directly relevant to explaining actual instances of overt class struggle. The same holds for legally ascribed status, which reflected society's self-image. As will be shown in the first half of this study, Tokugawa society was as much a status as a class society. And in the determination of both class and status, the state was a common overriding element. Hereditary statuses, ascribed by the wielders of state power, had some degree of shaping effect on class relations and, in turn, were shaped by those same class relations in all periods of Tokugawa history. But economic distinctions of class increasingly asserted themselves from the second half of the eighteenth century onward. So we may say that as commodity economy and manufacture developed, the degree of peasant "classness" tended to increase while their "statusness" decreased. During the first half of the nineteenth century, the status system and status ideology slowly began to break down. As that happened, social groups appeared that had "dropped out," or that no longer classified themselves (or could be classified) according to the old status ascriptions.

Another prefatory remark that must be made concerns the relationship between class and class consciousness. In Tokugawa class struggles, peasants did not always define their interests in militant class terms. Such a consciousness was not necessary for the development of their struggles. As one writer observed, "Classes have frequently existed whose members did not 'identify their antagonistic interests' in any process of common clarification or struggle. Indeed it is probable that for most of historical time this was the rule rather than the exception."[7] But the absence of a high degree (or indeed *any* degree) of class consciousness did not mean that resistance was exercised without consciousness. On the contrary, it is more than likely that the ideological struggle was being waged continuously. Given the shortcomings of the historical record, however, we can discern it only indirectly, through scrutiny of daily religious and symbolic practices, through examination of language and speech, or by studying actual demands raised by peasants and others in the course of countering oppression.

The next term requiring comment, *exploitation*, is also intimately related to class and class struggle. The *Encyclopaedia of the Social Sciences* derives it from "the idea ... that some individuals, groups or classes benefit unjustly and unfairly from the labor of or at the expense of others."[8] The idea of morally selfish and unjust action is certainly one side of the problem. The other is the idea of "surplus," which Marx captured by defining exploitation as "the appropriation of the unpaid labor of others" and "unpaid surplus labor" (*Capital*, vol. 3).

For our purposes three points should be noted. First, exploitation, like class, underscores the close connection between fact and value—their mutual interdependence—in the understanding and explanation of reality. Exploitation needs to be defined therefore both from the side of the social relations of production and from the side of the distribution wealth and power. In the latter case, the historical and moral dimensions, or the psychology and "feelings of the oppressed," are primary.[9] We shall be studying numerous examples of how peasants and others from whom tributes were extracted came to feel their exploitation unjust and to protest against it.

Second, the main relationship of exploitation in Tokugawa Japan was between peasant producers and the samurai wielders of state power. It involved the forcible extraction of ground rent and corvées. Lords used these and other forms of exploitation to consolidate their territorial domains and to enable their retainers to live without engaging in productive labor.

Third, "tribute" or "rice tribute" (nengu) is used throughout this study because of the peculiar political situation and social environment in which Tokugawa peasants lived out their lives. This use is also impelled by the fact that the Tokugawa state originally took shape as a type of failed conquest state which turned inward and battened on the peasant population. Tax or village tax is too modern and broad a term to fit this situation and will be avoided hereafter except where reasons of style dictate otherwise. Furthermore, annual tributes implied rent and state tax since the feudal lord was both the nominal owner of land and the governor of the domain. As time went on, peasants paid both tribute to lords and rent to landlords in various forms. But an enduring feature of the entire Tokugawa era was the joining of economic exploitation and political rule "in the same hands."[10]

That particular fusion of the economic and the political leads to our last key term, feudalism. Tokugawa society was essentially a type of feudal society—that is, one in which the main production relationship was between a military, landowning class and a subject peasantry. In such a society political sovereignty was fragmented in distinctive ways. Ground rent, in the form of tributes and corvée services, constituted virtually the whole of peasant surplus labor. And the warrior ruling class controlled the production process from the outside, depriving all ruled classes of the freedom to move about and alienate their labor power under conditions of their own choosing. The following pages will describe the details of such a society.

THE FORMS OF PROTEST

Turning from issues of terminology, let us introduce next the forms of protest we shall be studying. When feudal authorities confronted them with life-threatening crises, peasants responded pluralistically. Sometimes they resigned themselves to conditions that appeared inevitable, or they internalized their problems and did nothing. But when their options allowed and they could draw on a supportive past, many acted. Peasants protesting collectively usually began in accordance with legal procedures. When petitions failed, they would escalate their protests over a period of time, turning them into full-scale risings in which some peasants invariably died for the common good. These risings are called *ikki*, a term we shall tentatively define as public protests in rural areas involving significant numbers of armed people.

A typical ikki usually unfolded through successive stages. These included an initial, short, preparatory stage, noted by the designation "unrest" (*fuon*) or even "disturbance" (*sōdō*). In the process, some villages might seek redress of grievances through legal appeal or petition (*shūso*); others might take flight (*chōsan*). Simultaneously, instances of illegal appeal to higher levels of authority (*osso*), sometimes outside the fief itself, would appear once the situation burst into a full-fledged forceful appeal (*gōso*), that is, an ikki involving the entire fief, often accompanied by "house-smashing" (*uchikowashi*).

Thus we may say that the institutionalized forms of peasant struggles were often combined in practice. None of these active protest forms was unique to Japan. Petition to higher authority, flight, and house-smashing can all be found in the class struggle histories of many other peasant societies. The different struggle forms changed as the Tokugawa political economy developed; no change was more significant than the numerical increase in incidents of house-smashing, or uchikowashi. Uchikowashi was a traditional sanction in the form of total or partial property destruction levied on individuals considered guilty of intolerable social abuses. As a tactic and method of punishment, it was a disciplined action, seldom accompanied by looting and stealing or by physical harm to those being punished. House-smashing also went along with a keen sense of righteousness and, sometimes, a distinctive organizational structure.

Interestingly, many of these characteristics of punishment by property destruction can also be seen in the class struggle history of Russian peasants. The Russian peasant counterpart to the uchikowashi was *razobran*, which meant "to take apart." [11] Razobran was the disciplined sanction of taking apart rural noble estates, destroying their warehouses, and carting away their grain and fodder for equal division among peasant households. Usually, everything else would be left intact and the owners unmolested. When Russian peasants wanted to rid the area of the noble household, they would burn the estate to the ground. This was called, picturesquely, putting the "red cock to the roof" or the "red rooster." [12] The Japanese uchikowashi differed from Russian practice mainly in being more ritualized and specialized, particularly in the tools that peasants used to inflict degrees of house destruction.

Uchikowashi against merchants, village headmen and their assistants, and samurai officials characterized the protest actions of peasants through different stages of the fiscal and political decline of the Tokugawa state. But from the last quarter of the eighteenth century, they became particularly frequent. This rising trend of punitive property destruction (in connection with disputes at the village and district levels within fiefs) reflected an important structural development in the Tokugawa economy. This was the growth of a class of marginally situated people in villages and towns who were chronically in debt, probably propertyless, and perhaps barely able to provide for their daily physical subsistence.

Anti-Marxist scholarship on the history of the Tokugawa economy dutifully conjures away this problem of the poor.[13] Yet it was there, generated by the socioeconomic conditions of Tokugawa society. One factor was the steady commercialization of the rice-based economy. Another was the tendency for tributes and corvées to increase as a result of feudal administrative reforms. But the most historically important factor behind the growth of house-smashing incidents was the increase in the power of landlord families over the course of the eighteenth and nineteenth centuries. Landlords amassed the pawned land of large numbers of minute cultivators, who had been forced down into the status of tenants. Although landlords secured their tenants by contracts, which often specified strict payments of fixed (that is, non-interest bearing) tenant fees and punishments for violations, the landlord-tenant relationship was disguised by paternalism. Its chief effects were not only to place tenants in a new status relationship within the village but also to subject them to the dual exploitation of tenant rents and feudal tributes.

Thus, for a significant minority of the Tokugawa population, class was coming to be based on a nonfeudal relationship—one that was disguised and restrained by village customs, feudal laws, and the whole ensemble of institutions that composed a system of moral economy. Behind changes in the form of peasant struggles between 1590 and 1884, however, there clearly lay the growth of landlord-tenant relations. By studying the forms of protest, we can simultaneously address the relationship between state power and the class forces under construction in village society.

The protest forms that we shall be concerned with in this book are indicated in figures 1 and 2. They are the results of the work of historian Yokoyama Toshio, as revised by Yamanaka Kiyotaka. Yokoyama drew on the pioneering statistical work and chronology of Aoki Kōji in order to make charts that illustrate the slow but steady escalation in risings of all kinds starting from the second decade of the eighteenth century. Aoki's statistics (revised up to 1974) showed that Tokugawa Japan experienced 488 urban riots, 3,189 village disturbances, and as many as 3,212 peasant ikki.[14] Yokoyama revised these figures downward by eliminating hundreds of incidents that were either minor or unclear in nature. The result was a

FIGURE 1. Breakdown of 3,001 Peasant Risings between 1590 and 1871 and Their Seven Main Forms

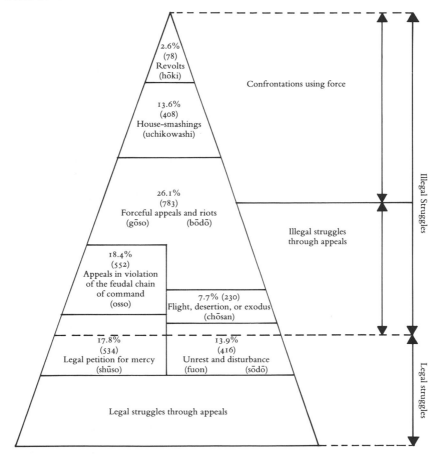

Source: Based on chart 1 in Yokoyama Toshio, *Hyakushō ikki to gimin denshō* (Tokyo, 1977), p. 38, as revised by Yamanaka Kiyotaka, "Hyakushō ikki no jidaisei to chiikisei," *Rekishi kōron,* June 1978, p. 52. I added "disturbance" (*sōdō*) to the category of "unrest" and "riot" (*bōdō*) to "forceful appeals." In both cases the reality behind the different terms was usually the same. The broken line drawn above the base and through the pyramid indicates the overlap and continuity—the indeterminate boundary— between legal and illegal struggles.

FIGURE 2. Changes in Forms of Peasant Risings (hyakushō ikki) in Different Periods

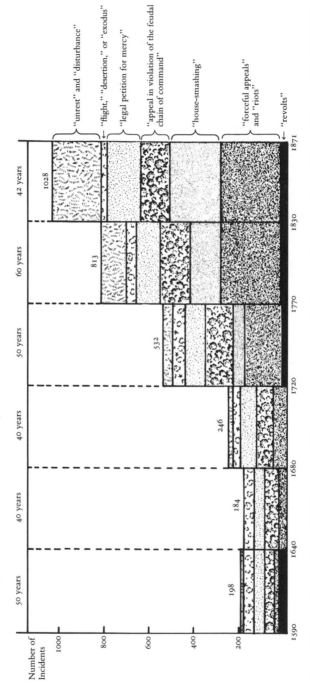

Source: Yokoyama Toshio, *Hyakushō ikki to gimin denshō* (Tokyo, 1977), as reproduced in Yamanaka Kiyotaka, "Hyakushō ikki no jidaisei to chiikisei," *Rekishi kōron*, June 1978, p. 55.

reduced figure of 2,750 peasant ikki between 1590, when Toyotomi Hideyoshi unified the country, and 1867, when the Tokugawa regime was finally overthrown. Adding another 251 incidents for the tumultuous years of the early Meiji Restoration, 1868 to 1871, Yokoyama then arrived at a new total of 3,001 ikki.

Using this provisional figure, Yokoyama next divided the incidents into seven categories according to their ramifying effects on society. To the 78 revolts (hōki) occurring between 1590 and 1871—most of which were samurai-led rebellions of the very early seventeenth century and the late 1860s and 1870s—he assigned the highest social and political weight. To cases of legal petition for mercy or fair treatment, exodus or desertion from villages and fiefs, and unrest, he gave the lowest weight.

The greatest proportion of all illegal struggles was composed of forceful appeals (gōso) and riots (bōdō), often accompanied by house-smashings (uchikowashi) and appeals to higher authority in violation of the feudal chain of command (osso). Over the long run, these types of protest action had the most political influence on society and the state. When Japanese historians refer to ikki, it is usually violent appeals, riots, and house-smashing that they have in mind.

By using Yokoyama's charts and examining the sites of the 3,001 incidents, we learn further that most peasant risings occurred in two regions spanning the length of the three main islands of Honshū, Shikoku, and Kyūshū. As indicated in map 1, the spawning grounds of protest were nine provinces stretching from the northeast through the central mountain region and eight western provinces spanning the Chūgoku region down to Shikoku. The smallest number of risings (nineteen or fewer) occurred mainly in three regions: the southwestern part of Kyūshū, Owari province, and parts of the Kinai and Hokuriku where, as Yamanaka speculates, there was high grain production and relatively more systematic and all-pervasive political repression.[15]

Since causes are assigned more easily to events than nonevents, and provinces where social upheavals seldom occurred have not been well studied, one can only speculate as to why some areas and not others experienced them. Generally speaking, where the political context was ripe and an acute crisis situation existed, risings tended to break out. In such situations a combination of factors was present. These factors included high levels of exploitation and the existence of clearly identifiable targets such as village officials, merchants, or landlords, who acted as agents of the government and were hated because of their glaring defiance of community norms. Also, many high-conflict areas had known past instances of collective protest that left behind, in some localities, all-embracing traditions of human sacrifice and the possibility of exposure to them in times of crisis. The traditions and practice of dramatic human sacrifice, of people victimized on behalf of their village com-

MAP 1. Outbreaks of Ikki by Province, 1590–1867

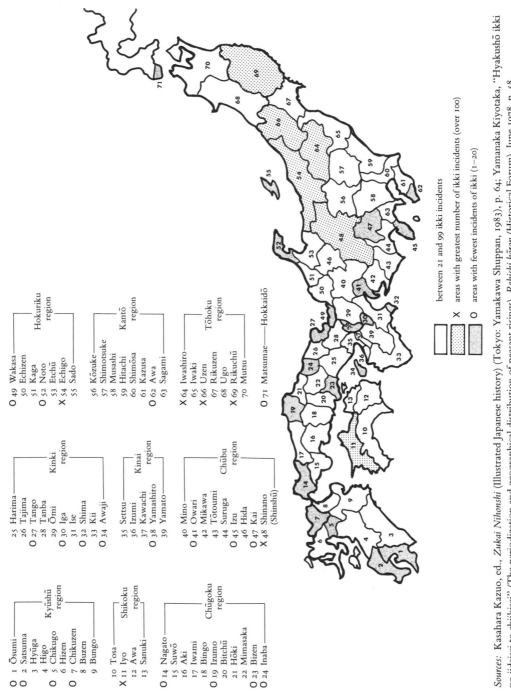

O 1 Ōsumi
O 2 Satsuma
   3 Hyūga
O 4 Higo ⎱ Kyūshū
O 5 Chikugo ⎰ region
O 6 Hizen
O 7 Chikuzen
   8 Buzen
   9 Bungo

   10 Tosa
X 11 Iyo ⎱ Shikoku
   12 Awa ⎰ region
   13 Sanuki

O 14 Nagato
   15 Suwō
   16 Aki
   17 Iwami
   18 Bingo ⎱ Chūgoku
O 19 Izumo ⎰ region
   20 Bitchū
   21 Hōki
   22 Mimasaka
O 23 Bizen
O 24 Inaba

   25 Harima
   26 Tajima
O 27 Tango
   28 Tanba
   29 Ōmi ⎱ Kinki
O 30 Iga ⎰ region
   31 Ise
O 32 Shima
   33 Kii
O 34 Awaji

   35 Settsu
   36 Izumi
   37 Kawachi ⎱ Kinai
O 38 Yamashiro ⎰ region
   39 Yamato

O 40 Mino
O 41 Owari
   42 Mikawa
   43 Tōtoumi ⎱ Chūbu
   44 Suruga ⎰ region
O 45 Izu
   46 Hida
O 47 Kai
X 48 Shinano
      (Shinshū)

O 49 Wakasa
   50 Echizen
O 51 Kaga ⎱ Hokuriku
   52 Noto ⎰ region
   53 Etchū
X 54 Echigo
   55 Sado

   56 Kōzuke
   57 Shimotsuke
   58 Musashi ⎱ Kantō
   59 Hitachi ⎰ region
   60 Shimōsa
   61 Kazusa
O 62 Awa
   63 Sagami

X 64 Iwashiro
   65 Iwaki
X 66 Uzen ⎱ Tōhoku
   67 Rikuzen ⎰ region
   68 Ugo
X 69 Rikuchū
   70 Mutsu

O 71 Matsumae ── Hokkaidō

[ ] between 21 and 99 ikki incidents

X areas with greatest number of ikki incidents (over 100)

O areas with fewest incidents of ikki (1–20)

Sources: Kasahara Kazuo, ed., Zukai Nihonshi (Illustrated Japanese history) (Tokyo: Yamakawa Shuppan, 1983), p. 64; Yamanaka Kiyotaka, "Hyakushō ikki no jidaisei to chiikisei" (The periodization and geographical distribution of peasant risings), Rekishi kōron (Historical Forum), June 1978, p. 58.

munities, helped peasants realize the righteousness of their cause and sustained them in pursuing it.

Keeping in mind now the picture of an ascending trend in specific forms of peasant protests, we shall take our first step toward re-creating, at a general level, the institutional setting in which they arose. Peasants lived out their lives within networks of interpenetrating power relationships constituted by class, state, and village community. It is these relationships to which we turn next.

THE BAKUHAN STATE

The first of the two main systems of formal organization to which peasants were subjected was the Tokugawa state. Like its Western counterparts, the feudal state in Japan enjoyed a monopoly in violence, specified and enforced property rights, and defined both the life roles that all classes could play and the rules for playing them.[16] Where it differed from Western feudal states was, among other things, in not having to contend historically with a Christian church that not only controlled vast wealth but actually participated in political power. The Japanese state in the Tokugawa era had no institutional rivals and was able to regulate closely virtually all aspects of social life.

The second formal organization shaping and restraining peasants in the conduct of their daily lives was the village community, which usually functioned as the tool of the state. Fief lords and intendants of the Tokugawa military government (*bakufu*) determined the village's internal power relations from the outside, often in ways that reinforced the social subjection already inherent in the villages' own internal hierarchy. Despite this overdetermination of the village by the state, however, the village still had the potential to become, under certain circumstances, the real defender of the peasants' common interests. When the claims of the state for tribute and labor were forced to yield to the physical and moral needs of peasants, the village became a community "imagined" in terms of justice. That happened most often whenever stepped-up exploitation and misfortune at the village level forced peasants to reshape their beliefs and the ways in which they processed the state's claims. But before going any further into the nature of the exploitation process, we had better explain how the Japanese feudal state actually related to peasant production.

For nearly three centuries prior to the 1870s, when the Meiji regime cleared the ground for the emergence of a unitary capitalist state, the Japanese lived under a semicentralized system of feudal rule. It consisted of over two hundred fiefs (*han*) differentially subordinated to a single military government (bakufu). Heading the government was a top military commander and holder of centralized power, called the *shogun* ("barbarian-quelling-generalissimo"). With his headquarters in Edo (present-day Tokyo) in the Kantō plain area, the shogun's domain occupied roughly the middle of the main island of Honshū. His bakufu, established on the basis of an incomplete subjugation of his territorial rivals, owned and governed directly only about 23 percent of Japan's entire land area. That area, called the "heavenly domain" (*tenryō*), was valued initially at about 7 million *koku* (one koku equaled about five American bushels), and included the major cities of Edo, Osaka, Nagasaki, and Kyoto, and most of the country's mines and ports.

Over the rest of Japan the bakufu was unable to levy taxes directly and had to tolerate a diffusion of power among the military families. As a result, after swearing allegiance to the shogun, hundreds of fief lords (*daimyo*) were entrusted with the administration of land and were divided into categories of relative trustworthiness to the Tokugawa house. Thereafter, the fief bureaucracies, headed by the lord and staffed by his loyal retainers, operated a system of tribute extraction (ground rent in kind and money) and exercised over all ruled classes within their territory a high degree of control. Unlike European feudalism, no essential difference existed in the social formations over which fiefs and bakufu ruled.

To this statelike framework, in which each daimyo fief was a branch or agent of a hegemonial super-fief, and society everywhere was organized on exactly the same principles of extreme status inequality and discrimination, modern Japanese historians have given a special name. They call it the *bakuhan* state. Western historians have preferred a different terminology: shogunate for the bakufu and Tokugawa rather than bakuhan state. Hereafter, rather than continue a Eurocentric practice which fails to do justice to the distinctiveness of the Japanese feudal state, we shall follow Japanese usage most of the time, except where reasons of style or excessive repetition dictate otherwise.

Starting in the 1590s, the bakuhan state was erected in stages, by military force, over an agrarian village-economy that had evolved out of several earlier, class-divided modes of production. Formalized in 1603 with the founding of the Tokugawa house, it remained essentially intact thereafter until the 1850s and 1860s, when, under the impact of multiple foreign and domestic crises, it underwent rapid breakdown.

The new state's first structural principle—the policy of seclusion—commenced only in the second quarter of the seventeenth century, some thirty years after the Japanese armies sent by Hideyoshi to invade the Korean peninsula had been brought home. In the interim, Tokugawa Ieyasu, a lieutenant of Hideyoshi, unified the warrior class under his hegemony. Afterwards, following the battles of Sekigahara (1600) and Osaka (1614–1615), Ieyasu's sons and successor Tokugawa shoguns banned the teaching of Christianity, ordered Japanese to stop traveling abroad, and confined foreign merchant activity to the tiny island of Deshima in Nagasaki harbor. Seclusion became the Tokugawa house's way of strengthening the new state and ensuring domestic security by keeping out foreign ideas. It was also their way of avoiding being drawn into a struggle with the European absolutist states for trade and empire in East Asia.[17]

Once the country was secluded and foreign trade confined to a single port, the samurai found themselves engaged in conflict with society's producers in a new and more sustained way. The physical and spatial separation of soldiers and peasants—*heinō bunri*—was designed to deal with that problem. This second principle of the new state was the product not of a specific historical conjuncture of foreign and domestic problems but of a long historical evolution. It must be understood, as Minegishi Kentarō noted, in connection with the stabilization of property rights in land. The practice of separating soldiers and peasants originated during Japan's warring-states period in the late fourteenth and fifteenth centuries, when samurai were conquering land and exercising direct personal control over peasants. But the policy was not fully implemented on a national scale until the very end of the seventeenth century. Only then were most samurai removed from a relationship of direct control over peasants.[18]

Meanwhile, Hideyoshi had earlier spurred the separation process by his national cadastral survey of 1582–1589, which registered nearly all land that had economic value. Ultimately, his survey helped consolidate the samurai class hierarchy while denying peasants the possibility of becoming warriors. After its completion, peasants alone experienced the phenomenon of class differentiation on the basis of landholding.

Hideyoshi's Sword Hunting Edict of 1588 further clarified the status of peasants by banning their possession of arms. He rationalized the ban as follows: "If peasants possess only agricultural implements and work exclusively on land, their fortune will last down to their far later descendants. This is so ordered out of sympathy for peasants. It is indeed to provide a basis for the safety of the land and the happiness of all the people."[19]

Because the real division of labor and classes in the bakuhan state was tied to landholding and the expropriation of the peasants' surplus, Hideyoshi's Sword Hunting Edict had to be supplemented. By itself it was not enough to ensure that peasants stayed put, bound to their land and to their villages. To make them willing and disciplined tribute bearers for the rest of society, other legal and institutional measures were required.

First, upon the custom-bound social groups of seventeenth-century Japan, the samurai forced a unique system of hereditary status discrimination. Its accompanying ideology of finely graded fixed status inculcated loyalty, discipline, and a spirit of inequality, which contrasted sharply with the egalitarianism preached by medieval Buddhism. Second, the samurai established within villages the five-family-group responsibility system to prevent desertion and ensure that tribute was paid in full. They also developed a system of indirect control and policing of villages by a hierarchy of peasant officials. The latter were quasi-samurai at a district or circuit level and peasants with some samurai perquisites at the lowest level. Imposed on villages by regional power holders and by daimyo, peasant officials sometimes acted to prevent domanial power from intervening too harshly in village affairs. But more often they initiated economic and political repression on behalf of the fief.

In either case, the existence of these intermediary agents, whose primary task was tribute collection, ensured that the samurai grip on the countryside was not lessened by the removal of warriors to the castle. Henceforth samurai managed intermediaries who, in turn, specialized in depriving peasants of the fruits of their labor. Moreover, samurai were not barred from villages. Some resided there as warehouse keepers and police officials; and all samurai could, if they wished, visit villages daily. The idea that villages were autonomous entities within the fief is a myth created largely by modern historians.[20]

Two other less effective mechanisms for controlling peasants were the use of Buddhist temples and Shintō shrines to legitimize state power and the propagation of neo-Confucian ideology in the service of tribute collection. Under the bakuhan state, samurai officials regulated the number of shrines and temples and attempted also to interdict and control the relationship between religious practices and the events of daily life. In this they were only partially successful. They forced peasants everywhere to register with Buddhist temples and to retain their sect affiliation permanently. But official control over organized religion and religious indoctrination could not be extended for long to control over the actual content of memorial services, annual religious functions, and shrine festivals. When the second, and largest ever, mass pilgrimage (*okage mairi*) to Ise Shrine swept over the country in 1705, involving over 3.6 million people in a fifty-day period, it was a clear sign that the samurai had lost their grip on popular religion. The people were doing things in the name of religion that the authorities had not anticipated and could not control.

Whether the bakufu and fief governments were any more successful in manipulating secular ideology as it bore on production may also be questioned. Certainly, from the outset of the new regime, official samurai propaganda put ideal attitudes toward work and paying taxes at the forefront. In fact, daimyo and shogun used all the moral machinery at their command to turn peasants into "economic animals" preoccupied with increasing output. Official ideology tried to weaken their will to resist exploitation by fostering an inner compulsion to work hard and render up tributes. In admonitory edicts of the seventeenth century, such as the widely disseminated Keian Circular (*Keian ofuregaki*), issued in 1649, the character for virtue (*toku*) was, as Minegishi Kentarō pointed out, synonymous with profits, while filial piety was linked to the performance of agricultural duties and the full payment of tributes. Article 1 of that document warned: "You should not neglect the laws of the Shogunate and never slight lords and intendants [*daikan*]. Also regard village heads and district heads as your real parents. Look up to provincial lords as the sun and moon and respect the lords [*jitō*] and intendants as your tutelary deities. Regard assistants to village officials as your real parents."

Such filial piety could best be rendered by producing lots of rice and paying tributes in full. And Articles 24 and 31 added that "If you peasants exert yourselves in cultivation, take good care of your crops and have a greater harvest, then you will have more profits and it will be to your advantage.... Since the lord may go but the peasants stay permanently on the land, they maintain their holdings [*mimochi* = also economy, wealth]. And if their economy improves, should not that be of great advantage to peasants?"[21] The Keian Circular also recommended that peasants "use foods sparingly and always in an attitude of tiding over the off-crop season of January, February and March.... [You] should depend entirely on miscellaneous grains. To that end, grow barley, millet, green vegetables, radish and any other crop so as not to waste rice by eating it."[22]

When disseminated by the shogunate and backed by overwhelming military force, easily deployed against villages, ideas such as these did influence peasants. But they did not have to be, and probably were not, believed completely and uniformly. What really compelled peasants to go on producing rice for their rulers and miscellaneous grains for themselves, generation after generation, was the tribute system, the power of the bakuhan state, and the level of development of the division of labor, not ruling class ideology per se. Moreover, the frequency of peasant protests, even in the seventeenth century, suggests that peasants not only doubted the teachings from above, but in times of crisis invariably transformed those aspects of official ideology that inhibited their capacity for remedial action. Like Christianity in medieval Europe, neo-Confucian ideology ultimately proved to be more important for ruling-class solidarity than for peasant indoctrination.[23]

The foregoing discussion now allows us to clarify the position of peasants in the bakuhan state at the dawn of seclusion, when they constituted over 80 percent of a population of about 20 million. First, peasants were defined as politically passive, obedient, immobile beings. Their putative protectors and cultural leaders were the samurai (together with the court nobles and emperor living in Kyōto): about 6 percent of the population at the beginning and 8 to 10 percent at the end of the Tokugawa period. Theoretically, unless peasants belonged to different kinds of backward, unfree statuses, they were landholders just like samurai. But as time went on, only lords were legally recognized owners of land. Samurai became their military-administrative servants, separated from agricultural production and concentrated in castle towns, from which they administered the fiefs.

Second, peasants were essentially freer than their ancestors had been when unfree statuses prevailed everywhere and land was owned by court nobles and the big temples of a Sinicized state. They were also freer than when land was owned by bailiffs who rose to power and usurped ownership over private agricultural domains. Since the fourteenth century they had stood up repeatedly to defend with arms their land and possessions and to force the cancelation of debts. But in the early seventeenth century, because of the daimyo's subordination to the bakufu, when economic exploitation became intolerable, peasants could appeal for justice to a higher authority (called the *kōgi*, or "public authority"). This meant that the reverse side of the subordination of daimyo to shogun was a situation in which peasants could become, within narrow limits, "negotiators" who played fiefs and bakufu against each other to their own advantage.[24]

In the early seventeenth century most peasants were disarmed and degraded by numerous restrictions. Institutions of class, status, and corvée deprived them of their time and a large part of the products of their labor. The more or less independent, subsistence-oriented, petty farming in which they engaged was on land they could not legally sell, which yielded produce they could not freely circulate. Moreover, these independent petty cultivators still had a weak sense of landownership. And they coexisted everywhere with "agricultural servants" who were entangled in relations of personal servitude within "blood-tie groups."[25] Given this general economic condition of inadequately developed petty commodity production, it is understandable that no daimyo was ever able to establish himself on a national scale in competition with the bakufu.[26]

Last, the peace and harmony that the Tokugawa house established was between ruling families, not necessarily with those over whom they ruled. For peasants, the Tokugawa peace existed within an elaborate framework of repression and policing of villages. What, then, can be said of the general political relation of the Tokugawa village to the new state?

THE STATE-VILLAGE RELATIONSHIP

The Tokugawa state-village relationship was highly mediated and bureaucratic in nature. The mediated side consisted of two rural hierarchies of control. Together cation. The acts of violence they engaged in were usually against property rather than persons. This pacifism expressed in the legends of gimin seems to distinguish the Japanese little tradition, and village society itself, until the last decades of the Tokugawa period, when the level of violence throughout Japan increased dramatically.

Third, the gimin idea was perfected and had its greatest appeal during a particular stage of social development: when Tokugawa society was weak and timid and the bakuhan state strong. Gimin legends flourished when feudal lords maintained a pervasive system of rural repression that kept alive the memory of harsh punishments. In order to offset that system of social repression and motivate themselves, peasants who lost out in confrontations with domanial and shogunal power nurtured the idea of gimin. By enshrining as deities precisely those whom the state regarded as criminals and outlaws, some village communities were able subjectively to resist the values imposed upon them by the ruling class. The very act of making a gimin holy once again—establishing closer mental contact with a spiritual being in whom the power to resist injustice and oppression was manifested— undoubtedly helped some peasants to increase their own individual powers of resistance.[33] Thus, under certain conditions, the recollection and worship of gimin could facilitate an exploitation of the past for purposes of rebellion.

Fourth, the concept of gimin connoted a historical situation in which peasants were at once deferential and outwardly compliant, and yet so deeply resentful of samurai misrule and repression that the only outlet for them was a psychological mythmaking one. In this sense also, the gimin who appeared after peasants yielded to repression represented both a mechanism of compensation for repression and a pledge not to forget the punishments endured.

Gimin can be found throughout the Tokugawa and Meiji periods, but their high tide was from the second half of the seventeenth century through the end of the eighteenth century. Thereafter they seemed to recede into the background. Their gradual disappearance from the historical stage occurred over the entire course of the nineteenth century. Partly it coincided with the growth of village communities that were more resistant to fief manipulation and more capable of rectifying local injustices without reliance on the local elite. But also contributing to their demise was a worsening historical situation, which forced many peasants to shift their concern from the deification of heroes to calls for *yonaoshi* (world renewal).

Even then, the gimin legends were still alive in 1884 when the peasants of Chichibu district, Saitama prefecture, rose up in a desperate armed attempt to cancel their debts and secure the yonaoshi leveling of all of Saitama prefecture. Twice on the eve of this transitional type of incident, in April and again in August, the problem of peasant protest by introducing a key concept produced by the political culture or "little tradition" of the Japanese peasantry.

GIMIN

In the Japanese little tradition, peasants sometimes regarded the shogun as a savior when, in violation of the law, they tried to appeal for mercy directly to him. But that was the exception rather than the rule. For the most part, Japanese peasants did not attempt to "adjust the terms of their subordination" to rulers by producing a Christ-like savior concept or by appealing to a "true Tsar Deliverer" "to save the peasants and set things right."[31] Instead, we find them apotheosizing local leaders and making a highly functional use of the past to justify their own assertion of rights.

Specifically, the repressive nature of bakufu and fief rule produced a mechanism of psychological redress which found its expression in the idea of gimin—literally, "righteous people" or "exemplary martyrs." The most celebrated gimin was Sakura Sōgorō, an official of Narita village who was crucified in 1653 for standing up in behalf of the people of Sakura fief (present-day Narita city, Chiba prefecture).[32] Later, starting in the mid-eighteenth century, Sōgorō's fame spread throughout the country as dissident peasants molded his alleged exploits to serve their own particular circumstances. We find his name invoked in protest actions right down to the late nineteenth century. In the first half of this study we shall meet three peasant leaders—Tokuemon, Hanbei, and Asanojō—around whom, like Sakura Sōgorō, contemporary accounts of peasant risings were woven. These gimin figures help unlock for us the subjective consciousness of Tokugawa risings. Much may be gained therefore by trying to understand their general features before tracing their appearance in actual historical situations.

Basically gimin were village representatives who pitted themselves against the bakuhan state, suffering torture and martyrdom for the sake of their villages. Because they saved others and preserved the community by their painful deaths, they attained in time the quality of deities. Four aspects of this peasant "social construction" of gimin deserve emphasis.

First, like the peasant uprisings they undergirded, the belief in gimin can be interpreted as an implicit rejection by peasants of the ruling-class claim that social relations within Tokugawa society were natural rather than man-made.

Second, gimin who led uprisings were often depicted in accounts by sympathetic contemporaries as fearless heroes. They commanded peasant troops and were invariably imbued with the martial virtues of true samurai. Yet they, and the protests they led, seldom intended to take human life no matter what the provo-

of common lands. A second type of village association disposed of transport corvées of rice and money ordered by the fief. A third type of ongoing village association emerged in the early nineteenth century in connection with religious festivals
and the collection of grain offerings for particular shrines and temples. Last, villages sometimes cooperated on a districtwide basis, at the behest of the fief, in order
to facilitate the rapid circulation of official instructions and messages. This form of
cooperation held the most potential for being turned against the fief.[29]

Individual villages also had the potential for making their internal power relations more democratic, thereby meliorating their external relationship with the
bakuhan state. Most of the time political and ideological repression prevented that
potential from being realized. Yet the state-village relationship was dynamic. Like
fief methods of exploitation, it tended to change from period to period, in connection with stages of market development. Under certain conditions, peasants realized a more democratic development and a less unilateral village relationship
with the state. Acting collectively, they sometimes forced their village officials to
adhere to certain norms and expectations, particularly where tribute matters, land
ownership, and land-use rights were involved. When local officials failed to act in
the interests of the majority, or when they were overly enthusiastic in enforcing
fief policies of tax exploitation, peasants formed autonomous groups outside their
reach. These would then threaten to break off the village's relationship to the state,
that is, to withhold labor and tribute payments. Divided as it was between imposed
groups and institutions, and temporarily formed autonomous ones, the Tokugawa
village was probably most united and harmonious in times of crisis. Only when
dependency relations were dissolving and residents joined together in autonomous
groups to resist samurai and landlord exploitation did a type of "democratic consensus" appear in villages.

From this brief sketch of the bakuhan state and its relationship to village
society, a number of points emerge. Tokugawa village society was formed for production and bound together by various types of political ties. But it was definitely
not an autonomous unit, arena, or world of activity in which peasants "shifted for
themselves" and samurai refrained from interfering. Nor can it be described either
as a "society without rights," even though in legal terms rights were not recognized.[30] On the contrary, the whole history of Tokugawa peasant resistance to
samurai and landlords attests to a developing sense of general rights among the
Japanese. The right to resist unjust exactions, the right to land, and the right to fair
treatment by privileged power holders were three such general rights repeatedly
expressed in rebellions. But there were other rights, of a more specific nature,
which became manifest as the Tokugawa political economy and its culture developed through specific historical stages. In what follows, we shall try to understand

they tied villages to the production process and to various levels of fief and bakufu administrators. Samurai officials, from senior councillors down to lowly foot soldiers and police bailiffs, staffed one rural chain of command. Peasant officials at the district and village level constituted a second, indigenous power network subordinated to samurai commands. Peasant officials were almost always recruited locally, usually from the wealthiest and most prestigious stratum in the countryside.[27] Generally, lords imposed them upon villages and subsequently invested them with some of the key attributes of samurai status. The prerogatives of such "peasants" included the right to use a surname, carry a sword, ride into the castle in a palanquin, and, on very special occasions, even be received in audience by the lord himself. Because the shogun and lords effected their control over villages indirectly, through village officials, the officials occupied an absolutely key position in the overall Tokugawa power network. One expression of the bureaucratic side of the village-state relationship was the issuing of orders by samurai in charge of rural affairs to peasant officials at different levels, telling them to forward written pledges signed by all the peasants under them, confirming that they would carry out commands as given.

A second feature of the state-village relationship was its unilateral nature. Certainly the political control of the bakufu and fief governments over villages was not total. But that did not mean that villages were governed by consensus, in what was "essentially a democratic resolution of village problems," as the conventional historiography asserts.[28] The state maintained coercive administrative and ideological control over villages because it was concerned primarily with ensuring the uninterrupted flow of tribute to the castle towns and cities. It was usually sufficient for samurai to issue orders bureaucratically and conduct frequent inspections of villages accompanied by small military contingents. Complete control over all aspects of village finances was unnecessary. Those details could be left to the privileged intermediaries whom most peasants had no say in choosing. Hence, in normal times, only relatively minor problems were ever resolved by what can be very loosely termed "democratic procedures." On matters such as the determination of work-free days, religious festivals, and arrangements for mutual aid in rendering corvée services, peasants probably could assert themselves freely. But for the most part the internal governance of village communities was consistently authoritarian.

Yet, under certain conditions, the nature of village governance could change and be made to serve peasants rather than the state. Village associations furnished a potential lever for such a transformation. Traditionally, villages cooperated with one another or formed federations to perform certain common functions related to agricultural production, such as water conservation and control and the utilization peasants in Nagatomi village, Chichibu, offered up memorial plaques and haiku poems to Sakura Sōgorō, god of peasants. These reaffirmations of Sōgorō occurred in a shrine erected specifically to honor his memory and in a village that, by the second day of the insurrection, had contributed to it 160 people out of 213 households.[34] Interestingly, an essential feature of the Chichibu incident was the final fusion of the gimin legend with the figure of ex-samurai politician Itagaki Taisuke, leader of the Liberal party. Peasants understood him not as a modern politician but as "Lord Itagaki," a genuine gimin figure with whom they would "join forces" and "transform the despotic [Meiji] rule into a good government and realize a world of freedom where the people can enjoy tranquility."[35]

THE STRUCTURE OF THE STUDY

By now it is clear that the concerns of this book are quite broad. We identified the main features of the bakuhan state and sketched the institutional and ideological world peasants inhabited. In what follows we shall attempt to reconstruct, systematically and in as much depth as the materials allow, the dynamic relationship between class struggle and the state under Tokugawa feudalism. Second, while focusing on the struggle between the power of lords and the peasantry, we shall reflect on what James C. Scott aptly terms "the shared values and goals which find expression through rebellion."[36]

Part I describes the slow ebbing of feudal strength as a result of economic growth and social conflict. Starting in the late seventeenth century and continuing into the early eighteenth century, a money economy intruded deeply into village life. Population growth slowed. There were food shortages and famines on a national scale. Disguised landlord-tenant relations began to change the quality of life in many villages. Also helping to prepare the ground for conflict were two other signs of structural change: increasing daimyo and samurai indebtedness to merchants and a decline in the price of rice, the main medium of exchange and value.

These developments signaled the end of the first century of stable Tokugawa rule. Now began a long period of social and economic change which slowly debilitated and transformed feudal political rule. The bakufu in the Kyōhō era (1716–1735) undertook its first series of reforms to overcome its deepening fiscal problems. Aimed at reconsolidating the original feudal framework, the Kyōhō reforms depended mainly on increasing the proportion of rice tributes that peasants paid to rulers. Partly in response to this development, as well as to specific conditions in different fiefs, conflict incidents escalated beyond anything experienced during the previous half-century. Chapters 1 through 4 of part I study the seventeenth- and early eighteenth-century events leading to the Sanchū rising of

1726–1727 in western Japan. This uprising occurred during uncertainty about the future of Tsuyama fief and was indicative of many problems that first surfaced at the start of the middle Tokugawa period, the 1710s through the 1780s.

As the eighteenth century unfolded, the fiscal crisis of the bakuhan state continued to deepen despite intensified exploitation of peasants, reductions in samurai stipends, and more forced loans from the urban merchant class. By the end of the Hōreki period (1751–1763), the trend of gradually increasing but unsynchronized protests by peasants and townsmen reached a new level. Chapters 5 through 8 of part II focus on the rising of 1761–1763 in mountainous Ueda fief, central Japan. This event symbolized a turning point in the ongoing struggle between peasants and lords. With unusual clarity, Ueda also prefigured many of the themes in peasant struggles and class relationships for the remainder of the Tokugawa period.

After the Ueda incident, the weaker daimyo throughout Japan drew closer to the bakufu, hoping to generate more legitimacy for their heavier tribute impositions. Conversely, instances multiplied of forceful bakufu intervention in the internal affairs of private fiefs. Realizing that their own replies to peasant demands would be subjected to closer bakufu scrutiny, many daimyo stiffened their resistance. But the full contours of the daimyo's class response to a century of popular protests did not become clear until the very end of the eighteenth century when the bakufu undertook its second major reform effort—the Kansei era reforms (1789–1800).

To illustrate that development, chapters 9, 10, and 11 of part III treat, very briefly, the uprising of 1786–1787 in Fukuyama fief, a cotton-growing area of lowlands and hills in western Japan. This event, seen primarily through the eyes of daimyo Abe Masatomo, sheds light on the emergence of the problem of mass poverty, involving substantial numbers of propertyless people. It also shows how the samurai aristocracy strengthened its position by coopting the landlord and rural merchant strata in support of the state. With the rising in Fukuyama and its aftermath in the Kansei reforms, the middle Tokugawa period comes symbolically to an end, and Japan passes into its last period of feudal decline: late Tokugawa or the transition to the modern era.

The description in parts I through III of different trans-fief risings of the eighteenth century turns on the analysis of political economy, political culture or "the subjective dimension of politics," and the structure of property. By making class struggle and exploitation the central concepts, it sets the past as much as possible in relation to the present.

Furthermore, this portion of the book attempts to reveal the ideology of peasants and lords in moments of crisis by drawing on a limited number of documents. The documents were chosen because they are authentic contemporary accounts of the events they describe, and also because they are relatively accessible. In the cases of the "Mikoku shimin ranpōki" (Account of the People's Revolt in the Province of Mimasaka) and the "Ueda sōdō jikki" (Account of the Peasant Uprising in Ueda), studied in parts I and II, respectively, their provenance and degree of trustworthiness are explained in the text. The unknown authors of these accounts were close to, perhaps even actual witnesses of, the events they described. They reproduced orders from samurai officials to village chiefs, together with the names and ages of peasants and others who were later punished for their roles in the protests. The documents thus aid us in understanding what exploitation actually meant to peasants. At the same time, the documents help in reconstructing the chronology of local events connected with each rising. Equally important are the obviously fictional passages in which the authors portray the public executions of peasant leaders. The public executions illuminate the objective and subjective dimensions of the eighteenth-century crisis with which peasants and samurai grappled.

Part IV addresses the history of nineteenth-century risings. During the nineteenth century a dramatic increase occurred in protests by peasants and townspeople. The earlier portrayal found in eighteenth-century documentary accounts of stylized, two-sided conflict, embellished by legends, gave way to a more confused, historically realistic picture. All the risings in part IV occurred during worsening stages of political crises, fiscal decline of the fiefs, and growing hardship for both samurai and peasants. They differed from eighteenth-century risings in their form, content, scale, and frequency of occurrence, as well as in some but not all of their underlying premises.

Chapter 12 of part IV begins with a reflection on the semantics of Tokugawa peasant protest and goes on to examine problems of justice, right, and property-consciousness encountered in their interpretation. Chapter 13 shifts the focus to the socioeconomic background and the periodization of the nineteenth-century crises. Attending first to the cultural developments affecting peasants and townsmen between 1800 and 1830, it argues that the emergence of a growing class of poor people in villages and towns manifested itself in new forms of religious activity. Next it proceeds to examine the Osaka insurrection of 1837 and the world renewal (yonaoshi) movements that erupted after the opening of the treaty ports in 1860. These actions culminated in the second half of 1867 in a distorted, orgiastic form of protest known as *Ee jya nai ka* ("who cares what happens" or "isn't it good"). Chapter 13 also compares Russian and Japanese peasants and the different social structures within which they struggled to remove the causes of their suffering.

After the overthrow of the Tokugawa bakufu, rural and urban protests flared up again in reaction to the policies of the new Meiji government. In chapters 14 and 15 we return to Tsuyama and Ueda fiefs over a century after their eighteenth-century risings. The objective is to show the changes that had occurred in the interim while also treating the demands raised in two yonaoshi incidents that occurred at the beginning (1866) and end (1870) of the last great wave of Tokugawa uprisings. Chapter 14 explains the phenomenon of "role reversals," the growth of precapitalist tenancy as a form of debt bondage, and the emergence onto the historical stage of the semiproletariat. Chapter 15 then discusses the monetary crises of early Meiji and its effects on people's lives. In the debased-currency risings in Shinshū province, peasant demands reflected both the old and the new ways in which the economic and political aspects of class domination joined to shape their lives. Analysis of the Shinshū disturbances serves a dual purpose. It affords a glimpse of the lineup of class antagonists in the Japanese countryside for the remainder of the nineteenth century. And it allows us to measure changes that occurred over the next decade and a half, ending with the last peak year of activity by armed peasant rebels: 1884. Finally, in chapter 16, the highlights of all four parts of the study are summarized.

Notes on the Text

Dates

The lunar calendar (reflecting the phases of the moon and with the civil month as its basic unit of measure) was used in Japan from the early seventh century until 1872. Thereafter the modern solar calendar was adopted. The solar calendar employs the natural year as its main unit of measurement. The difference between the lunar and solar calendars can vary from two weeks to one or even two months each year. In all direct quotations from, and citations to, primary documents, the lunar months are converted here into modern English equivalents.

Japanese words

Technical terms and office names, unless singled out for special treatment in the introduction, are given English equivalents. Japanese proper names are given surname first, except where citing material in which the normal Japanese order is reversed. In the sources, occasional alternate readings of Japanese names are given in parentheses.

Notes

To help readers locate easily quotations from the documents used in parts I, II, and III, note citations specify the upper (*jōdan*) and the lower (*gedan*) half of the page.

PART I

Defeat:
The Onset of Feudal Decline

Class Structure and Dynamics in Seventeenth-Century Tsuyama

T HE quiet border area of present-day northern Okayama prefecture offers to view a highland of mountain passes, terraced hillsides, and plateau. Here, in the Hiruzen Heights, the Asahi River rises up and, fed by many tributaries, flows downward through the ancient provinces of Mimasaka and Bizen before emptying into the Inland Sea at Okayama city. Cold rough winter weather and debilitatingly hot summers characterize this western part of Honshū island. But the land is equally well known for the richness of its human history. The dead remains of earlier periods of the Japanese past issue from its soil and haunt its landscape. They remind us of social and moral orders now partially or wholly transcended. Besides stone tumuli from the sixth and seventh centuries, one can see here Zen temples from the fourteenth century; besides wall-enclosed residential compounds of Tokugawa rural officials, there are rows of erect gravestones set in the hills and mountains, marking the sites where the remains of peasant martyrs repose. To travel through this Mimasaka region is truly to be reminded of the compacted, multilayered culture of Japan, and of the crucial role of the class struggle in shaping it.[1]

In 1726–1727 Tsuyama fief, embracing nearly all of Mimasaka, was shaken by a bloody convulsion known as the Sanchū ikki. Many of the historical conditions that led to it existed elsewhere in Japan at that time and were reflected in other large-scale, trans-fief disturbances of the early Kyōhō period (1716–1735): Fukuyama (1717), Tottori (1717), Hiroshima (1718), and Kurume (1728), to name just a few. In the Sanchū action, peasants demanded substantial reductions in the amount of rice tribute and went on to eliminate the village control system through which the fief extracted tributes. Like other peasant struggles of that time, it revealed the growing conflict between towns and villages, besides being clearly related to shogunate and fief bureaucratic reform efforts. On the other hand, many aspects of later peasant revolts had yet to make an appearance. There were no millenarian aspects, nor social strata on their way to becoming new semiproletarians in this ikki. The historical process that was slowly transforming peasant, communal property into its opposite was still at an early stage. Thus, by starting with the unsuccessful Sanchū revolt, the progress of Japanese peasants in the course of later class struggles may be measured in a general way.

Let us begin by reviewing Tsuyama fief's seventeenth-century background. In early 1603, three years after winning the battle of Sekigahara, and shortly before having himself appointed shogun in the name of the emperor, Tokugawa Ieyasu enfeoffed his trusted vassal, the veteran warrior Mori Tadamasa, in the ancient province of Mimasaka. The estimated official productive value of its land was then set by the bakufu at 186,500 koku. The area over which the Mori house of "outside" lords ruled for the next ninety-five years came to be known, variously and interchangeably, as Mimasaka, Sakushū, or Tsuyama han. Five other provinces constituted its borders: Hoki and Inaba in the north, Bizen in the south, Harima in the east, and Bitchū in the west.

When Tadamasa and his retainers arrived in Tsuyama, agricultural production, artisanal manufacture, and mining had already gone through a long process of development. The underlying population was divided into a complex hierarchy of classes, old and new, existing in close proximity to one another. At the bottom of the heap was a large mass of serflike peasants having the status of *nago* and *kerai*, with roots going back to the manorial stage of feudalism. Landless peasants, called *mizunomi-byakushō*, not bound in direct personal servitude to household heads, were equally numerous.

Standing above the nago, kerai and mizunomi, and exploiting their labor power, were two layers of rural elite. The first consisted of a small number of senior peasants and a much larger number of full-status peasants (*honbyakushō*), both of whom owned over 10 koku of land. Standing above both, at the very top of the rural hierarchy, was a thin stratum of local samurai, known as *kunizamurai* and *kokujin*. Their roots went back to the warring-states period: a time when "fief" meant simply a league of small lords and not a territorially integrated unit. Kunizamurai and kokujin were both the traditional warriors of the Mimasaka region, serving overlords, and landowners in their own right, using the services of many unfree peasants. Some of these local samurai, such as Namba Munemori, a retainer of the Kobayakawa family of small lords, contemplated armed resistance to Mori

Tadamasa. But, apparently at the last minute, they realized the futility of such an action and yielded quietly to Tadamasa.[2]

When, in 1604, Tadamasa ordered his new fief surveyed, it was these people who, on the basis of long-established tradition, exercised firm hegemony over Tsuyama's villages. To secure revenue for provisioning his warriors and establishing his daimyo rule, Tadamasa needed to control all the peasants, and for that, the cooperation of the rural elite of kunizamurai and kokujin was essential. With their help his own samurai retainers rapidly surveyed the land and classified the villages themselves as high, middle, and low according to the quality of their fields.[3] In the process, samurai officials, with the cooperation of village headmen (shōya), registered in village account ledgers each taxpaying peasant—nago, kerai, and mizunomi were not listed—and the area and productivity of the plots of cultivated land they possessed. They then assigned the annual amount of tribute required of each peasant in order to meet the village quota. In addition, they delimited the boundaries of villages, thereby simplifying the pattern of farming inherited from late medieval times. On the basis of this cadastral survey, Tadamasa and his successors were able to bar samurai and, to a much lesser extent, merchants from living permanently in villages and to make other changes that sharpened the line between samurai and peasants.[4]

Thereafter, step by step, social estate or status was introduced into the life of Tsuyama's villages, fixing people's occupational positions by birth and their social roles for life. The hereditary status system was deeply embedded in Japanese history and had already played a central role in the formation of the Yamato state and the Kamakura and Ashikaga shogunates of the twelfth to sixteenth centuries. But this ancient institutional inheritance came fully into play only in the more developed agrarian society of the Tokugawa period. Then, for the first time, it was grounded in the principle of the separation of soldiers and peasants.[5] With its graded privileges and carefully fostered spirit of discrimination, status became, more than ever, a restraint on all classes. Mainly, however, it functioned as a mechanism for dividing peasants from one another so as to be better able to rule them.

Even the kunizamurai, who were allies of the Mori, were not immune from this separation process. Tadamasa eventually expropriated their landholdings (chigyōchi), deprived them of surnames, lowered their status to peasants, and made them the objects of a sword hunt that yielded thousands of weapons. Then, having completed the disarmament of the ruled classes, which began on a national level during the previous century, he partly compensated the kunizamurai for having lowered their status by giving them the special new designation of kashira-byakushō and allowing them two of the insignia of samurai rank: short swords and cere-

monial garments woven of hemp.[6] In time, because the Mori recruited its local
and district-level officials from this land-possessing stratum, many were able to re-
build their power. Imposed peasant status in this case did not fundamentally alter a
key class relationship.

No sooner had Tadamasa surveyed his fief and made an official assessment of
what his land produced in rice, which approximated its actual productive value at
that time, than he set in motion other great projects. The *History of Tsuyama City*
notes that Tadamasa preserved the system of twelve administrative regions (*gun*)
and many smaller "circular instruction districts" (*fure*) into which Tsuyama was
already divided.[7] (The districts were the areas within which fief instructions and
orders circulated.) But to administer them he appointed officials called district
headmen (*ōjōya*) and deputy district headmen (*chūjōya*, but at that time termed
kimoiri). These intermediaries between the fief and the villages were chosen from
the kunizamurai and kokujin. They seemed to have the largest wealth and, at that
time, the biggest landholdings in the countryside.

While his system of local control was still taking shape, Tadamasa ordered the
building of Tsuyama castle near an important marketplace on a plain in the vicinity
of the Yoshii and Kamo rivers. Peasants, conscripted from neighboring villages,
labored thirteen years to complete it, but experienced no easing of hardships at its
finish. For in 1615, when the battle was fought that resolved Tokugawa Ieyasu's
succession problem, Tadamasa sent them by the thousands outside the fief to repair
Ōsaka castle.[8] All these costly undertakings forced him in the end to raise the ratio
of crop tributes that peasants paid to their lord from 50 percent of the harvest, set
in 1605, to 60 percent after the Battle of Ōsaka.[9]

When Tadamasa died in 1634, the process of constructing the bakuhan state
was nearing completion under the leadership of the third shogun, Iemitsu. But
neither the proscription of Christianity nor the seclusion policy were yet fully in
effect. They became so only during the reign of Tadamasa's grandson and successor
Nagatsugu. The 1630s and 1640s saw the bakufu turn inward. By firming up a
specific, though highly limited, relationship with the countries of East Asia and
with Holland, the bakufu was able to keep at bay the first wave of European imperialist advance. Seclusion, the external form of the bakuhan state, by cutting Japan
off from most contact with foreigners and instilling xenophobia into all classes, had
an extraordinarily profound influence on the development of its internal structure.
Daimyo and shogunate alike were henceforth obliged to monopolize internal
trade, while directing their full attention to increasing agricultural production and
eliminating the influence not only of Western culture but of all forms of proscribed
thought.

Nagatsugu did not stand aloof from the events of this critical period of reorganization of the bakuhan system. He participated in them by persecuting Tsuyama's Christians as well as members of an uncompromising heterodox sect of Nichiren Buddhism.[10] He may also have changed the fief's methods of managing peasants. For oppressed people in many areas of Japan during the second quarter of the seventeenth century were beginning to revive popular tradition and to act against ruthless domanial overtaxation. Throwing off their legally imposed status distinctions, they returned to the medieval rituals for forming solidarity bands. Swearing solemn oaths to the gods, they drank "holy water" and pledged themselves to cooperate, one and all, in villagewide associations which would express their common grievances.[11] Of course, all such oath taking and secret political activity the bakufu harshly proscribed. But just how far Nagatsugu himself had to go in personally enforcing such proscriptions is not known. Circumstances in provinces bordering the Chūgoku region, however, suggest the powerful momentum of peasant movements during this period.

In 1637, after twenty-two years of uninterrupted Tokugawa "peace," there occurred a peasant revolt of unsurpassed ferocity. Some thirty-seven thousand peasants from the fiefs of Shimabara and Karatsu (Amakusa Island), led by their village headmen and forty masterless samurai (rōnin), rose up under the overall leadership of one Amakusa Shirō, a self-styled "people's commander" (taishō). The bakufu responded to this Shimabara Revolt with a campaign of annihilation and ordered Nagatsugu to mobilize his warriors in preparation for sending them south by ship into Hizen province in Kyūshū, neighboring on the area of revolt.[12] But before the samurai of Tsuyama could enter the fray, bakufu armies numbering over 120,000 soldiers stormed the rebel's Shimabara fortress, wiping out every last starving man, woman, and child in it. Whereupon Edo ordered Matsukura Katsuie, the disgraced lord of Shimabara, placed in the custody of Tsuyama fief. Matsukura remained in the castle of Tsuyama until ordered to Edo. Like the lord of Karatsu, he too was later forced to commit suicide for having allowed a peasant uprising to occur in his territory.[13]

The remarkable Shimabara Revolt, in whose defeat Tsuyama fief was indirectly involved, shocked the daimyo class as a whole and everywhere left lasting memories of peasant resistance to tyrannical lordship. After this watershed event, the bakufu stepped up its repression of all organized, politicized expression of heterodox thought. The Japanese people were thus deprived of the possibility of a powerful unity against feudal oppression based squarely on a religious movement. But even after Shimabara popular religion never failed to be turned against authority when economic circumstances dictated. Although everywhere disarmed by sword hunts, physically separated from the warrior class, and forced into hereditary statuses, peasants quickly learned how to forge their externally imposed statuses into weapons of resistance.[14] In fact, popular resistance to misrule by daimyo and bakufu officials continued for the remainder of the seventeenth century. Village headmen throughout the country made direct appeals to lords and brought lawsuits to Edo magistrates in violation of the feudal chain of command.

But the most effective form of resistance during the second half of the seventeenth century was exodus or desertion (chōsan). This particular response to oppression is universal and has appeared in many different historical contexts. In the ancient Greek and Roman worlds exodus "was essentially a strike, taking the form of a collective departure (preferably to a nearby temple where asylum could be claimed) and a refusal to resume work until grievances were remedied."[15] In medieval Japan, where exodus was also a type of strike, the term included the political act of resisting warriors and their tax-collecting agents by erecting barricades and sealing off the village from all outside contact.[16] In early modern Japan the term was usually applied to situations where entire villages (sometimes in defiance of their headman's wishes or even without his knowledge) deserted en masse from oppressive fiefs. But it also denoted the action of peasants who fled their villages in search of sanctuary in the mountains or an even more illusory liberation in castle towns and large cities. The most famous mass exodus of the entire Tokugawa era occurred in 1853 in the "three Hei districts" of Nanbu fief, northeast Japan. Then, sixteen to seventeen thousand peasants took to the road in a movement that proclaimed the illegitimacy of the fief itself.[17] All such random but persistent acts of resistance, in the form of exodus, suggest that even after Shimabara a hidden issue in class struggles continued to be the character of the bakuhan state, which excluded peasants and commoners in principle from all serious political activity.

Unfortunately, the documentation does not exist that would permit the construction of a continuous narrative of overt struggles involving peasants, lords, merchants, and low-status samurai in seventeenth century Tsuyama. There one can aspire, at best, to isolate certain trends and events that affected the differentiation of the peasantry, setting the stage for the fief's later struggles of the eighteenth and nineteenth centuries. One such event—Nagatsugu's more detailed resurvey of fields in the mid-1660s—may have been ordered to resolve peasant complaints stemming from Tadamasa's original cadastral survey of 1604–1605. The resurvey further divided the fields of each village into grades of productivity: from one to six in some cases and as many as ten in others, with different tribute rates assigned to each grade.[18] As a result, some villages registered a slight tax decrease but the real productivity assessment for the fief as a whole rose to about 229,000 koku and went on increasing as new land was reclaimed for cultivation. In the last year of the Mori, 1697, it stood at 259,327 koku.[19]

The reigns of Mori Nagatsugu's two nephews, the third and fourth lords of

Tsuyama, spanned the years 1674 to 1697. In this final quarter of the seventeenth century, the last samurai with direct experience of war died off, intellectuals concentrated on absolutizing the martial virtues, and popular culture flourished in the big cities. Meanwhile, in the rural areas of the hundreds of domains into which Japan was divided, the cover of "perpetual peace" allowed overstaffed fief bureaucracies to settle into a more single-minded struggle with peasants for the fruits of their labor.

In Tsuyama, important changes occurred in the fief bureaucratic apparatus and in the conditions of rural life. Rule over peasants was now being supervised by the highest stratum of Mori retainers, who exercised all real power in the name of a figurehead lord. Nagatsugu watched over the fief's several mansions in Edo and attended to ceremonial from a position of retirement while his nephews alternated as fief lords. Economic development, meanwhile, continued in the villages, stimulated by a number of different factors. Indirectly, the fief's well-developed system of highways and waterways contributed to it, as did the geographical peculiarities of the region. In many parts of Tsuyama a small amount of arable land forced peasants, in order to pay their tributes, to depend on the local production of special products. In addition, the Mori pursued some policies that favored full-status peasants (honbyakushō) of the kind who exploited their own independent family labor rather than the corvée labor of non-tribute-paying nago and kerai. This was in accord with basic Tokugawa policy at that time. The idea behind it was to maximize tributes by getting all able-bodied peasants listed on the tribute registers.

Decrees of the late 1670s, based on a bakufu policy of 1673, reflected the Mori's increasing concern for the preservation of such full-status, self-cultivating peasants.[20] Some of them prohibited smallholders with less than ten koku of land from dividing up their inheritance. These, insofar as they contravened the interests of the rising stratum of minute self-cultivators, were often disregarded. But where the Mori's efforts to foster full-status peasants did not clash with the land hunger and desire for greater freedom of minute cultivators—those who were in the process of rising out of servile statuses—they were more successful. The following regulation of May 1682 was, in fact, protective of the interests of nago and kerai: "Human traffic shall be strictly banned and the term for servants, men or women, employed seasonally shall be limited to ten years. Any excess over this fixed term shall be regarded as a crime. ADDENDA: Those hereditary servants or visiting people who have moved out to other places for work, and have wives or children, shall not be called back."[21]

By the time of this decree, the village hierarchy of full-status peasants, landless mizunomi-byakushō, nago, and kerai had already started to collapse in places where rice fields were scarce and necessity dictated bringing new land under cultivation. To attribute the increase in Tsuyama fief's real grain output to the efforts of a growing number of peasants who aspired to rise out of nago and kerai statuses and become minute full-status cultivators, utilizing the labor power of their immediate family members, does not, therefore, seem unreasonable. But in fostering this trend toward independent petty cultivators who paid land rent in kind, the Mori were also, inadvertently, promoting a significant growth of rural merchant activity.

Kamei Masao, in his important study of the historical background to the Sanchū ikki of 1726– 1727, called attention to peasants who, from the late 1680s onward, were selling directly to merchants "such things as miscellaneous grains, bamboo, lumber, tobacco, paper, cotton plants, perilla oil from mint seeds [used in making varnish and printing ink], sesame, charcoal, indigo, oil and firewood."[22] Mori tax policy, he suggests, while helping to free some peasants from direct personal bondage to patriarchal family heads, was also furthering the intermediate exploitation of peasants by rural merchants. The latter (eventually with the fief's blessing) exchanged the miscellaneous grains and upland products of peasants for rice and cash with which the peasants paid their tributes.

Toward the end of the seventeenth century, merchant activities developed and spread throughout the entire western and northern parts of Tsuyama fief, centering on the relatively remote and economically vulnerable "Sanchū" area. This was the name for the three administrative districts of Hijiya, Yumoto, and Mitsue. Geographically, the Sanchū straddled the upper reaches of the meandering Asahi River, which rises in the Hiruzen Heights and then flows downward to the Inland Sea. With the Chūgoku Mountains and the Hiruzen Heights as its background, the Sanchū encompassed steep valleys, sloping fields, stone quarries, iron mines, and comparatively little arable land. Yet "everywhere within it—Doi, Shinjō, Kuginuki, Ogawa, Yumoto and especially Kuse village—post stations and wholesalers could be seen."[23]

Three points should be noted about this diffusion of rural merchant trading activities. First, it occurred in a general context of increasing agricultural output. This increase was due partly to the development of independent families of full-status peasants and partly to fief policies that favored that stratum of tribute bearers. Second, the increase in rural commercial activities was also accompanied by a collapse of the lower stratum of minute full-status peasants. The fief's tribute exploitation deprived many minute landholders of an excessive amount of surplus. Simultaneously, a rigid status system in villages limited their possibilities for participation in village affairs. Under such circumstances, the increased exposure by the poor to merchant moneylenders accelerated a debt cycle in villages and defaults on land, hence social poverty.

Third, peasant production of miscellaneous products that could be marketed commercially did not, it is true, automatically mean more exploitation by merchants. However, merchants went on making tax loans to peasants (authenticated by village and district headmen) and they continued to be drawn into the fief's financial structure. As that happened, the local trading relationships, which peasants preferred to keep personalized, may have become impersonal and antagonistic.

Thus a deterioration in the social atmosphere surrounding the merchant-peasant exchange relationship also accompanied the complex process whereby more and more minute landholding peasants entered into conditions of poverty. What some of those conditions were has been spelled out by historian Nakano Michiko in her excellent study, "The Sanchū Rising of the Kyōhō Era." She cites an appeal to the Edo financial magistrate brought by peasants from eighty-seven Tsuyama fief villages in the year 1726. Before their villages came under direct bakufu administration, these peasants claimed that the tax rate was so high that, starting in the late 1680s, an average of from "five to ten peasants died of starvation each year, and in each village an equal number of bankrupt peasants, unable to pay taxes, had their fields and properties confiscated and were expelled from their villages." [24]

Thus, stimulated by the mechanism of overtaxation and by increased peasant production, both merchant activities and poverty spread throughout rural Tsuyama. Equally important, these developments were attended by a proliferation of intravillage and fief-village disputes over usage rights to common grass fields and mountain forests. As early as 1655, Tsuyama fief levied a tax on mountain forests which took account of the difficulty of transporting timber over long distances to the castle town. In theory, as Kamei's study notes, ownership of the fief's mountain forests was supposed to have accrued to the lord, as one of his domanial rights. But, in fact, custom dictated the division of forests into three categories: those owned by the fief, by villages, and by individual full-status peasants. As the seventeenth century drew to a close, peasant demand increased for "forests and for weeding fields, hills and tree stubs which furnished firewood, piled leaves and manure for cultivated fields." [25]

But Tsuyama fief also had a growing need for forests as sources of charcoal for its ironworks, iron mining being one of its earliest and most important fief monopolies. [26] Thus, in proportion as peasant farming required greater access to forests and common fields, and as fief income also came to depend more heavily on iron mining, conflicts grew between the castle authorities and the villages. So the dynamics of economic development was heating up the class struggle as the seventeenth century drew to a close in Tsuyama.

It is a truism that ruling classes and groups in every age actively encourage obsessions that serve their own convenience.[27] In our own time consumerism, deterrence, and anticommunism are dominant obsessions. In Tokugawa Japan the ruling families embraced the cult of the warrior and esteemed loyalty and filial piety in order not only to strengthen their status relations to one another but also to wring huge sacrifices and enormous work effort from their subjects. But because the loyalty of lords to the Tokugawa shogun was so unilateral and obsessive, it tended at times to work against the very principle of hereditary succession it was meant to reinforce. Thus, whenever a lord or a shogun died without specifying a direct successor, a great crisis would arise at the castle compound. The resolution of such a succession crisis often spelled disaster for daimyo families, as happened to the Mori in the summer of 1697.

The fourth Tsuyama lord, twenty-seven-year-old Naganari, died childless in that year and the fief elders designated as his successor the twelfth son of the polygamous Nagatsugu. When their candidate allegedly went mad while en route to Edo, the bakufu decided to confiscate Tsuyama fief. The ostensible ground for the confiscation was that the Mori had failed to designate a legitimate heir; the real reason remains hidden.[28] After announcing the death sentence on the Mori house to old Nagatsugu, whom they had summoned to Chiyoda castle, the bakufu councillors sent their death tidings on by courier to Tsuyama. On August 10 the fief elders in Tsuyama learned of the domain's confiscation. Quickly perceiving their own utter helplessness against the state power, they ordered the retainers to capitulate without resistance. Then, after informing the villages of the new situation, they closed the fief's grain warehouses in Edo, Ōsaka, and Kyōto. At the same time, they ordered the return of all retainers residing outside the fief. All that remained—their last official act—was to surrender Tsuyama castle itself to troops and officials from other fiefs ordered into Mimasaka by the bakufu.[29]

The subsequent dispersal of the Mori retainers, mostly to places within Mimasaka, the reduction in the size of Tsuyama fief to 40 percent of its original area (equivalent to 100,000 koku), and the temporary transfer of its government to three intendants (daikan) dispatched from Edo were three decisive steps on the road to the Sanchū rising of 1726–1727.

What an impression that panicky, but increasingly typical, scene at the castle town presented of abject daimyo weakness before the bakufu's almighty power. One can easily imagine some peasants sensing, suddenly, at that point, how bakufu power could be used to advantage in the struggle against daimyo misrule. Watching in their villages as the Mori retainers exited their fortress to become roaming, unemployed rōnin, local doctors, and even cultivators of the soil, Tsuyama's peasants certainly had reason to yearn for change in that drought year 1697—and to feel cheated when it was not forthcoming.

To see why change was so desperately needed, let us consider separately the issue of tributes and then Tsuyama's system of local control, and what happened to both during the next few years. In Tokugawa Japan, as we have seen, the burden of rice tributes varied with the productivity of land. It was quite heavy in certain periods and literally tremendous right before risings. Moreover, even during periods of little overt class struggle, the general question of taxation was then, as it is today, a source of anxiety for the majority. Yet many historians who write on Japan in the English-speaking West tend nowadays to shy away from or minimize the oppressiveness of taxation. Some readers may therefore question the reliability of the high rates cited here for Tsuyama fief. There is no reason to doubt them, however. Average tribute rates declined over the course of the Tokugawa period, but within fiefs some villages always had rates higher or lower than the average; and even when average rates were in decline, they were usually at a level high enough to cause distress to the poorest in the villages.

More specifically, on bakufu lands at the end of the seventeenth century, villages usually paid in taxes from 50 to 60 percent of their harvest. But in Tsuyama the rice tribute (*nengu*) on the eve of the Mori's departure amounted, on the average, to nearly 70 percent (69.6 percent) of the total harvest on all wet and dry fields. Villages with poor or insufficient croplands paid less: as in the northwestern part of the fief—Ōba region, Yumoto district—where in 1696 the average rate of tribute on 23 villages was 64 percent, and in the remote Hiruzen plateau area (where most peasants possessed less than 5 koku of land) 10 villages paid tributes averaging 60 percent. But in Tsuyama's other 254 villages the rice tribute rate when the Mori left was close to 70 percent.[30]

An interesting verification of this fact, cited by Nakano, takes the form of an inquiry sent by two Matsudaira retainers in the summer of 1698 to the bakufu intendants in Tsuyama. Their inquiry concerning the future management of local affairs mentions these figures:

The previous lord ordered that 70 percent of the harvest be taken, leaving the peasants 30 percent as rice profits. The past practice in bakufu domains has been for the lord to collect 50 percent of the crops and the peasants 50 percent. But in recent years in the western part of the country the crop ratio has been 40 percent to the lord and 60 percent to peasants. How should the matter be ordered?

The bakufu intendants replied as follows:

In the matter of rice tributes and rice profits, the bakufu practice has been a 5 to 5 ratio or in the western part of the country a 4 to 6 ratio. But in this fief we understand from the fief instructions that the officials ordered tributes of 70 percent, leaving peasants rice profits of 30 percent. However, with rice profits of 30 percent peasants are bound to suffer. Since we hear that in the case of growing barley after the rice crop, tributes are deducted from both crops, it seems not unreasonable to fix the ratio at 40 percent [for the lord] and 60 percent [for peasants].[31]

The Matsudaira however were to be no less extortionate than the Mori, for they too eventually adopted a 6-to-4 ratio rather than the one recommended by the bakufu intendants. The important point here is the tremendously heavy tax pressure that the predecessors of the Matsudaira put on peasants. To maintain it, the Mori evolved a system of rural control based on the hierarchic investiture of men descended from small resident lords and old local samurai families. It started with fifty-one district headmen (ōjōya) and their deputies (chūjōya). Technically, these were peasants selected for office because they possessed considerable landed wealth and also because of their apparently close identification with the interests of the samurai class. These middle-level intermediaries were under the direct jurisdiction of six samurai intendants, known initially as koribugyō and later as daikan. The latter reported upward to a higher ranking superintendent of local affairs (gundai). The chain of rural command then worked downward from the middle-level intermediaries—district headmen and their deputies—to village headmen and various lesser ranks.

It was the district headmen and their deputies (both of peasant status), and not the officials of samurai status, who were the centerpieces of this entire system. These men, whom peasants knew better than to regard as equals, were the real managers of the yearly forced transfer of their surpluses: the estimators, apportioners, and collectors of the taxes upon which daimyo rule depended.[32] With wealth and major landholdings in the countryside, the district headmen could best enhance their own positions, under most circumstances, by siding with the fief.

In the winter of 1697, following the Mori's departure and also taking account of a drought during the previous year, the bakufu intendants in Tsuyama ordered these economically and politically powerful rural agents to make for all villages large tribute discounts averaging around 23 percent: a tax reduction never before experienced by Tsuyama's peasants. These reductions, as Nakano notes, were in line with bakufu tax policy at the time. They also made political sense since the reductions assuaged peasant anxieties about what would occur in the wake of the Mori's removal and were easily represented as acts of genuine feudal benevolence. The intendant's action, however, set a precedent which peasants would not soon forget.[33]

On January 14, 1698, the bakufu appointed the lord of Bizen, Matsudaira Naganori, as Tsuyama's new lord. This post the Matsudaira daimyo family, direct relations of a branch of the Tokugawa house, retained for the next 175 years, down to the Meiji Restoration. Five months later the bakufu intendants transferred Tsuyama castle itself to Naganori (later changed to Nobutomi), effectively ending their direct administration of Tsuyama.[34] The Matsudaira now controlled a greatly reduced fief of 100,000 koku, consisting of eight administrative regions in the northern and western parts of Mimasaka province. Specifically, the new lord's writ extended over about 254 villages occupying 35 percent of Majima region, 15 percent of Kumenanjō, 9 percent of Katsunan, and all of Ōba, Seihokujō, Seiseijō, Tōhokujō, and Tōnanjō regions.[35]

It was to the twenty-two district headmen in these eight regions that Matsudaira Naganori directed his earliest actions affecting peasants (see map 2 and figure 3). First, he instructed them to continue administering taxes in their districts, each of which came to average about 5,000 koku.[36] Then, to the villages in all districts, he sent an even clearer signal of his determination to maintain the Mori's system of rural control and so keep peasants in the same old rut. In 1698, the first year in which he had responsibility for exacting tributes from his entire fief, Naganori restored Tsuyama's taxes to their traditional 68 to 70 percent level and allowed the district headmen and the deputy district headmen (averaging one to three per district), together with the village headmen, to increase their respective official salaries or office expenses.

This last action was really worse than it sounds. The district headmen and their deputies were not only officially appointed tax administrators and intermediaries between peasants and samurai officials. They were also the major landholders and moneylenders of the countryside. Now, while everyone else's taxes were being raised, Naganori allowed his rich agents, the main exploiters of unfree nago and kerai labor, to lower their own taxes by deducting higher office fees from that portion of the main nengu which they, as holders of peasant status, were obliged to pay. And he did this while the impact of the intendants' tax reductions of the previous year, and the more generous tax practices in adjoining villages under direct bakufu administration, were still fresh in peasant minds.

Thus it was that, less than a year after assuming charge of his reduced inheritance, Matsudaira Naganori faced his first major peasant protest. This was not a protest against the removal of the Mori but a demonstration in the eastern districts against Matsudaira tax policy. The confrontation was mediated by a district headman and an unknown village headman, both of whom acted as spokesmen for peasants. Unfortunately, very little is known about it.

On November 11, 1698, village couriers called out several hundred peasants by means of unsigned circulars distributed secretly in the villages. Unable to contain their anger at the new lord's tax policies, they prepared to make a peaceful

MAP 2. Tsuyama: A 100,000-Koku Fief, Showing the District Boundaries of Its District Headmen in 1698

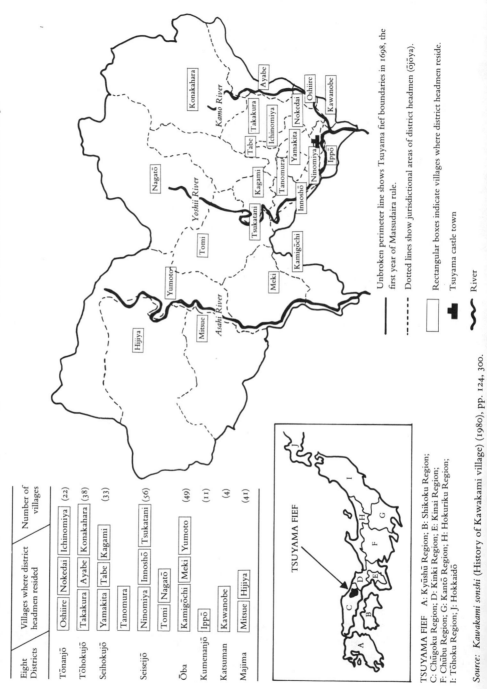

Eight Districts	Villages where district headmen resided		Number of villages
Tōnanjō	Oshiire Nokedai Ichinomiya		(22)
Tōhokujō	Takakura Ayabe Konakahara		(38)
Seihokujō	Yamakita Tabe Kagami		(33)
	Tanomura		
Seiseijō	Ninomiya Innoshō Tsukatani		(56)
	Tomi Nagatō		
Ōba	Kamigōchi Meki Yumoto		(49)
Kumenanjō	Ippō		(11)
Katsuman	Kawanobe		(4)
Majima	Mitsue Hijiya		(41)

Unbroken perimeter line shows Tsuyama fief boundaries in 1698, the first year of Matsudaira rule.

Dotted lines show jurisdictional areas of district headmen (ōjōya).

Rectangular boxes indicate villages where district headmen reside.

Tsuyama castle town

River

TSUYAMA FIEF   A: Kyūshū Region; B: Shikoku Region;
C: Chūgoku Region; D: Kinki Region; E: Kinai Region;
F: Chūbu Region; G: Kantō Region; H: Hokuriku Region;
I: Tōhoku Region; J: Hokkaidō

Source: Kawakami sonshi (History of Kawakami village) (1980), pp. 124, 300.

FIGURE 3. A Simplified Chart of Official Positions: The Matsudaira Family's Rural Chain of Command in Tsuyama Fief, 1698–1727

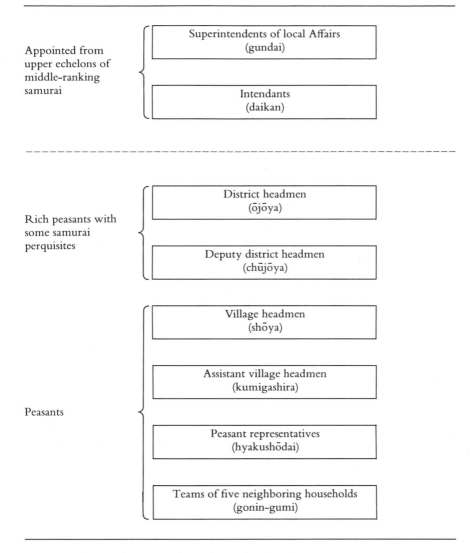

Appointed from
upper echelons of
middle-ranking
samurai

> Superintendents of local Affairs
> (gundai)

> Intendants
> (daikan)

Rich peasants with
some samurai
perquisites

> District headmen
> (ōjōya)

> Deputy district headmen
> (chūjōya)

Peasants

> Village headmen
> (shōya)

> Assistant village headmen
> (kumigashira)

> Peasant representatives
> (hyakushōdai)

> Teams of five neighboring households
> (gonin-gumi)

Source: *Kawakami sonshi* (History of Kawakami Village) (1980), pp. 128–135, 178–185, 309–312.

appeal near the castle town. When their secret rally occurred, however, seven district headmen who were in the vicinity received word of what was happening. Immediately, they rushed to the scene and tried to get the protesters to desist. But the aroused peasants would brook no interference and chased them for their efforts into the town. In this incident the tax officials revealed their Janus-faced role. While serving their samurai masters, they also tried to shield the peasants in their own communities where they were subject to sanctions if they beared down too heavily.

Later, some of the peasants rioted, while others succeeded in the main purpose of the demonstration: to get one of the two fief superintendents of local affairs to call a meeting of all district headmen. The details surrounding subsequent events are much less clear. Apparently, when the meeting convened, Saburōemon, the headman of Takakura district in the Tōhoku region, came forward and defended the peasants' action, saying that they would never be satisfied until the fief lowered its tax rate to the level obtaining in adjoining bakufu domains. All that is known about Saburōmon is that he came from a family of hereditary district headmen who had served the Mori.[37] Why he defended the peasants is not clear; neither is it known why the protest ended as quickly as it did.

Tsuyama fief made two responses to this first peasant demonstration against its tax policies. First, in late 1698, it granted some temporary tax concessions. Then, four months later in March 1699, it turned right around and publicly executed Saburōemon, one village headman who had defended him at the meeting, and two unknown peasants accused of having staged the original demonstration. Thereafter, to eliminate any possibility of peasants again gaining political access through the mediation of sympathetic district and village headmen, the Matsudaira reduced its districts to twenty and strengthened its system of rural control. It made district headmen swear oaths of allegiance and granted them, in 1717, the right to have surnames and pass them on to their legal descendants. Though legally still defined as peasants, the district headmen were, by this time, quasi samurai—addressed by peasants as samurai (gōzamurai)—with incomes in some cases equal to that of high-ranking samurai officials. Nakano reports that on the eve of the Sanchū rising, the richest district headman had acquired landholdings worth about 430 koku; the next richest had holdings worth about 200 koku; three had holdings of from 100 to 200 koku; five had 50 to 100 koku; and the remaining ten around 50 koku.[38] But the main consequence of the closer ties between Tsuyama fief and its district headmen was that, later on during the Sanchū rising, all the headmen sided with the fief and helped to lead the attack against peasants.

To recapitulate: the "violent appeal" of November 1698, followed by the execution of the peasants' defenders, speeded up the Matsudaira's policy of strengthening ties with district officials: the rustic samurai. In the long run, however, both developments exacerbated problems of fief administration by ending peasant political apathy. For the appeal of 1698 also established a precedent that, in time of need, could serve peasant ends. Henceforth, Tsuyama's peasants would not stand so much in awe of the castle authorities. They would react in a more politically self-conscious way to achieve relief from the burden of oppressive taxes. And just as the bakufu used every accession of a daimyo to strengthen its own power, so peasants would learn to turn to their own advantage any change in the fortunes of their feudal masters.

Yet the transformation of "precedent" and "custom" into "right" is a painfully slow process. Another twenty-eight years were to elapse before peasants were ready to be their own spokesmen, registering in their own voices the full range of their grievances against the fief. During that time many material, institutional, and ideological conditions had to be fulfilled in order to bring all social groups and classes closer in relations of mutual conflict and cooperation. It is to those complex, subjective-objective conditions that we turn next.

CHAPTER TWO

The Coming Conflict: Taxes, Competition, and Reform

LIKE the feudal monarchies of Western Europe, the bakuhan state was constructed to facilitate the collection of taxes from peasants. Hence the issues of identifying and measuring wealth, taxing it, and gauging peasant reactions to taxes and corvées were at the forefront of its official considerations.[1] Moreover, because the Tokugawa house rejected the policy of overseas mercantilism, the ruling class was forced to develop a particular type of fiscal system: one that promoted petty agricultural production and urban monopolies in trade and manufacturing, but also taxed both quite harshly, thereby driving peasants and merchants into market development. In turning now to Tsuyama fief during the early eighteenth century, we find that high taxes, often levied arbitrarily, together with steadily worsening relations among peasants, rich merchants, and rural officials, had become abiding aspects of village life. Let us examine each element of this situation in turn.

TAXES

On the basis of local village records for the first quarter of the eighteenth century—table 1—it appears that the fief collected annually about 58 percent of peasant harvests. Still, the tax question was forever on peasant minds in a way it had not been before the bakufu split the fief. Generally speaking, there was considerable economic inequality among different regions within Tsuyama fief, so that the tax picture remained one of high but geographically uneven rates. According to the *Gonarika yosechō* (Collected Accounts of Annual Tributes), the tribute rate over the two decades from 1716 to 1736 averaged about 60 percent for the entire fief. How-

TABLE 1. Rice Tribute Payments in Tsuyama Fief

Before the Sanchū Rising (100,000 koku)

Year	Officially assessed production (koku)	Amount of crop harvested (koku)	Lord's gross share of total harvest (koku)	Deductions for district headmen, village office expenses, and social relief (koku)	Lord's final (net) share of harvest (koku)	Actual percentage of harvest surrendered as tribute
1702	100,177.310	89,435.179	54,752.278	7,064.609	47,687.669	53.3
1719	100,670.442	89,262.075	55,189.240	2,588.644	52,600.596	58.9
1720	100,737.518	89,330.813	55,212.907	3,573.224	51,639.683	57.8
1726	101,670.725	90,247.834	55,537.339	3,237.993	52,299.346	58.0

After the Sanchū Rising (50,000 koku)

Year	Officially assessed production (koku)	Amount of crop harvested (koku)	Lord's gross share of total harvest (koku)	Deductions for district headmen, village office expenses, and social relief (koku)	Lord's final (net) share of harvest (koku)	Actual percentage of harvest surrendered as tribute
1727	50,867.214	46,486.160	29,600.900	2,526.739	27,074.161	58.2
28	50,887.779	46,522.003	29,621.948	1,824.353	27,797.593	59.8
29	50,911.998	46,536.136	29,625.245	2,933.882	26,691.363	57.4
30	50,925.872	46,549.688	29,630.672	2,050.371	27,580.301	59.2
31	50,935.802	46,559.360	29,634.224	2,529.828	27,104.396	58.2
32	50,936.929	46,556.705	29,633.684	2,966.180	26,667.504	57.3
33	50,942.300	46,562.870	29,638.186	2,398.481	27,239.705	58.5
34	50,947.404	46,567.556	29,640.638	2,646.869	26,993.769	58.0
35	50,956.858	46,574.868	29,642.531	2,554.827	27,087.704	58.2
36	50,962.046	46,570.292	29,638.853	4,322.604	25,316.249	54.4
37	50,966.872	46,571.025	29,637.877	2,524.202	27,113.675	58.2
38	50,970.466	46,574.448	29,639.285	3,863.271	25,776.014	55.3
1751	51,015.363	46,546.821	29,703.669	4,177.868	25,525.801	54.8
1752	51,016.017	46,504.918	29,711.808	4,332.543	25,389.265	54.5

Source: Figures compiled from local village records by Nakano Michiko in *Kawakami sonshi* (History of Kawakami village) (1980), pp. 317, 369.

ever, in 1719, half of Tsuyama's districts had tribute rates that were far above this
60 percent fief average by as much as 10 to 16 percent. Districts with tax rates of
from 62 to 76 percent included the central wet-field zone in the vicinity of Tsuyama
castle and the river plain along the Asahi centering on Kuse village. On the other
hand, ten districts in the northern and western border regions, including the three
that composed the mountainous Sanchū area, paid much less than the fief average
of 60 percent. But in these same northern and western districts the rate of tribute
reductions for office fees for rural officials and relief rice—a combined category
called *okuhikimai*—exceeded the fief average for such deductions by about 12 to 15
percent.[2]

On top of paying the basic rice tribute, Tsuyama's peasants were also forced
to pay levies (*komononari*) on products from the seas, rivers, and mountains and
enterprise taxes (*unjōkin*), which were tributes levied on forges, wine brewing,
forestry work, and water transport. These two taxes apparently remained unchanged until 1726, when, as part of the Kyōhō reforms, enterprise taxes were
abruptly increased on mountain products, forestry work, and iron mining.

RELATIONS WITH OFFICIALS AND MERCHANTS

Peasant–rural official relations worsened over the two decades preceding the rising. But this decline in the prestige of district and village headmen, as a result of
their role as exploiters of peasants and servitors of fief power, was also a feature of
the entire eighteenth century, observable in many other domains besides Tsuyama.
As the rural tribute administrators drew closer to the castle and away from peasants, peasant dissatisfaction with their conduct of local affairs mounted. By the
winter of 1726, villagers in every region of Tsuyama were unanimous in demanding their removal and replacement by "honest officials" chosen by ordinary peasants from their own ranks, together with the surrender of village account registers
and tax instructions.

Peasant hatred of rural officials also implied a growing rift between town and
countryside, merchants and peasants. This aspect of peasant social relations anticipated the maturation of a more complex agrarian economy in which coercion via
the market paralleled feudal extra-economic coercion. Throughout the first quarter of the eighteenth century, the enmity of Tsuyama's peasants was not confined
just to local officials and tax administrators. It extended to merchants as well
because the tribute system also operated to subordinate poor peasants to merchants.
In peasant eyes, towns and strategically located market villages were places of residence of privileged merchants who made interest-bearing tax loans.

On the other hand, in many parts of Tsuyama, peasant existence was predicated on cooperation with merchants through "upland products associations," so that the peasant-merchant relationship was not only an exploitative one. Indeed, within the framework of routine village life the two classes were mutually indispensable.

Thus, understanding of the Sanchū rising requires that different layers of merchants be distinguished and that those merchants be identified who were not in a mutually supportive relationship with fief authorities. For when revolt engulfed Tsuyama, a majority of merchants shied away from any open collaboration with peasants. But in the Sanchū revolt, a tiny handful of rice and iron merchants did just the opposite: like the iron mine owner and merchant, Otaniya Heibei, they gave strong support to the peasants upon whom their trade depended.[3]

Increasing social and economic inequality within villages was another central feature of the social scene in early eighteenth-century Tsuyama. As noted earlier, ever since the second half of the seventeenth century, the fief had been promoting the growth of petty proprietorships by full-status peasants (honbyakushō). Such peasants already predominated in the wet-field and river plains areas. But in the remote Sanchū region late medieval economic institutions fused with early modern ones to produce a more complex class structure. There, even in the Kyōhō period, we still find many nago and kerai peasants locked into exploitative relationships of personal dependency to big landlords of the district headmen stratum and to full-status peasants—relationships that prevented them from appropriating property on their own authority.

On the other hand, the climate in the Sanchū villages was hostile to ex-nago and kerai who had recently risen to higher status. Even when listed in cadastral registers as payers of tribute, they may not have actually been treated as full-status peasants within the villages. Yet such peasants, farming one to five koku of land, together with landless tenants, who combined farming on mortgaged land with migrant nonagricultural labor, constituted the overwhelming majority by the 1720s.

During the agricultural slack season—December through early March—the migrant workers crossed the borders of villages and districts in tightly knit bands and worked together as day laborers in iron mines at the foot of the Chūgoku Mountains, in a region which, at the time, was said to have produced nearly half of Japan's iron.[4] Migrant iron mining was then the Sanchū peasants' main off-season employment. The operators of the mines, mountain huts, and blacksmith shops in which they worked were the Tsuyama merchants living in districts along both sides of the Asahi River—villages such as Ochiai, Kuse, and Katsuyama. Tsuyama fief also operated three iron mountains of its own, which gave employment to such peasants, besides having close ties to private operators of ironworks who made contributions to fief finances.[5]

Apart from mining, the Sanchū peasants specialized in growing miscellaneous grains such as wheat, soybeans, and tobacco, or else they specialized in lumbering, woodworking, and animal husbandry. In 1725, Tsuda Shigemichi, a retainer of the Matsudaira, noted in his *Sakushūki* (Sakushū Account) that:

Tsuyama has little rice and produces many miscellaneous grains. They have the institution of "upland products association" [*hatamonoza*] which merchants finance so that peasants pay in grains in exchange for rice, which they pay out again as tribute. This practice is called upland products exchange. Such associations exist, for instance, in Kuse village [in the Sanchū region].[6]

Tsuda's comment is important for two reasons. It underscores the complexity, diversification, and backwardness of Tsuyama fief's agrarian economy on the eve of the Kyōhō rising. At the same time, it points to the antagonistic unity of peasant-merchant existence, mediated by the upland products association which functioned within the larger unity of the fief's political economy. By Kyōhō, the tribute system, with its impossibly high tax rates, had fostered conditions that kept a large part of the peasantry in perpetual debt. The poor, caught in a complex web of exploitative relationships, were at the mercy of iron and rice merchants, who in turn were linked to both village officials and the higher echelons of fief power.

How were such linkages effected? One mechanism was rice loans at high interest certificated by fief officials. Typically, when winter came and crops were bad—as they frequently were—poor peasants borrowed rice in order to complete payment of their annual tributes. If they borrowed from their village headman, the latter, charged with ensuring that the entire village met its tax quota, would invariably lend the needed rice in the form of a stamped ticket for the required amount. The borrower would take this "rice exchange ticket" to the district headman for that official's endorsement. Once endorsed by the district headman the peasant could take the paper to a merchant and ask for rice. The merchant would then agree to go by a fixed date to one of the three rural warehouses established by Tsuyama fief for the collection and storage of grain tributes, bringing with him the necessary amount of tax rice in the name of the peasant who had made the original loan request to the village headman. Thereupon the warehouse official issued to the merchant another rice receipt ticket, which would go back to the village headman as tangible proof that the peasant had completed payment of his taxes. Of course, not all peasants borrowed rice from village and district headmen. Some made deals directly with rice-exchange merchants and received tickets themselves from the officials at the fief's Kuse, Nishihara, or Takada warehouses located in Majima and Ōba regions.[7] These tickets had also to be presented to the headmen for recording in the village tax account register as proof of payment made to one of the rural warehouses.[8]

Ultimately, this complicated procedure left many peasants in debt to merchants and others who paid their taxes and gave them stamped receipts for the amount lent. If they failed to repay such loans, together with the high interest on them, the district headman would hold the village headman responsible for the unpaid borrowings of their charges. In 1722, when bad crops made it impossible for many villages to complete payment of their tributes, the fief accountant, Kubo Shimbei (Chikahira), granted permission for the deficits to be made up in the form of loaned rice guaranteed or certificated by the district headmen. Nakano Michiko, citing fief records of this transaction, notes that "the rice was loaned at 30 percent interest for six years. But 18 percent of the interest was designated as relief rice and deducted from the *okuhikimai*. The remaining 12 percent interest was assumed by villages which borrowed the rice."[9] Significantly, throughout the Sanchū rising, peasants who owned fields insisted most vehemently on being released from returning borrowed rice that had been endorsed by the stamps of the district headmen.

THE KYŌHŌ REFORMS AND TSUYAMA FIEF

By the start of the second decade of the eighteenth century, Tsuyama fief faced a crisis of feudal revenues of undetermined proportions. Its finances depended mainly on a steady influx of peasant tributes in rice and cash. But that input was being eroded by a slow process of quiet peasant resistance to exploitation on the one hand and, on the other, a vicious cycle of repeated crop failures which forced the fief to grant tribute reductions to peasants in order to tide them over really bad crop seasons. For samurai who lived off of peasant production, the practical consequence of this financial decay was the cutting of their stipends and the lowering of their standard of living.

But by this time the bakufu and nearly all the private domains were also in distress. There had been typhoons and floods in many parts of Japan in 1720–1721. In bakufu warehouses rice stockpiles were low. Many samurai were not receiving their customary stipends while peasants in certain areas of the "heavenly domain" were experiencing even worse deprivation in the form of starvation.[10] For the eighth shogun, Yoshimune, and his finance councillors, destroyed food supplies, inadequate or delayed tribute payments, and starving peasants signified something more serious than a transient natural disaster. Starting in 1721 and continuing in stages for the next three decades, the finance councillors in shogun's capital drafted a series of reforms, which intensified the exploitation of peasants, effected reductions in samurai stipends, and forced various loans upon the merchant class. Essentially, these Kyōhō reforms addressed three distinct economic problems: feudal tenancy, declining rice prices, and the narrowing of the rice tribute base upon which the bakufu depended. Let us consider each one briefly.

Throughout the second half of the seventeenth century, poor peasants who needed a loan to help meet their tribute payments placed their land in the custody of better-off landholders. When they could not continue repaying the principal on the loan, they sometimes lost part or all of their cultivators' rights to the land which they had pledged as security. Since one of the main aims of the Kyōhō reforms was to reconstruct small-scale farming, the practice of illegal land transfers and sales among peasants had to be curbed. In June 1722 (A.D.) the bakufu issued a "ban on the forfeiture of land." It forbid the forfeiture of pawned fields even if the debt on them had not been repaid within the alloted time period. In cases where debts could not be repaid, it ordered holders of pawned fields to rewrite the contract specifying that the principal would be repaid in annual installments without interest, and when repayment was completed, the land would revert to the person who had originally pawned it. All pawned land forfeited after 1717 could be recovered by repaying the debts on it; and moneylenders who allowed pawners to continue occupying the land as tenants were told to make the annual tenant fee less than 15 percent of the loan.[11]

Soon after issuing this ban, a mass protest movement erupted on bakufu territory in Murayama district, Dewa province, and Nagakubiki district, Echigo province. In both cases peasants, interpreting the ban to suit their purposes, forcibly confiscated records pertaining to pawned and forfeited land. These disturbances were harshly suppressed, and the next year, 1723, the bakufu withdrew its ban. Private fiefs throughout the country are believed to have registered the failure of this particular reform and drawn conclusions from it in shaping their own land policy.[12]

The second problem addressed by Yoshimune's reforms was the price of rice. The rice price first began to decline simultaneously in many parts of the country in 1723–1724, and the decline did not bottom out until the middle of the next decade. Since rice was the main Tokugawa medium of exchange and value, the bakufu and fief economies evolved price systems that constrained other commodities to rise or fall along with fluctuations in the rice price. So long as the urban population was increasing fairly rapidly, as had been the case during the seventeenth century, the rice price also tended to rise. But when the population boom ended early in the first quarter of the eighteenth century, a situation emerged wherein the rice price began a long, slow descent while prices for all other commodities continued to rise. The daimyo and their retainer bands were thus caught in a vicious cycle. They strove to market more rice every year in Osaka and Edo—only to see its price fall, thereby driving them deeper into debt to merchants.

This was the situation that the bakufu now tried to counter. First, it attempted to corner the market in tribute rice, remove restrictions on rice for wine brewing, and sanction future transactions by rice wholesalers. Later it began the practice on a small scale of forcing merchants who handled commodities other than rice to form restrictive guilds.[13] Out of this last policy, as Totman notes, came the practice of giving official recognition to federations of craft guilds and extracting from them fees at regular intervals.[14]

However, at this time, the main source of bakufu income was not the taxation of commercial wealth but the rice tax. And the most decisive issue confronting the shogun's bureaucratic reformers was the problem of the state's stagnating rice tribute base. Here arose the problem of tribute assessment. The customary method for assessing tribute had long been annual direct field inspections (kemi), conducted in normal times by officials on the average crops of the entire village. In bad crop years some fiefs inspected the fields of individual peasants in order to estimate the average crops.[15] But regardless of how it was conducted, from the viewpoint of the bakufu such annual direct inspections had two disadvantages. Villagers intent on preventing increases in their rice tributes often bribed local officials to reduce their rates. Second, annual direct inspection was time consuming and "involved the possibility of losing time for harvesting early, middle or late rice crops, or sowing a secondary crop of winter wheat on the same fields."[16]

In 1722 the bakufu abandoned annual field inspection and switched to jōmen: the practice of fixing the tribute rate on the basis of the average gross assessment over a fixed period in the past, ranging usually from three to seven, ten, or even twenty years. This opened the way to raising the tribute rate after the end of each fixed assessment period. Accompanying this reform was a tightening up of the conditions under which bakufu officials were allowed to grant discounts on fields damaged by bad weather. This particular reform, which had already been adopted by some private fiefs, did succeed eventually in increasing the exploitation of peasants on bakufu lands. According to different estimates, tribute income on directly administered bakufu territories averaged from 1,600,000 to 1,800,000 koku for eight years from 1737 to 1744: the highest amount recorded until the last decades of the Tokugawa era.[17]

So much for the reforms unfolding in the shogun's capital during the early 1720s. While they were being implemented, the fief official Kubo Shimbei appeared on the scene in Tsuyama fief. Kubo introduced his own version of the

Kyōhō reforms to Tsuyama in an effort to stem its financial decline. The exact proportions of that deterioration cannot be established for want of data. But it is known that Tsuyama's finances were being undermined by forced rice contributions to the bakufu and the mounting expenses associated with the Tokugawa hostage system. The latter required the daimyo's attendance at the shogun's court in alternate years and the permanent residence of their families in Edo. Poor crops in the years 1719, 1720, and 1722 had been detrimental to the fief's finances. In 1723 Kubo cut the stipends of the Matsudaira retainers by half. He was planning to introduce the next year a shift-over from annual field inspection (kemi) to fixed-period tribute assessment (jōmen). But the repercussion in 1724 of new natural disasters on agricultural production forced him to delay. For that year typhoons and floods hit Tsuyama, causing widespread crop damage, hunger, and malnutrition. In 1725 villages in all districts of the fief suffered from "the worst drought in a century" and successfully protested the introduction of fixed-period tribute assessment. Again, Kubo postponed its implementation and, instead, discharged over twenty low-ranking samurai.[18] But facing an ever worsening revenue situation the next drought year, he resolved to delay no longer.

As we approach the eve of the Sanchū rising, Tsuyama's financial difficulties need to be carefully distinguished from the political crisis into which the fief government was plunged during October and November 1726. The former was serious but certainly not as acute as it would become by the middle of the eighteenth century. Further, when Kubo, whose career up to that time had been meteoric, attained on September 26 the two additional posts of superintendent of local affairs (gundai) and general superintendent of all rural areas (zaichū sōnomikomi), his reform proposals had the support of the highest fief officials. Having concentrated in his own hands full authority for all aspects of fief economy, Kubo took direct charge of a tax collection team of four intendants. Two of them—Miki Jinzaemon, responsible for the three Sanchū districts of Hijiya, Yumoto, and Mitsue, and Yamada Bumpachi, in charge of the two adjacent flatland districts of Meki and Kamigōchi—were soon to play leading roles in pacifying peasants. Now Kubo was ready to implement his solution to the problem of fief finances by making the ruled population shoulder a heavier burden.[19]

But let us stop and back up a bit. In the fall of 1726, something much more serious than falling samurai incomes and a generally gloomy economic picture preoccupied the fief government in Tsuyama castle. Five years earlier, in 1721, at exactly the time Yoshimune commenced his Kyōhō reforms at Edo, Naganori's adopted six-year-old son, Asagorō, succeeded to the lordship of Tsuyama. Now in September 1726, Asagorō lay gravely ill in the fief's Edo mansion. In October his condition worsened. As he had no direct successor, the very survival of the Mat-

sudaira house hung on his life. Thus, when Kubo Shimbei ordered the rural officials to implement his new tax policy, the bakufu was already preparing to strike
at the Matsudaira house and the warriors in Tsuyama castle had the strongest possible reason for attempting to speed up the collection of the maximum amount of
taxes from peasants. These might be the last tributes they would ever get their
hands on. These circumstances help to explain Kubo's fall tax order, the initial pro-
vocation that set in motion a direct appeal out of which developed a virtual general
insurrection, the first ever experienced by Tsuyama fief: "For this year move up
your Fall work so that you can complete the payment of your tributes by October
15. Until then, wheat sowing is totally prohibited. In addition, we order you to
increase taxes by 4 percent."[20] Thus was the die cast and a shock administered to
Tsuyama's villagers which awakened their sense of past injustices.

Before going on to examine in detail the inner dynamics of the Sanchū revolt,
there are two further matters to consider. First, the question of alternatives. In that
harsh winter of 1726, was there no alternative for Tsuyama's financially pressed
samurai other than to increase their exploitation of peasants? Why, for instance,
did Kubo not wait in implementing his tax reforms until agricultural conditions
had improved? Why, in implementing his tax orders, did the rural agents act so
harshly toward peasants? The peasants, in a sense, answered both questions at the
time by charging that the fief government and its agents were corrupt. Their
answer undoubtedly contains a large measure of truth.

But further reflection reveals the shortcomings of the questions themselves.
That is the second matter. The moral criteria by which peasants and sympathetic
contemporaries judged events implied the external, accidental nature of the
rising—as if it could have been avoided if only the feudal power holders had practiced their own moral teachings and treated peasants benevolently. But Tokugawa
feudal society was an inherently and profoundly unjust society. Despite the
samurai's promises of services to the people—a feature of all ruling ideologies—
their whole past experience was one of treating all but the top stratum of wealthy,
elite peasants with disrespect. Since at least the late sixteenth century, samurai had
deprived peasants of political rights, maintained them as mere rice-producing ma-
chines, and punished them cruelly for behavior that challenged the samurai way of
rule. Moreover, although samurai may have wanted, at times, to curb corruption
in their own ranks, that was not their overriding priority; but keeping peasants in a
state of feudal bondage was.

Therefore, insofar as the dominant class exercised rights unilaterally, without
ensuring the basic security of peasants, revolts had to occur. Moreover, the
samurai, as a class, had organized the basic processes of production and distribution
in such a way that their own constantly growing needs conflicted continually with

the expanding needs of the overwhelming majority of society's producers. What made class relations antagonistic and uprisings unavoidable was the Tokugawa political economy (with its authoritarian principles of organization and exploitative conditions of production), together with the dislocations generated by the process of economic change itself. This system inextricably welded together political domination and economic exploitation, so that even when protesting peasants made only economic demands, they reflected a situation in which the issue of feudal political control was usually latent.

Who today would claim that feudal economy is comparable with capitalist economy? Yet both are regimes of class exploitation in which economic and political power are inseparably fused, though in very different ways. Feudalism and capitalism have in common a regulative social principle of treating people in the process of production as means of gain rather than ends in themselves. In both, a major function of the state is to sustain and intensify production relations. And just as peasant struggles were structurally inevitable under feudalism, so the unjust organization of production in modern capitalist society creates circumstances in which workers' strikes and popular protests become structurally inevitable.

Similarly, if we view the state as historically coexistent with and constitutive of class, then whenever the state, under feudalism or capitalism, adopts harsh policies that increase sharply an existing level of economic exploitation, the chances are strong that resistance activity from below will also increase, though never in a mechanical, one-to-one relationship. And when resistance does occur under specific historical conditions, it will usually fail unless it is broad based and persistent. And last, under both historical modes of production, the area in which class struggle occurs is hardly ever confined to just distributive or economic issues but entails, as well, issues of control over the sphere of production. We shall now see that for Tsuyama's peasants that meant securing control over their own villages by ousting the fief's intermediate exploiters. For the fief controlled the relations of production through the villages and, more specifically, through the mechanism of appointing and dismissing village and district headmen.

CHAPTER THREE

The Sanchū Rising of 1726–1727

THE Sanchū rising lasted approximately ten weeks and unfolded in two stages. Stage I—November 20–21 to December 22, 1726—was the period of the trans-fief ikki waged by a peasantry loosely united in its major demands. The major events were: the Nishihara and Kuse warehouse incidents; the uprising of the peasants in the western districts in a struggle for local political power and tax concessions; their successful negotiations over a period of four days with fief representatives at Ōdankōge; the spread of the struggle to the eastern and central districts, where the pattern of collective negotiations was repeated successfully; and, finally, the seeming victory of peasants throughout the entire fief confirmed by written pledges of the intendants.

Stage II began around December 21–22 in the western districts that were the scene of the original rising and ended there on January 30, 1727, when the fief's military forces withdrew to Tsuyama castle. Although a clear picture of events and their meaning in this crucial second stage is lacking, the main contours of what happened can be established fairly accurately. Stage II saw the virtual liberation of the Sanchū from Tsuyama's control and the establishment there of a system of dual control in villages. Peasant "message receivers," who cooperated with the ikki leaders in resisting the Matsudaira's control, displaced the old ruling elite. The subsequent exodus of some of the fief's rural agents to Tsuyama castle and their appeals for fief assistance in crushing the insurrection hastened the final settlement of accounts. After a few days of deliberations, the fief leaders opted for a two-pronged invasion of the Sanchū, from front and rear, by military forces under the command of Miki Jinzaemon and Yamada Bumpachi. After a week of skirmishing they succeeded in arresting the ikki leaders. There followed: the capture of most of their

31

followers; on-the-spot executions of forty-five peasant captives; and finally, the withdrawal of the fief army from the Sanchū and its return to Tsuyama castle.

A third stage or aftermath followed the defeat of the Sanchū rising. This was the period February 1 to late April 1727, when Tokuemon and five other leaders who had been dragged back to Tsuyama castle were imprisoned, tortured, and executed, finally, in a small public ceremony at a river beach outside the castle walls. The fief, to punish the peasants, withdrew all but one of the concessions it had made earlier—the 4 percent tax increase—and forced them to sign loyalty oaths in which they swore never again to disobey any order of the authorities. In the countryside the district and village headmen returned to power. Mass arrests of peasants and their reindoctrination in obedience went forward. But from late February the main concern of fief leaders shifted to personnel retrenchment—the disbanding of military units—in preparation for the dreaded day when the bakufu would dispossess the Matsudaira of lands worth fifty thousand koku.

Many contemporary accounts remain of the events that occurred in Tsuyama during the fateful years 1726–1727. But what follows draws especially heavily on one classic document in particular: the "Mikoku shimin ranpōki" (An Account of the People's Revolt in the Province of Mimasaka; hereafter "Ranpōki"). Its unknown author signed himself "Shimpūken Chikuō"—literally, "Divine Wind House, Bamboo Old Man." This was the sort of pen name that anonymous storytellers often affixed to war tales. Shimpūken completed his record in June 1727 while residing in the market village of Takada, not far from the scene of the events he describes. Historian Nagamitsu Norikazu summed up nearly all that can be inferred about Shimpūken by remarking that he was "an intellectual hidden among the people, such as a rōnin, doctor, itinerant priest or member of a professional family of readers of the Taiheiki." [1]

Since the Taiheiki (or "Chronicle of Grand Pacification") was clearly on Shimpūken's mind when he thought of Tokuemon, the main leader of the Sanchū peasants, that fourteenth-century anonymous war chronicle requires a word before proceeding. The Taiheiki centers on the theme of Japan's ruling-class families at war, with the court and Emperor Go-Daigo pitted in a losing battle against the military houses. Much of the action in the latter half of the work is set in central and western Japan, in Harima, Bizen, Mimasaka, and Hōki. Two other facts are also relevant. The Taiheiki was written in the third person by several authors, and one of its main heroes was the warrior Kusunoki Masashige, a paragon of samurai loyalty and filial piety, but also a symbol of rebellion and righteousness. Similarly, the "Ranpōki" is also written in the third person. In chronicling an uprising of poor peasants, Shimpūken likens their leader to, among others, Kusunoki. However, writing in an age in which the samurai have banned all ikki, he takes pains throughout his narrative to make the people's position crystal clear by employing sharply different terms for peasants and their oppressors.

Shimpūken's document is obviously an invaluable source on peasant beliefs and culture. No other contemporary account yet uncovered captures better than the "Ranpōki" the moral tone and atmosphere of this particular struggle. The "Ranpōki" also yields vital information on samurai tax measures and on such contemporary economic activities as grain storage, marketing, and the struggle between fief and peasantry over grazing and forestry rights. But it must be handled critically and its accuracy on details established, wherever possible, by comparison with official records and with the later accounts of historians. For Shimpūken was no stenographer, taking down the words of peasants as they spoke. Rather, in recounting their struggle under conditions of censorship and military repression, he drew on preexisting oral and literary traditions which deliberately mixed fact and fiction for purposes of moral exhortation as well as self-protection. Nevertheless, the "Ranpōki" is true to the spirit of the times and to certain values of the classes it depicts.

STAGE I

On November 11, 1726, Matsudaira Asagorō died in Edo without ever having set foot in his fief. His retainers and their families in Tsuyama learned the news six days later on November 17. Their panicky response was, for peasants, an unexpected stroke of good fortune. Contemporary accounts of the Sanchū rising contain no explicit references to the Mori's removal in 1697 or to the events that followed on its heels. But peasant actions suggest that they carried forward into the 1720s collective memories of those earlier events and that in 1726 they were motivated significantly by inferences from their own late seventeenth-century past.

By the start of the third week in November, the countryside was alive with rumors of the fief's imminent confiscation and the sale of tribute rice stored in warehouses by officials preparing to flee. "Another rumor, rampant here and there, was that all the loans and debts in the fief, along with the village headmen's certificated rice loans, would be cancelled."[2] Meanwhile, bitter denunciations were hurled at Kubo Shimbei for his harsh tax orders and at the rural tax administrators for their mercilessly strict implementation of them.

Then two minor incidents, occurring one after the other, allowed peasants to unleash their anger. In the Sanchū area, rice tribute was shipped downstream on flat-bottom riverboats to the fief's warehouses in Kuse, Nishihara, and Takada. There some of the grain was converted into cash by privileged merchants and some sent on by packhorses and cows to Tsuyama castle town. The trouble started on the night of November 21 at the fief's Nishihara warehouse, located beside a sharp bend in the Asahi River (at the site of what today is the Nishihara railway station in Ochiai City). Anticipating that samurai officials were getting ready to seal up the warehouses and sell off the peasants' tribute grains, the district headman of Kamigōchi, Ōba region, Kondō Masatsune and the deputy district headman of Shimo village, one Saburobei, began secretly removing eighty-four bales of their own rice from the warehouse in the dark of night. Their apparent objective was to retrieve, for their own purposes, tribute rice consigned to the Matsudaira. Fearing just such a move from their headmen and creditors, some peasants had been watching the warehouse from a distance. When these lookouts spotted the pair, they imagined it was their own tribute rice being stolen and gave the alarm.

By taking account now of three points, the peasants' original motivation at the start of the uprising becomes readily understandable. First, the district headmen and deputies were generally hated. The people considered them too merciless in carrying out fief reforms and believed they had long been interpreting official instructions to suit their own purposes. Second, the tensions aroused by Kubo's 4 percent tax increase order had been heightened by rumors that the Sanchū region might possibly escape the rule of the Matsudaira if the bakufu confiscated the fief. Once that happened, no tax official had any right whatsoever to remove any portion of the tribute from the region. Third, the people strongly believed in the likelihood of an edict of debt cancelation because of the abnormal conditions prevailing at the time.

Given these elements affecting their state of mind, we can appreciate the colorful narrative of what happened next, given in the "Ranpōki":

When the people of the nearby villages heard that this district headman Kondō Masatsune . . . secretly removed all the rice from the warehouse and had it loaded onto river boats hidden in the vicinity, a people's army of over 100 men quickly descended upon them. Raising a battle cry, they surrounded the warehouse and pounced upon Kondō. He narrowly escaped from the place. Hearing of this incident, the deputy district headman of Akano village, Chūzaemon, from a wealthy family, lent rice to the peasants. He also kept his rice in that warehouse in Nishihara along with others. He said that because the fief was in danger, "I thought we would be unable to dispose freely of our own things, so I indiscreetly had my rice loaded at night." Whether this was true or not is unclear. The next day a messenger arrived from Tsuyama saying that these two men [Kondō Masatsune and Chūzaemon] are ordered to come to the castle. Accepting this instruction, they fled while on their way to the castle town. Their associates . . . (also) fled here and there just like baby spiders. Encouraged by this, the people withdrew individually.[3]

The four intendants completed their own initial account of the Tsuyama rising on January 15, 1727, while their troops were billeted in the Kuse area and mopping up operations were still underway in Sanchū. From their official version of the Nishihara incident, we learn further that on the night of November 21, the peasants from ten villages came out and yelled that it was an act of outright theft [for Kondō Chūzaemon and Saburobei] to take rice from a warehouse without permission. Other district headmen and deputies appeared and tried to stop the peasants by saying they must be quiet during the period of mourning for the death of the lord. But the peasants from the ten villages did not agree because many years before they had made an appeal and delivered both rice and soybeans to the Nishihara warehouse. In time of an emergency, these villages understood that they should consult with one another and pledge to make payments together. That's why they were given collective responsibility. Nevertheless, the owner of the warehouse at Nishihara . . . serving in the capacity of district headman and other offices, completed payment last summer by returning borrowed rice to the intendants. (Concerning the borrowed rice: since peasants would borrow from the warehouse, the district headman of the ten villages had been allocating rice there.) Because the district headmen and deputy district headmen were badgering peasants on the matter of returning borrowed rice, the disturbance would not subside. Fortunately, officials from Tsuyama came to Kuse village on November 22 to investigate and then, on the same day, to Nishihara village, where they placated the peasants.[4]

When Miki Jinzaemon and Yamada Bumpachi arrived in Nishihara, they confiscated the properties of its district headman and his deputy and entrusted their various account books to Fukushima Zenbei, the district headman of Meki. But no sooner had the two intendants settled the Nishihara incident when new troubles broke out up river at the fief's other warehouse in Kuse village. Once again peasants discovered local officials trying to sneak rice downstream. Interdicting three of the fully loaded riverboats, they brought the rice back to Kuse and demanded of the fief accountant Ide Kudayū a complete cessation of all river traffic in rice during the period of mourning for the lord. The promise was given, but the very next night the warehouse officials at Kuse rushed more boats downstream loaded with rice.

These repeated provocations by the fief brought the Sanchū peasants' feelings of outrage to the boiling point. When the officials in Kuse refused to accept their appeal to "desist from the 4 percent tax increase," the more politically aware peasants turned that anger into a political force.

The Nishihara and Kuse incidents, occurring in a context of political crisis and economic hardship, ignited the fires of the Sanchū revolt. But of its actual preparation little is known. Subversive gatherings of peasants with a view to challenging Kubo's tax orders—perhaps by a mass appeal and march in force on the castle— seem not to have occurred until very late in November, that is, after the intendants had settled matters at Nishihara. Only then did unsigned circulars appear in the Kuse village area and further upstream calling on peasants to "come to the warehouse at Kuse to investigate our rice." Soon Kuse was humming with rumors, as peasant couriers went racing through the Sanchū districts telling everybody that "Tsuyama has become a 50,000 koku fief. This region is far from the castle and will undoubtedly become a direct vassal domain. The unpaid tribute and the loans accumulated up to now are going to be cancelled. . . . Let's safeguard the tribute rice for ourselves." [5]

So, their decision to challenge Tsuyama was made in the belief that, at that crucial moment, their chances for success were great. They did indeed imagine that the fief, in its moment of acute crisis, would grant them an edict of debt cancelation.

In the "Ranpōki," the peasants' leaders reveal themselves, on signal, as soon as illegal circulars reach Tokuemon of Maki branch village (an extension of Nakama village, some forty kilometers from Tsuyama castle town) and Higuchi Yajirō, the assistant headman of Mio village. These two were real representatives and leaders of poor peasants at this time. But the unknown author of the "Ranpōki," moved by sympathy for the peasants and the miserable way in which their revolt ended, writes in such a way as to elevate their tragedy by giving it a greater content than it really had. He makes Tokuemon—a cattle or horse grazer by occupation—the direct descendant of the famous Amakusa Shirō Tokisada, leader of the Shimabara revolt, which western Japan experienced ninety years earlier.[6] Drawing his inspiration from the past, Shimpūken transforms a real leader of poor humble people into a "people's commander" fully equal to any samurai who could possibly take the field against them.

By giving Tokuemon the name Amano Tokisada, and later by likening Tokuemon to that famed paradigm of samurai loyalty, Kusunoki Masashige—the hero of the *Taiheiki*—Shimpūken evokes a number of past references that his early eighteenth-century audience could easily recognize and sympathize with. In the service of resistance to feudal oppression, he has connected Tokuemon to real historical events and personages, one of whom, Kusunoki, also figured in the consciousness of ordinary people at that time. But his precedents are most ambiguous. For to the extent that Shimpūken, particularly in his fictional opening pages, emphasizes Tokuemon's samurai birth and extraordinary talents, he is not at all a true class representative of peasants. The perspective that Shimpūken brings to depicting Tokuemon actually reveals the limits of the realism a nonpeasant sympathizer with their rebellion was capable of in that era.

At the same time, Shimpūken's perspective tells us that a sympathetic reporter on peasant problems structured his understanding (or "reading") of actual events in terms of derived literary images of peasants. To convey to the literate what had occurred, he was obliged to alter stories and values from the military chronicles of the ruling class and to adapt samurai heroes to peasant settings and experiences. That did not mean that the Japanese people, at that stage of their history, lacked independent literary images of themselves. But it did mean that such images as existed in folk culture, folktales, and songs did not get registered in accounts of the literati, which belonged to a different genre.

Let us turn next to the Kuse events of December 4–6, as summarized by Shimpūken. By comparing his account with the intendants' version we can glimpse how the two sides conceived the struggle in which they were locked, and one of the techniques peasants used for mobilizing resistance. Shimpūken:

> It was heard that "on the evening of December 4, 1726, someone loaded rice from the warehouse in Kuse onto riverboats"; and so, when unsigned circulars were sent to Maki [Tōsuke—Shimpūken's pseudonym for Tokuemon] and Higuchi [Yajirō], each of them investigated and said, "We can't do anything without a people's commander [taishō] and since Tōsuke is old ..." Thus, because of his talents, they [presumably Maki Tōsuke and Higuchi Yajirō] chose Tokuemon as the taishō. He changed his name to Amano [Amakusa] Shirō no Saemonnosuke Fujiwara Tokisada. His followers at this time were: from Majima region, 42 villages, 3,000 rebels [ki]; from Ōba region, 37 villages, 5,000 rebels.
>
> The above force numbered over 8,000 rebels. They raced out, over 100 of them with hunting guns, and guns that fired only powder, and the others carrying in their hands boar hunting spears, bamboo spears, hatchets and axes. Roaring like the hills would crumble, they pursued and captured the boats loaded with rice from the Kuse warehouse. After cornering them and retrieving the rice without anyone identifying them, they brought it back to Kuse and placed guards over it.[7]

Now the intendants' more factual but no less varnished account of these same events:

> How the peasants from the Sanchū ... districts went up to appeal to Kuse village was like this. Lord Matsudaira Asagorō died on November 11 and ... Matagorō was ordered by the bakufu to succeed him with a fief of 50,000 koku. But before the amount of the inheritance was set, Tokuemon ... and Yajirō ... acting as the ringleaders, joined with other malicious minds from the villages. They staged a rally and said that the Sanchū area lay outside the fief's [new] inheritance of 50,000 koku. They circulated notices in the villages telling the peasants that it had become part of the Shogunal domains.
>
> On the evening of [December 4] they went to Kuse village and, from about 7:30 P.M., announced loudly in the town [sic] for everybody to assemble: "rice robbers are in the warehouse." They created a disturbance in the town, rushed here and there to the local warehouse and inexcusably rioted. Ide Kudayū, the Fief Magistrate Accountant for Upland Fields [hatake gokanjō gobugyō] proceeded to Kuse. The rioting peasants went to his inn and asked him to listen. Ide Kudayū said that since this was a critical time, if they stayed calm, he would return to Tsuyama to have their appeal heard. So he instructed them to wait there.... On the evening of [December] 4, rice [for Osaka] was ordered loaded onto three riverboats. Hearing of this, the peasants from the three districts suddenly rose up.... On the morning of the 5th, they unjustifiably interdicted the rice in the town and set watchmen to guard it. The remaining peasants, appealing to go up to Tsuyama, made assignments to neighboring villages and ran from door to door saying that those peasants who would not join them would suffer destruction. They assembled on the wild plain of Ōdankōge in Daikanaya village, near Kuse.... Altogether the peasants of six districts—on the evening of the 5th—rioted on their way to the residence compound of the district headman, Fukushima Zenbei, and the deputy district headman, Chūjirō of Meki village. They destroyed various household implements, burnt village account records, and also stole many things. In addition, they com-

mitted various outrageous actions. Thereupon Tsuyama fief's intendants arrived at Kuse village.[8]

Two features of this long official explanation deserve comment. First, the intendants' text, constructed for a constituency of village headmen to aid them in answering inquiries, omits mention of anything that could undermine the correctness of the fief's stance toward peasants. The samurai officials take their own legal and systematic plunder of peasants for granted. Bound by rules of their own making, they have to regard the peasants as thieves. But the peasants, having made their rupture with the fief, see correctly that the real rice thieves are the Matsudaira and their rural intermediaries, both of whom have been defrauding them of the fruits of their labor.

Second, the intendants deny a crucial moral and rational ground on which the peasants, at the start of the rising, stand. The intendants do so by their claim that the ringleaders, "before the amount of the inheritance was set, . . . joined with other malicious minds from the villages." But approximately two weeks earlier, on November 18, the bakufu informed Tsuyama castle that it had unilaterally divested it of lands worth 50,000 koku while, at the same time, granting permission for a nephew of the Matsudaira to inherit the reduced fief. Later, on November 24, that information was conveyed to all district headmen and deputy district headmen offices throughout the fief.[9] Thus, before the peasants acted at Kuse, the castle authorities knew not only that the Matsudaira house was saved but that they would be losing the Majima and Ōba regions. Thus Tokuemon and Yajirō read the situation correctly and were telling peasants the truth when they said that Sanchū "had become part of the Shogunal domains."

By the beginning of December, masses of peasants in the seven western districts—Hijiya, Mitsue, Yumoto, Meki, Kamigōchi, Tomi, and Nagatō—had organized themselves on a quasi-military basis and were taking part in antifief, antimerchant actions. About the men who led them little is known other than that most were migrant agricultural laborers and full-status peasants. Tokuemon the "people's commander" and Yajirō, his second in command, were their overall leaders. Under them were Yajirō's nephew, the iron worker Higuchi Shichirōbei, Hanroku of Hinata village, Shichizaemon of the Ōmori branch village of Higashi Kayabe village, Kiheiji of Nishikayabe village, Yamane Gorōemon, and Chūemon of Doi village. Organized in bands led by these men, the peasants struck three initial blows against Tsuyama fief: they confiscated and stockpiled hundreds of bales of rice in several Kuse warehouses; they stripped power from the district headmen and their deputies in the vicinity of Kuse; and, ignoring their leader's injunction not to attack property, they destroyed the houses and confiscated the property of at least three rich merchants.[10]

At that point, having received reports of the worsening situation in the western circuit area from Ide Kudayū, the fief leaders in Tsuyama castle dispatched
Miki Jinzaemon and Yamada Bumpachi to Kuse to pacify the peasants. Emboldened by their successes, the peasants met the two intendants on the afternoon of
December 6, 1726, at Ōdankōge, a broad plain about two kilometers from the
center of Kuse, roughly equidistant between Kuse and Meki village. There they
disclosed their grievances in a memorable scene whose spirit is captured in this long
passage from the "Ranpōki":

As the sun was beginning to set, the two intendants arrived in the vicinity of Kuse and
called for the people to assemble. But, fearing that they would be held as hostages, they
didn't appear and instead sent a message saying: "If you have any business with us, come to
Ōdankōge [wild plain] and we people will explain briefly to you." When they came out to
Ōdankōge, the peasants pressed in upon them from all sides.... Everyone was lined up and
the magistrates looked endangered. The leaders began saying:
    "First of all, we can't understand why you tacked on a special notice to this year's order
for the payment of rice tributes raising taxes by 4 percent; and then, on top of that, ordered
us to complete payment of it all within this year. When the previous lord was alive his
benevolence was known even in other provinces, so that people in the shōgun's domain
wished to live in Tsuyama fief. But after Kubo took over the administration, he did many
evil things. For example, the gōshi [rural samurai, that is, district headmen and their deputies]
in association with Kubo, suspended the sowing of the autumn wheat crop and ordered seals
to be put on cow and horse plows. We don't think it was the Shogunate's order for us to pay
rice tributes as quickly as possible. Nevertheless, the district headmen and their deputies circulated such an instruction and threatened to manacle late payers. The various pressures they
applied made the peasants suffer beyond description. In addition, Chikahira, in league with
Tsuyama townsmen, issued thousands of rice tickets and sold them at any price. Chikahira
stole the money gained from their sale and bought a house in Osaka. Many people said, 'He's
getting ready to flee because Tsuyama is endangered!' Truly, the peasants' first concern is
growing wheat to shield themselves against starvation in the spring. We can't understand
why you would stop us from doing this. Falsely claiming the lord's official appointment,
you announced the levying of money taxes in the town and countryside to meet the expenses involved. That was a serious act of injustice. Then a messenger came from Harima
to express sympathy. The granduncle of the fief's lord was surprised and said it is a lawless
action to levy taxes [on such a pretext]: 'return everything immediately.' Such was the attitude that a virtuous lord should take. Next, the district headmen collected their own loaned
rice [from the people] before collecting the rice tribute. They deceived the authorities into
thinking that the peasants had not paid their taxes. Are the authorities not aware of this act of
contempt for peasants? The accumulated frustrations of the peasants have thus resulted in
this action." [11]

Having voiced their anger against the unjust policies and practices of the fief in the
presence of its high officials, the peasant leaders presented eight political-economic
demands. They demanded, first, (in supplicatory fashion) the retraction of Kubo's
4 percent tax increase and, second, having already paid 86 percent of that year's rice

tribute, the cancelation of the remainder. "We will make payment of rice bran, straw and various forms of tribute rice and cash payments. Therefore we wish to be exempted from other rice payments." [12]

Third, fourth, and fifth, they called for the dismissal of all village headmen, deputy district headmen, and district headmen, the turning over to peasants of the written instructions and account books belonging to those officials, and their replacement by popularly designated message receivers.[13] These message receivers once operated districtwide courier relay systems, linking together all the villages of the fief. Their exact nature and duties, however, pose a problem. Nakano speculates that a stipended office of "message headman" (*jōsashi shōya*) existed in Tsuyama during the Mori period (1603–1697). And a contemporary document ("Official Record of the Sakuyō Region"), which she also cites, indicates that in 1698 when the Matsudaira took over there were 135 message receivers employed in delivering instructions from superintendents and intendants to district headmen and from the latter to village headmen.[14] We also know that message receivers assisted village headmen in organizing common functions between villages and that they presumably had detailed knowledge of fief communication routes. But that is all we know. Some time after the Matsudaira assumed control, the office was apparently eliminated. The Sanchū peasants probably wanted the older system of message receivers restored because they believed the district and deputy headmen were cheating them by falsifying fief instructions.

In short, these particular demands pertaining to taxes and officials were intended to eliminate the main embodiments of repressive fief power in the countryside. Their realization would give peasants of high and middling economic status a chance to regulate village affairs. It would also mean a return to a simpler, more familiar mode of dealing with common administrative duties imposed upon villages from above. But from the Matsudaira viewpoint, whoever commanded the villages controlled production. The receipt of these peasant demands, calling for the elimination of the very agents who implemented samurai class rule, must have made the Matsudaira officials realize they were in a life-or-death struggle.

The remaining demands were for the cancelation of all outstanding rice loans endorsed by the district headmen's stamp and exemption from all miscellaneous taxes (unjōkin) on soya beans and tributes on forestry work (*yamabataraki nengu*). These demands reflected the deeply felt interests of the poorest stratum of peasants who were heavily indebted to rice merchants and rural officials.

After four days of negotiating, Miki and Yamada acceded to the peasants' demands and exchanged documents with them promising to put the agreement into effect. The intendants returned to Tsuyama castle on December 11 and the anger in the western districts subsided temporarily. But unperceived by the authorities, cir-

culars had begun spreading in the eastern districts telling of the victory in the western area. On the night of December 12, peasants from five eastern districts—
Konakahara, Ayabe, Kawabe, Ichinomiya, and Nokedai—rallied in preparation
for a march on the castle. Once again the intendants made the rounds in an effort to
appease the peasants. Disaffected peasants in the richer eastern area (destined to remain under Matsudaira control) put forward demands that were essentially similar
to but more detailed than those of their western compatriots. Recorded on December 13, 1726, in extremely polite language, no doubt by fief officials, some of
them are worth quoting in full.

"We Would Be Grateful If" [*arigataku zonji tatematsuri sōrō*] . . .
- We are troubled by the order that forest tributes be paid in new silver coins and at an
  increased rate of 10 percent. From this year on we want it ordered as in previous years and
  we want a refund of the overpaid silver.
- In recent years taxes were ordered paid on hunting guns as a result of which the small-
  income hunters are suffering. Hereafter rescind this tax.
- Although wheat tributes have been ordered paid in recent years, we wish hereafter to be
  exempted from them and we want the wheat tributes paid to date returned to us.
- We suffer from the practice of paying more than the normal of 3 *to* [$\frac{1}{10}$ of a koku or 4.65
  U.S. gallons] 4 *shō* of rice whenever we deliver rice to the storage warehouse. Therefore
  we appeal that rice be delivered in a regular bale of 3 to 4 shō.
- In the matter of payment of standard quality soybeans, in some years 1 koku of standard
  soybeans could be purchased for 1.2 or 1.3 koku of rice. But according to the fief's exchange rate, 1 koku of soybeans is only equivalent to 6 to of rice. . . . From now on set the
  yearly market exchange rate so as to eliminate any loss of rice.
- If interests are collected on various borrowings, such as annual certificated loans of rice
  and other loans made at the district headman level and above, it will create receivers of aid
  in the villages, and their support will cause trouble for villagers. Today when peasants are
  in distress and the lord is being changed, we wish to have matters ordered exactly as in
  Sanchū. . . .
- . . . the district headmen and deputy district headmen be relieved of their offices. We wish
  to replace them with honest officials. . . .
- . . . make repayments of rice to villages where overpayment was made and collect rice
  from villages where payment has not been completed.[15]

The day after presenting these demands and receiving soothing assurances from the
intendants that the tax increases would be rescinded and their appeal heard, the
eastern area quieted down.

 But still the fatigued intendants had no rest, for just then peasants in the central districts rose up and destroyed property. Again the pattern was repeated,
though this time the intendants yielded to their demands quickly without protracted negotiations. By December 19 the central area too had quieted down.

 Three days later, however, on December 22, all four intendants—Miki,

Yamada, Arakawa, and Yamaoka—issued a formal response to the eastern area
peasants in which they rescinded the 4 percent tax increase but were unwilling to
return immediately all overpaid rice or to desist from collecting forestry tributes
and miscellaneous enterprise taxes. Nor did they bother to mention removing
from office any of the district headmen or deputy district headmen.

Although we do not know the thinking and the value judgments behind the
intendants' December 22 reply, the stiffening of position it expressed vis-à-vis the
demands of the eastern district peasants may reasonably be interpreted as indicating
that, by that time—though not necessarily on the specific day they made their
reply—the rising had already ended. The second stage was to commence almost
immediately afterwards, when the western area alone renewed the struggle. But
before proceeding to it, let us summarize what the peasants gained in one month of
struggle, with relatively little advance preparation.

• Kubo Shimbei, who had introduced the Kyōhō reforms in Tsuyama, was
dismissed from office in early December and ordered into domiciliary confinement.
Four months later, on April 16, 1727, he was expelled from the fief, a common fate
of reforming ("evil") retainers.[16]

• The peasants forced Tsuyama fief to rescind its 4 percent tax increase and to
write off approximately 14 percent in uncollected taxes. Further, if all the promises
made by the intendants had actually been kept, and if the rice confiscated from fief
warehouses is included, then, according to Nakano's estimate, the peasants forced
the fief to sustain a revenue loss of approximately 11,500 koku, or about 20 percent
of a normal year's tribute.[17]

• Historically most important in the long run, the peasants made the fief
abolish its system of rural intermediaries. By December 26, when Tsuyama's
highest authorities finally got around to authorizing the superintendents of local
affairs and the intendants to dismiss their district headmen and deputies, many villages in the Sanchū had already established message receivers who were in contact
with peasants in other districts.[18] That ordinary peasants were capable of realizing,
albeit briefly and in a limited area, an approximation of the idea of local self-
government was the highest achievement of the Sanchū rising.

Yet, at the end of Stage I, serious problems remained which would soon offset
these gains. First, on the peasant side, the unity of the different regions was only
tactical and temporary. In many areas, peasants seem to have discontinued the
struggle as soon as the intendants compromised on the tax increases and promised
to remove hated rural officials. Once community punishment had been meted out
and anger vented, no obstacle seemed to stand in the way of peasants resuming the
obligations of feudal submission. One reason peasants failed to maintain strong
unity may have had something to do with their lack of an adequate ideology of
struggle. Let us consider this point.

As seen through the prism of Shimpūken's "Ranpōki," Tsuyama's peasants made use of a heterodox (and contradictory) religious concept of heaven. A popular—as opposed to a ruling-class—belief in heaven did not figure in peasant demands against the fief. But such an ethical idea at least circulated in every period of Tokugawa history and was as influential in the outbreaks of the eighteenth century as in the riots and property destruction of the last decades of the bakufu.[19] Sometimes heaven was a punitive concept, useful for rationalizing anger and vengeance, but offering no positive idea for which to struggle. More often it was a synonym for justice. In punishing the fief's rural allies and local merchants, the peasants of 1726–1727 saw themselves as moral agents, executing the judgments of a vengeful, punitive heaven. In a sense, the heaven of popular ideology existed to help effect political changes in the real world or, more concretely, to remove obstacles to the people's welfare.

One must note, however, that peasants also invoked heaven as a standard for judging and rationalizing their own private actions. Thus, in attacking the home of the headman of Shinjō village, Fukushima Zenbei, the peasants are made to say, "We're really grateful for heaven's judgment on his greed and evil." And in another scene, Higuchi Yajirō is hiding in a cave, on the verge of capture by the intendants. He observes his mother "bound up [like a criminal] and walked about on a prominent mountain spot." Seeing her from a distance, he drops his sword, bursts into tears, and cries out: "I wanted to fight but now have lost all hope. . . . If I let my mother die right before my very eyes, I would be deserving of heaven's punishment and lose the way of filial piety."[20]

Interestingly, this particular scene of Yajirō and his mother also illustrates an important point about the suppression of armed protests in various historical contexts. One of the most effective holds that rulers have over protesters is control over their families. When the target of official violence eludes capture, his family can be made to suffer. It was entirely typical, therefore, that in the final stage of the Sanchū rising the intendants threatened punishments to the families of peasant leaders like Yajirō. (In a different age, the 1930s, Japanese "thought police" practiced intimidation against the families of left-wing dissidents who refused to recant. In the same way, though more brutally, the counterrevolutionary policy of the United States in Vietnam during the 1960s and early 1970s specifically targeted for destruction the noncombatant families of Vietnamese Communist ["Viet Cong"] sympathizers, who were easier to get at than armed guerrillas hiding in the jungle.)

But returning to the question of the weakness of peasant unity against the fief, another factor that may be cited was the unequal economic development of Tsuyama's different regions, hence the conflicting material interests and demands of different strata of peasants. Such horizontal conflicts may have contributed to making peasants in the eastern and central areas mere passive bystanders during the second, insurrectionary stage. Conflicting material interests may also explain why some peasants defected to the samurai side almost from the start of the fief's counteroffensive in early January. The main fruits of victory, after all, accrued to the upper stratum of landowning peasants. From their ranks came, first, the new message receivers and, later, in the final weeks of the struggle, those peasants who responded to the intendants' use of spies by turning traitor. But the concessions won at Ōdankōge two weeks earlier were not a victory for the poorest stratum of indebted peasants, especially forestry workers and migrant iron miners. They were unable to secure even such modest demands as cancelation of forestry tributes and taxes on soybeans.

Turning to the samurai side, the most striking feature of the opening weeks of stage 1 had been the political crisis that kept the fief's highest retainers preoccupied and psychologically disposed to grant concessions. For the intendants, negotiations with peasants always served a dual purpose: to quiet them down in order to gain time for assessing the situation and to learn who their leaders were. The one thing negotiations did not connote was a serious intention of actually implementing concessions granted to peasants under compulsion. With strong military forces available to them at the castle, it was only a matter of time before the fief magistrates would use them. And the temptation would be greatest to use force against peasants who would soon come under bakufu jurisdiction: those living in remote areas in which Tsuyama was acting as a proxy for the bakufu.

STAGE II

In the second stage of the uprising, peasants in Sanchū took the offensive against Tsuyama. Their anger, fed by the pent-up resentments of the poorest among them, exploded in attacks against local officials and usurious merchants. Unable to see anything but their own local strategic situation, they acted without bothering to forward demands for negotiation and also without realizing that the Matsudaira retainers were now in a stronger position than before for mobilizing all their military strength against them. But what emerges most clearly at the start of this second stage is the peasants' critical capacity to question and repudiate the Matsudaira's entitlement to tribute (let alone its right to physically remove the tribute from the district), once the bakufu had confiscated some portion of the fief.

Around December 21–22, at approximately the time the intendants made their final reply to the villagers of eastern districts, the West began to stir again. Fearing perhaps that Tsuyama's officials were meditating some act of treachery and had no intention of fulfilling their written promises, peasants in Tomi and Meki districts staged attacks on the homes of deputy district headmen and village headmen. During these incidents they demanded the return of excess rice tributes and the handing over to message receivers of the village account books. Miki and Yamada, however, heard about them almost immediately and rushed to the trouble spots, where, in order to quiet the peasants, they issued tickets worth 1,800 bales of rice.

No sooner did news of this latest fief concession reach neighboring villages within Sanchū than peasants there became emboldened and began a struggle of their own to convert rice bills or tickets into real rice. At this point, in the middle of the "Ranpōki," Shimpūken Chikuō links the failure of the uprising to the very same concept of heaven that he had earlier invoked to justify it.

According to an old saying, "When you are too proud, you receive heaven's punishment and when you betray heaven's rules, you are bound to perish." Truly, whereas it may be said that "Up to the present the peasants are justified," are they now to perish because they were unaware of their evil mind, discarded the Buddhist and Shintō teachings, and made light of Tsuyama?[21]

Peasants in Sanchū had indeed laid aside all fear of Tsuyama and were now acting under the spell of leaders like Tokuemon who told them that unless they acted immediately, before their tickets became void, they would lose their chance to convert them into real rice. "If Tsuyama fief is cut in half, the western regions will become, without doubt, *bakufu* domains and in that event the intendants will change the law. We will not be able to easily borrow money. Before that happens, let's take back our rice." [22]

Thus began the struggle to convert rice bills into real rice and break the hold of feudal rule in the Sanchū. First Tokuemon and Yajirō led attacks on the district headmen of Hijiya and Mitsue, from whom they confiscated over three hundred bales of rice. Then, during the last days of December 1726, bands of thousands of peasants under Tokuemon and other leaders fanned out through the Sanchū in a series of raids on other village and district level headmen. By New Year 1727, many of the district headmen and their deputies, perhaps together with some village headmen, had fled to Tsuyama castle town. With the intermediate structure of control over the rural areas destroyed or paralyzed, the fief was deprived of its chief instrument of rural control. In that sense, one may say that virtually the entire Sanchū district had been liberated by peasants from Tsuyama's effective political control, and newly chosen message receivers were managing village civil administration.

Had a list been drawn up at that point of all the "wealthy people" the peasants attacked for their "greed and evil," it would have included river transport agents, innkeepers, iron wholesalers, woodworks merchants (*kiji ton'ya*), sake brewers, oil merchants, warehouse officials who were, technically, merchants in the employ of the fief, and numerous rice exchange merchants with stores along the Izumo, Ōyama, and Hōki highways.[23]

Looking closer at the conflict in the village of Mikamo, we learn that one portion of it was a "town" (*machi*) wherein rural merchants outside the reach of the castle town authorities sold their wares and conducted business. There the merchant Tsukataniya Ichirōemon of Takada (further downstream beside the Asahi River) had a branch store where he sold wine, lent money, and also stored rice for exchange. On the night of December 29 the peasants

besieged it demanding rice. The store apprentice [*tedai*] said: "I can't do it on my own authority." But the peasants wouldn't listen and raced to take out over 3,000 kilograms of iron ore and over 150 bales of rice, which they placed in the custody of two peasants living nearby—Yahei and Heiemon. In addition, there was a rumor that peasants were going to "destroy the town [of Mikamo]." Taking wives and children and entire households, everybody raced to escape.[24]

Further intimations of the deepening conflict of town and countryside, which Mikamo, like many other rural villages, bore in itself, appear at two other points in the "Ranpōki": first, a week after the above incident, when Tokuemon recounts a rumor he has heard to the effect that "Chikahira [Kubo Shinbei] relieved the foot soldiers of their stipends and on this occasion has done the extraordinary thing of hiring townsmen to make their [suppression] force a mixture of different elements";[25] and second, when a "townsman" of Mikamo village, one Rokuemon, gathers fifty-six people (merchants and their apprentices?) and makes them pledge to resist if the ikki strikes at Mikamo:

"We will be outnumbered when the enemy attacks and must therefore put strategy first. Pile up scores of bales of ash atop the gate and throw it on the enemy the minute they enter. It will get into their eyes and throw them into a panic. Only then unsheath your swords and rush out to fight. Don't be cowardly out of fear of losing your lives. Just value your [family] names." He opened a fan and cheered them on. They all unsheathed spears and long swords and looked determined to make this their last day. Shrinking from their air of determination, the people's army did not dare to approach them.[26]

The year 1727 opened in Tsuyama fief with the central and eastern districts returned to normal. But in the three Sanchū districts the rising had taken on the characteristics of a full-scale revolt. The old village rulers had been attacked one after another. And message receivers rather than traditional headmen were now conducting village affairs. But about the details of this new village administration we know nothing. Nor do we know what specific powers they seized and exercised during the short time they were in charge. It is known, however, that in the effort to retrieve their own excess grain and cash tributes, peasants terrorized the wealthy by destroying their homes and warehouses.

Meanwhile, some forty kilometers away in Tsuyama castle, January 3 and 4 were spent in deliberations among the highest fief officials on how to handle the peasants. The issue now was who would control the villages: the peasants themselves through their new message receivers, or Tsuyama fief through its hierarchy of rural officials? Miki and Yamada argued for a quick military solution with the strictest punishments, meted out on the spot, for all peasants who had participated. Their advice was accepted, and the next day, January 5, an initial punitive force of seventy soldiers made ready to invade the Sanchū. Their commanders were Miki and Yamada together with Yamada Heinai, the chief inspector for the interior, who would function as the judge, ensuring legality for the planned executions. Early next morning, January 6, two lines of samurai soldiers, clad in full battle dress, filed out of the castle gate preceded by the intendants mounted on horses. Guided by deposed local officials, they headed for Kuse village, intent on making it their staging base for a frontal attack on Sanchū.

The final battle between the fief and the "peoples army" lasted about two weeks and involved an estimated 350 to 500 samurai soldiers, some of whom deployed cannon. It resulted in the massacre of at least forty-five peasants, many of them message receivers, captured and disarmed deep in Sanchū. When the six "ringleaders" brought back to the castle for later public execution are included, the number rises to fifty-one. Older accounts give even higher estimates of from seventy to eighty peasants executed and over two hundred imprisoned.[27] There are apparently no extant figures on samurai casualties. With the rebellion crushed, the peasants were made to swear in writing never again to disobey fief officials in any matter whatsoever. The oaths were then sealed with sign-impressions by their old local officials, all of whom returned to power.[28] On January 30 the intendants and their troops quit the mountains to return to Tsuyama castle.

Contemporary accounts of the January events differ sharply as to the nature and degree of peasant resistance. The initial intendants' report of January 15, 1727, insisted that once the ringleaders had been captured,

peasants in different villages uncovered other evil elements and the officials took them away. In this way the riot was suppressed without particular difficulty. By no means were there reinforcements from neighboring provinces. The intendants could suppress the peasants and keep order because they could, in normal times, hear quickly from their men whatever news there was about any misdemeanors and unrest against the authorities.[29]

By contrast, Shimpūken, drawing on his knowledge of the medieval war chronicles, invested the peasants and particularly their leaders with exemplary heroism. What mattered most for him was precisely their courage and the utter futility of their desperate efforts to defy Tsuyama.

Thus the picture that emerged from his account of the January days was, first of all, one of passive resistance by the majority and active defense by a large minority who marched back and forth in armed bands intent on defending Sanchū. On the approach of the samurai soldiers, whole villages fled. Tokuemon and his lieutenants rallied peasant fighters, and at least several hundred took the field. Expecting the samurai camped at Kuse village to enter their region through the Misaka mountain pass, they fortified it and waited, hoping to counter the superior-armed samurai by using guerilla-style tactics. When the suppression force failed to appear, they rushed to contain other samurai troops approaching from their rear. Night marches accomplished nothing, and ambushes, painstakingly staged, were avoided by the enemy. More samurai reinforcements with guns and even cannon arrived. A blizzard then hit the region, adding to the misery of the peasant fighters. There were defections from their ranks. The Mikamo and Shinjō village message receivers, once comrades of the rebel leaders, turned traitor. As peasants were killed and their heads displayed on poles in villages and along mountain roads, the number of dropouts increased. In vain, Tokuemon tried to arrange a cease-fire. But, alerted to his hiding place, the intendants launched a night raid on Doi village. They arrested him before he could resist. Bereft of their main leader, the remaining armed bands quickly disintegrated. Thousands fled their villages and hundreds were arrested. By the end of January, the last spark of resistance had been crushed.

What was Shimpūken's evaluation of the whole rebellion? His opening lines seem to be offering a slightly optimistic reading of a failed revolt: "When beset with doubts your judgment is wrong. In your dreams nothing is real. It is only because they are so firmly committed to attaining their own objectives that the mantis challenges the ax or the monkey grasps for the moon." [30] In short, the rebellion, he is saying, was doomed from the outset. But some men shed their doubts and were able to act. If you are free of doubts, strong of judgment, and determined, then even the impossible can come within the realm of striving.

But this hopeful reading of the text turns on banishing unwelcome realities. Shimpūken is also saying that the peasants did not calculate the consequences of their actions or weigh their chances for success, because the officials drove them beyond the point of caring. And, in fact, the "Ranpōki" conveys primarily a mood of extreme bitterness and hatred of officials—all that was left after the fire in Sanchū had been extinguished.

Near the end of his account, Shimpūken multiplies his dark warnings to officials, as in this speech put into the mouth of Tokuemon (alias "Tokisada"). Bound with ropes and heavily guarded, Tokisada was en route to Tsuyama castle when he noticed

the rural samurai Shinshi hurriedly passing by. Tokisada called out: "You over there! Wait a minute!" Looking at Shinshi with angry eyes, Tokisada said: "Truly, when you have committed a crime you look ugly. You must be one of Kubo's gang. Ever since the excessive taxes were levied, the rural samurai of all six districts have been in league with Kubo. I don't have to go into the details of what you did with the rice tickets, which was just like stealing. You know very well what you did. We people in revolt have no personal grudge whatsoever against the lord of Tsuyama. But it just so happened that I was asked to become the commander of all the peasants, though I am not qualified for such a position. So I resolved to end the long accumulated frustrations of the peasants by cutting you down with a stroke of my sword. But while time was wasted because of last night's big snow storm, I lost the chance and was unexpectedly captured, much to my regret." . . . He gritted his teeth and trembled. "Though my corpse turns into white bones, my firm hatred is bound to express itself throughout the course of six worlds where one is reborn four times." [31]

Fevered warnings and exhortations such as this one were often used by the anonymous authors of unofficial accounts of Tokugawa peasant revolts in order to impress their readers and listeners. Other favorite devices were to comment on the punishments meted out to peasant leaders and to use execution scenes to inculcate a moral message. For Shimpūken, the execution of the "people's commanders" was an opportunity to record for posterity the emotions of the people before and after their defeat. The "Ranpōki" ends on a note of impotent rage and bitterness at the corrupt behavior of Tsuyama's local officials. The time was March 20, 1727; and from the castle and nearby vicinities an audience of officials and commoners had converged on Numeri river beach, along the Izumo road, not far from Tsuyama castle.[32] Suddenly Tokisada appeared, "shedding bitter tears." For his opening remark he evokes the ancient, archetypal theme of all the ages all over the world: of the people betrayed by their leaders.

We have an old saying that when the upper reaches of the river are unclean, the downstream becomes muddy. When the country is poorly governed, the people become rebellious. Well, look for yourselves! Within seven years the rural samurai will lead the country to destruction. All the sycophants will receive heaven's punishment. Even though I become a demon or a snake, I will surely reap my revenge.

Then, by means of the curse on Tokisada's lips, Shimpūken skillfully links the Sanchū peasant martyrs to the world of the living.

When his final moment came, they pulled Tokisada to the top of a tree and with eyes wide open he said, "For three weeks after my death, neither my color nor the shape of my face will change or decay. I shall take my revenge even after death!" Saying this, he cut off his own tongue with his teeth, filled his cheeks with blood and spit to heaven. "Gods in heaven! I beseech you! Take the lives of those sycophants!" Then he shut his eyes and fell silent. The outcasts, hearing his cry, came with spears and gave several thrusts through his sides. Not minding this, he again opened his eyes and said: "My life is over; my soul is bound for the other world. But I want you all to know that my spirit remains in this world and will be reborn forever." . . . All of this is now an old story. As Tokisada said, his color, curiously, did not change for seven days. It was said that those who are conscious of guilt should be afraid.[33]

But another version of Tokuemon's last words (provenance unknown) cleverly turns it to the advantage of the authorities. In this rendering, he died not with a curse against officials on his lips but with a warning to peasants: "Even when you are in an advantageous position, you peasants should be cautious in dealing with the fief officials. Just as I find myself now in an extreme situation, everybody should learn from the example of my death."[34]

When Shimpūken finished writing his own last lines on Tokuemon's death, the bloody upheaval that shook Tsuyama fief was over, though the social abuses that had produced it remained. Yet he could only warn "those who are conscious of guilt" that they "should be afraid." He too had no political ideology, only a moral creed.

Historian Nagamitsu Norikazu called the last lines of the "Ranpōki" the key for a propeasant reading. It touches, indirectly, on the nature of Tokugawa thought control, reminding us that even to write on peasant dissent—the most serious social issue of the entire Tokugawa epoch—was to court imprisonment and death. Constrained by censorship, Japanese authors who pursued the illegal tradition of writing secret accounts of ikki had to protect their anonymity at all costs. The use of pseudonyms was one obvious way, and the use of literary devices that deliberately glossed over their true intentions was another. Shimpūken closes his account with these memorable lines:

Those who read this should not think that everything contained herein is true. Such may be what is meant by the fiction in fact and the fact in fiction. But that is precisely what this writer does not know.

> Sakushū, Majima district, Takada
> Shimpūken Chikuō, 1727, mid-June[35]

When the punitive expedition returned to the castle after suppressing the revolt, Tsuyama fief prepared to face its reduced circumstances. On four occasions between late January and the end of March 1727, it discharged as many as 366 samurai, perhaps a third of its retainer force, ranging from lowly foot soldiers to high-ranking company commanders.[36] Only then, with the Matsudaira's personnel retrenchment completed, did the bakufu step into the picture, just as it had done in 1697. In April 1727, Tsuyama was divested of its rebellious regions (including most of Ōba and Majima) and became a fifty-thousand-koku domain. While that was happening, the spirits of the fifty-one peasant victims were enshrined in the Sanchū region, never thereafter to be entirely forgotten. The Shingon and Zen temples celebrated mass for them and before long a stone iconography appeared to mark the spots where they died.

CHAPTER FOUR

Epilogue: Tsuyama after 1727

A S Japan moved into the second half of the eighteenth century, struggles for social justice began to accomplish more, and to foreshadow more clearly than had the Sanchū rising, the approaching end of the Tokugawa regime. Yet certain features of this incident in western Japan are worth summarizing for the light they shed on that time and on what lay ahead.

There were, first of all, the fief bureaucratic "reforms" undertaken in parallel with bakufu's Kyōhō era reforms. These, centering on increased taxes, added to the suffering that peasants were already experiencing because of crop failures, and triggered the uprising. But right down to 1867, reactionary bureaucratic reforms by fief officials, carried out usually in the midst of natural disasters, continued to precipitate violent protests in Tsuyama and throughout the Chūgoku region. Indeed, hereafter, fief and bakufu actions that threatened to leave peasants with less than the minimum of food needed for their subsistence were to be a major precipitator of peasant rebellions. And when goaded into violent protests, peasants in other fiefs often would do exactly as the Sanchū peasants did: not stop at making merely economic demands but seek to effect local political reforms.

Second, fighting to overthrow a rural administrative hierarchy inherited from the early seventeenth century, and to replace it with their own message receivers, the Sanchū peasants conjured up historical memories of an earlier past, including such local heroes as Amakusa Shirō Tokisada. After their revolt was crushed, the figure of Tokuemon was equated with both Tokisada and Kusunoki Masashige. Having led the revolt against Tsuyama, Tokuemon and the other leaders became gimin: literally, "righteous people" who sacrificed themselves for the preservation of the community.

Another dimension to the Sanchū peasants' rebellion was their belief in the punishment of heaven, which reinforced the strongly anachronistic coloration of their rising. This feature, together with their belief in gimin, meant that the ideological traditions and the value structures on which peasant ikki drew were continuing ones. Long before the Tokugawa era, a belief in heaven and in the punitive powers of Buddhist and Shintō gods, or a belief in village tutelary deities, figured in the radicalism of peasants. Whenever collective energies were required to right social wrongs or defend subsistence rights, peasants would appeal to such beliefs in the course of taking remedial action. Since no other beliefs were available to help them, they were compelled to abstract, creatively, from their own little tradition versions of Buddhism and Shintō in order to meet their immediate needs. In that sense, a religious component, as seen in the Sanchū peasants' ideology, was invariably present thereafter in the history of virtually all later peasant ikki.

Third, the very essence of feudal exploitation was the political inability of peasants who owned their own labor power and their means of production to withdraw them from the system of tribute extraction in order to obtain better terms elsewhere under which to be exploited. But precisely that is what the Sanchū peasants attempted to do. Although their rising spread quickly in succession through all the administrative regions of Tsuyama, it lacked stamina, trans-district unity, and, in a sense, even intelligence. Merely by promising to meet most of their demands, the Matsudaira intendants succeeded, after only two weeks, in sequestering the revolt in the remote Sanchū area. Within another two weeks, the samurai defeated it with the aid of peasant defectors and spies. In the process, they vented their own frustrations against fifty-one helpless peasants, all but six of whom they executed summarily on the spot. Shortly afterwards, the elders of the Echizen Matsudaira clan forced 366 of their loyal military and administrative servants to pay the entire costs of the bloody victory. They had no scruples about dismissing them for economic reasons because, at that juncture, anxiety about serious political conflicts within their own samurai ranks was virtually nonexistent. Ruling-class unity could still be taken for granted but peasant unity was ephemeral. So, the struggle in Tsuyama failed to change the servile condition of peasants or to weaken feudal fetters in any visible way. But fief power was definitely weakened by being cut in half by the bakufu.

Fourth, the late seventeenth- and early eighteenth-century political economy and, in particular, the growth of the productive base in Tsuyama fief prepared the ground for this uprising. Beginning in the late seventeenth century, increased grain output and a more diversified economic development (centering on mining, lumbering, horse and cattle grazing, and so on) began to forge a complex network of commercial-political relationships. Economic diversification reduced some peasants to submission to grain and iron merchants while forcing others into fiercer competition with the fief for scarce land and forestry resources. The important role of moneylender and tax creditor in this system was played by rural merchants, store operators, and mine owners tied to castle authorities and sometimes to town merchants, and also by the fief's tax-collecting intermediaries. The latter resided as officials in villages and were delegated power and authority to oversee the upaid labor of peasants.

This whole system may be termed a feudal structure of exploitation and indebtedness, born of the Mori and the Matsudaira's oppressive tax practices. This substructure of the feudal economy guaranteed the steady economic differentiation of strata and the nurturance of economic and power relations that benefited some families while dooming many others to a state of propertylessness and even vagabondage. That fact needs to be kept in mind when considering recent discussions of "premodern human capital formation" in Tokugawa Japan. For the proponents of that theory celebrate uncritically the "market consciousness" and "skills" that Japanese peasants developed as a result of such institutions as the alternative attendance system and the growth of castle towns. However, they fail to notice at all the formidable system of tribute exploitation, and the way in which skill development in rural areas usually corresponded to the existing hierarchy of class and status among peasants. And just as the human capital theorists do not comment on the enhanced resistance of peasants that often accompanied their increased knowledge and skills, so too are they silent on the creation of a class of impoverished people through the process of market development and economic diversification. Yet precisely these features of impoverishment and resistance to it may have had the most bearing on the distinctive Japanese process of precapitalist economic growth.[1]

The last feature to note is that after 1727 the essentials of the situation, which embittered the poor and drove them into open confrontation both with Tsuyama fief and with those who handled its local finances, continued to exist. The lords of Tsuyama castle quickly restored their system of rural control through district headmen and deputy district headmen. All through the 1730s and 1740s, they exacted from their remaining peasants the same high level of tribute as before the rising. And the population fared not a whit better in those regions that had been wrested from Tsuyama in 1727 and placed under direct shogunal administration. In fact, everywhere throughout the province of Mimasaka, despite area differences in productive output, tribute rates remained near the 58 percent Matsudaira level. Not until the second half of the eighteenth century did they begin a slow decline.[2]

Because the material conditions of their daily lives were often so harsh, the burdens of taxation weighing upon them so great, and misgovernment by both upper and intermediate levels of officials so persistent, resistance by peasants could never be suppressed entirely. In Tsuyama, peasant traditions of armed public protest and of legal protest persisted well into the nineteenth century.[3] So also did more quiet, stubborn, symbolic resistance to everyday situations of perceived injustice. Interestingly, Tokuemon continued to be remembered and worshiped as a martyr by peasants from his home village. In a large uprising in 1871, one peasant leader even set out from his village carrying on his back a memorial tablet inscribed with the name "Tokuemon."[4]

Matters therefore cannot be left as they stood in the 1720s. Samurai rule too often could not guarantee the safety of the peasants, nor could the official ideology always fulfill its promises of services to them. Indeed, in certain circumstances, the professed ruling-class values of benevolence and humanity contained in the dominant ideology could themselves become an "incitement" to peasant protest.[5] For all these reasons and more, the class struggle and the ideological struggle in Tsuyama continued of its own internal necessity, even when it did not take either violent or public forms. In order to achieve an adequate evaluation of their histories, particularly the objective circumstances and the class practices that gave rise to later conflicts, we must follow the story of Tsuyama's peasants to its end in the last years of the Tokugawa bakufu. But before attempting that, a deeper acquaintance is required of peasant movements, their creativity, and their results during the second half of the eighteenth century, when the crisis of feudalism assumed fuller proportions and most of the key elements in the struggles of the 1850s and 1860s first made their appearance.

PART II

Forward Again:
Readjusting the Social Contract

Historical Setting in Eighteenth-Century Ueda

M OVING now into volcanic central Japan, we come to Shinshū, or Shinano Ueda, scene of the next rising. Here a slightly harsher climate, in a latitude about one degree farther north than Tsuyama, complements more rugged and higher mountainous terrain.[1]

Ueda was once a 95,000-koku fief extending over the whole of ancient Chiisagata district (gun) within Shinshū province and part of Jōshū province. But by the early eighteenth century, it had been reduced to the confines of Chiisagata, with a seigneurial ranking of only 53,000 koku: smaller by half than Tsuyama's. Basically, Ueda comprehended Chiisagata's main granary—the fertile Shioda Plain—plus stretches of mountainous land on both sides of the Chikuma River. Five roads linked Ueda to neighboring private domains and shogunal lands, which encircled it on all sides. Traversing the fief east and west was the Hokkokukaidō, a major highway frequented by daimyo processions and comparable in importance to Tsuyama's less officially traveled Ōyama and Izumo highways. The Hokkokukaidō tied Ueda to the large "outside lord" (tozama) fief of Matsushiro (100,000 koku) in the North and to the tiny (15,000 koku) "hereditary lord" (fudai) fief of Komoro. In the West, the Hofukujikaidō tied Ueda to the fudai fief of Matsumoto (60,000 koku), and other roads connected through heavily guarded barriers to Jōshū province and Shogunal territories.

The weather in Ueda is cold and sharp in winter, dry in summer, with frequent droughts. Along the banks of the Chikuma River, it is windy nearly all year round. Once its valley sides were covered with a blanket of fairly tractable forests, but this presented no insurmountable problem for peasant cultivators. Rather, for dwellers of the river plain, the real struggle for survival centered on controlling the swift-flowing Chikuma, which regularly overflowed its banks, wreaking destruction on fields and dwellings.

In several striking respects the landlocked fief of Ueda resembled Tsuyama. The Chikuma River, which bisected it into roughly equal parts, conditioned the fief's agriculture, just as the Asahi, Kamo, and Yoshii rivers did in Tsuyama. The Chikuma and its tributaries, together with the region's many roads, also mitigated Ueda's isolation by providing routes over which political and commercial news could travel quickly. Common to both fiefs, moreover, were extensive mountain and hill areas with long traditions of resistance to feudal misrule. Urano district, spawning ground of virtually all of Ueda's risings, resembled Tsuyama's rebellious Majima and Ōba regions: both had harsh climates, rugged terrain, single-crop rice fields on terraced hillsides, and rice harvests per unit of cultivated land that were comparatively small and of poor quality. Yet these same remote mountain areas, with their extreme paucity of wet rice fields, also offered opportunities for augmenting rice supplies by the cultivation of commercial crops, such as wheat, soybeans, tobacco, and rapeseed, and, in the case of the Sanchū, by animal husbandry and migrant wage-work in iron mines. Furthermore, villages ensconced in mountains often sheltered many hidden fields on which peasants paid no taxes whatever.

For all these reasons, in Ueda, just as in Tsuyama, most peasants did not, ordinarily, live in utter destitution. Had it not been for tribute officials who dunned them perpetually, even in abnormally bad crop years, the inhabitants of even its remotest villages would have produced enough food supplies to stave off starvation. But to say more than that is difficult. For here too the weather was frequently bad and the vast majority of villagers, despite their cash crop opportunities, were locked into feudal exchange relationships that kept them living fairly close to subsistence level, while their rulers and taskmasters lived in conditions of relative, if austere, comfort.

At the start of the eighteenth century a new daimyo of the important Matsudaira line and his retainers, numbering about 256 households, took control of Ueda fief and began ruling over approximately fifty thousand peasants.[2] From a castle fortress situated above the narrow river plain on high ground on the Chikuma's east bank, the samurai guards on duty in their watchtowers looked out over peasants toiling in the fields below. While the daimyo came and went on attendance to the shogun at Edo, these peasants remained in the manner of their ancestors. Clinging tenaciously to the land, they tilled it, harvested crops, rendered up tribute, and imposed on themselves, in countless ways, to meet the needs of their rulers. But at the same time they also endeavored, from generation to generation, to make small improvements in their situation, even if that meant resisting their rulers in hidden, indirect, and only symbolic ways.

But new circumstances and experiences were about to make these peasants stand up and challenge Ueda's taxation practices openly and in a major way. And once they launched their struggle to realize exclusive demands that pertained only to them, the entire fief became paralyzed. From townsmen and artisans down to "outcasts" (*eta*), all the other ruled classes of Ueda joined in to protest those specific forms of exploitation that bore most directly on them. In the end, as the following detailed account will show, the Ueda uprising weakened irrevocably the foundations of daimyo rule in Ueda and had lasting effects on future social and economic conditions within that fief.

More important, the next struggle illustrates just how much the strength of all oppressed classes had increased by the second half of the eighteenth century. It is the starting point for, and a microcosm of, later peasant and townsmen struggles that would erode the foundations of the bakuhan state itself, until direct Western intervention a century later forced open the treaty ports, drastically speeding up its final collapse.

Serious financial problems of fief management first appeared in Ueda, as in other domains of the bakuhan system, during the last quarter of the seventeenth century, when the lords of Ueda began borrowing money from rich merchants. By 1697, Sengoku Masaaki was forced to expropriate half the stipends of his retainers in the first direct assault on their material well-being.[3] When the time came for his administrative transfer, ordered by the bakufu in 1706, he had already accumulated 1,558 *ryō* in unpaid debts just to Ueda's castle town merchants. That large amount was equivalent to a real rice income at the time of 1,416 koku or about three times the annual rice stipend income of the highest Sengoku retainer.[4]

The eighty-four-year reign of the Sengoku family bequeathed to the peasants of Ueda fief a mixed legacy. The removal of samurai from the villages and the ending of the practice of giving large rice tribute discounts to former retainers of the previous Sanada daimyo family could be counted as gains from the viewpoint of the institutional evolution of fief government.[5] But such gains were purchased at the cost of deepening the cleavage between peasants and samurai and increasing the tax and corvée burdens on peasants. On the other hand, even after three generations of rule, the power of Ueda's peasants was such that the Sengoku had never been able to conduct a successful cadastral survey of the entire fief. Thus, when Ueda became the patrimony of the Matsudaira lineage, the Sengoku clan left them not the *kokudaka* system for measuring the amount of rice harvest, which by then had become universalized in domains throughout the country, but the medieval *kandaka* system of land-area assessment by monetary units called *kan*.[6]

The arrival in Ueda castle of Matsudaira Tadachika, in 1706, signaled a changed approach to Ueda's economic difficulties. To compensate for the fief's financial deficiencies, the newly promoted Tadachika launched an assault on both samurai, the embodiments of fief power, and peasants, upon whom they fed. One of his first acts was to order all samurai stipends drawn directly from fief storage warehouses, thereby curbing the authority of enfeoffed retainers and further centralizing fief power. Henceforth only samurai officials could secure rice directly from peasant producers.[7]

Naturally, it was upon the peasants that Tadachika's heaviest blow fell. In new regulations to the villages he lost no time in warning them to

cultivate agriculture diligently. If you let the fields lie fallow even a little, then not only will the five-man groups be blamed, but it will be considered the fault of the entire village.... There should not be even the smallest strip of hidden land, not to speak of newly reclaimed fields or fields reclaimed after many years of devastation, and other worthless land. If it comes out later that you have done so, the person responsible will certainly be seriously punished, as will the village headman and elders.[8]

Two specific measures for increasing fief income accompanied this threat. In 1706 Tadachika changed the form of rice tribute collection from unhulled paddy payments in bale (*mominō*) to unpolished rice (*genmai* or *beinō*), thereby effectively increasing the basic tax burden from 0.35 koku (1.75 bushels) of genmai to 0.38 koku (1.9 bushels) of genmai.[9] Then, hoping to gain firmer control over peasants, he altered the village control structure inherited from the Sengoku. The latter had first divided Ueda administratively into seven districts (see map 3). The three largest—Koizumi, Urano, and Shioda, with eleven, fifteen, and twenty-two villages, respectively—lay to the west of the Chikuma, embracing most of the Shioda Plain. Four districts occupied the land east of the river: Tanaka, Kokubunji, Seba and Shiojiri, with eighteen, thirteen, ten, and twelve villages, respectively. The remainder of Ueda consisted of the large village of Takeshi, equivalent to a district, and (commencing in 1728) the small (5,000 koku), but strategically located, subfief of Kawanakajima, which was given to the lord's son.

To facilitate the collection of tribute, the Sengoku developed a two-tier chain of command, going from district magistrates (*kōribugyō*) to intendants and their assistants (*daikan* and *tedai*). Beneath the intendants stood the hierarchy of village tribute-collecting contractors: village headmen (*shōya*), assistant headmen (*kumigashira*), senior peasants (*osabyakushō*), and peasant representatives (*hyakushōdai*). The village headmen were akin to salaried village chiefs-of-staff. As in other parts of Japan, some of them are thought to have originated from the samurai class and been imposed on the villages from above, though documentary evidence to that effect for Ueda is not readily available. It is known, however, that the office was hereditary and would often alternate within each village between the two or three most prominent families.[10] A headman's commands were usually obeyed, but

MAP 3. Ueda: A 53,000-Koku Fief within Shinshū (Shinano)

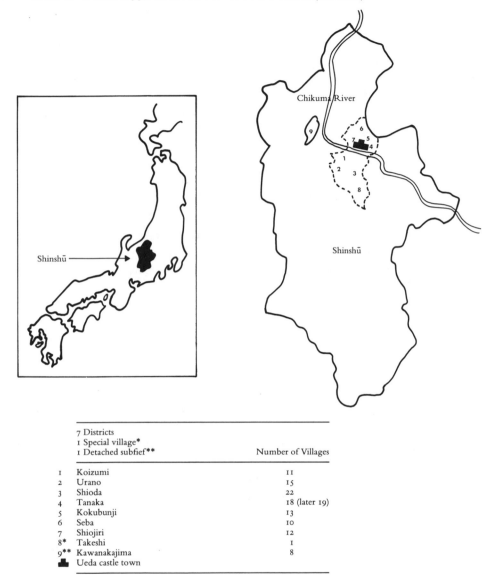

		Number of Villages
7 Districts		
1 Special village*		
1 Detached subfief**		
1	Koizumi	11
2	Urano	15
3	Shioda	22
4	Tanaka	18 (later 19)
5	Kokubunji	13
6	Seba	10
7	Shiojiri	12
8*	Takeshi	1
9**	Kawanakajima	8
⚓	Ueda castle town	

Source: Ueda shishi (The history of Ueda city), vol. 1 (1974), pp. 634–635.

the legitimacy of his financial practices was not always accepted by the poorer peasants.

Tadachika's innovation was to place in each district two new hereditary officials with immense authority vis-à-vis peasants (see figure 4). These were the *wariban*, or district tribute officers, the highest stratum of peasant officials above the village headmen. The wariban originated from the small landed-retainer class of the late Warring-States period. Some of them could trace their ancestry back to followers of Yazawa Yorisada, a sixteenth-century retainer of the Sanada who employed many subretainers and successfully carved out his own small fief within Chiisagata. After the arrival of the Sengoku family in the region, he and others like him were reduced to peasant status, though they remained powerful landed notables.[11]

Beginning in 1718, while absent from the fief serving as the bakufu's Kyoto administrator (*shoshidai*), Tadachika added another level of hereditary officialdom above the district tribute officers. These were the district headmen (*ōjōya*), the most powerful and influential men in the local areas. For the next twenty-three years district headmen and tribute officers assisted samurai magistrates and intendants in operating the tribute system. Not the least of the many privileges enjoyed by the district headmen and tribute officers were the right of free access to the castle on horseback and the right to have surnames, wear swords, draw a token salary of 20 *kanmon*, and enjoy exemption from corvées.[12]

Matsudaira Tadachika obviously hoped to increase fief income and reinforce his control over villages through the use of district headmen. But interposing additional levels of rural officialdom—men who had been, in a sense, coopted by stipends and various samurai perquisites—only increased the estrangement between the fief and peasants in the villages, besides allowing the district headmen, as officially sanctioned middlemen, to siphon off some of the surplus for themselves. It was hardly a substitute for reforming the kandaka system, let alone curtailing the scale of fief expenditures, neither of which Tadachika nor any of his successors were able to accomplish.

Lord Tadazane, the second Matsudaira, ruled from 1728 to his retirement in 1749 and was noted for his profligate living and irrational behavior. He was said to have had restaurants built in the castle modeled on the fifty–three stages of the Tōkaidō highway.[13] Such expenditures might have been suffered to pass without any effect on fief government were it not for an unfortunate coincidence. Tadazane's twenty-year reign spanned a period of protracted economic stagnation all over Japan. In Ueda, it was marked not only by fires and floods but also by declining revenues from rice tribute. Ueda's actual tribute income in 1716 was

FIGURE 4. A Simplified Chart of Official Positions: The Rural Chain of Command in Ueda Fief during the 1740s

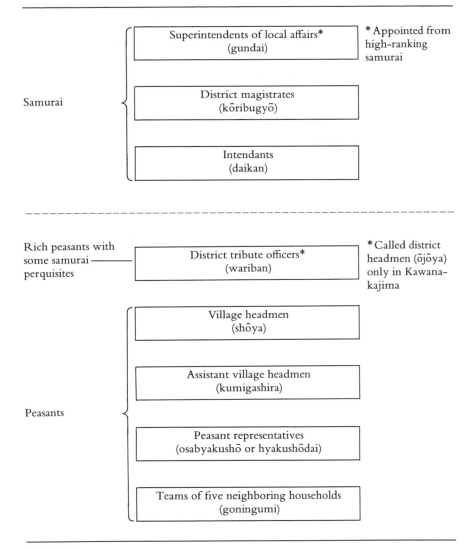

Source: Ueda shishi (History of Ueda City), vol. 1 (1974), pp. 613, 168.

over 32,200 koku. Nearly a century later by 1812, it had fallen to 27,800 koku, a decrease in rice income of 4,400 koku or to 83.6 percent of the 1716 income. And the biggest decline occurred almost precisely in the latter half of Tadazane's reign, the years 1736 to 1743; for after 1743 no great fluctuation in rice tribute income can be seen except in years of bad harvests.[14]

Against this setting of continuing decay in fief finances, Tadazane undertook his only major administrative reforms. In 1740 he discharged the district headmen and, except in the subfief of Kawanakajima, abolished their office, thereby leaving those next in rank, the district tribute officers, with more power than before.[15] Tadazane then changed the method of collecting tribute from annual field inspection (*kemihō*) to fixed tribute (*jōmenhō*). Theoretically, this meant the stabilization of tribute on the basis of average gross ground rent paid over a preceding period of five years or longer. During a famine, or when harvests were bad, peasants under the jōmen system were, in theory, to be given a "fixed discount," called *jōbiki*. But when famine conditions actually arose in the reign of Tadazane's successor, the twenty-five-year-old Iganokami Tadayori (1749–1783), no feudal charity was allowed. The fief simply abolished jōmen and switched back to annual field inspection.[16]

CHAPTER SIX

A Decade of Polarization, 1751–1761

THREE developments in young Tadayori's first decade of rule during the 1750s set the stage for the Ueda uprising. First was the deepening rift between castle town and countryside, or between commerce and administration on the one hand and farming on the other. Although both town and countryside were still fully enmeshed in the structure of tribute relations, the town was then the main representative of merchant activities, more convergent with samurai than with peasant interests. In the Hōreki era, Ueda's commercial agricultural production was still quite underdeveloped. Normal methods of extraction yielded only a relatively minimal surplus from peasants, who were mostly either minute landholders or entirely landless tenants.

Confined to their villages and subjected to the indirect power of merchants living in the castle town, these tiny producers were just beginning to develop commercialized agriculture in the form of silk, tobacco, dyestuff, and paper production. Peasants who developed the fief's paper industry, however, soon found it monopolized by wholesale merchants in Ueda town who prohibited them from selling paper to anyone else. The fief then participated in securing their new source of income by means of an enterprise tax on paper (*kamisuki unjōkin*), which peasants were required to pay in cash.[1] Part of what they received from the paper wholesale merchants went to the authorities in new taxes.

It was hardly remarkable therefore that such new levies made the town itself a symbol of cruel exploitation by privileged merchants and samurai officials. Ueda castle dominated the river plain and looked out on the distant villages, which clung to the sides of grassy hills and wooded mountains. On a clear day its high watchtowers were visible even from Ogami village in remote Urano district, where planning for the great uprising was eventually to begin. During the second quarter of the eighteenth century, some 1,236 samurai lived within the castle, physically sequestered by walls, moats, and gates from the merchant quarters of the town.[2] Law and experience had commanded them to keep peasants in ignorance of political matters. But, in fact, peasants were keenly sensitive to samurai affairs when their own interests were concerned, though that did not prevent them from also wrongly imagining the town itself as a theater of lavish spending and luxurious living by the high samurai officials.

In numerous ways this town-countryside antagonism reflected and expressed the deterioration in samurai-peasant relationships. Amamiya Yuki, in her detailed study of Ueda, reports that in 1752 Ueda's artisans began withholding delivery of articles to the samurai of the castle in retaliation for their refusal to pay for work ordered previously. In 1755 the castle had to warn the villages against selecting bad quality rice for supply to the retainers.[3] More significant still, the impact of fief extortion policies was contributing to the declining image of Lord Tadayori, the foremost symbol of domanial power. When not neglecting his official duties at Edo for the pleasures of Yoshiwara, he was absorbed in falconry and boar hunting, samurai pastimes that devastated crop land and entailed the requisitioning of peasant labor services, usually at harvest time when every hand was needed. Significantly, by late 1758 the castle authorities were forced to deny rumors, widespread in all the districts, to the effect that the bakufu was planning to rotate Tadayori to another fief.[4]

The second major development of the Hōreki era (1751–1763) was the complex struggle within villages throughout Ueda to resist further tax encroachments by undercutting the power of the hated district tribute officers and village headmen. These struggles, pitting the poorer peasants against the agents of fief power, centered on various issues: demands by peasants for impartial investigation of the village headman's account books; disputes over forestry rights or the common usage of forest land (*iriaichi*); lawsuits by villages against some unspecified malpractices or against the autocratic behavior of individual district tribute officers and village headmen. In one unsuccessful suit brought by Umagōshi village in Urano against its headman, Kozaemon, the village was punished. In another, involving feuding villages in Koizumi district, the fief forcibly suppressed the opposition to the granting of common land rights to one of the villages. Interestingly, nearly all the tribute officers and headmen whose property was destroyed in the winter of 1761–1762—Saburōbei (district tribute officer, Uedahara village), Magoemon and his son Jūzō (district tribute officer, Komaki village), Heijirō (district tribute officer, Fumiiri village), Dangoemon (headman, Sanada village), and so on—had earlier been objects of peasant protests in the village disputes of the 1750s, and many were also owners of mortgaged land.[5]

Third, and integrally related to the first two developments, the 1750s witnessed a recrudescence of antidomanial ideology. As the fief's deepening financial insolvency brought the peasants' struggle with samurai officials to the boiling point, some peasants learned more about their own past history of struggle. Such knowledge was history, not myth, because it had been inscribed on gravestones and passed down orally, in the form of "tales of exemplary martyrs" (*gimin denshō*) within a time span of only three or four generations. In other words, a tradition of peasant resistance to samurai oppression in Ueda could be dated accurately from about the middle of the seventeenth century, when Koyama Kyūsuke became the first to protest excessive feudal burdens. Originally a retainer of the Sanada, he stayed behind in Ueda when the Sanadas were transferred to Matsushiro fief in 1622 and later suffered a reduction to peasant status. Koyama Kyūsuke was executed in 1653 after having made a direct appeal to the lord of Ueda castle in behalf of the peasants of Takeishi village. Later, the peasants of Amari village established a religious association (called *Kyūsuke kō*) in his honor.[6] Hayashi Tokuemon, the headman of Hiraide village, became the second peasant martyr when he was executed in 1675, after the fief had accepted his appeal for a tax reduction during a famine year.[7] A short time later, in 1682, Masuda Yohei was ordered executed by Lord Sengoku Masaaki after he had protested the fact that the headman of Irinaramoto village was levying a heavier rice tribute on the village than the castle authorities had authorized.[8] The last of the peasant martyrs before the Hōreki uprising was Hirabayashi Shinshichi, a kumigashira from Nakabasami village who was executed in 1721, after winning a tax reduction for his village.[9]

In 1758, amidst the rising agitation against fief tax policies, peasants from the nearby hamlets of Shimonaramoto and Irinaramoto, in Urano, enshrined Masuda Yohei, for what might have been a second time, and elevated him to a higher status. This event occurred on the eve of the Hōreki uprising, exactly seventy-eight years after Yohei's execution for having made a "legal appeal" (*sogan*) for reduction of rice tributes. It is thought to have reinforced the militancy of peasants in what was traditionally Ueda's most rebellious district by giving it an added if nebulous religious dimension.[10] More concretely, by enabling the peasants to conceptualize and enlarge upon an earlier event in their history, Yohei's deification ceremony represented a simulation or rehearsal for their own protest against the fief.

Thus it was that the revival of a hitherto dormant, but now traditional, ideology of resistance to oppression together with the growing rift between town and countryside and the ferment in the villages to replace headmen and tribute officers contributed to the uprising of 1761.

But in order for peasants to take direct action to change the situation they were in, many psychological obstacles had to be overcome. They had to abandon their usual avoidance strategies for dealing with oppression, such as outward submission and petty cheating. Their ordinary expectations of benevolent treatment from the lord and his officials had to be replaced by a more critical mode of thinking. And feelings of hatred and revenge against those in positions of authority had to be awakened. It seems likely that such changes could have occurred only in peasants who already had a sense of identity and worth as productive human beings and members of a sustaining community.[11]

When the fief authorities intensified their exploitation during an abnormal period of famine and drought, they struck at the peasants' very existence and, by extension, threatened the integrity of local village society. The samurai failed to perceive that they were inflicting a shock similar to several earlier instances of dramatic tax increase that had led to different forms of peasant protest (and fatalities) in the past; nor did they imagine that peasants would connect that shock with their own evolving tradition of martyrs. But precisely that sudden, morally unjustifiable increase in taxes led directly to the 1761 uprising. Since the Ueda revolt was primarily a feudal land rent struggle—"eleven out of the peasants' twenty-seven [written] demands related directly to rice tribute in its various forms and methods of exaction"[12]—the taxes Ueda peasants paid, unprotestingly, under ordinary conditions of Tokugawa "peace" are now worth describing.

Hōreki, meaning literally "era of affluence," was a name misapplied by the bakufu to a time of unusual hardship and famine, as well as declining rice prices for Japanese peasant.[13] In Ueda it connected a period of intermittent drought and anti-tax struggles, when no less than eight major categories of taxes bore heavily upon the ruled: *nengu, debito, zōzei, unjōkin, komonomari, goyōkin*, and *sukegō* (also called *tenma*). The first is a key to understanding the 1761 uprising.

Ueda derived surplus value from its peasants chiefly in the form of nengu or rice tribute. Upon it rested, throughout the long Tokugawa period, the entire edifice of feudal class domination. Traditionally, peasants yielded as tribute to the lords of Ueda at least 50 percent of their harvest. One small portion (*gozenmai*) they grew specifically for his consumption; another portion they supplied as glutinous rice (*mochigome*) for the retainers; but the vast bulk of the tribute was surrendered up as commissariat rice, or *jōmai*. Paid partly in kind and partly in cash for the convenience of the authorities, the mechanism for extorting jōmai worked roughly as follows. Twice a year peasants paid tribute both in Ueda castle town and outside the fief borders in Jōshū, Matsuida (present-day Gunma prefecture). The Matsuida price, however, determined the exchange rate for the cash payment portion of the tribute. That arrangement worked well enough as long as the market price at Matsuida and at Ueda fluctuated in parallel. During most of the period from 1736 to 1772, it did just that as the difference between the two rice markets was only about two-tenths to three-tenths of a koku. But beginning in 1759 and lasting until the winter of 1761, the difference increased to over seven-tenths of a koku.[14]

This discrepancy, as Amamiya Yuki has shown, was no accident. Worried about the decline in its rice tribute income because of the general fall in the price of rice throughout Japan, the fief had called in a "tax specialist," one Funakoshi Banuemon, and in January 1759 appointed him rice sales magistrate (komeuri bugyō) at Matsuida.[15] There Funakoshi operated a conversion racket. At a time when the official conversion rate set by the fief at the rice market in Ueda town was 1 ryō per 1.4 koku, Funakoshi forced the peasants to pay much more in order to meet the cash portion of their tribute obligations. At Matsuida they would have to sell 2.1 koku of rice to obtain 1 ryō of cash. As Yokoyama Toshio illustrated the situation, this meant that a village assessed 21 koku should have paid at the official rate, in cash, only 15 ryō (21 ÷ 1.4). Yet, beginning in 1759 when its rice carriers went to Ueda town to sell their 21 koku, they received only 10 ryō (21 ÷ 2.1). At the higher Matsudaira rate of 2.1 koku per ryō, they had, therefore, to sell an additional 10.5 koku in order to secure the remaining 5 ryō. Thus, by manipulating the rice-cash conversion rate, the fief leaders succeeded in raising the basic tribute tax by nearly 50 percent at a single stroke.[16]

This conversion rate trickery may be compared to "cheating tenants by the use of fraudulent measures," which de Ste. Croix says was "very common" in the late Roman Empire; or it may be likened to landlord manipulation of weights and measures, which Scott described in twentieth-century Southeast Asia.[17] An important point in such cases is that the misbehavior also indicated that the officials and landlords themselves recognized the existence of a moral limit on the economic claims that they could legitimately make against peasants. In the Japanese case, at the very least, a direct change in tribute was not legitimate.

More important, however, official misbehavior meant acute suffering and dislocation in every village and hamlet in Ueda. No wonder then that manipulation of the rice tribute had a galvanizing effect: it immediately created an issue around which local communities in all districts could unite. And the keen sense of injustice that peasants felt toward the fief for having created discrepancies in the cash exchange rate for tribute also carried over to the burden of transporting the rice. Reimbursed at the rate of 4 shō, 2 gō, 7 shaku, 5 sai per bale of commissariat rice carried as far as Komoro fief (a two-day journey), they had then to haul it the remainder of the way to Matsuida at their own expense over distances ranging from seventy-two to ninety-two kilometers—a journey of another three to four days one way.[18] The peasants were forced to bear all the expenses of the return leg of the tax trip, including feed for their horses. Even those who could manage to feed themselves received no remuneration whatsoever for their labors.

During 1760 the financial manipulation of the rice tribute caused peasant opposition to expand in scope, producing two distinct effects in the villages. Peasants wanting to appeal directly to the castle to get the officials to desist came into heated conflict with village headmen who cautioned against taking such action. Second, the basic division within the village headman stratum itself came to the surface as the antagonism worsened between them and the ordinary peasants. Reasonably well-off headmen, those whose positions allowed them to benefit from fief policies, sided with the fief and urged patience. Poor headmen, who often borrowed money in order to pay their village taxes and were as wretched as the peasants they represented, echoed the call from below for direct action and provided the leadership during the planning stage of the great uprising.[19] In structural terms, therefore, the manipulation of the rice tribute exacerbated horizontal conflict within the top stratum of the peasant class, but in a way that produced leaders for the deepening vertical struggle between peasants and samurai.

A direct precipitating cause of the Hōreki uprising in Ueda was certainly the sudden increase in feudal rent on agricultural produce, beginning in 1759. But peasants were also deprived of other parts of their surplus through a multiplication of enterprise taxes (unjōkin), the repeal of which also figured in their demands. By the 1750s there were seven types of unjōkin on everything from the use of guns and the gathering of mushrooms to papermaking and fishing in the Chikuma River and its tributaries. And all types of unjōkin had to be paid in cash.[20]

In addition, forced loans (goyōkin) were usually levied on merchants and on the district and village headmen stratum. But they could also be imposed directly on entire villages. In the final analysis, merchants (via the market price mechanism) were able to make peasants shoulder part of the burden of goyōkin. For peasants were their customers and, more important, their commodity suppliers almost as much as the primary urban dwellers. Merchants would pass forced loans onto peasants by keeping prices down for them as suppliers of products and raising prices for them as consumers of commodities and services.

Also contributing to the rebellion were increased corvée duties. Originally, during the shōen, or manorial period, which lasted until the end of the fifteenth century, the main form of ground rent in Japan was the corvée labor system. By the Tokugawa period, however, corvée had become subordinate in relative importance to agricultural production itself.[21] Nevertheless, corvées were important and extremely onerous everywhere. The lord's mansion at Edo, his castle in Ueda, the residences of the retainers and the daimyo's processions in alternate years to Edo—all these required personal servant services, called *debito* or *denin*. And each debito meant a reduction in the number of men engaged in rice production. Moreover, the demand for debito grew in inverse proportion to the samurai's ability to pay for their essential upkeep. By 1759, when for the second time in only six years Tadayori cut samurai stipends, he also "ordered the peasants to supply *debito* to all the samurai families." [22] But he had made it impossible for the retainers to pay for their sustenance. In 1759 alone the villages had to send out, just within the fief, over nine-hundred domestic servant laborers and to shoulder, in addition, part of the cost of their board while away. The latter, a tax called *debito moyaikin*, amounted to over nine-hundred ryō and its reduction was a major demand during the uprising.

To recapitulate: by the end of the 1750s, causes that antedated but were mostly specific to the Hōreki period had prepared the Ueda uprising. The uprising itself may be conceived as the culmination of a protracted class struggle, in the course of which fief policy approached financial bankruptcy. In desperation, the top fief officials fell back upon the traditional practice of naked, direct tax extortion. Feeling hampered by a lack of information as to actual conditions in the villages, and unable because of peasant protests to undertake inspection surveys of newly reclaimed land, they began to call in tax specialists, tough men skilled in treating peasants harshly, like Nakamura Yazaemon. In return for raising cash revenues, the regime rewarded them with samurai privileges.

The years 1759–1761 were a period of drought and drastically reduced crop yields in Ueda. The authorities knew they had to make reductions in tribute to which peasants were entitled in famine years if peasants were not to starve. But hating the thought of sustaining cuts in their own living standards, they went ahead anyway over repeated peasant protests and allowed Nakamura Yazaemon to eliminate fixed discounts. In January 1761, Nakamura was promoted to assistant district magistrate. He immediately prepared to eliminate the fixed tribute system (jōmen) and return to the practice, abandoned twenty years earlier, of annual field inspection (kemi).[23]

Before long winter turned to spring. But, once again, little rain fell in Ueda. Then in May 1761, while prayers for rain were being offered in the Buddhist temples of all the districts, Lord Tadayori departed the fief for alternate attendance duty and the pleasures of Edo.[24] Addicted, while in Ueda, to hunting wild animals and inclined to follow advisers such as Suzuki Sukenoshin, who urged reliance on the *jikata kōsha* (newly elevated samurai), he left behind a famished, angry, and resentful peasantry, as well as a retainer force demoralized by repeated stipend cuts. De facto control of Ueda devolved immediately upon Morooka Kahei, the superintendent of local affairs (gundai) and senior councillor, Okabe Kurobei, the young associate superintendent of local affairs (gundai) and junior councillor (who was also a relative by marriage to Tadayori), and Hisamatsu Shume, a karō, or senior councillor.[25] Fateful events were about to unfold in which these three would play major roles. For in September 1761, annual field inspection was resumed,[26] creating a desperate situation for peasants, but also, at the same time, dispelling their doubts that now the only way out was the surprise attack of the ikki.

CHAPTER SEVEN

Prologue and Periodization of the Ueda Hōreki Rising, 1761–1763

W E know that early in 1761 there were some secret preparations for a peaceful mass protest at the castle town by a united front of villages. The actual protest was planned for the next slack season. These preparations were hastened by the renewal of kemi in September and then gained further momentum as the peasants marketed their tribute rice at Jōshū Matsuida. But exactly how the peasants mobilized for their confrontation with the castle, and what mood encompassed their actions at the moment of revolt, is largely unknown. Here we must draw on our knowledge of the ikki tradition as it had evolved down to mid-Tokugawa times, keeping in mind that the real initiators of an ikki often acted behind the scenes while others, who were not as careful in concealing their identities, actually led in organizing dissent and presenting demands. Such seems to have been the case in Ueda.

By all accounts, Hanbei, a common peasant, and Asanojō, an assistant headman, both from Ogami village in Urano (located at the foot of Kanjyadake), were the prime movers. But acting behind the scenes, assisting them in various ways, were three others of higher status. One of these men, who was later to receive a comparatively light punishment, was the rural samurai from Umagōshi village, Hayashi Tōshiro. Hayashi was on close terms with many fief retainers and had been given a rifle and charged with the duty of serving guard during a fief emergency. The other two were Magojirō, the district tribute officer of Tazawa village and Denzaemon, the headman of Koshido village.[1]

The turning out of the peasants was achieved by the agitation of Hanbei and Asanojō who went from village to village preaching, conspiring, inflaming. After Urano had begun its preparations for a march on the castle, Shioda district joined

73

in, then Koizumi, and finally the entire fief. No doubt some village headmen took a leading part in the protest because they were thoroughly fed up with samurai inconsistency in issuing commands and the disorder in administering the fief; and their participation facilitated the task of communicating information and hastening peasant mobilization through the villages' five-man team or *gonin-gumi* organization for collective responsibility and mutual surveillance. Other headmen may have defected to the peasants' side because they had a strong moral incentive to do so.

Another possibility that cannot be overlooked, though Ueda's records make no mention of it, is that some villages were coerced into participating in the protest action. Coercive recruitment occurred in a minor way during the Sanchū rising in Tsuyama and has been a ubiquitous feature of peasant revolts throughout the world. If the threat of sanctions was, in fact, applied, by leaders such as Hanbei and Asanojō, against reluctant villages which might have wanted to sit out the protest action yet reap whatever benefits might later arise from it, then it needs no apology. For it was the sanction of equals, not backed by systematic relations of domination and exploitation, and certainly not intrinsically barbaric or unfocused. Moreover, whenever coercion functioned as a secondary recruitment method, it was a socially constructive action because it helped make needed change possible by communicating and strengthening the belief in change to the widest number of peasants, during the crucial initial stage of mobilization. Such coercive techniques, like the violent sanctions later meted out by peasants to the property of wrong-doers, thus subserved the widely shared, rational political objectives that the community viewed as just. But, unfortunately, of recruitment and peasant methods for ensuring collective action in Ueda, the contemporary sources say nothing.

Instead, what we are allowed to see, in the months and weeks immediately preceding the uprising, is an event that casts its shadow ahead in the form of miraculous occurrences: a mysterious play of light and shadow charged with deep significance because it is enacted in the mountains, where peasants in distress traditionally gathered to establish their oneness with the punitive mountain gods.

Around this time several strange things happened. Already from mid-February 1761 frequent earthquakes occurred only in Chiisagata. Also Mt. Kanjya in Urano, where the ikki leader Sugihara Shirobei entrenched himself at the time of the battle of Ueda, rumbled terribly and the sound traveled a distance of twenty *ri* [eighty kilometers]. "What a strange phenomenon" thought the lord, and he ordered two or three foot soldiers to go there and investigate. They came to this region and investigated for three days and nights. Upon receiving their report, the lord thought it an evil omen for the fief and ordered special prayers offered in the Daihōji temple of the Tendai sect of this region, in Hakusanji of Sanada village and in Zenzanji of the Shinshū sect in Shioda. Special prayers were said in these three temples by order of the lord.

In addition, from December 1 there was an omen of crows roosting in the forest of the castle and making tremendous noises throughout the night, until the night of the fifth day. But when it came to the eleventh night, not a single crow was to be found in the forest. This was seen as a sign of the outbreak of the uprising. And there were still stranger happenings. From around November unknown persons in Shioda spread a rumor that every night "thieves are sneaking around the village." Whereupon the villages consulted together and formed groups. They searched about the forests and woods trying to catch the scoundrels, but it proved to be only a groundless rumor. Another strange occurrence: one saw numerous fires in the mountains and the wet fields. Pine torches appeared and there was noise everywhere, yet nobody knew what it all meant. When thinking about it now, there is no doubt it was a harbinger of the uprising. How strange that it all started from the base of Mt. Kanjya.[2]

Thus passed nearly a year of detailed planning and organizing along district lines during which time there was even talk in at least one village of appealing directly to the bakufu in Edo.[3] Finally, with the lighting of signal fires in Ogami village early on the night of December 11, 1761, Ueda's first mass uprising erupted. It lasted for approximately fifteen months and passed through five stages, which may be summarized roughly as follows: December 11 to 14, mobilization and invasion of the castle town; December 15 to 26, stalemate and confusion; December 27 to January 9, 1762, recommencement; January 10, 1762, to March 1, 1763, "vertical" discussions, conciliation, reintegration, and repression; and finally, on March 2, 1763, the public execution of Hanbei and Asanojō, followed by more group discussions throughout the fief.

Once the uprising commenced, spontaneous disconnected riots, demonstrations, and agitations broke out in the early and middle stages, across the fief and at all levels of society. For most of this period the main struggle was the vertical one between rulers and ruled or, in other words, samurai officials and their village agents versus a peasantry that was united on the two primary issues of (a) excessive rice tributes and corvée duties and (b) the need for local political reform. The one secondary issue most peasants agreed on was that the fief overtaxed profits from commercialized agriculture.

But, at every stage, this vertical conflict also involved horizontal struggles within different classes and stratum. A growing class of poor, landless tenants and minute landholders fought richer peasant landlords, village officials, and privileged merchants who engaged in agriculture (zaikata shōnin); townsmen were pitted against fief officials; low-ranking samurai were in conflict with senior retainers; artisans rose in protest against the practices of their guild chiefs; even social outcasts (eta) stirred themselves against the abuses of their caste chief. Because the samurai of Ueda were demoralized and divided from the outset, and because the struggles dragged on for so long, the peasants were able to undermine fief stability and even threaten the survival of Matsudaira rule. Reluctantly, in the interest of safeguarding their command and restoring at least the appearance of normalcy, the fief rulers agreed to change their methods of surplus extraction.

MOBILIZATION AND INVASION OF UEDA CASTLE TOWN, DECEMBER 11–14, 1761

In the course of a single night, the sixty-year-old Hanbei, the thirty-six-year-old Asanojō, and the headman Tarobei—all from Ogami village—together with Kinjirō, the headman of Tazawa village and other headmen from the villages of Muramatsu, Tōgō, and Koshido (all in Urano), succeeded in mobilizing the entire fief by means of signal fires and messengers. The latter were sent running through the villages shouting, "We're going to Ueda tomorrow to appeal the manipulated pricing of the rice tribute. If you agree with us, push forward to Suwabe village in the morning before six o'clock." [4] Before dawn the next day, scores of villages, organized along district lines, were out in force along the plain of the Chikuma River, six or seven thousand strong. The *Sōdō jikki* describes them

carrying several thousand pine torches ... [and] push[ing] forward as if competing with each other. They were clad in rags and straw raincoats. Tied to their backs inside their raincoats were paper bags filled with baked flour and one wooden bowl per person. Tucked into their belts were broad axes, hatchets and their handy [farming] tools.[5]

From the rendezvous point of the vanguard near Suwabe village, the march to the castle town took about thirty minutes. As an orderly column of two to three hundred peasants neared the entrance to the town, a tiny contingent of sixteen staff-wielding bailiffs attempted to intercept them, but were easily disarmed by the peasants and sent fleeing for their lives.[6]

By this time, the watchtower guards having sounded an alert, the cabinet of senior councillors (karō) was in session under Tadayori's chief representatives: Morooka, Okabe, and Hisamatsu. With a sizable peasant force fast approaching the wooden door of the main castle gate—and thousands more in their wake—they probably imagined an illegal mass appeal was in progress. Hence their first move was to call out police and tower and gate guards, deploying them to reinforce all strategic positions.[7] The original aim of the ikki leaders was indeed "an appeal to the authorities at the main gate of the castle." [8] But when the peasants (whose vanguard conceivably might have been led by old Hanbei) arrived there, Okabe and Hisamatsu issued two new orders. The commander of foot soldiers (omonogashira), one Hattori Jūrōbei, was told to defend with ten soldiers per place, the second earthwork-enclosed access area to the inner castle (Ninokuruwa) and the guard-houses, and all the district magistrates and intendants were ordered to go out and meet the peasants at the gate.[9] Accordingly,

Nakamura Yazaemon ... Katsura Kakuemon ... and Iwasaki Kichirōji made an appearance and were forced to allow the peasants into the castle. On this occasion, Umedo Yozōemon was away on duty at Edo. Since these four people mishandled the rice tributes, miscellaneous taxes and commodity tax money, the peasants came to appeal to them. Then these four local officals, saying they would transmit their appeal to the lord as the peasants wished, drew them into the castle because they thought it was a group of two to three hundred peasants. It was said that the four officials were truly lacking in wisdom. The peasants poured into the castle area and at the main gate of Okabe Kurobei's residence the officials said again to the peasants that they would transmit their appeal to the lord. But the peasants did not listen to them and insisted on appealing directly to the superintendents of local affairs. "We intend to hold these five people: Nakamura Yazaemon, Iwaski Kichirōji, Magoemon the district tribute officer of Komaki village in Koizumi district, Saburōbei the tribute officer of Uedahara village in Koizumi district, and Kozaemon the headman of Umagōshi village in Urano district." The four officials repeated again and again that they would transmit the appeal to the lord. But the power of four was nothing compared to that of six or seven thousand.

At this point in the *Sōdō jikki*, the Ueda events seem to be colored, momentarily at least, by dependence on the theatrical techniques of eighteenth-century kabuki. Although the bakufu banned the convulsions of the rural scene from being depicted on the kabuki stage, unknown authors of accounts of peasant ikki drew naturally on kabuki stylistic conventions. What better way was there to heighten popular emotions than by magnifying gestures or by pitting bare human passions against the oppressive feudal authorities in a striking tableau? The next lines are not only a good example of this use of kabuki technique to sum up a real historical event; they also suggest how the underground popular literature of that time was a part of the larger cultural world of Tokugawa Japan.

The officials said they would give in evidence a note guaranteeing the report they would make to the lord. They presented the peasants with three written notes which the latter received and examined. Saying that these documents were unacceptable, they tore them up and immediately threw them back. The four officials got angry, uncovered their spears and brandished them in the air. The courageous peasants bared their chests and gestured to them to go ahead and strike, while they walked toward the four officials, forcing them to retreat inside Okabe's courtyard.

Having retreated inside the courtyard, one of the samurai officials, using a ladder as his prop, strikes a different, almost comic pose.

The four officials locked the gate and from within raised a ladder against the wall. Nakamura Yazaemon, holding the three documents, waved them from the top of the wall. A scream went up: "Hey, don't let that thieving upstart [literally, "new fox"] samurai escape over the wall." [10]

And with that cry, the indignation of the peasants exploded at the inhuman treatment of the officials. A passage from *The History of Ueda City* (*Ueda shishi*, 1940), somewhat at variance with the above account from the *Sōdō jikki*, helps us follow what happened next as the ikki entered its violent phase.

> Some shouted: "We took action to make an appeal like this because you collect tributes in an unjust manner. This is the time we satisfy our revenge. Kill them!" But others stopped them saying "If we kill them, that will obstruct our appeals." Katsura Kakuemon and Nakamura Yazaemon fled into Okabe's residence compound and the peasants, running after them, did not dare to enter. At about four o'clock there were many people coming up from villages in Ueda to take part in the ikki. They marched up to the front gate of the lord's residence, where they roared loudly and used abusive language to the officials. It was in the cold winter. The water of the moat was frozen so hard that some crossed the ice and ran up the bank on the other side, where they pulled out bamboo stake poles and threw them inside the compound.
>
> Prior to this the associate superintendent of local affairs, Okabe Kurobei, summoned all the retainers to the meeting room to admonish them, saying that even a single casualty among the peasants would lead to a serious situation. "Take all precautions." So the samurai guards refrained from taking action before the peasants raged into the courtyard compound. At that moment it seemed that anything could happen. But after a while a piece of paper was thrown out from the residence which read as follows: "Each item of the peasants at this time will be reported to the lord at Edo, so that all items may be accepted as you appeal. December 12. Okabe Kurobei, Morooka Kahei." [11]

Clearly, the thoughts of the fief leaders focused on the bakufu's despotism, and fear of that governed their actions toward the peasants. In other words, on the late afternoon of December 12, it was from Edo, and not directly from a revolt powered by peasants, that they felt themselves most endangered.

So, with darkness beginning to descend and the air still filled with clashing words, Hisamatsu and other senior councillors emerged from the castle and tried to calm the rebellious peasants. [12] Finally, Okabe himself came riding out escorted by more than thirty armed samurai one of whom apparently copied down the peasants' demands. [13] Although the *Uedajima kuzuregōshi* (1762) lists only eighteen, Amamiya has differentiated as many as twenty-eight separate demands conveyed orally. [14] Eleven of them, as noted before, concerned the basic rice tribute; three called for a reduction in corvée labor services connected with rice tributes; four protested miscellaneous enterprise taxes and surcharges on production other than rice; one called for exemption from forced loans levied on the villages in the form of "voluntary gifts" (*saikakukin*); another for ending the practice of commandeering laborers at hunting time; and still others for the rotation of all village headmen

and an end to their oppression and that of the district tribute officers and field in-
specting officials. But the one demand that best captured the peasants' mood that
evening, and also revealed how far the previously well-defined rules governing
samurai-peasant relations had broken down, was their request "that the various
officials who go around the circuit on field inspection be delivered over to the peasants. Since they are so skilled in local affairs, we wish to learn from them how to
grow rice."[15]

Recollecting that tumultous and confusing first day of the uprising, the
author of the *Sōdō jikki* describes the peasants' riot in such a way as to celebrate
Okabe's daring and finesse in curbing it. He shows the peasants from the villages
west of the Chikuma River arriving first, allegedly destroying Okabe's gate and
high wall, and practically taking over the town, which at the time had a population
of only a little over 2,600 residents:[16] "Their roaring voices, shouting 'eiya, eiya,'
sounded like a thunderstorm and the scene made a picture with which even the
sight of the Heike battle could not compare."[17]

And with that as background—but omitting any mention of the strong possibility of the peasants' physical exhaustion after a day and night of continual marching and agitating—he offers evidence of Okabe's skill in cultivating the personal
obedience of peasants:

Okabe rode out from the castle in a serious air, wearing his ceremonial dress. He was reputed
for his abilities and features so that everybody looked up to him as a splendid gundai. All the
peasants removed the hoods and towels from around their heads and gathered round him.
With some grabbing his legs and others clinging to his sleeves, they left him no space to get
through and all the while appealed to him. Okabe listened to everything they had to say.
"That is truly a reasonable request. I, Kurobei, will go on your behalf and inform my lord
and will immediately make your wish come true. But first of all, you must calm down."
Whereupon everyone bowed down and understood what Kurobei said. The peasants from
the villages west of the river (amounting to 30,000 koku) then departed—after receiving a
letter of certification [*goshōmon*].[18]

Here was the real hero of the *Sōdō jikki*, the ideal embodiment of the samurais'
spiritual and cultural hegemony in eighteenth-century Japan. Here was the only
person who knew his duty and acted with a sense of his own class's historic mission
to rule. At the commencement of the *Sōdō jikki*, Okabe had invoked Confucian
classics and Buddhist scriptures to admonish Tadayori for "killing living things"
and ordering peasant laborers to accompany him on his hunting forays. Now, at
the Matsudaira family's most critical hour, he still remained the good and righteous adviser, applying his skills to deflect the peasants' anger away from the
samurai class. But, in the circumstances, whether righteous or not, he had also to
give them a written promise to fulfill their demands.

Next, a great commotion erupts at the main castle gate as some thirteen thousand peasants from the districts east of the river ("twenty-eight thousand koku") begin to pour in "at the appointed hour of six o'clock in the evening." After watching the demonstration for a while from a platform built for reviewing cavalry parades,[19] Okabe

once again came out and repeated what he had said earlier to the peasants. All of them were grateful for what he said but they appealed to Okabe that five persons . . . be given to them. Then Okabe said, "Why don't you peasants place yourself in my position? The lord is away. You asked for five people; but if you really want that, then why don't you take me, Kurobei?" Yielding to this argument, they all desisted from making further demands. Then Okabe said, "I'm going to set off immediately for Edo and report all this to the lord so that your wishes will be met." Instead of returning to his residence, he departed at seven o'clock for Edo. On his departure, he said to the peasants, "I'm going to Edo on your behalf and report everything to the lord. Depending on the lord's mind, I may or may not return. So a few of you may even come with me." Then 4–5,000 peasants, accepting with awe what he said, followed him to Ōmiya shrine, there to pray to Ōmiya Daimyōjin for a successful journey. Here Okabe said, ". . . this may be the last time I say farewell to you. So let us drink to a lucky start." He drank and passed the cup to all the major peasants, not to mention the ordinary peasants. Everybody was moved to tears. Then, after receiving a cup of sake, the peasants bid farewell and Okabe departed for Edo.[20]

Thus, at the end of the first night on which the issue was joined, at the height of their rebellious anger, some peasants, perhaps exhausted and confused by the ceaseless agitation, apparently allowed Okabe to cast a spell over them, to dissipate and momentarily deflate their energies. And while they were acknowledging Okabe's virtuous leadership (thereby indirectly confirming their own bondage), the momentum of their united front seemed to slow. The wine-drinking scene at Ōmiya shrine thus affords a rare glimpse of that structure of consciousness which holds together any class-stratified society almost as much as the ruling class's monopoly of legal force, which is why we must look closer at what actually occurred in it.

In a situation fraught with tension and anger, Okabe not only came down off his horse and talked kindly to the lowly peasants. He also showed them he did not even mind drinking with them. ("He drank and passed the cup. . . . Everybody was moved to tears.") The peasants were acutely conscious of Okabe's exalted status and of the fact that he was a relative of the lord. No wonder they reacted emotionally and positively to his paternalistic treatment and even offered prayers, for his successful return, to the deity of Ōmiya Shrine (Ōmiya daimyōjin). The weakness and confusion of peasant class consciousness in this particular encounter is unmistakable. Although he was responsible for crushing them down, the peasants willingly allowed themselves to be manipulated by Okabe, once he demonstrated benevolent concern. Later, after Okabe departed, they displaced their anger and frustration onto the "middle managers" (the village headmen, district tribute officers, and merchants), leaving the lord and his highest retainers alone. But there would be other times and situations when the peasants themselves manipulated the noblesse oblige obligations of their local rulers, when their servility itself was a form of manipulation.

The incident at Ōmiya Shrine should not therefore be exaggerated. The alliance of villages east and west of the Chikuma held for approximately three days until a meeting of peasants from districts west of the river on December 14, at a place called Ubugawa, dissolved it.[21] Recapitulating that initial stage of the Ueda uprising, the mass of peasants controlled the situation in both town and countryside, and their violence seems to have been occasioned—as is invariably the case with major social upheavals—by a trifling incident, concerning which contemporary accounts disagree. According to the *Ueda City History*, it started on the morning of the first day when Fujiya, a fairly large tobacconist of Yokomachi, unwittingly insulted the peasant demonstrators. Mistaking them for beggars, he observed aloud that "this morning so many poor souls [*hinindomo*] are passing through." Whereupon some of the marching peasants remarked that on their way back he would "see what hinindomo can do."[22] Other sources locate the start of the riot in Haramachi. But the *Sōdō jikki* merely notes that the peasants, seized by an intense hatred of fief power, vented their anger against its agents and servitors.

After bidding farewell [to Okabe] the peasants came back. Then an unprecedented event occurred. They pushed into the house of Zen'emon (a silk merchant) of Ueno district, a man who made contributions to the lord, and destroyed his property, including his warehouse. They also smashed the shop windows in Unno. The next day, on the thirteenth, a really frightening scene occurred when, in various places, they knocked down and trampled upon altogether a total of twenty houses belonging to district tribute officers and village headmen.

It was right after this property destruction occurred that some unknown persons scribbled the following satirical lines on fences and walls:

To the district tribute officers we gave crushed egg soup. The bean paste was too strong and broke the yolks.
Magoemon, with a fringe of hair, should be tonsured.
Jūzō, his son, with his swords taken away, is also culpable.
Saburobei emerged from the mountain areas as a beggar clad in straw.
Later his fortune was baked in a casserole.
Whither is the village headman Ikushima going with his properties destroyed, when he says to his wife and children: "come on this way."[23]

Here the coarse food (salty *miso* and egg) served up to local officials and the rich symbolized their punishment. Based squarely on the peasants' daily experience, this sort of graffiti may not have enhanced their understanding of political conditions in the fief, but it was, nevertheless, instructive. As a type of black humor, it evoked delight by simultaneously identifying the guilty and noting their punishment. The guilty, as everyone in the community knew, were Magoemon, Saburōbei, Jūzō, and Ikushima. By destroying their property, the peasants brought them down to a level beneath the poor. Such a rebirth was a fitting punishment for their crimes. Although no physical violence was done to their persons, their fortunes presumably went to a Buddhist hell, which was the association carried by "baked in a casserole." Clearly, the use of such satire, directed against their immediate tormentors, gave instruction as well as pleasure to peasants. Yet seen in conjunction with the Ubugawa meeting, when the peasants west of the river met and failed to agree on whether to continue the riot, it also suggests that their hopes had become diverted. By the fourth day, the peasant struggle against samurai had diminished almost in proportion as that against district tribute officers and village headmen increased.

STALEMATE AND CONFUSION, DECEMBER 15–26, 1761

Two distant centers of action and of power dominated the second phase of class struggle in Ueda: Edo, where the fief's highest officials had gone to confer with Tadayori, and rural Ueda, some two hundred kilometers away, where feudal administration remained paralyzed and the highest fief authorities were reduced to pleading with the peasants (via written messages sent in their own name because the district magistrates were too unpopular) to calm down, stop pillaging, renounce the demand for samurai hostages, and wait patiently for Okabe's return.[24] Once again cleavages appeared in peasant ranks as the conflict with the district tribute officers and headmen in the villages took precedence over the vertical struggle against the fief. But Ueda's middle-level samurai officials who were in direct charge of rural affairs, such as the district magistrates and the senior fief leaders who set overall policy, also were unable to reach a policy consensus on the basis of which the uprising could be brought to an end. The joint council system of rule, which technically obtained in normal times, had broken down in the emergency.

When Okabe and Hisamatsu arrived in Edo on December 16, they reported immediately to the lord, in full, on the uprising and on the retainers' latent sympathy for the peasants' cause. But they failed to bring any policy for dealing with the crisis, nor did they even know what their junior officials in charge of peasants were thinking. As the district magistrate Katsura Kakuemon was to charge a few weeks later in a personal letter to the elder Morooka Kahei, Okabe and Hisamatsu should have gone up to Edo with the officials in charge of rural affairs in order to decide what the proper policy of the fief should be and also to learn the lord's intentions. But nobody voiced such an opinion. Instead, everybody worried about flattering his superiors and they all asked for instructions on even the most trivial matters, thereby obstructing the administration of the fief.[25]

Lord Tadayori, for his part, seems to have lacked knowledge of how to use his power and had nothing constructive to offer. Interestingly, the *Sōdō jikki* projects this image of heated political conflict at the highest echelons of fief government, which may be partly, but not entirely, fictionalized. Standing by Tadayori's side, Suzuki Sukenoshin, his chief adviser, is made to say, boastfully,

> "Unlike your high-ranking offices, you are very timid in handling mere peasants who count for nothing. Why, the measures you took were cowardly. Unworthy though I am, if I had been in the domain, I would not have allowed them to go so far."
>
> Without replying [Hisamatsu and Okabe] pulled off their outer ceremonial robes and seemed ready to commit suicide. Frightened by their touching determination, the lord angrily ordered Sukenoshin to exit. He retreated to a lower seat and bowed in awe to show his acceptance of the order [that is, he forfeited his right thereafter to advise the lord]. . . . The lord listened and understood everything the two officials said. He called them praiseworthy for having faultlessly pacified such a large number of peasants.[26]

If one assumes that Okabe and Hisamatsu represented an opposition faction dissatisfied with past treatment of the retainers and desirous of reviving their morale, then this encounter, held against a background of insurrection within the fief, may have signaled its triumph.[27] In any case, having been won over by the two retainers, Tadayori acknowledged his indebtedness to them by bestowing upon them his own long sword and crepe *haori*, a short coat worn over a kimono. He then ordered them to handle matters until his return. On the eighteenth Okabe and Hisamatsu reported informally to the shogunal councillor, Itakura Sado no Kami, husband of Tadayori's younger sister.[28] Because of the unusually heavy snowstorm that day, they were unable to depart Edo until the nineteenth.

While the fief leaders in Edo worked to overcome differences among themselves, coordinate a strategy of repression with the bakufu, and then transit the difficult snow-covered highways during the storm of mid-December, the peasants waited for their answer. Disunity among the retainers in Ueda also contributed to the delay. Finally, on December 20, a messenger arrived from Edo bearing Lord Tadayori's instruction to suspend temporarily, though not formally dismiss, certain village headmen, district tribute officers, district magistrates, and intendants. Thus the villages learned that new officials were to be provisionally appointed in place of Funakoshi Banemon, the magistrates Nakamura Yazaemon and Katsura Kakuemon, the accountant Iwasaki Kichirōji, the tribute officer Magoemon, and the headman Kozaemon. Four intendants were also named for replacement.[29]

This apparent firing of a small number of rural officials whom peasants blamed for their suffering (even though the fief leaders secretly regarded them as men who had rendered distinguished service) was the fief's answer to the mass protests of December 12 and 13. Apparently, Okabe, Morooka, and the others had entertained the comforting thought that a mere wave of house-smashings, if allowed to run its course, would not necessarily turn into an antifief action. Hoping to escape blame themselves, they had stood by and allowed the full force of peasant wrath to be vented against the district tribute officer–village headman stratum. But now a counterstrategy of repression had been formulated with the bakufu, while at the same time the peasants had shown their determination. In these circumstances the fief leaders wanted to restore order and gain time to consider how to handle the peasants' economic challenge. By appearing to meet their one explicitly political demand before announcing any economic concessions, they succeeded momentarily in defusing the situation without threatening the retainers.

Three or four days later, Okabe and Hisamatsu reached Kazawa village on the Ueda border, where a mixed retinue of samurai and peasants met and escorted them back to the castle town. Although the fief leaders were unaware of it, the most dangerous moment for the Matsudaira family had already been weathered. Their own positions were politically stronger now than when they had left for Edo at the height of the uprising. Since they were in firmer control of fief administration, Okabe, Hisamatsu, and Morooka could try to force the peasants to accept minimal concessions. Anything more could be only at the retainers' expense and would surely worsen their already low morale.

But popular passions had not burned out, either in the countryside, where the ikki leaders were still at large and unknown to the authorities, or in the castle town, as Okabe and Hisamatsu were about to learn. During their stay in Edo, life in Ueda castle town had been completely disrupted. Business ceased for twelve days while the fief struggled helplessly to control the peasants. Meanwhile, the town magistrate, his two administrative assistants (called *tonya*), and the latter's more numerous helpers (called *machidōshin*) did what they could to restore calm in the eight districts into which the castle town was divided. But frightening rumors circulated of renewed disturbances by peasants. On December 16, day and night patrols were started to prevent looting. On the seventeenth, Katō Sachū, the town magistrate, personally inspected burnt-out stores and homes.[30]

As they watched the progress of the peasants' struggle with the fief, many residents of the town districts must have reacted unhappily, if not with unconcealed contempt, at the impotent racing around of samurai in full armor. But, whatever their thoughts, they refrained from action of their own until they learned, on the twenty-first, that the fief had finally given in to the peasants and agreed to suspend, temporarily, the most hated of the senior rural officials. Only then, after having conferred earlier in small groups, did townsmen meet en masse and decide to immediately press their own long-standing grievances against the authorities. Thus the apparent initial success of peasants inspired townsmen to act on their own concerns. Here, as Francis Piven and Richard Cloward observe in a more contemporary context, the general point about the contagious nature of mass protests "is not simply that people mimic each other; it is that mobilization among some groups provokes the hopes and aspirations of other groups and shows them a way to act on those hopes."[31]

Around December 22, a few days before Okabe and Hisamatsu arrived back at the castle, townsmen petitioned Katō Sachū at his official residence within the castle walls. Drawn up in the name of merchants of Hara and Yanagi districts (machi), their demands embraced fourteen separate items,[32] of which the most important are quoted below. Before looking at them, however, a brief sketch of the castle town's development will help explain the townsmen's complaints.

Up to the last quarter of the seventeenth century, the lords of Ueda were fairly successful in their policy of minimizing contacts between peasants and merchants and of banning peasant participation in a wide range of essential commercial activities, such as the marketing of rice, soybeans, silk thread (pongee), buckwheat, and cotton. This relative commercial isolation of the rural population, together with the growth in population throughout the country in the seventeenth century, contributed to the early prosperity of the two oldest town districts: Hara and Unno. By the 1670s, Ueda castle town had absorbed five other geographically related market villages: Kaji, Yoko, Yanagi, Konya, and Ta. And by the close of the seventeenth century, as it neared the peak of its development, the silk thread of Unno and the iron plows of Kaji were being marketed widely throughout Shinshū, Jōshū, and the Kantō plain.[33]

But early in the eighteenth century, the castle town in Ueda, as in many other fiefs, began to experience a slow decline in its registered population and internal contradictions in both the domanial and national market spheres. Specifically, fief officials, though they exercised strict control over trade in strategic commodities, never attempted to exclude peasants from all market activities. In other words, from the outset of the Tokugawa regime, peasants were not completely self-sufficient. In Ueda, for example, they made their own clothing but brought their cotton material to the artisans of Konya for dyeing. When their horses needed shoeing, they brought them to the blacksmiths of Kaji. They also participated in monthly and bimonthly markets in designated rural areas. And because the authorities needed to raise revenues in every possible way, they allowed peasants from all seven districts, in increasing numbers, to sell certain commodities in their villages under commercial license.[34]

Another departure from feudal economic principle was Ueda's tolerance of "town peasants" (*machi byakushō*), or townsmen who were not employed in commerce and industry but engaged in agricultural production in surrounding areas. In the Kyōhō era such townsmen paid tributes of at least 680 koku. Their existence should be kept in mind because it figured in later peasant efforts to legitimate their own commercial activities whenever guild merchants called for their suppression.[35]

By the Hōreki era—largely as a result of (a) increasing commercial activity in rural areas and (b) the blurring of the line between the lowest stratum of town residents who worked the land in outside areas and peasants residing in villages on the periphery of the town districts—the castle town of Ueda ceased to be the fief's sole and exclusive center for the distribution of essential goods and services. The townsmen's demands should thus be read against this background of long-term structural decline and widespread grievances against their rural competitors and against the fief authorities who overtaxed and overregulated them almost as much as peasants.

They began, as they had on earlier occasions, by complaining of personal ruin and demoralization as a result of onerous day-labor services, forced loans, and additional tenma—the furnishing of men and horses to shogunal officials and court nobles who were in transit on official business. They then went on to protest having to pay the costs of food and lodging incurred by visiting shogunal and other officials who came through the town bearing red-sealed certificates (*goshuin goshō-mon*) or circular notices (*ofure*). They also protested the loss of business and the property destruction caused by the peasants' "disturbance." "We are not sure we can collect bills any longer. We appeal therefore for your relief measures." But perhaps their most instructive complaints concerned the inroads being made by peasants on their own control of rural markets.

- In recent years, many stores have opened in rural villages to do business. As a result, [our own] village markets are automatically declining. We sincerely appeal that the authorities ban the opening of shops in remote rural villages where we town merchants have transported goods to markets.
- Concerning the matter of merchants from other places coming into the rural areas, we appeal that the practice be banned as it was ordered.[36]

The restrained, even humble language in which all these appeals were couched should not obscure the militancy of the townsmen's action. If the account given in the *Sōdō jikki* is to be believed, it was carried out amidst shouts and threats by hundreds of angry men who milled about the residence compound of Town Magistrate Katō Sachū: "They gathered at his gate and shouted in one voice: 'Because of the recent uprising, we are unable to do any business and each man is suffering in getting his daily rice allotment. Lend us rice. If you refuse to accept this appeal, we will crush your house.'"[37] The townsmen not only got their appeal accepted for consideration, they also received immediate delivery of two hundred bales of rice, enough for each household to receive four shō.

On December 25, shortly after their return from Edo, Okabe, Hisamatsu, and Morooka took a series of small steps toward appeasing the peasants and restoring public confidence in the institution of the lord as a technique of ideological control. After having received the townsmen's petition, they discharged thirty-one of Tadayori's thirty-six maid servants or ladies-in-waiting and also ordered the release of about 350 of his wild ducks, hawks, and falcons. Whether the *Kuzuregōshi* has recorded the details of this incident accurately or not, it does suggest that they acted quickly to eliminate superfluous expenses of the fief and to reestablish an image of high moral conduct by the lord. Okabe also had the district intendants notify the villages of his return and of the lord's approval of one of their demands: henceforth peasants were to be reimbursed for expenses incurred by the billeting of field inspection officials.

The peasants were then told to send representatives to the castle by 8 o'clock on the morning of the next day, December 26: "It is instructed by Okabe in yesterday's notice that you consult together. Either village officials alone, or a certain number of peasants as well, depending on how you wish, are to come up to the castle accompanied by village headmen, assistant headmen, peasant representatives and heads of five-man groups."[38] The "depending on how you wish" may have been another concession to the peasants allowing them to protect the anonymity of their leaders by going to the castle en masse.[39]

The meeting of December 26, 1761, brought the second phase of the Ueda uprising to a close. The villages sent six or seven representatives each to accompany their officials to the castle town. Nearly six hundred filled the inns on that day of the great meeting. From the intendant's office came a message instructing them to assemble in the garden of Okabe's residence compound. There, in a large wall-enclosed garden, the next to last scene of the *Kuzuregōshi* unfolded. At one end was an open meeting room elevated above the ground like a stage and commanding a view of the entire inner compound. In rows facing the garden sat Ueda's highest ranking officials. In front, the high councillors: Okabe Kurobei, Hisamatsu Shume, Morooka Kahei, and Kimura Kageyu; behind them, the chamberlains: Murakami Sahei, Nakamura Seidayū, Saji Hachiemon, Yasuhara Tarō, and Saji Ichiemon; next the intendants: Hayakawa Rinpei, Hara Zendayū, Noma Koemon, and Hayashi Hachirōji; then the commanders and their deputies in charge of foot soldiers; and last, adjutants with spears and rifles. Two hundred foot soldiers (*ashigaru*) and police bailiffs (*dōshin*) with six-foot-long sticks stood guard in the rear of the garden and outside around the compound. Hunched down on the cold snow-covered ground were unarmed village officials and peasant representatives.

Okabe stepped forward to give the fief's reply to the peasants: "I went up to Edo and reported your wishes to the lord. Now I pass to you this written instruction." [40] And he read out to them a five-point statement bearing his and Morooka's signatures. It began with an admonition: "The lord was of the opinion that peasants should make orderly requests in a proper manner, starting with the assistant headmen and headmen and going on upward to the fief officials." [41] Then followed a partial acceptance of the peasants' demands of the twelfth. The fief agreed to refund the price of soybeans, abolish the practice of advance cash payments, and refund payments already made. But it deferred for future investigation any action on the key problem of discrepancies in cash payments for grain at Matsuida and Ueda, while not even mentioning the problem of servant services (debito).

As for the peasants' request for a five-year rotation of village headmen, Okabe insisted it was not a matter that small men in villages should be allowed to deliberate. So,

there should not be a change in each village. If for the time being there is a change, then the peasants' accounts will be thrown into confusion. Therefore the authorities will, in due course, investigate the matter and later there may possibly be a change.

Other items of your appeal are difficult for the various offices [yakusho] to fully investigate. They will therefore be studied in due course. After investigations have been made it will be ordered that peasants do not suffer. [42]

When Okabe finished speaking, the meeting dispersed. The anger of the first two weeks seemed to have subsided. To all appearances the uprising seemed over, as the village officials returned home intent, perhaps, on securing compliance with Okabe's terms. On the twenty-eighth Okabe and Morooka issued a second circular notice to all the village headmen and assistant headmen, making some partial concessions. On that same day the village headmen and their assistants from Kokubunji district (adjacent to the castle on the left bank of the Chikuma River) were able to forward written acceptances of Okabe's terms. [43] But from the vast majority of peasants such acceptances were not immediately forthcoming. Recognizing the inadequacy of what had been offered them, and unhappy with the fief's mixture of high-handedness and partial, mostly unspecific concessions to be implemented "in due time after investigation," the peasants refused to submit either to the fief authorities or to their own village officials. And thus, "with each peasant insisting on his own opinion, they were unable to reach a consensus. Because what they were told at that time was not agreeable to them, the whole domain was thrown into turmoil." [44]

RECOMMENCEMENT, DECEMBER 27–28, 1761, TO JANUARY 9, 1762

The third phase began with the refusal of a majority of peasants to accept the fief's initial settlement offer and ended with a reconciliation of the two sides on the basis of much greater concessions offered by the fief on January 9. In between, the poorer peasants, against the wishes of the economically dominant stratum in the villages, refused to end the struggle and continued sporadic acts of violent protest. Still in position to suppress them, the authorities refrained from using military force and used the last week of the year to continually sound out the peasants. When nothing happened, they reached a consensus among themselves on the necessity of making still further concessions to the peasants' demands.

One incentive that led them to make additional concessions in such circumstances was their obvious need of peasants to manage the fief. But a more important factor was their belief that the use of force, and the bloodshed that might result from it, would be a clear admission of the Matsudaira family's administrative incompetence. The bakufu would see it as prima facie evidence of their misgovernment and loss of control. They would then be liable to punishment, even removal. Ultimately, fear of the bakufu was the real source of the fief elders' noblesse oblige toward peasants.

After loudly trumpeting their own long-awaited return to the domain and fostering high expectations about the great occasion of the lord's reply to the peasants' demands, Okabe and Morooka on the twenty-sixth and again on the twenty-eighth failed to formally dismiss the village headmen en masse, threatened the peasants with a display of repressive military force, and ended up offering them only partial concessions on relatively nonurgent issues. In adopting such an approach, Okabe and company may have imagined the peasants were exhausted by this time, ready to end their protest and go down on their knees at the first display of samurai benevolence. But the fief's official reply of the twenty-sixth, followed two days later by its circular notice, had just the opposite effect. Rather than intimidating them into submission, it rekindled their spirit of resistance to samurai and deepened unrest throughout the fief. On December 31, as a gesture of their dissatisfaction, the peasants refused to celebrate the New Year, and most village officials absented themselves from making the customary New Year's calls at the castle.

Caught between an aroused and distrustful peasantry, which appeared to be winning new strength, and a suspicious bakufu waiting to see how the Matsudaira family would handle matters, Okabe and the others now had little room left for maneuver. They could contemplate either giving to peasants by taking from the retainers or else running the risk of another uprising and with it the likelihood of losing the fief through shogunal intervention. Although we do not know how great the danger of shogunal confiscation of the fief really was, it seems reasonable to suppose that the high retainers momentarily feared confiscation.

Whether or not that was the case at this time, Okabe's response was another circular notice to all village officials—headmen, assistant headmen, and peasant representatives—ordering them to appear before the castle gate on January 9, 1762, accompanied by one or two of the more vocal peasants. Sent out to the villages on December 30 and 31, this notice was interpreted to mean that the fief authorities were about to redress the major unresolved grievances.

Meanwhile, the more radical component of the peasants mobilized to resolve the problem of unpopular village headmen. If the fief would not rotate them out of office, they would attack and burn them out. During the first few days of January 1762, limited assaults were launched against fifteen homes of "privileged merchants, district tribute officers and above." In some cases, too, "peasants attacked not only the village headmen, but also their assistants and peasant representatives, saying that there were injustices in the account books and they had broken in [to the offices] in order to investigate." And once again, as during the first week of the rising, political lampoons appeared on gates and walls mocking both the district tribute officers and, for the first time, the fief administration. One line evoked the usual food metaphor: "We crushed district tribute officers like eggs to make bean paste soup and with too much paste the egg yolks broke." The other employed the metaphors of Japanese chess (shōgi): "Look at those peasants rushing toward the main gate (ōte); even with gold and silver [playing] pieces taken away, they can still check the King if they wish." [45] Here, the class struggle between peasants and their rulers is likened to a chess match. After losing their income (gold and silver playing pieces) and being driven into a corner, the peasants cry out a warning to the king to move. We still have the power to march directly on the castle and frustrate you if we wish. Easily decipherable, the symbolism of peasant graffiti carried a New Year's message of defiance to the feudal authorities.

Actions such as these, physical and symbolic, continued in different places throughout Ueda until the mass meeting that restored outward peace with the peasants was finally held as scheduled. On January 9, 1762, two days after the end of the New Year's holiday, Okabe Kurobei read out the nine-point document and the four-point accompanying explanation quoted, in part, below. In the first, the feudal authorities were unable to explain the cause of the price discrepancy at Jōshū, Matsuida, and Ueda. To the peasants' demands for rice tribute reductions and reductions in labor services for senior retainers and for those in official fief employment, they could give only partial satisfaction. To the peasants' demand for exemption from new enterprise taxes, they could only promise an answer after having made investigations. They also deferred until later answers to several requests concerning circumstances in one village only. Overall, the document showed the authorities clinging unyieldingly to the basic pattern of rulers and ruled, while at the same time acknowledging their own subordination to the national market and the political order controlled by the bakufu. Thus,

- ... as a special relief measure on this occasion, we shall discount for you 4 to 5 shō from the amount of rice you have to pay for 1 ryō.... But we cannot break the previously established rule. Recently, the peasants requested to make payments according to the selling price in the local villages. That cannot be permitted because it will be harmful to neighboring domains.... However, whenever prices [at Jōshū, Matsuida, and Ueda] are especially different, we shall, at our discretion, make exemptions at the fief's expense.
- ... in time of military duties, we shall call for servant services [debito] in accordance with our needs. This is an official matter ordered by the Shogunate.
- The matter of alternate attendance [sankin kōtai] is also a duty ordered by the shogunate. So ... there will be an additional need for servant services. But since there are not enough servants [hōkōnin] recently in the villages ... the authorities shall avoid as much as possible giving orders to the villages for servants....
- ... One is free to become a servant in samurai families or in towns, villages and other places. But villages should first meet the retainers' need for employees. Afterwards, they may go anywhere they wish to serve, provided they request the usual permission in writing.

After this pronouncement was read out, the accompanying explanation told the assembled peasants that the fief's "judgment on less urgent matters" would be rendered later. Meanwhile, they were to:

- Return and inform all the peasants of the contents of the above document; then come back here on the 12th, after having obtained everyone's consent, and bring a document of guarantee [ukesho]).
- As we told you the other time, since we will handle all matters justly, you peasants too quickly consult one another and conduct yourselves in an orderly manner. Hereafter, even if you have a complaint, your appeals should not be unreasonable. Since the higher are treating the lower with benevolence, change your behavior and observe all the laws of the authorities. As noted in the provisions of law [gojōmoku], parents and children, brothers and sisters should get along well with one another, maintain harmony inside the villages, and be circumspect in behavior. When you return to your villages, discuss this matter and make sure everyone understands that hereafter it will not be good for those who act contrary to this order.
- Know that anyone spreading rumors about a matter of inquiry will be relieved of the post of servant. Be well aware of these points. Return to your villages now and discuss them thoroughly.[46]

In this compromise pronouncement of the fief, the principle of feudal benevolence was invoked to justify the promotion of the welfare of the oppressed and, at the same time, to legitimate their continued repression. Relying on shogunal authority to justify their actions, the fief officials managed to avoid making any firm promise of a decrease in the number of servants supplied by villages. By now accepting the fief's terms and agreeing to desist from the further successful use of violence, the peasants of Ueda were not saying that their discontent was at an end. But they were saying that they had never subjectively desired the overthrow of feudal rule as such: the fief's central institutions were, in their eyes, still legitimate. In fact, their highest goal all along had really been a different type of feudal rule, with lighter taxes of all kinds, an end to samurai corruption and interference in agricultural work, and greater political control by peasants over all their activities at the local level.

Interestingly, this absence of revolutionary sentiments in the demands of ordinary peasants in revolt—their latent desire for a reform of the existing order rather than its radical overthrow—is not confined just to peasants under a feudal mode of production in a nonrevolutionary situation. It has also been a feature of the rank-and-file industrial proletariat, even under genuinely revolutionary circumstances. As Barrington Moore, Jr., noted, concerning the initial phase of the Bolshevik Revolution (February-March 1917), "nearly all the demands that surfaced with the end of Tsarism had to do with wages and working conditions." In general, what workers and peasants want politically "is the present order with its most disagreeable features softened or eliminated." [47]

In Ueda, after the fief made concessions to them on January 9, and again in later weeks, most peasants could consider their conflict with the fief settled, their sacrifices rewarded. But for its part, the fief could not consider the matter settled until it had first exacted admonitory punishment for what had occurred. Hence the manner of its capitulation to the peasants also prefigured what was to occur next: the arrest and torture of the leaders who first focused the peasants' discontent and led them against the fief.

TOWARD CONCILIATION AND REINTEGRATION, JANUARY 10, 1762, TO MARCH 1, 1763

Within a month of the January 9 settlement by the fief, most, if not all, of Ueda's eighty-two villages returned to the castle written acceptances of a contractual though nonreciprocal nature, thereby binding themselves once again in feudal submission to the authorities. "Regarding the authorities' inquiries," they ended with a formulistic profession of servility: "We have no word of explanation and we sincerely apologize. We shall be most obliged if you would pardon us with your mercy from now on as well. [signed] All the peasants, all the villages." [48]

This appeal to the value of "mercy" can be read as false consciousness. But it can also be read as a deliberate peasant strategem: an attempt to exploit the ruling values for their own ends. Significantly, it occurred when the repercussions of the uprising had by no means spent themselves.

By successfully protesting specific forms of oppression, the Ueda peasants had indirectly raised the general question of oppression itself. Now other subordinated groups, inspired by the peasants' action, asserted their own claims for redress of specific grievances. These nonpeasant struggles, though organizationally detached from one another, were reactions to roughly similar situations of economic exploitation and extreme status discrimination. As summarized in the *Sōdō jikki*:

On January 17 a complaint was made by all the Buddhist temples of the domain concerning the tribute on . . . forest lands within temples [*tachidashiyama*]. In addition, a five-article request was submitted in the name of all the temples and shrines.

On January 18 all the carpenters of the domain went en masse and requested that the authorities provide them with bags of rice, counted per head, in compensation for the mishandling of water-service allowances and per head payments to carpenters.

On January 19 all the coopers of the domain went en masse to the office of the head cooper and made the same complaint as the carpenters.

On January 28 all the social outcasts [eta] of the domain descended en masse on Kojuro of Suwabe village, the head of the outcasts [chōrigashira], and presented him with a total of thirteen different complaints such as the matter of unjust collection of *busen* [cash charges in lieu of labor services] and the manner of assigning various duties, including night duty services and other illegitimate practices. Shouting they would destroy everything if he did not listen, Kojuro was frightened by their demonstration and accepted their demands, thereby settling the matter.

Seen in this way, the recent uprising involved not only peasants but Buddhist priests, Shinto priests, artisans, townsmen and even the chief of the social outcasts. Everybody's attention was attracted. The authorities investigated these uprisings together with the complaints of the peasants. Soon the agitation settled down.[49]

Meanwhile the fief, learning at last the identities of the peasant ringleaders, and particularly of Hanbei and Asanojō, went on the offensive. Early on the evening of January 19 Okabe dispatched to Urano district, "the breeding ground of disturbances," an official raiding party of 138 heavily armed men. According to the *Sōdō jikki*,

when they arrived at the village which was their place of destination . . . [they] surrounded the houses and called out "Come out! This is official business of the lord!" Although they had long been aware of and prepared for such an eventuality, when the time came to be arrested, there was some confusion and the peasants were easily taken alive.[50]

After the eight peasant leaders from Ogami and Tōgō villages in Urano were brought back to Ueda castle and jailed, Okabe Kurobei is depicted as having personally interrogated them by asking: "Do you in the humble status of peasants know the proper manner for getting the person of a samurai and killing him? The proper practice is that the death of one samurai will be compensated for by the death of seven peasants."[51] To this threat of reprisal and claim of superiority over peasants—scaled by feudal justice at seven peasant lives for one samurai life—the prisoners responded by shifting the issue. They at once denied ever having had any intention to do harm and asserted a moral-economic claim to greater social recognition and consideration: "In our humble capacity we never dreamed of such a thing as asking for the person of a samurai in order to kill him. But since you officials think that 'peasants' are particularly useful beings, we wanted to let the samurai do the hard work of peasants and see for themselves how profitable we are."[52]

By this juxtaposition of quotations, the unknown author of the *Sōdō jikki* has given expression to a significant peasant feeling not only of revenge but also of contempt for samurai. That contempt was grounded in the peasants' own sense of personal worth apart from inherited status, which, in the absence of contrary evidence, we may presume to have always existed. The implicit mockery of samurai by oppressed peasants also tells us that much of their behavior that appeared respectful and deferential of samurai was perhaps ritualized and even calculating.[53]

Okabe, conceding the reasonableness of this reply, answered with an "indeed" and then continued: "Field inspection is ordered according to law throughout the country. Why do you complain about your hardships? In reply, the peasants said: 'We may respectfully answer you this way: Field inspection is to us what an investigation by a traveling inspector from Edo is to the lord.' To this Okabe again replied 'Yes indeed' and smiled slightly."[54]

But notwithstanding Okabe's smiles and "indeeds," which the author would have us take as further proof of his hero's admirable nature, Hanbei, Asanojō, and the other six prisoners were tortured to determine who else led the uprising. When, after various interrogations and tortures, they still refused to confess, they

were subjected to *ebizeme* [shrimp torture, or bending the body in the shape of a shrimp], *mokuba* [stretching the body with weights between wooden horses] or *hashigozeme* [ladder torture in which the body was stretched on a ladder]. They were tortured with various methods but uttered not a word. Because they unanimously repeated the same statement they made before and never confessed, they were put to a new torture called the *seirōzeme* [box torture].

Sharp stones were lined up inside a box; the [eight] were made to squat down on them and a board was placed across their thighs to which increasingly heavier weights were added. From eight o'clock in the morning until four in the afternoon they were tortured in this way. By that time they seemed half dead and no longer looked like human beings. They were like a picture of hell, so awful that nobody could bear to behold them. Finally, after this continuous torture, they confessed. Thereupon the identity of the criminals gradually became clear.[55]

Following the torture of the main peasant leaders in late January, the fief leaders launched mass arrests and investigations throughout Ueda. This had gone on for some time when from the temples and shrines in each of the districts, priests began arriving at the castle to appeal directly for mercy for the peasants. But the fief, ignoring their appeals, went on examining each complaint and bombarding the villages with orders demanding the peasants' written assent. Because its aim was to restore not only outward social order but also sovereignty over the minds of its peasants, Ueda fief ordered the villages to meet repeatedly for over a year— from February 1762 to late March 1763—to discuss and report on what had happened.

On such occasions, the officials sought to foster a sort of childlike acceptance of paternal feudal authority. Maintain harmony, comply with the laws and the village chain of command, always behave with circumspection and sensitivity to rank, they repeated endlessly, week after week, month after month. Finally, the peasants relearned the terms of the feudal compact by which they let the samurai exercise domination over them. But if this ideological remolding of peasants in ideas of personal submission and service to hereditary superiors was designed to negate the experience of the December days, that aim would eventually be countered by the peasants' careful efforts to keep alive the memory of their leaders.

Then in May 1762, two significant things happened. In Ueda, the first heavy rain fell in over two years, signaling the end of the drought and the return to more normal farming conditions.[56] And in Edo, the bakufu took important new steps in a systematic policy of political repression of peasants. Responding to the unprecedented wave of successful uprisings that had swept different parts of the country since 1759, it issued a proclamation to all private fiefs and shogunal lands. As Hayashi Motoi pointed out, the May 1762 edict publicly acknowledged the peasants' right of appeal for redress of grievances. It also clearly specified for the first time that "this document must be copied down in each village and posted on the headman's house or on a high public bulletin board [kōsatsu] and at the entrance and exit of the village. All village officials had better have a good understanding of it and also explain it in detail to all the peasants."[57]

In this way, as Hayashi notes, the bakufu signaled its abandonment of the original Tokugawa principle that "people should be kept uninformed and made to depend on the authorities." On the other hand, the main thrust of the May 1762 edict was a stern warning to peasants who, "acting in concert, enter capital cities and make forceful appeals before the gates of lords and magistrates. When that occurs their demands, whether right or wrong, are not to be taken up. When the leaders are unknown, the first names on the census registers of the participating villages are to be selected. They will be considered the ringleaders and executed."[58] Following this edict, the bakufu multiplied its prior warnings to fief lords, telling them to be ever more vigilant and take all possible police precautions against "disorderly" peasants.

Then, in September 1767, Edo went out of its way to call attention to the "obstinacy" of peasants in the western provinces of Kyūshū, who were defying prohibitions and refusing to accept orders from intendants, shogunal magistrates, and lords. In an edict summarized by Hayashi, the peasants were described as often deserting their villages and making appeals in other domains.

> Lords who receive their appeals hesitate to immediately drive them back to where they came from. For such lords to say they will allow the deserting peasants to return to their villages only on the condition that their original lord does not punish them is inexcusable. Hereafter, lords who receive such appeals must make the peasants return immediately to their home villages and punish them severely.[59]

After this warning to lords in the western provinces, the bakufu, in 1769, formally empowered fief lords throughout the country to use guns to put down peasant uprisings. Then, in 1770, it ordered the posting in all villages of a "signboard to give encouragement to informers about conspiratorial groups, violent appeals and collective desertions."[60]

It would seem from such evidence that the bakufu was, in fact, moving toward a complex policy of making traditionally harsh repression more systematic and, at the same time, combining it with indirect, oblique concessions. The latter may have been intended to draw peasants into the process of legal appeals. If that was the case, then Ueda fief's program of concessions, "moderate" punishments, and constant reindoctrination meetings was fully in accord with such a policy.

Exactly how many peasants suffered punishment in Ueda shall probably never be known. No doubt there were a great many, though the Sōdō jikki records the names of "only those who were most severely punished." Naturally, the lightest chastisement was reserved for the offending officials, twenty-five of whom were ordered into domiciliary confinement in May and then pardoned the following February. By contrast, punishments prescribed for peasants ran the gamut from expulsion from the fief (seven cases), domiciliary confinement (four cases), and manacling (eleven cases) to life imprisonment (three cases) and execution (two cases). Interestingly, the fief officials first suspended from office on December 21, 1761 (among whom Nakamura Yazaemon, Katsura Kakuemon, and Umedo Yozōemon were the most infamous) were not formally dismissed until March 16, a full two weeks after the peasant leaders, Hanbei and Asanojō, had been publicly executed.[61] And three years later in 1765, one who had been most critical of the fief's handling of the uprising, Katsura Kakuemon, was appointed to the important post of censor in Edo.

But let us pause a moment at this point to make a short comparison of the Ueda and Tsuyama events. The geographical similarities between the two regions have already been noted in chapter 5. We may now add two other facts. First, both risings began in winter, reflecting the fact that peasant struggles are invariably shaped by the labor process in agriculture, which in turn depends on the "seasonal climatic cycle." Second, the two risings began in areas where there were a comparatively large number of village deities, shrines, and temples.

Apart from these similarities of season and physical setting, and an abundance of institutions for religious remembrance and expression, both risings incorporated a large number of characteristic peasant protest actions. Of these, the most important were the presentation of detailed collective demands concerning taxes and local officials. The former were to be lowered and the latter removed, thereby bringing about a more just and compassionate rural regime. Demands pertaining to supplementary income—taxes on commercial production—were not as important as the desire for local (village-level) political power.

Quantitative differences between the two risings were also conspicuous at every stage of the unfolding of the struggles within their respective contexts. The destruction of the houses and warehouses of village headmen, district officials, and rural merchants occurred on a somewhat greater scale in 1761–1763 than in 1726–1727, partly because by the later date commodity economy itself was more developed. The townspeople of Ueda castle town also participated in demonstrations against the fief after peasants had shown them the way. Nothing at all like that happened in Tsuyama. Despite its obvious intensity, the Tsuyama rising was quickly sequestered in Sanchū and bloodily crushed there. By contrast, the Ueda rising was protracted and displayed a somewhat higher level of peasant organization. Acts of defiance continued in Ueda for over a year, and there the fief authorities made a much greater effort at appeasement.

Last, the picture of repression in Ueda (albeit incomplete) shows it to have been much less severe than in Tsuyama fief during the years 1726–1727. What distinguished the two situations and helped curb the degree of repression was, first, the latent sympathy of many of Ueda's lower status samurai with the general mood of the peasants' discontent. Peasant frustration with the fief was not unlike their own unhappiness with the stipend-cutting policies of the senior retainers. Second, since Ueda fief was not threatened from the outset with imminent confiscation by the bakufu, its senior officials could afford to take a more conciliatory attitude toward peasants. Moreover, unlike the leaders of Tsuyama fief in 1726, Ueda's senior retainers had considerable political leverage in Edo, which allowed them to lobby in bakufu corridors, while continuing to appease the peasants in Ueda. Last, the Ueda rising involved the entire fief through all its stages, whereas the peasants of

Tsuyama were able to maintain trans-fief unity only during the first stage of their struggle.

In Chapter 16 of this study, "Results and Conclusion," we shall return to this question of the historical comparison of different uprisings. But for now let us focus once again on Hanbei and Asanojō.

THE EXECUTION OF HANBEI AND ASANOJŌ, MARCH 2, 1763

Ueda fief's most memorable discussion with its peasants took the form of the execution of Hanbei and Asanojō. Announced on March 1, 1763, it was carried out before the people on the next day. We realize by now how difficult it is to describe individual peasants in feudal Japan, much less to judge realistically those who appear in documents written from a position sympathetic to peasants. In these especially, they tend to be portrayed as heroes who embody the samurai virtues. So it is with Hanbei and Asanojō, about whose lives we know virtually nothing. As we read now the romanticized account of their execution from the concluding portion of the *Sōdō jikki*, we should bear in mind two points.[62] First, its main purpose was to afford consolation, as well as pleasure and instruction, to contemporary readers. Second, even an obviously fictionalized scene in a document such as this can be analyzed to reveal the worldview and emotional life of peasants at the time.

When the scene opens, we are told that people of the fief had "competed to get to the execution ground" at Nakajima river beach and were there waiting, "with not a bit of room to spare," when Hanbei and Asanojō arrived. The two ringleaders, conscious of the crowd that was there to observe how they conducted themselves at the moment of death, "walked falteringly, as if in a dream, just like sheep on their way to slaughter." With riflemen, bowmen, cavalry, and assorted guards ringing their execution spot—formed by a wall of crossed bamboo poles sixty feet square—and their spears and long swords glittering in the sun, the whole scene "was enough to terrify people out of their wits." Finally, the condemned men sat down on the ground, facing west, and regained their composure. Hanbei then turned to Asanojō and said:

"Now is our last moment in this world. Let us die as honorable a death as possible. Do not let people laugh at our timid actions." Asanojō replied, "Why should I, at this last moment, have anything to regret."

Hanbei said, "I agree. Yet I am sixty-two years old and it was for me, as the proverb says, to do something before leaving. But you, at thirty-eight, are still in the prime of life and may think regrettably fully of your wife and children."

Then Asanojō raised his voice and said, "Foolish as I am, I know that Shakamuni taught of the sorrow that those who meet are bound to depart, while those who live are bound to die. For the old to die before the young is neither unusual nor surprising. How splendid and blessed we are. Once I, a man of lowly peasant status, have become the commander of a fief worth fifty-eight thousand koku, my name will certainly remain to posterity. Should the wife or children of such a man not be resolved [to see his fate]? Therefore, I have nothing in this world to regret."

... Noticing that Asanojō looked dispirited, Hanbei said, "We hear by tradition that Kannoshōkō [popular name for Sugawara no Michizane] was demoted and transferred to the remote office of Dazaifu, for no fault of his own but because of a false charge against him made by [Fujiwara] Tokihira. Daitōnomiya [Prince Morinaga, son of Emperor Godaigo] suffered imprisonment in a cave because of Ashikaga Tadayoshi and was finally murdered by Fuchinobe Yoshihiro [an Ashikaga retainer]. If even noble people of high ranking cannot evade the laws of destiny, how much less can a common man. But I, relying on the mercy of Amida Nyorai, wish to go to the peaceful world in the West and be reborn to enjoy life together on the same lotus leaf."

Asanojō said, "Such sinful creatures as us cannot expect to go to paradise. On the contrary, we will be brought down to the abyss of hell where eternal suffering is unavoidable."

Upon hearing that Hanbei said, "*Ōjōyōshū* says 'a scoundrel of the blackest dye has no other means than citing Buddha's name to attain life in paradise.' Thus even a villain can be saved in paradise if he recites the *nenbutsu*. How could Buddha utter a false word. So pray with all your might. You and I have become the heads of a fief worth fifty-eight thousand koku and, as we see, our army now numbers seven hundred to eight hundred men. How could that number be insufficient, particularly the beautifully clad retinue. A fifty-thousand-to sixty-thousand-koku daimyo is no match for that. We really are commanders of fifty-eight-thousand koku."

When Hanbei said this unworriedly, Asanojō remarked, "What a wonderful spirit. Well then, let us make our last verse."

After remaining silent for a while, Hanbei intoned, "Too long have I lived in this world. Today in this fine spring dawn, I make room for others. Dropping behind I leave a trail for you, Asanojō."

And Asanojō continued, "The abode we finally head for is in the Western sky, but I shall go first and blaze the trail."

And with that voices of praise welled up, "What splendid, heroic spirits."

In this moving execution scene, Hanbei and Asanojō, who broke the laws of the shogunate, implicitly deny their guilt and treat their own deaths as a reward rather than a punishment. Moreover, they are depicted as dying for a cause, for public and not for private reasons. The *Sōdō jikki* describes them as having "become the ringleaders of a violent appeal" not because they sought something for themselves but because they were "compelled by circumstances," as were all peasants who rebelled against the fief. Hanbei and Asanojō—real historical figures—are thus recast sympathetically for later generations as exemplary martyrs (gimin) who acted sacrificially in behalf of peasants. But neither their lives nor the lives of peasants in general are seen as being inherently tragic. Nor are their premature deaths—the fate meted out to them for their leadership role in the rebellion—regarded that way. Finally, from the surrounding crowd, whose members are conscious of the events that led them to be there watching on that solemn public occasion, their deaths elicit tears of grief. But Hanbei and Asanojō show only the emotion of eager expectancy as they look ahead to the reward that lies in store for them.

We can see clearly now that the unknown author of the *Sōdō jikki* is expressing a Buddhist view of life and death. For a Buddhist, death means to live eternally in another world. By stressing that aspect, by reminding his eighteenth-century audience that even lowly peasants could free themselves from the painful fetters of a feudal existence and find repose in another world, he is hoping to console them and mitigate the loss to the peasant community caused by the deaths of Hanbei and Asanojō and the punishment of scores of others.

Also of great significance is the form in which Hanbei and Asanojō expressly visualize their freedom: as commanders of a fifty-eight-thousand-koku fief in the western sky. Of course, the passive glorification of an afterlife conceived in feudal terms, qualitatively similar to Tokugawa society, is what could be expected of peasants who were physically and spiritually isolated in the villages of eighteenth-century Japan. And yet, the making of Hanbei and Asanojō into imaginary lords of their own domain must also be counted one of the achievements of the Ueda uprising. Thanks to their capacity for focusing the peasants' righteous anger, demands that might have been compromised in local struggles were successfully raised to an action on a fief scale. In the course of that first trans-fief struggle, the numerous restrictions inhibiting the growth of peasant consciousness were, temporarily, thrust aside; samurai lost some ground to peasants; and Ueda castle learned to never again seek direct access to the villages or to increase the basic rice tribute. Of the many achievements symbolized by Hanbei and Asanojō, not the least was the capacity of a united peasantry to effect changes in a way of life that had appeared, to those who lived it, static and unchangeable.

After Hanbei and Asanojō intone their last verse, another premise of the *Sōdō jikki* is revealed. As we saw at that point, the crowd, swept with emotion, can hardly contain its admiration of the two peasants. Suddenly, an official steps forward and tells the doomed men that their suffering really exceeds their ranks: "If samurai should do that [that is, act self-sacrificingly], they would have been looked upon as brave men. But regrettably [you are not samurai]." According to the conventional wisdom of Tokugawa feudalism, samurai, by definition, were brave people; peasants, even if they fulfilled the factual conditions for such a virtue, were not. But in this case, these two peasants, being as brave as samurai, are exceptions. Thus, even while extolling peasants, the author, by his choice of epithets, is still singing the praises of samurai and, indirectly, lamenting the absence of bravery in their ranks. In the final analysis, the author's sympathy for peasants is conditioned by his recognition of, and higher commitment to, the concept of feudal discrimination.

The same official is then compelled to simultaneously justify the lord's death sentence, shift the blame for it onto the bakufu, and appease the martyrs' ghosts. Apparently, even officialdom looked upon Hanbei and Asanojō as potential or soon-to-be gods, capable, as spirits, of doing harm: "Although the lord gave thoughtful consideration to this matter, he had to order you executed because it was unavoidable under the law [of the bakufu]. By all means be sure you bear no grudges."

Then, kneeling upon the ground, "their heads bowed down," Hanbei and Asanojō listened while the same official read the final charge.

"When the peasants made violent appeals [gōso] on December 12, 1761, Asanojō and Hanbei consulted together as ringleaders and the people of the domain rioted. The lord thought this unlawful and ought to have ordered the more painful and frightful sentence of death by crucifixion, but, in his mercy, he simply gave them death [by beheading, a quicker punishment]." When he had finished reading, the sword flickered in the sun and instantly heads fell forward. Asanojō . . . and Hanbei . . . lost their lives like a bubble on the water at Nakajima River beach. Thousands of onlookers, including officials, all wept in sorrow. Through the karma of a previous life, the two were compelled by circumstances to become the ringleaders of a violent appeal and had their lives, which might have lasted for a hundred years, cut short by the sword, leaving behind lasting sorrow for their wives and relatives. How cruel it is.

No popular reaction followed this execution. But sometime later, flat vertical stones, inscribed with "Hanbei" and "Asanojō" and their ages at the time of death, were erected in the quiet of two different mountain slopes. And three weeks later, on March 25, 1763, the peasants of Ueda met under the direction of their district magistrates to be instructed once again on how to behave. Rebelliousness having given way to servility, the poorest peasants returned to the command of their upper stratum, and Ueda's Hōreki uprising passed into history. The peasants returned to their fields to build up production; and somewhere in Ueda, the unknown author of the *Sōdō jikki* sat down to record what had happened. Symbolically, when the next New Year arrived, the fief mourned the principal figure in quelling the uprising. For on December 29, 1763, the proud Okabe Kurobei, who had once bowed his head to the people and begged them to accept his apology, died of illness at age thirty-one.[63]

CHAPTER EIGHT

Results and Aftermath

TO effect change in Ueda fief's taxation practices, the peasants had to riot; and in rioting they sent shock waves through Ueda that were not thereafter forgotten. The fief had to meet most of their economic demands and stand by helplessly while they meted out justice to village headmen, district tribute officers, and rich merchants who had been their enemies for at least a decade. In the actual process of struggle and revolt, some peasants learned that they themselves were a force for change as well as for production.

If we were to view Ueda's peasants, from the outset, as passive bearers of an ideology brought to them from above, we would see only a hereditary status consciousness informing their battle for tribute relief and local political reform. They, and the other dominated classes, would then appear to be motivated primarily by a spontaneous feeling of indispensability to the fief—a belief in their own worth as "honorable peasants," artisans, townsmen, and so on with important customary rights, who count in feudal society. And since hierarchical status consciousness persisted throughout the struggle, we would also tend to be sensitive only to how they remained active if unwitting agents in their own oppression.

But, in fact, the peasants were not ideologically passive creatures. Even prior to the actual uprising, they were manipulating ruling ideology and quietly resisting ruling-class values and policies to serve their own material interests in concrete everyday situations. Peasants accepted, and were thus limited by, certain elements of the ruling class's definition of their existential situation. But at other levels, and in other instances, they creatively used particular elements of ruling-class teaching to simultaneously defend themselves and impose limitations on their rulers.

Men, as Marx said, are not free to make their own history "just as they please"; they are only free to make it under given circumstances. Ueda's peasants can be charged with having left the top echelons of fief administration unchanged, no more capable than before of analyzing and remedying the common economic problems of the fief. But that did not mean they were unrealistic to aim at the punishment of and revenge upon local, identifiable wrongdoers. Such action was safer and more likely to succeed than any direct attack on well-armed samurai forces, let alone an absentee lord in Edo.

The peasant movement in Ueda can be charged with failure to forge alliances with other oppressed groups. Specifically, even the participation of nonpeasant outcasts in an ikki organized by common peasants had its limitations. That small incident, which occurred on January 28, 1762, signaled an important future trend toward cooperation in struggle between peasants and hereditary outcasts. But it did not denote a trend toward their active solidarity in risings over the course of the next century. Despite the confluence of their protests, the gap between peasants and pariah groups was never to be fully overcome. On the contrary, it was actually solidified during the 1860s and 1870s, when Japan began its own unique passage to a distinctive type of capitalist rural development. This failure of cooperation between peasants and outcasts suggests the powerful influence of hereditary status prejudice within the peasant class in structuring social movements in Japan. But such a phenomenon is by no means uniquely Japanese. The functional counterpart to it, in a non-Japanese setting, is "the existence of deep racial cleavages (particularly between blacks and whites) in the American working class." [1]

Yet divisions within and between the subordinate classes in Ueda did not prevent gains from being made. The peasants did not leave the world as it was for those who ruled over them. With the resources they were able to command, they succeeded in redrawing the line over the issue of tributes, thereby defining an altered economic relationship with their rulers. In short, the Hōreki rising in Ueda managed to advance beyond its point of departure. After the protests died away, Ueda was different from before. Let us review why.

At the beginning of the rising, many members of the village elite were willing to act against the fief in concert with their fellow villagers. They joined in the destruction of the homes of hereditary headmen and district tribute officers who had sided with the lord against the interests of villages. In that sense, the line between the peasants' world and the world of samurai officialdom was still sharply drawn in many peasant minds. But, at the same time and generally throughout Japan from the 1760s onward, the division of peasants along economic lines was slowly beginning to override their unity along status lines.

Insufficient study of the extant data on landholdings (expressed in kanmon monetary units) makes it extremely difficult to demonstrate empirically such economic divisions in Ueda.[2] But we know that in the mountain villages, more than on the river plain, minute-scale landholders constituted the majority. There were also many "pawned land servants" and landless peasants throughout the fief, together with a thin stratum of landlords. Historically, the trend was for commodity economy to increasingly develop and shape more complex boundaries between these strata. One may reasonably hypothesize, therefore, that class and income stratification was starting to introduce distinctions between households, which, in turn, reduced the likelihood that mere status could continue to serve as a firm basis of solidarity.

Of course, many areas of Japan continued to experience struggles based on the unity between village officials and the peasant rank and file right down to the middle of the nineteenth century. But the issues and actions revealed in the unfolding of the Ueda events foreshadowed what was to be the numerically dominant type of disturbance from the late eighteenth century onward. That was the struggle that expressed the deepening structural rift between rich and poor households within villages and was resolved in the form of punitive property destruction, usually against the homes of village officials and landlords.

The development of commodity economy in Ueda was also reflected in the issue of the rice price. Peasants operated within the confines of the fief's market control system and were subjected to domanial manipulation of the rice-cash exchange rate as well as to rice price fluctuations beyond the control of fief officials.

Proceeding further, we may also say that in the Ueda incident the fief unit itself was challenged, and in the process, the Matsudaira family was taught—in the most graphic way, and by peasants whose leaders came from both the low and the middle strata of the peasantry—that it could not go on plundering the villages. It was taught that attempts to increase the basic rice tribute and proliferate corvée duties and enterprise taxes were contradictory and liable to produce the opposite result: a struggle involving the entire peasantry, with consequent loss of revenue. Thereafter, whenever revenues had to be expanded, the fief could do so only by developing new, less brutal and direct approaches. Thus, for both rulers and ruled alike, the Hōreki rising became a reference by means of which later events in the fief were measured. When, in chapter 15, we return to Ueda in the year 1869, we shall see that its peasants recollected this particular incident when they again rose up against the fief.

Increasingly, as the eighteenth century drew to a close, the authorities in Ueda diversified their sources of income. Not only did they enter into alliance with merchant capital; they also imposed forced loans (goyōkin) and "thanks money" (myō-gakin) on the upper stratum of peasants who had become rural silk merchants, producing and marketing the famous Uedajima and Ueda pongee. And there is some evidence that they might have sold samurai ranks with increasing frequency to rich peasants and merchants. The Takizawa family of wholesale merchants in Hara district, for example, were allowed to wear swords in 1763, and five years later, in 1768, a merchant named Tsuchiya Kaemon was given a three-man stipend and appointed a financial affairs officer of the fief.[3] Clearly, these later developments signified the rising weight of Ueda's sericulture industry, the declining status of its warriors, and the very slow but continuous transformation of the most active segments of the peasant and merchant classes into rich landowning peasants and rich merchants. In short, a new social stratification was emerging within the feudal classes based on the further development of social and economic conditions in the villages and castle town.

This process implied a deepening of two kinds of contradictions: one was the main, unsolvable contradiction between peasants and lords within the feudal socioeconomic system; the other was the secondary level or horizontal contradiction occurring between different strata and groups within the dominant ruled class. The bakufu, by its May 1762 edict, showed a readiness to respond to the main (polar) contradiction—between the peasant producers of "surplus" wealth and their samurai appropriators—by a policy of increased repression combined with persuasion and reeducation. But it would be hard-pressed to resolve contradictions born of the continuous evolution of a more complex commodity economy, which, in turn, shaped a more complex class and status structure within villages. Structurally, as the Ueda uprising revealed, Tokugawa feudalism was becoming ineffective as a system of administration for the purpose of stabilizing the general relationship between society's producers of wealth and all its appropriators. The original Tokugawa policy of establishing full-status peasants and basing the state upon them had clearly failed.

The Ueda Hōreki uprising also sheds light on the aging process of a feudalistic administrative organization. By the second half of the eighteenth century, the fief organization—a rather simple apparatus of bureaucratic-military rule—had entered a mid-term stage of stagnation, which manifested itself in various ways. Excessive elitism had developed, which reflected deep divisions between hereditary statuses. Subsequently, breakdowns occurred in the chain of command at several levels, but especially the lines of communication linking lower level samurai officials with village chiefs. And, most important, demoralization, corruption, and venality spread through all ranks.

Katsura Kakuemon, the district magistrate who was one of those held responsible for what happened because of his official position, left behind a remarkable postmortem on the uprising, which speaks to just this aspect of organizational malaise and ossification. Drafted while he was in domiciliary confinement during

January 1762, it revealed his hostility to Okabe Kurobei while, at the same time, attacking middle levels of samurai officialdom as well as the fief elders for opportunism and shallowness of intellect. The troubles, he noted, did not arise, as some claimed, because of the peasants' "selfishness." Rather, the real cause lay in the fact that "the lord and the retainers lacked the will to consider the well-being of the fief."

Without excessive levies, the peasants would not have been in distress. But since, for the past several years, we deceived them, they do not believe anything we may say and suspect all officials. Recently, the measures taken were increasingly inconsistent. Even persons not in charge of rural affairs gave orders individually to village chiefs. Since orders of this official would be completely contradicted by orders from some other office, the village chiefs would not only suspect the samurai officials but also see through the fief's designs.[4]

We do not know what measures of reform Ueda's rulers adopted to revitalize their fief organization and restore samurai morale. But we do know that high officials in other fiefs were soon to become increasingly sensitive to, and fearful of, the unknown potential of disaffected samurai and of samurai-peasant collaboration. In a sense, the sympathetic samurai who hovered in the background of the Ueda rising represented the germ of a new self-consciousness. As the samurai who were aware of problems and more critical of the system itself increased in number, that new self-consciousness would prove as threatening to the old order of things as the rebellious peasants.

We also know that, once having been alerted to the danger of village headmen being driven into the arms of disaffected peasants, the rulers of Ueda acted over the next few decades to end the headmen's marginal status vis-á-vis the samurai bureaucracy. This they did by separating headmen more sharply from peasants and bringing them, as well as the district tribute officers, into closer political and social ties with the castle. In so doing, the Matsudaira clan actually helped pave the way for the next stage of peasant risings: struggles in villages and towns focusing on commercial profiteering and on the tribute contracting system.

PART III

Reaction:
Social Developments of
the Late Eighteenth Century

CHAPTER NINE

The Crisis of Tenmei

L ET us now quickly survey some of the major political and economic changes of the last three decades of the eighteenth century, when the shortcomings of the bakuhan state became clearly apparent among different segments of the ruling class.

Generally speaking, during the period spanning late Meiwa through Tenmei and Kansei—from 1765 to 1800—the bakufu moved toward a uniform system of punishments designed to curb peasant and commoner behavior labeled "obstinate," "insolent," "unlawful," and "disrespectful." But it met with only limited success. Peasants and townspeople refused to remain politically mute. Their need for direct action and for criticism of bakuhan politics forced them, repeatedly, to breach the law, which in turn drew daimyo and shogunal officials into a greater reliance on military and police methods of suppression. In March 1767, the bakufu ordered all intendants in its direct domains in Kōshū province (Yamanashi) to take vigilant suppressive measures because there "the people are of violent and stubborn temper and disorderly elements come out of them." [1] The attempt, in 1770, to step up police surveillance over the countryside in the form of the famous "signboard to give encouragement to informers" has already been noted. There the object was to reward informers with cash and status symbols for telling the authorities about signs of political dissent. Since Tokugawa villages, as official units of taxation, were already organized like prisons, this measure signified more than just the strengthening of traditional mechanisms for mutual surveillance and discipline within villages. In fact, it marked the start of a bakufu effort to supplement its official information sources by creating a network of political informers.[2]

Interestingly, as the 1770s unfolded, the bakufu also issued more and more edicts reaffirming its earlier one of 1765 against the practice of infanticide, then widespread in many parts of Japan. But the bakufu's main concern was to curb violent disorder from below. And here only meager results were gained from its harsher repression of ikki and its greater discrimination in differentiating types of lesser offenses, such as appeals made at the gates of official residences. As long as protest actions and violent disorders met deeply felt social needs and were supported by the norms of village society, the law and its punishments, however onerous or discriminating, could not deter them. In its last century of existence the bakufu confronted an unresolvable class struggle under gradually worsening political conditions that led, eventually, to its dissolution.

Economically, the period under consideration may be termed the dawn of the age of generalized commodity production. Its most notable characteristic was the emergence of major regional markets specializing in cotton, silk, tea, tobacco, and other agricultural products. Although this new commercial production was only just getting started in the 1760s and 1770s, it signified the emergence of different types of rural economy with a wider variety of social relationships than had been the case earlier in the century. It also meant the development, in many areas, of a social division of labor on a regional rather than fief scale.

The increasing interventionism of the bakuhan state during the second half of the eighteenth century was motivated by the need to manage this ongoing structural change in Japan's agrarian economy. Working along lines set out in Yoshimune's time, a succession of bribe-taking senior councillors and grand chamberlains set about strengthening the bakufu's centralizing powers at the expense of the daimyo. One of them, Tanuma Okitsugu, rose to high office from lowly footsoldier descent and left his name on the age. After serving for nearly a decade as a chamberlain to the ninth shogun, Ieshige, Tanuma, in 1760, became the favorite of Ieshige's successor, Shogun Ieharu. In 1767, Ieharu elevated him to the position of grand chamberlain, and five years later, in 1772, he became senior councillor. The so-called Tanuma period traditionally spans the late 1760s down to 1786; but in fact he came fully into his own only during the early years of Tenmei, and after 1784 his power was on the wane.

The distinguishing feature of the Tanuma period was the bakufu's political failure to exercise moral leadership over the dominant classes in a time of economic crisis and natural disasters. During the 1770s, when Finance Councillor Matsudaira Taketomo, and not Tanuma, was mainly responsible for setting economic policy, rice tribute revenues continued to decline, throwing the bakufu treasury deeper into the red. The search for new revenue sources focused on forced loans from merchants, on the establishment (begun in 1767) of a cotton monopoly in the Kantō plains area, and on frequent recoinages. A major recoinage ordered in 1772 took the form of minting a new one-eighth-ryō silver coin denominated in gold units. (This was the *nishu-gin* or *nanryō nishu* coin that thenceforth played the role of a "token subsidiary money.")[3] Most important, as the country's agricultural tax base weakened, the bakufu as well as the daimyo became increasingly dependent on merchants to whom they gave grants of monopoly privilege for dealing in various products. This intertwining of ruling-class and big-merchant interests advanced rapidly all during the 1770s and 1780s. More and more, big merchants, particularly rice brokers, came into official service as commercial agents for different domains and as consultants in the techniques of exploitation. In the famine and natural disaster years of the early and mid-1780s, Tanuma Okitsugu continued these and other policies of his predecessors designed to incorporate the profits from commerce into a total system of feudal rule based on mercantile principles.[4]

But while Tanuma's bakufu was trying to harness the late eighteenth-century growth process and make money out of it by mercantilist practices, a new internal organization of the peasant class unfolded and weak points accumulated all over Japan. In the most economically developed regions, the middle stratum of peasants attacked long-established village elites for unjust economic activities. Backing them in their attacks were the poorest peasants, who were finding life harder than ever in this period. In their efforts to pay off taxes and escape chronic poverty in villages, many migrated to cities and rural towns. Others pawned their land and entered into a tenancy relationship of some sort with a landlord, often a village official or local merchant.

For the power holders of Tokugawa society who viewed this process from afar, the last decades of the eighteenth century offered additional reasons for believing that the social order was in an advanced state of decay, which somehow had to be checked. Everywhere corruption seemed more rampant than usual. Merchants in large numbers had risen to official employment as financiers of the bakuhan state. And in the countryside, multitudes of oppressed and hungry people stood up, told the authorities what they did not want to hear, and succeeded sometimes in getting them to change course. Reinforcing the perception of social breakdown were the terrible fires and volcanic eruptions of Tenmei, which laid waste whole provinces. Famine and pestilence on a national scale added to the suffering of people in these years. In the northeastern fiefs, natural disasters interrupted grain production to such an extent that deaths from starvation occurred by the hundreds of thousands. In this period, nationwide, over a million people are estimated to have died from starvation and related causes.

Finally, in 1786–1787, when normal agricultural production in most regions had been cut in half by bad weather, a great wave of popular risings occurred, far more destructive and larger in scale than those of the Hōreki era. Of ninety-five recorded incidents of just urban riots during Tenmei, over fifty occurred in a twelve-month period during 1786–1787 and nineteen of them erupted in the month of May alone. The ikki, urban riots, and house-smashings shook entire fiefs, as well as large inland cities, rural towns, post stations, and port cities throughout the country. Those that occurred simultaneously in May 1787 in the great market centers of Edo and Osaka involved the lowest stratum of town dwellers, including shop servants and the homeless poor who had flocked to the nation's two biggest cities during the previous decade. Other riots erupted in Nara, Kyoto and the coastal cities of Hiroshima, Nagasaki, Shimonoseki, and Hakata, to name just a few.

Incensed by the high price of rice and sake, as well as by the severity of feudal restrictions governing urban living, town dwellers carefully organized themselves according to strict rules of conduct and launched well-aimed attacks against the upper stratum of the merchant class responsible for urban food supply. In Edo they destroyed 980 rice shops and hundreds of licensed merchant stores, pawnshops, and sake shops in the first clear yonaoshi-type urban riot of the eighteenth century. In his study of the period, Ooms notes that "the destruction was carried out by people who, in their desperation, hoped in a semireligious way for a new, more egalitarian world order. Low-class Shugendō exorcists and magico-religious reciters seem to have been the spiritual leaders of the movement, which obviously had political overtones." [5] In the countryside, where the disturbances were far more numerous, peasants directed their main blows at particular village officials and local merchants who, because of their collusion with fief officials, were perceived as the financiers of peasant oppression.

Clearly, the consciousness of peasants and commoners regarding the worth of their labor and their skills as producers had outgrown the limits that hereditary status imposed upon them. But the daimyo and their retainers all lived by taking from and oppressing peasants, and could conceive of no other way of life than feudalism. Hence these geographically scattered but nearly simultaneous protests, riots, and revolts (involving the entire country) created in them a profound sense of crisis, which they now struggled to overcome by instituting reforms designed to preserve the status quo.

With the ferment from below undermining bakufu and fief finances, with distinctions of rank becoming blurred, with merchant capitalists, organized since 1724 in a licensed rice brokers guild (fudasashi kabunakama), manipulating the rice market and exercising autonomous power, and with the samurai developing an insatiable taste for bourgeois living—under these conditions the long equilibrium at the center of the bakuhan state began to weaken. In late 1783, the Tanuma regime took two actions which stiffened its daimyo opponents within the ruling class. First, it attempted to strengthen bakufu control over the Osaka rice market; then it decreed an end, for seven years, "to all assistance the bakufu customarily granted to financially-strapped daimyo, who now, in a year of great famine, were left to their own resources." [6] Three years later, in 1786, the opposition placed the entire blame for peasant insurrections and for the decline of samurai morale upon the officials, led by Tanuma and the finance magistrates Matsumoto Hidemichi and Akai Tadaakira, who had been setting bakufu policy since the start of Tenmei.

The incident that galvanized the opposition from all ranks of daimyo (fudai, tozama, and the three Tokugawa collateral houses) was a plan drawn up by Tanuma and the finance magistrates "to requisition a nationwide loan on all property of temples, shrines, peasants, merchants, and artisans in the bakufu territories and in all domains. This loan . . . was in fact a national property tax." [7] No sooner had the plan been revealed than from the collateral houses, the Senior Council, and the fudai daimyo stratum of high officials demands arose for an immediate change in bakufu direction in ruling the country. In all these circles, concern focused on the key problem of controlling the class struggle that manifested itself in factional splits within retainer bands, in peaceful legal disputes, and in violent insurrections and riots. But no advance on that front could occur, it was believed, without first removing the sources of "corruption": Tanuma Okitsugu and the veteran administrators who had set financial policy ever since 1781. For the vassal daimyo in particular, Tanuma was a special target of wrath because his entire career symbolized the loosening up of the old rigid hierarchical society and the strengthening of bakufu hegemony at the expense of daimyo economic independence.

On August 20, 1786, Shogun Ieharu died under mysterious circumstances, perhaps, as contemporaries alleged, by poison. In a matter of days, with his patron eliminated, Tanuma's enemies moved to dismiss him in a bloodless palace coup d'état (August 27, 1786). [8] A bitter ten-month-long political purge of the Tanuma faction followed, during which over fifty senior officials were dismissed. It was in this period of intensified class struggles in towns and provinces that the reform regime of Matsudaira Sadanobu was born, one month after the worst riot in the history of Edo. On June 19, 1787, twenty-nine-year-old Matsudaira Sadanobu, who had been Tanuma's most implacable enemy, assumed the post of senior councillor. With a fourteen-year-old boy as the new shogun, the fudai daimyo and the families collateral to the shogun at the center of bakufu affairs could look forward to an improvement on what had gone before.

CHAPTER TEN

The Tenmei Rising in Fukuyama, 1786–1787

I T is useful now to focus on the connections between the political agitation at the top of Tokugawa society, which resulted in Sadanobu's appointment as senior councillor, and the simultaneous background risings of commoners and peasants, which made that event possible. From the late 1780s onward, every generation of high officials at the center of bakufu affairs, as well as every generation of active daimyo and fief administrators, worried about how to solve the economic problem (rising prices and a declining tax base) while at the same time containing the powerful stirrings from below of peasants and commoners.

The Tenmei rising in Fukuyama fief in the southwestern part of Bingo province began approximately four months after Tanuma's removal from office and while a historically unprecedented purge of his entire faction was still unfolding. It thus sheds light on the interaction between the bakufu and private domains during a peak period of internal tension. More than in previous ventures into microhistory, we shall be interested this time in the view from the top, as reflected in two types of documentary evidence. One is the correspondence of Abe Masatomo, the proud vassal daimyo of Fukuyama whose ancestor had been Ieyasu's comrade in arms and whose family owed its subsequent success to its loyal vassal service to the Tokugawa.[1] Masatomo, daimyo ruler of Fukuyama from 1769 to 1805, was serving as a bakufu magistrate in Edo, in line for higher promotion, when the rising erupted in his own domain. While it unfolded, his chief inspectors (ōmetsuke) kept him well informed of the samurai's behavior and of all police matters relating to the rural areas. Masatomo's correspondence with them, first introduced in an important study by Michishige Tatsuo, reflected the evolution of his thinking during the crisis.[2] It also testified to his own deep need to justify his life as a ruler by rejecting the changes that peasants wished to bring about.

A second contemporary source is the famous *Abeno dōjimon* (Account of the Boy from Abeno), which circulated widely in the Fukuyama area after the rising. Its unknown author signed himself "Naniwa jōnan inshi": literally, "a retired man from the south of Osaka." From the literary allusions and categories he used to explain the rising, Naniwa jōnan inshi appears to have been a Confucian scholar with detailed knowledge of Fukuyama's history and its bureaucratic administration—knowledge of the sort one would expect of someone who had participated in it. The *Abeno dōjimon* is similar to previous ikki documents we have studied in its concession to censorship, which forced the author to cast events in a semific-tional mold. It also had more to say about the worldview and values of the ruling class than of peasants. And, as always, it was explicitly tendentious: "Hereafter I shall put down, by way of a warning on government, what I happened to witness while traveling in the western region." [3]

But the *Abeno dōjimon* also differs in a number of ways from many earlier unofficial ikki accounts. First, it reveals indirectly the split in top ruling-class circles that had developed on the eve of the Kansei Reforms over the issue of how and where to intervene in the feudal economy. By distinguishing among "military arts," "civil arts," and—a new factor—"profits," the author of *Abeno dōjimon* gave ideological expression to that split. "Only when civil and military arts are both maintained is the country secure and the government able to continue. Now-adays they are both abandoned and profits are pursued. Disasters follow one an-other and even good people are helpless to do anything about it." [4] In other words, responsibility for the uprising lay, ultimately, with a low-born retainer of Masa-tomo, one Endō Benzō, who took over the management of the fief's economy and, in order to pursue profits, neglected the military and civil arts. The terms of this explanation of the crisis were, of course, thoroughly Confucian and anticom-mercial. But by means of it, a moralist such as Naniwa jōnan inshi was able to express the ruling class's indignation, at that juncture, at the growth of a commod-ity money economy and at the new morality of profits it was bringing about.

The second way in which *Abeno dōjimon* differs from previous documents of its kind is in the prominence it gives to the workings of the "evil-minister" mech-anism. This ideological device is quite common in all societies with autocratic regimes in which the information needed for understanding how state institutions work is limited to a tiny minority. In Fukuyama, the peasants were encouraged to channel most of their criticism and discontent in the direction of subordinate officials whose dismissal from office in no way effected the later direction of policy. By overpersonalizing the problems of the fief, ascribing them to a single odious individual who had to be overthrown, the peasants inadvertently absolved the bakuhan state itself of blame. Precisely to leave unquestioned the ultimate author-ity of the state—thereby preventing peasants from ever grasping wherein lay the real source of their difficulties and revolting against it—was the function of the evil-minister mechanism.

Third, *Abeno dōjimon* shows the lower stratum of samurai discredited in the person of a single retainer and in that respect is similar to other documents of its kind. But it is distinctive in depicting as the people's protagonist an entire village rather than an individual peasant. Since there were no peasant martyrs in this incident, it was possible to depict as the headquarters and driving force of the entire ikki a single village (or composite group recruited from a few neighboring villages), which operated, under the name of the "Ōhira band," mainly in the fief's second largest district, Numakuma. So much for the surviving evidence. Let us now turn to the incident.

Fukuyama, a 100,000-koku fudai domain (part of present-day Hiroshima prefecture) occupied a rich farming region bordered by the Inland Sea on one side and low rolling hills and mountains on the other (see map 4). In 1816, its six administrative districts had a total ruled population of approximately 120,655 people.[5] We may safely estimate a figure only slightly smaller at the time of the 1786 rising. Some of its inhabitants, who lived in the coastal villages of the Inland Sea, were fishermen and salt workers, but the overwhelming majority were rice and cotton farmers. The fief's ruling stratum consisted of approximately 2,200 samurai of whom about 40 percent (over 920) were usually on duty year-round in Edo.[6]

The first point to note about Fukuyama was its earlier history of protest against the tax policies of the Abe family of Ise, which ruled the fief from 1710, repeatedly taxing peasants beyond their physical limit. Starting in December 1717, Fukuyama experienced its first rising on a trans-fief scale. A contemporary account describes "Genzaemon of Miyauchi village" marching with hundreds of peasants on the castle of Fukuyama. They were clad like beggars in the ritual ikki garb of woven straw matting, "with loosely bundled hair and bearing scythes, wooden swords and other tools."[7] Although their struggle was short-lived and ill prepared, they somehow managed to get most of their fifteen tax demands accepted.

The next partially successful rising started in late February 1752, triggered by a drastic rise in enterprise taxes on cotton imposed after several years of bad crops and near famine conditions. This second rising lasted about a week and was much better organized than the first.[8] Interestingly, this incident renewed the medieval practice of ringing temple bells to signal the start of a protest mobilization. What political or symbolic connotations this had in 1752 is difficult to say. But during the fifteenth and sixteenth centuries, when "*tokusei* bells" were rung quite frequently in the Inland Sea region, they indicated the start of a new era in which ordinary peasants would seek to cancel loan contracts, recover pawned land, or redeem pawned goods with only token money payments.[9]

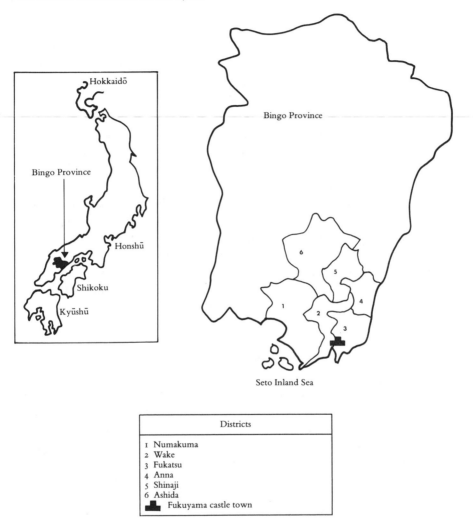

Seto Inland Sea

Districts	
1	Numakuma
2	Wake
3	Fukatsu
4	Anna
5	Shinaji
6	Ashida
■	Fukuyama castle town

Source: Fukuyama shishi (The history of Fukuyama city), vol. 2, pp. 197, 490, 500.

In the summer of the drought year of 1770, a year after the accession of the fourth Abe lord, Masatomo, the peasants of Fukuyama stood up a third time. In the process, they articulated some entirely new demands indicative of the growth of commodity production and the spread of money economy in the region. These new demands called for reductions in tenant rents and in enterprise taxes on cotton as well as for deferral of loan payments. But, by this time, the economic plight of the Abe retainers had also worsened and the new lord decided to stiffen his policy toward peasants. After granting them a hearing and accepting a few of their nineteen demands, Abe Masatomo rejected outright those calling for rent reductions and for the dismissal of all village headmen and assistant headmen. Two years later he exercised his judicial right to punish the peasants for their earlier delinquency and destruction of property by ordering the execution of their leaders.[10]

Also, around this time, the castle authorities in Fukuyama reduced the amount of grain tribute that village officials were allowed to deduct from their taxes as office expenses.[11] This move was another antecedent to the events of 1786–1787 because it affected internal relations within the peasant class. Specifically, it hastened the transference downward of aggression by spurring the village elite—many of whom were also owners of pawned land—to a more energetic exploitation of the financially poorer middle stratum of the villages. Significantly, ten of the thirty peasant demands of 1786 were directly related to abuses by village headmen and sixty of the ninety-six homes destroyed during that upheaval belonged to headmen.[12]

To sum up, on three different occasions—1717, 1752, and 1770—the peasants of Fukuyama challenged the Abe clan in a conflict over taxes and tax collection. And during each confrontation they expressed new discontents and more precisely defined demands and improved their organizational skills. In 1786, when they clashed for a fourth time with the power of their feudal rulers, they were able to recollect and revalue those earlier experiences, making them not a mere passive preliminary to the Tenmei rising but an active ingredient in its very preparation. In other words, just as the peasants of Tsuyama and Ueda gained politically from their recollection of exemplary peasant martyrs on the eve of the Sanchū and Hōreki risings, respectively, so the peasants of Fukuyama revived their memories of past struggles and derived values from them which then shaped their political attitudes to the situation that existed in 1786.

The second point concerns the causes of the Tenmei rising in Fukuyama. Important gaps in the historical record and inadequate study of extant documents make it difficult to reconstruct the full context in which it occurred. We can determine accurately enough, however, who was responsible and who and what set the stage. For all practical purposes, the rising that marked the culmination of peasant struggles in eighteenth-century Fukuyama had its roots, first, in the fief's worsening financial situation. A second cause was the behavior of Abe Masatomo who, during the 1770s, turned away from the problems of his own fief in order to begin his rise to power in Shogun Ieharu's service at Edo. A third cause was the actions and policies of Masatomo's most trusted retainers in Fukuyama during the Tenmei period.

In 1774, Masatomo was appointed to the inner office of chamberlain. He became magistrate on probation for shrines and temples two years later and in 1778 full magistrate for shrines and temples. While he was advancing in the shogun's service, the tax burden on the peasants of Fukuyama increased and the stipends of his retainers were cut back. In 1781, Masatomo ordered the fief administration in Fukuyama to embark on a program of financial reconstruction.

Between 1781 and the start of the rising in mid-December 1786, the senior person in charge of fief reforms in Fukuyama was Masatomo's uncle, the senior councillor Andō Motome. Under him, holding concurrent posts and in direct contact with villages and rural towns, was Endō Benzō, an official whom Masatomo in the mid-1770s elevated from inspector of foot soldiers to high office. In the early 1780s, as his stipend rose and his offices accumulated, Benzō, though he was never at the top, became the symbol of the fief reform effort. Since he was to the peasants of Fukuyama what Tanuma Okitsugu was to the country as a whole, let us dwell a moment on Benzō. Here is how Naniwa jōnan inshi refers to him in the author's preface to the *Abeno dōjimon*.

Here there was a certain Endō, the treacherous retainer of lord Abe, and formerly a man of mere humble origins. But within several years he came to rank next to the fief elders with the largest stipend among high ranking retainers. He rose like the sun and exercised power like thunderbolts. Who would dare to overthrow him? The high and the low wrung their hands to do his bidding as if he were their lord. Assuming the shape of a predatory bird, he would torment the people like a tiger or a wolf. Those who agreed with him were increasingly favored; those who disagreed he thrust aside and punished. By forming a faction at court he made his position unshakable. In all affairs internal and external he decided alone. On both official and private levels they looked up to him with frightened eyes and feared him like a ferocious tiger. A large number of officials ... were killed when they invited Endō's anger. Even Emperor Chin's close net of persecution was not comparable. The people were driven to extreme impoverishment.[13]

This sociological and psychological pattern of the evil retainer, described in the *Abeno dōjimon*, prevailed at one time or other in nearly every fief. In most cases, the dynamic bad retainer got his chance to overcome the disadvantages of humble status when the lord gave him a household appointment. But the sheer speed with which he subsequently rose to high position within the structure of domanial clique politics earned him the enmity of the dominant clique of officials who had been unable to furnish an alternative realistic policy for handling the problem. The bright upstart had then either to appease his resentful opposition or, failing that, to suppress them. Often he did both. Forming his own private faction, he decided matters alone, as if he were equal to the lord. This further deepened the resentment of the injured opposition. Meanwhile, he was working all the time in a social context that forced him to pursue profits, thereby controverting established Confucian teaching. Once one of his policies started to fail because of circumstances beyond his control, all his reforms had to end in failure.

The cause of the Tenmei rising cannot of course be imputed to Endō Benzō alone when the whole trend of historical development in Fukuyama also helped prepare it. Yet Benzō fitted this pattern sufficiently to become the scapegoat for all of Fukuyama's ills. He was partly the front man for Masatomo's reforms and partly his own man: a person who liked to show his powers whenever possible and of whom everyone would say, "Ah, this is Benzō's order." In a society whose dominant considerations were fixed status and hierarchy, his initially low status but subsequent upward placement (implying illegitimate authority) was an irrational subjective element, working to heighten the animosity that peasants already felt toward him because of his flagrant abuse of power.

In 1781, when Andō Motome and Benzō set about rebuilding Fukuyama's treasury, they struck bargains with three breeds of merchants: powerful grain brokers in Osaka, favored merchants of high status living in the many town districts surrounding Fukuyama castle, and rich merchants living in the district towns of the fief. The cash assistance of these three groups enabled them to finance the issue of new fief silver notes. In 1784, they ordered the fief's inspectors to interdict the use of the silver notes of other domains. In a short time their protectionist policies succeeded in establishing firm control over all currency circulation within Fukuyama. Then, in August 1785, they set up a Cotton Office to regulate illegal raw cotton shipments to other fiefs.

These policies governing the circulation and control of goods attacked the efficient uncontrolled economy that had started to develop in Fukuyama. Understandably, they made Benzō the hated adversary of peasants and small rural merchants who had been steadily building up the fief's cotton industry in trade with neighboring fiefs. But at some point during the 1780s, Benzō also earned the fierce enmity of some of his local financial backers who had made substantial contributions to the fief. Apparently, in order to avoid repercussions from the bakufu and to sustain the fief's much more important merchant creditors in Osaka, he repudiated its domestic debts, including silver loans made by the merchants of Kamishimo village, an outpost of the bakufu-owned Ōmori silver mine.[14] Afterwards, starting in 1785, perhaps in an effort to dissociate the fief from responsibility for the silver loans, he expelled from Fukuyama three powerful merchants involved in the Kamishimo silver problem. How this particular double cross was engineered, and what role Masatomo himself had in it, the historical record fails, so far, to indicate. But we do know that by the mid-1780s yet another element in Fukuyama's deteriorating social and financial situation was the quarrel between the fief, represented by Benzō, and three of Fukuyama's leading merchants: Satō Shinshirō, a wealthy district headman of Moriwaki village, Sumiya Sōjirō, and Yamamoto Bensuke, the younger brother of a Fukuyama samurai who was a close retainer of Tanuma Okitsugu. We also know that Masatomo personally obtained the support of the Tanuma faction in getting a freeze put on the Kamishimo silver loans.

Throughout Japan 1786 was a year of reduced grain production and rising food prices. The bad weather that had plagued the country off and on over the preceding five years continued. In the western Bingo region, rain fell continuously between May and October, unleashing floods that caused tremendous losses to rice and cotton crops. In September 1786, the rice price in Fukuyama stood at about 80 *momme* per koku. By December, one koku sold for the unprecedented amount of 105–106 momme and did not come down again below 80 until the following September.[15] It was during this period of natural calamity that Benzō ordered additional taxes and early tribute payments from peasants on no less than thirteen different occasions. Where before the peasants had made their advance tribute payment in July and their first cash payment by August 15, Benzō now moved these payment dates up to late February and mid-March, thereby making it impossible for many peasants to avoid punishment for being in arrears on tribute without going into debt. At the same time, he authorized all district offices to give seal impressions on tribute loans whenever villages borrowed money from wealthy merchants for the purpose of completing payment of their tributes. Merchants willingly assumed the risk entailed in such loans because they could charge interest and later ask the fief for payment if the borrower defaulted.[16]

Yet another unjust tax catalyzing unrest in the spring of 1786 was the "congratulation rice": an order to villages for four thousand koku of rice to be presented to Lord Masatomo on his appointment to high bakufu office. Since Masatomo was always advancing bureaucratically in Edo, the renewal of this particular levy in March could only be regarded as yet another tax squeeze. New tax orders followed in May, July, August, and October. One authorized new cash surcharges on tatami matting; another ordered the commutation of certain transportation and courier duties into large cash payments. As the end of the year approached, the tax orders multiplied. On November 2, an order came down telling all villages to open immediately "mutual financing associations" (*tanomoshikō*) in order to repay a money loan owed by the fief to the bakufu.[17] The final barrage of tax orders, issued between November 6 and December 12, were all characterized by payment periods of from one to ten days and stipulated interest surcharges on the unpaid portion.[18]

It was this intensification of exploitation in a time of economic hardship, together with the harsh manner in which officials collected taxes that winter, that provoked the peasants' outburst, just as it had in 1717, 1752, and 1770. Here is the standard summary description of the start of the rising as recorded in the *Abeno dōjimon*:

In 1786, year of the horse [that is, an inauspicious zodiac year portending disaster], on the night of a full moon, the entire populace rose up like a disturbed nest of bees. Signal fires lit up the night sky while battle cries shook the mountains and rivers. It so happened that over forty thousand people gathered and they all said "Let's get Endō to satisfy ourselves!" Ultimately, they lived outdoors for over sixty days. Discipline was broken and the government and public terrorized.[19]

The first stage of the Tenmei rising began dramatically on the night of December 15 with the pealing of temple warning bells and the blaring of bamboo horns in the villages of the Shinaji and Ashida districts in the western corner of the fief. Right from the start, the target of attack was not only Endō Benzō's taxes but also the property of village headmen and merchants, which the peasants could hardly wait to smash to pieces. When the fief elders in Fukuyama castle learned of the mobilization and the attacks on the headmen's property, they sought to diffuse the situation by adopting a conciliatory strategy. Officials and company commanders, leading teams of from twenty to fifty men each, went into the countryside and confronted peasants at meetings at which they promised to forward all demands to Lord Masatomo in Edo. Since the peasants had not formulated a unified set of demands at the outset, they were turned around, particularly as the officials also promised to make allotments of millet to the villages. Responding to the samurai officials' entreaties, many peasants, around December 19 and 20, returned to their villages to await the lord's reply, while still demanding that Benzo be turned over to them. The first stage of the rising did not fully end until a week later. But on December 20, at a meeting at the residence of the headman of Tokuda village in Anna district, the fief's chief inspectors (*ōmetsuke*) and company commanders (*omonogashira*) formally accepted a document containing thirty peasant demands.[20]

For Abe Masatomo, bakufu magistrate and absentee lord, the people he ruled were important mainly as sources of ground rent. Thus, when couriers from Fukuyama reached his Edo mansion ten days later, bearing reports on the rising and the peasants' demands, he read them from contradictory standpoints: as an independent fief holder concerned with securing his ground rent income, as a bakufu magistrate charged with upholding shogunal law everywhere in Japan, and as an official in line for promotion to the highest bakufu post during a time of political purges. Immediately, he countermanded the promises given by his senior officials to the peasants, in effect responding to the "national" pole of his thought and character. Here, in a long letter, dated January 7, 1787, addressed to his chief inspectors, he revealed the glaring limitations of his understanding of what had just occurred.

> I have looked over the bundle of peasant petitions and grievances sent to me. Each of them is merely a selfish request. Really, in this case, the fact that our domains in neighboring provinces were simultaneously stirred up is due ultimately to the widespread distress prevailing during the year.
> All violent appeals and conspiratorial groups are utterly unlawful actions in view of the bakufu's strict orders.... The writing in the passage where they [peasants] remind the officials of heavy responsibilities is disrespectful and unlawful.... I did not order anything to cause them difficulties. Ultimately, pushing from behind, were those who pursued selfish gains among the people ordered to come up to Fukuyama and get connected with the fief's financial affairs. First note that Satō Shinshirō, Sumiya Sōjirō and recently Yamamoto Bensuke and others had a grudge. They seem to be totally responsible for the writing about Endō Benzō.
> Recently, I did not order contributions [forced cash levies] from the countryside.... But if I had ordered it, the answer should not have been negative. Since I didn't order even that, no particular difficulty was caused to the livelihood of the lowly people (*shitakatadomo*). Yet they rose up because popular sentiments in all the neighboring provinces lured them out.
> If we comply with their demands in their interests, then afterwards the peasants will grow impudent and feel that whenever they make a stir their requests may be met. That should never be allowed to happen.... [He adds a postscript.] ... I am afraid Benzō will be made a target for disrepute.... take into account when making your report the truth or falsity of the information you receive. There is jealousy and envy among retainers over important posts.... By all means consult among yourselves and do not jump to hasty conclusions.[21]

Thus it was that Masatomo took issue with the way his own fief "elders" had handled the peasants. He did so by rejecting the peasants' demands and implying that the real instigators of their rebellion were the fief's creditors in the guise of three disgruntled merchants. He also disclaimed any personal responsibility for ordering "anything to cause them difficulties." In addition, he went out of his way to protect his loyal servant Benzō, while labeling as "selfish" the peasant victims who protested Benzō's extortionate tax practices. In short, by his letter of January 7, 1787, Lord Abe Masatomo showed he had not the faintest notion which way the wind was blowing back in Fukuyama.

Abe Masatomo, by his heartfelt concern for upholding his own prestige as a high-born hereditary ruler, triggered the second stage of the Tenmei rising. On the basis of his January 7 letter, the fief notified all villages on January 16 of its rejection of their demands, thereby reneging also on earlier promises of tax relief. The peasants' reply came ten days later (January 26) when the temple bells and gongs again rang out, sending them off by the thousands to rallying sites along riverbanks and in the mountains. Their tax strike was now on in full fury.

The fief elders in Fukuyama castle mobilized their entire retainer force within the domain, over twelve hundred samurai, and sent several units into the countryside accompanied by sword-bearing outcasts who assisted in police matters. But these actions only added fuel to the fire and ended in the defeat of samurai forces at the hands of rock-hurling peasants who far outnumbered them. Throughout the month of February the situation appeared deadlocked, though in fact the peasants were preparing the ground for a drastic reversal of the fief's hard-line position. On February 6, when the rising was at its height, about two thousand armed peasants gathered near the border with neighboring Okayama fief in Bizen province. There followed long hours of discussion in which it was decided that the most effective method for expressing their grievances—really the most unpleasant signal they could possibly send the castle authorities—was to break Fukuyama's entire chain of command and bring upon the lord himself the prospect of removal by a higher authority. After a tearful leave-taking, a party of six hundred peasants, risking death, crossed over into Okayama.

Their professed objective was to deliver a petition to Lord Ikeda asking for his intercession in their grievances, the most prominent of which were the abolition of the fief's Cotton Office, the return of pawned articles, and the deferment of loan repayments.[22] Since such matters were totally beyond the jurisdiction of a neighboring daimyo, it is obvious that their real intention was to provoke the bakufu's intervention. This particular incident ended peacefully, though only after a large contingent of Okayama soldiers met the peasants within their territory and turned them back.

The peasant foray into Okayama in defiance of fief and bakufu law finally brought about a change in Masatomo's situation. It shocked him into the painful realization that his own peasants had effectively raised the personal cost to him of allowing the struggle to continue by not granting their demands. In this new situation, he had not only to settle with his own peasants but also to deal with the lord of the fief in which they had sought redress of their grievances, not to mention his bakufu colleagues who would judge him on how well or how poorly he handled the disturbance in his own fief. Ending the rising remained, of course, his chief public responsibility. But as the peasants escalated their pressure, upholding bakufu law no longer seemed to him the main consideration in accomplishing that objective. If sacrificing the loyal Benzō by relieving him from his posts would serve to appease the peasants, then Benzō had to go. The first shift in Masatomo's thinking, forced by the intensity of the peasants' resistance, is registered in this short letter to his chief inspectors, dated February 18.

The courier letter of February 11 arrived.... there is still considerable feeling of unrest. Recently, many of them crossed over into Okayama domain. But since Okayama sent forces nothing particular happened. I understand that Endō Benzō was primarily responsible for causing the peasants to rise up and so have ordered him deprived of office and confined at home. By this action, I wonder if the people's minds could be appeased.... In any case, I wish to calm the situation by this action.... As for the peasants' requests, I order compliance with all of them. Since I will also order as they wish regarding Benzō, there should no longer be reasons for appeals and commotions. If there is further unrest, it will be the result of agitation by truly evil minds. Hastily, [signed] Bitchū.[23]

But back in Fukuyama, the peasants still held out for the punishment of Benzō, the release of captured peasants, no reprisals, and more concessions on demands. Fearing what would happen to him if their resistance continued, Masatomo wrote what, so far, has turned out to be his last available testimony on the rising. It is also the most interesting. In this next letter, to his chief inspectors, dated February 28, 1787—approximately ten days prior to his appointment to the Senior Council—we see Masatomo anguishing over Benzō and going to extremes to rationalize his decision not to use coercion against the peasants, as clearly specified by the bakufu instructions he was pledged to uphold.

I found the agreement you reached reasonable as you reported it. In a previous letter, I said you were so frightened by the disturbance as to forget the instructions issued previously by the bakufu [literally, "public authority," kōgi] and, in fear of the bakufu, you would not work out uniform action. So I sent the fief elders a package of bakufu instructions, requesting them to read it. There I stated that their action was deficient. Meanwhile I learned that the situation in the districts had become tranquil. So it is reasonable that fairly lenient measures were taken. Therefore nobody is to blame for rashness in taking measures. It was hardly possible to act upon the bakufu's frequently issued written instructions. Since the matter concerns the affairs of a private domain, it is difficult to take the strong measures that they stipulate.

    ... In the matter of the peasants' recent requests, it is insolent that violent appeals and other illegal acts developed because of failure in conveying my instructions in response to inquiries. It will be ruinous to the prestige and authority of the lord to conform readily to the peasants' requests no matter how much they rise up.

    ... Nevertheless, once popular sentiments have burst out and not returned to order, we are compelled to conform to their requests. But that cannot be the proper way of government [seidō to wa mōshigataku sōrō]....

    Although we have not heard that Benzō gave unjust orders to peasants, as long as popular sentiment does not return to order, no matter how much he worked in our interests,

it should not result in a change of the fief [that is, in their being removed to another fief]. . . .
Take rather lenient actions now. After investigations, in due course, peasants will also be
subjected to punishment. Although the matter arose, after all, from Benzō's actions, the
situation will not last for long that peasants gain too much.[24]

Abe Masatomo, without conforming to bakufu law, did succeed in settling
the rising in his own domain. Because of his success, he became a senior councillor
on March 7, 1787. But less than a year later, on February 29, 1788, for reasons that
are unclear, he resigned from the cabinet dominated by Matsudaira Sadanobu and
prepared to return to Fukuyama.

The date of Masatomo's appointment to the Senior Council, March 7, 1787,
may be taken as marking the end of the Fukuyama rising. The fief elders, citing it as
a face-saving pretext, announced the release from jail of seventy peasants arrested
earlier during the course of the rising. They had already removed Endō Benzō
from office (around February 7) and placed him under house arrest (February 18).
His imprisonment in solitary confinement followed ten days later (February 28).
Then on March 8, as a further show to peasants of the fief's sincerity in punishing
wrongdoers, the elders removed from office thirteen village headmen and assistant
headmen and reprimanded for wrongdoing certain district officials and their
assistants.[25]

What had the peasants accomplished? The fief elders, once Masatomo shifted
from a hard to a soft line, accepted twenty of their thirty demands, returned excessive rice tributes to villages, and attempted to rectify abuses by local officials.
Clearly, surrender on these issues attested to the weakening of their capacity to
extract rice tribute. But their ability and determination to obtain commercial
profits was not similarly impaired. On general issues having a direct bearing on
its plans for financial reconstruction, the Abe regime refused to budge. Thus it
did not rotate all village officials or abolish surcharges on tatami matting, as the
peasants had demanded. Neither did it abolish its newly established Cotton Office,
though it did agree to reduce some of its monopolistic functions. And although
it made concessions on the repayment of rice loans and unpaid back taxes, they
were not major ones.[26] Finally, the fief refused to intervene to regulate tenant
rents and pawned items, the main concerns of poor peasants. A further growth of
tenancy in Fukuyama was the long-term sequel to its refusal to protect the poor
from the undermining effects of tenant rents and loans.

CHAPTER ELEVEN

Dealing In the Landlords:
The Kansei Reforms and Fukuyama Fief,
1790–1805

THE fourth peasant rising in Fukuyama came and went "victoriously," but apparently without leading to much understanding by peasants of its real causes and without leaving behind any struggle organizations to actively combat the renewed growth of samurai tax oppression. When Abe Masatomo returned to his fief in 1790 to concentrate on overcoming its internal crisis, there seemed to be nothing to prevent him from redirecting peasants into the traditional feudal path. For the next quarter of a century, Fukuyama's general direction of development followed along lines Masatomo laid out between 1790 and his retirement in 1803. Since his reform strategy was part of a nationwide daimyo movement for restoring the country's peasant tax base, we shall start by first summarizing the bakufu's Kansei Reform, after which it will be easier to envisage Masatomo's program, which was essentially similar in intent and direction.[1]

Matsudaira Sadanobu carried out the Kansei Reform between 1789 and his retirement in 1793. His successors in the Senior Council, particularly Matsudaira Nobuaki, continued his basic policies, while daimyo in private domains implemented similar reforms throughout the 1790s and 1800s. Politically, Sadanobu's overall perspective, upon which he based his reforms, was that the entire bakufu organization had reached an impasse, which could be overcome only by returning to Shogun Yoshimune's example and adhering, rigidly, to original institutional structures. In other words, Japan's future, as most daimyo defined it, required holding firm to, rather than breaking with, its past.

The backward-looking nature of many of the Kansei Reforms followed from this general assumption. Challenges of various sorts had been mounted against the seclusion policy and even the authority of the shogun himself. And the effectiveness of feudal laws had been gradually undermined by peasant class struggles. Masatomo's response was, in effect, to stress moral revitalization of the samurai class and to supplement the regime of harsh punishments and threats with new ideological indoctrination and thought control. This shift of emphasis presupposed educational reform. Starting in the 1790s, fief schools were established to restore discipline and morale among retainers and to train bureaucrats in neo-Confucian state orthodoxy. At the same time, practical and moral instruction began to be given to peasants and townsmen, largely for the purpose of restoring political passivity, rectifying wrong thoughts, and inculcating proper attitudes of subjection to superiors. The establishment of the Hayashi school as a bakufu college for training bureaucrats in neo-Confucian ideology satisfied the former objective, while the Confucian indoctrination given to the poor and homeless at the bakufu's newly established (1790) public workhouse on Ishikawa Island in Edo Bay pointed to the new direction in social control.

Having committed itself under Sadanobu to preserving a full-blown feudal system, the bakufu organization pushed ahead with the encouragement of an official state ideology and of feudal, militaristic values and social norms. However, in working out economic policy, it revealed a more flexible approach to the problem of reform. Sadanobu not only emphasized the reinforcement of the seclusion policy and the suppression of heterodox thought but also promoted the establishment of grain warehouses as a famine relief measure and the strict enforcement of sumptuary regulations. In fact, the central economic problem he addressed concerned the bakufu's relationship to its own agricultural tax base. Sadanobu aimed at extricating Kantō Plains villages and towns from economic blight, establishing Edo's commercial superiority over Osaka, and easing the financial burden on deeply indebted domains.

In the six-year period 1788 to 1793, his key reforms succeeded in forcing many impoverished peasants and small townsmen to return to their villages by furnishing them with relief loans. The assistance covered their return travel plus the cost of purchasing fields, seeds, and equipment. Other relief measures pertained to lightening the burdens of transportation and courier service corvées, deferring loan repayments in provinces that had suffered severe crop damage, and establishing grain warehouses in all fiefs to protect against famine and also to help regulate the price of rice. In all these reforms, the primary aim was to secure and maintain minute-scale peasant farming on bakufu lands.[2] But their ultimate effect was somewhat different from what Sadanobu intended. For the loan money for most of the relief programs came from the top stratum of village officials, who were also landlords.

The bakufu, in other words, now gave its sanction to landlords who made loans to peasants at fixed but high rates of interest. The same landlordism of pawned land that in practice contravened the bakuhan state, by eroding its economic base of minute proprietors, thus became, simultaneously, one of its main structural supports.[3] By tacitly dealing in the landlords—that is, making allies of the rich peasant stratum, rather than trying to suppress them—the Kansei Reform prolonged the political life of the daimyo ruling stratum and regenerated the agrarian economy in areas worst hit by famine and natural disasters. His economic policies also encouraged a renewed concentration on economic goals in all regions of the country and imparted to all political units a sense of having to make do with limited resources. But, like Yoshimune's Kyōhō era reforms upon which they were professedly modeled, the overall effects of the Kansei Reforms were decidedly contradictory: although they strengthened the bakufu and extended its life, they did so only at the cost of furthering the gradual disintegration of the total bakuhan system.

Turning briefly now to Masatomo's reforms, we find that upon returning to Fukuyama castle in late 1790, he gave cash awards to his senior retainers and then waited a few months before announcing the start of new reforms. Significantly, he began in January 1791 by distributing to every village and town official in the fief a scroll composed of two characters, inscribed: "The Proper [Moral] way of Doing Things [seidō]." Then, at the same time, a long instruction went out to all village headmen and peasant representatives (hyakushō sōdai) with orders that it be read to peasants every month. This document, entitled "Instructions to the People on Civil Adminstration [minsei kyōsho]," represented the first of "various reforms to improve the habits of the people."[4] As summarized by historian Fujii Masao, it stipulated the general principles for rebuilding strong feudal control after nearly a century of peasant disturbances. One provision called for good conduct certificates to be given to peasants who excelled in filial piety and were diligent in carrying out their tax duties. Another emphasized strictness in the observance of the fief's laws and the high moral obligation of rendering up tribute. "Surrender as tribute to the lord the first rice crop of the year. You should put your whole heart into the making of rice and even if you are late in paying taxes, you will not be urged to pay more."[5] Another provision of the "Instructions" read:

Recently, some peasants behave improperly by seeking after profits and making light of important tribute matters. When village headmen and other officials strongly press them, they circulate stories that they are being subjected to unjust collections. Some of them, saying that even honest people plot bad things, talk about freely changing the village officials. In view of the laws of this country, there are no reasons to allow small peasants to seize tribute rice in their own selfish interest. Hereafter those who neglect the duties of these days will be punished severely as laid down by law.[6]

For the tardy in paying taxes, for those who manifested disobedience and a complaining nature, the "Instructions" threatened severe sanctions. All such behavior was "the selfishness of small holders [*kozura no wagamama*]" and subject to punishment according to law.[7] Lately, the "Instructions" contained provisions promising fief support to those who undertook to reclaim abandoned fields and restore impoverished villages. In practice, this meant giving a fairly free hand to merchants and wealthy peasants to overlord the regeneration of villages.

Masatomo's second reform consisted of new "Fief Articles for Five-Man Groups [*goryō goningumi kajōgaki*]." In these detailed articles, issued in January 1791, Fukuyama fief again responded indirectly and partially to peasant demands that it had earlier rejected. To guard against corruption by village officials, the articles specified that all expenses connected with village government were to be made public. They also fixed the amount of money that could be paid to samurai who visited villages on official business. Since most landowning peasants preferred to pawn their land in times of need rather than sell it, the new articles prohibited the permanent selling of land. At the same time, however, they accorded official recognition to the pawning of land for up to ten years, thereby blocking the growth of large-unit landowning. Finally, other articles encouraged the return of docile, obedient peasants who practiced mutual surveillance and the virtues of frugality, diligence, thrift, and filial piety.[8]

The third reform consisted of new sumptuary regulations, issued first in 1797 and again in 1815 under the regime of Abe Masakiyo. These established, with respect to patterns of dress and food consumption, roughly common provisions for all Abe retainers and their families as well as for all town and village officials. Separate sumptuary regulations governed the dress of townsmen and peasants.[9] Like the bakufu's sumptuary laws of the late 1780s and 1790s, Masatomo's sought to maintain social control over peasants and commoners by eliminating the most visible components of material inequality—those upon which perceptions of injustice were most easily grounded and envy and dissension engendered. They regulated, in other words, only the psychological effects of economic inequality but left its structure carefully intact. They were also intended to lower material expectations and to make "diligence" and "frugality" the common watchwords for all people.

Let us now see what light Masatomo's Kansei period reforms throw on class relations in Fukuyama at the end of the eighteenth century. Through his "Instructions to the People on Civil Government," his "Fief Articles for Five-Man Groups," and his sumptuary regulations, Masatomo and his chief retainers tried to regenerate a traditional status orientation to work and life. In one crucial area, however, they were obliged to leave the initiative for feudal regeneration to their allies: the rural elite of rich peasants and merchants. During the rising of 1786–1787, the fief elders had shown a willingness to sacrifice these upper strata of wealthy merchants and peasants to appease "small holders." Later, when the rising had ended, the elders failed to immediately ease the plight of the poor, who had been most militant in attacking the property of village headmen and rural merchants. In these circumstances of default by the Abe regime, many rich merchants and peasant landlords were compelled to take out their own local protection insurance.

Starting in 1788, nearly three years before Masatomo promulgated his "Instructions," the cotton merchant and assistant headman Kyūzaburō drew up plans for establishing the fief's first community warehouse (shasō) in Fuchū, Ashida district.[10] Thereafter, over the course of the next fifteen years, the fief elders gave official support to merchants, artisans, and "benevolent" village officials who established many community warehouses and poor relief warehouses (gisō) in all six districts of the domain. The warehouses, as historian Fujii Masao noted, "conducted various public welfare activities and frequently saved distressed people from starvation. . . . But in Fukuyama fief their real historical significance lay more in the builder's own self-defense."[11]

From the description of the poor relief warehouses given in the History of Fukuyama City, we learn further that they were, in economic essence, a type of profit-making company run jointly by groups of rich peasants and rural merchants. In fact, most of their founders were landlords and one of their major objectives was to accumulate paddy fields, dry fields, and salt marshes. To work their warehouse-attached fields and marshes they used tenant labor. They paid tribute on their fields and then sold the remaining tenant rice and salt on the market, making profits in the process. Documents showing warehouse receipts and expenditures do not reveal the number of tenants who worked on warehouse fields. But as a group they may be regarded as a farming "semiproletariat."[12]

The warehouses also aided the fief in financial reconstruction by performing banking functions. They handled its money and made loans to other wealthy merchants, accumulating and safekeeping the interest for later transfer to the fief. In addition, during the period 1805 to 1810, warehouse funds amounting to twenty kan of silver annually were spent on "repair of shrines and temples, relief for samurai retainers, lecture fees for Shintō and Buddhist priests, and training for medical students." This meant that a considerable part of their funds were used "to develop instruction in feudal ethics for the leading strata of all circles, thereby placing peasants and townsmen at large under the influence of such feudal virtues."[13]

Thus the essential points about the warehouses were these. Money-making and ideological indoctrination were their primary functions; relief of the poor was of secondary importance. Second, in the warehouses we see the rise of the big land-lords who, during the course of the nineteenth century, would come to dominate the Fukuyama countryside. The establishment of public warehouses during the course of Masatomo's reforms, therefore, was a manifestation of the crucial com-plementary role that the upper strata of rich merchants and peasants began to play in stabilizing daimyo rule at the end of the eighteenth and beginning of the nineteenth centuries. The political importance of such a development can hardly be overemphasized.

In conclusion, then, the social and economic contradictions that shaped daily life in Fukuyama were typical of the contradictions shaping the social situation in other fiefs and bakufu territories at the end of the eighteenth century. Starting in the 1790s, daimyo like Abe Masatomo, with the indispensable assistance of the rich peasant and merchant class, worked successfully to regain the political and moral ground that had been lost to peasants as a result of their mass actions in the middle and late 1780s. The daimyos' strategy aimed ultimately at maintaining and, when possible, increasing the fief's take. This was to be done by lowering the standard of living of all ruled classes, but especially the small-holding peasants who constituted the overwhelming majority, to a level where they could continue to endure the imposition of heavy taxes and corvées without revolting. At the same time, the daimyo sought to restore the lost authority of rural officials, recruited from the upper strata of peasants, so that their orders could once more command respect from a pacified peasantry.

Their success in achieving these aims is undeniable. Not until the 1830s and early 1840s, a period of even more acute economic distress than the 1780s, did Japan experience another nationwide explosion of violent social struggles. The follow-ing questions may therefore be posed: Why did the dissident peasants of the 1780s so quickly assume the yoke after having succeeded, momentarily, in throwing it off? More specifically, why did Fukuyama's peasants follow quietly for over thirty years in the direction of Masatomo's reforms?

The main point to keep in mind is that the 1790s was a period of forceful and sustained bakufu leadership on the terrain of politics and ideology. Inevitably, fief reformers in the provinces benefited from the leadership furnished by Sadanobu and his successors. But there were two other circumstantial reasons for the lull in the class struggle, pertaining to Fukuyama fief but valid, more or less, for other domains nationwide during the 1790s and 1800s.

First, peasants could not really oppose the fief-ordered practice of diligence and frugality because such "self-exploitation," practiced day in and day out, contributed to the rebuilding of their own household economies, hence increased their own surplus. In that sense, Fukuyama fief appeared to be making demands that were genuinely in the interests of peasants. Just this appearance of genuine benevolence, even though not fully actualized, helped forestall further protest actions.

Second, the fief easily countered the educative role of armed mass struggle by playing on the conditions of economic crisis under which agricultural production was resumed during the late 1780s and 1790s. It exploited the situation by arguing that the retainers should all work and sacrifice together, observing the sumptuary rules, for then similar or much more stringent rules would be easier to enforce on townsmen and peasants.

These were reasons enough for the decrease in incidents of violent public protest in the villages of Japan at the very end of the eighteenth century and the beginning of the nineteenth century. But a third consideration must also be added. It seems likely that many peasants accepted and went along with bakufu and fief reforms from their own standpoint in accordance with private goals that were not identical with the fief's. Moreover, they did so while still retaining a predisposition to resist feudal oppression. Such inclinations toward noncompliance may have expressed themselves in hidden or indirect ways, such as cultural and religious activities.

Thus, one cannot directly attribute the lull in the class struggle to peasant acceptance of feudal hegemony. For, historically, peasants have struggled against a variety of different forms of both feudal and capitalist regimes while still operating firmly within the framework of their respective overall hegemonies. The acceptance of a particular hegemony, whether labeled feudal or capitalist, is never sufficient to eliminate struggle or violent protest. But what most definitely does affect the goals and even the forms of popular struggle is the degree to which oppressed classes—whether peasants or workers—submit to ruling-class definitions of what is realistic and sensible for them to aspire to.[14]

Here is where the disciplining ideology of fixed status (applied to all classes) came into the picture. The degree to which the Japanese common people internalized that ideology affected their actual behavior in protest movements. It did not affect, however, the development of their beliefs. During the first half of the nineteenth century, in fact, the spread of literacy in villages and the growth of new religious and cultural activities among peasants would pose the most serious challenge yet to the bakuhan state. But at the very end of the eighteenth century, ruling-class culture and ideology still outweighed rural village culture and ideology. The task of the next few chapters will be to explore how that relationship of dominance was challenged and changed from below.

PART IV

Transition to a New Order: Class Conflicts up to the Late Nineteenth Century

CHAPTER TWELVE

Problems of Interpretation

THREE historical probes in depth have now been conducted into peasant class struggles of the early, middle, and last decades of the eighteenth century. Before moving on to the nineteenth century to examine incidents from the second and third peak periods of Tokugawa peasant agitation—the 1830s and 1866 to 1873—let us give some further thought to problems in the interpretation of peasant movements.

Statistics show clearly that the inclination of Japanese peasants to form active resistance groups against feudal exploitation was gradually on the rise nearly everywhere during the second half of the eighteenth century and throughout most of the nineteenth century. And there is no question either that changing economic grounds for social conflict were helping to bring into view, more openly and more often, a consciousness of struggle that was socially subversive and potentially anti-feudal. The persistent demands of peasants and townsmen for more freedoms, and for more of the fruits of their own labor, could not dislodge the privileged daimyo from their unassailably strong positions. But they did have an effect on the policies of the feudal ruling class as a whole. Slowly but steadily, they were forcing it to modify or to rescind altogether those policies that peasants would not tolerate.

In that sense, Ueda's peasants waged a struggle that was paradigmatic. It contained most of the forms and themes that were to appear later on in the history of the peasantry's emergence as a shaping political force. That force made constant thrusts within and even, occasionally, outside the framework of the bakuhan state. But all the while it was peacefully building up the conditions for its destruction. The samurai could crush such revolts as occurred but they could not prevent peasants from making gains over the centuries by minimizing village population registers, concealing grains, or cheating on corvées. Nor could they prevent the prestige and authority of daimyo and local officials from being undermined by peasants and townsmen who persisted in making formal demands that pertained to the lessening of exploitation—that is, to tribute and its collectors, or to corvée and guild restrictions.

It was also the actions of peasants, both peaceful and violent, that opened the way for more favorably situated samurai, such as the physician Andō Shōeki and Yamagata Daini, to call into question during the 1750s and 1760s, the very legitimacy of the entire feudal order. Significantly, Shōeki, through his intimate knowledge of the social situation of peasants in northeastern Japan, regarded all aspects of life from the viewpoint of the exploited peasantry. He taught that the essence of life was productive labor in the form of "direct cultivation," and he rejected totally the notion of a rigidly hierarchic society. Shōeki was the first Japanese to find a theoretical solution to the problems of feudal society in a full-blown philosophy of agrarian communism. But he was too far in advance of his age, and the cultural tradition he represented had little popular influence.[1] Shōeki's work really belonged to the future of Japan rather than to its Tokugawa past.

At this stage of social development, the eighteenth century, the efforts of peasants to change their objective situation could go only so far. Again, as the events in Ueda and Fukuyama demonstrated, even when rural protest movements happened to coincide with urban movements, they never actively merged with them. Nor, with one notable exception, did the dissident consciousness of peasant organizers lead to any synchronized resistance to bakuhan rule involving peasants in many different fiefs acting in unison. Furthermore, irrespective of how a particular rising ended, whether in clear defeat or apparent victory, a period of ideological reindoctrination followed. During it, feudal authorities meted out severe penalties to ikki leaders. This repeated subjection of peasants to police repression and to innumerable forms of thought control can hardly be overestimated. Together with the unconscious discipline imposed by daily agricultural life itself—the constant necessity of meeting immediate, practical needs—they were major factors setting back their horizons and contributing to their depoliticalization.

But taken by itself, feudal ideology alone did not always have the desired internal effect. The epitaphs of stone and wood, erected swiftly after the event in honor of peasant martyrs (gimin), reversed the judgment of officialdom. Tokuemon, Hanbei, and Asanojō, symbolically restored to their local communities, outlived their executioners, as did many other peasant martyrs. And from the middle of the eighteenth century, the shrine erected in honor of Sakura Sōgorō became so famous as to attract worshipers from all over Japan.[2] That ideological repression or thought control failed should not be surprising. Throughout history powerless people have allowed their thoughts at least to run in directions their rulers never approved. Despite their actual social positions, they have found innumerable symbolic ways to modify or reverse entirely the burden of dominant teachings imposed upon them by rulers.[3]

There is, however, another reason of a different order for repression sometimes failing. Participation in class struggle was a profound emotional experience, which became in turn a reference for individuals for judging other events. That is to say, the experience of resisting injustice invariably changed some people inwardly, just as it does today. The tension and danger of the confrontation with daimyo and bakufu law sharpened social perceptions. New feelings and insights were absorbed and then passed on to (or perhaps rediscovered by) the next generation, which faced the same problems as its parents. When the time came for it to stand up, the new generation would negate the memory of repression by nurturing the memory of gimin. As a result, the full consequences of a major peasant rising often did not manifest themselves until much later in time. But, as we saw in moving from Tsuyama and Ueda to Fukuyama, some changes in peasant political consciousness, methods of struggle, and degree of organization did actually occur over the course of the eighteenth century.

This lends all the more point to a related question: when protesters in such formidable numbers were so often making radical demands against bakuhan economic and political policies, why did their antifeudal consciousness not evolve at a much faster rate, despite the progress they sometimes showed during times of intense struggle? Let us consider this problem by focusing on the complex relationship between the feudal economic context and peasant class consciousness.

One reply to the question of the slowness of peasant consciousness to develop is simply to point out that elites too have great difficulty in developing their political horizons and imagining alternative socioeconomic systems. Another is to note, as Scott has done, that such imaginings are both possible and frequent. In fact, history is filled with examples of oppressed classes—whether slaves, serfs, or illiterate "free" peasants—who succeeded in imagining a different, less cruel political order than the one they suffered under. Invariably, a distinguishing feature of such ideal communities has been their reversal or negation of an existing social hierarchy.[4]

None of this is to deny the social determination of consciousness or the need to give it the closest attention. In Tokugawa Japan a slowly rising level of relations of production obviously set limits to both peasant and elite consciousness. Moreover, Japan was not yet a civil society in which economic, political, and military spheres of social control were clearly distinguished on the basis of a prior existential separation of the individual from society. On the contrary, here one sphere implied all the others. And in the period roughly from the 1760s through the early 1800s, social and historical processes changed slowly.

The general state of the Japanese economy was still at an early stage of commoditized money economy. In virtually all areas, its science and technology were, without question, extremely backward. Village industries that employed wage laborers, such as the salt, sake-brewing, and textile industries as well as mining and handicraft industries, were developing very slowly. They had not yet become important sources of employment for large numbers of workers. Everywhere the norm was for masses of serflike peasants to carry on minute-scale farming while the feudal ruling class tightly regulated the circulation and distribution of commodities. Certainly the prestige of wealthy merchants was on the rise while that of low-status samurai was on the wane. But in the villages moral considerations still predominated over cold market calculation in matters of lending and borrowing and in market exchange in general. Meanwhile, the social division of labor and commerce continued to be organized politically by hereditary statuses, which also determined most people's occupations and places of residence.

Conditions of status, work, and physical and moral environment thus shaped the character as well as the content of the peasants' response to oppression and exploitation. But cultural and ideological factors also gave form to their life situations and feelings, hence their style of politics. These, however, are best approached indirectly, by means of a digression on a famous incident, which occurred about a year after the conclusion of the Ueda uprising.

THE TENMA DISTURBANCE

Between December 1764 and early January 1765, the bakufu was shaken by a huge disturbance known to history as the "Tenma sōdō." It was triggered by two previous bakufu actions: (1) a heavy money tax levied on villages in the Kantō Plains area in order to cover entertainment expenses for a Korean delegation which visited the tenth shogun, Ieharu, at his Edo headquarters in the spring of 1764, and (2) the assigning of special corvées to 195 villages located within forty kilometers north and south of the bustling Nakasendō. This road was the second most important of five strategic post roads originating from Nihonbashi in Edo and joining Japan's major provinces and cities. Official courier traffic and private merchant freight traffic had been increasing on the Nakasendō ever since the early eighteenth century. In December 1764, the epicenter of the struggle was the Honjō post station, located in the northern part of Musashi province.[5]

From here thousands of leaflets began to circulate secretly to villages and post stations along the Nakasendō. They called upon peasants, already infuriated by the rising burden of compulsory requisitions of horses and men, to protest the bakufu's latest tax actions. From all along the highway peasants flocked to join. The demonstration took shape and moved toward Edo, with peasants bearing flags inscribed with their village names. At nocturnal meetings, during which all torch fires were extinguished in order to protect the anonymity of speakers, a strategy was worked out for presenting grievances to the bakufu. Then, on January 6, 1765, during the last days of the demonstration, a meeting of village chiefs from 110 villages in Musashi province elected three representatives to enter Edo and present a petition of grievances directly to the bakufu accountant magistrate. The Tenma protest ended shortly afterward. The bakufu's reply soon followed. It executed a small number of leaders and had 381 participants imprisoned and tortured.[6]

What makes the Tenma disturbance so interesting historically is, first, its numerical size—nothing like it had occurred since the great Amakusa-Shimabara revolt—and, second, its geographical scale. Where the Ueda Hōreki uprising had been confined to just one fief, on this occasion over 200,000 peasants, porters, and day laborers from affected villages and post stations spread their protests through parts of four provinces: Kōzuke (modern-day Gumma), Shimotsuke (Tochigi), Shinano (Nagano), and Musashi (part of Saitama, Kanagawa, and Tokyo).

Second, it demonstrated a shifting of targets, which was quite common to peasant struggles from Hōreki onward. Initially, the protest aimed at the bakufu's transportation and courier service policy. That guaranteed from the outset a broad-based alliance of all tax-affected villages. But the rank and file of respondents to the organizers' leaflets were really protesting the nexus of corrupt dealings among bakufu officials who arbitrarily allotted quotas of horses and men for un-paid courier and transport service duties, post station officials (such as tonya) who profited unfairly from the system, and privileged merchants and village officials who exploited the entire system to their own advantage.

Therefore, third, no sooner had all villages been fully mobilized around the single issue of transportation corvées than the poorest peasants turned their wrath against the ruling hierarchy in the villages through which they passed. As that occurred, the enthusiasm of participating village headmen and other village officials—the top stratum of the demonstration—fell off abruptly. Thus, a main factor contributing to the shattering of peasant unity in the final stage was the opposition of the village elite. But another limiting factor can also be detected. The lowest level of bakuhan popular control comprised Buddhist temples and Shinto shrines. In the Tenma incident priests played almost as crucial a role as village officials in blunting peasant militancy and sabotaging their unity.

Precisely to counter such activity, however, the village contingents from

Musashi, where the Tenma agitation came to be centered, raised aloft poles bearing not their village names and insignia but long strips of paper, knotted at the top and symbolizing the god of purification, "Bonten," meaning Brahma-Deva.[7] This incident, perhaps the most significant of the entire demonstration, is what deserves careful consideration. It seems to have represented one of the first attempts, since the peasant revolts of the fifteenth and sixteenth centuries, to appropriate a symbol of religious authority in a quest for class unity against samurai misrule. Moreover, Bonten was a harbinger of those frequent instances during the second and third peak periods of resistance from below—the 1830s and early 1840s and the late 1860s and early 1870s—when religious slogans and symbols moved closer to the foreground in the course of peasant uprisings. For example, in a peasant rising of 1836 in Kamo district, Mikawa province (present-day Aichi prefecture), the peasants called their ikki a "yonaoshi festival" and referred to themselves as "the gods of renewal." "Did you come out to meet the gods of renewal?" they asked.[8] Earlier, in Tsuyama, we witnessed peasants making themselves, in the act of property destruction, the agents of a punitive heaven. In Ueda some participants in the ikki may have believed themselves to have embodied the spirit of the punitive mountain gods that protected agriculture.

IKKI, ICHIMI DŌSHIN, AND YONAOSHI

What all this suggests is the need to reckon with peasant traditions at both the trans-fief and local community levels. In general, Japanese peasant culture was a matter of religious pilgrimages, rites, and daily practices; of itinerant teachers and traveling entertainers such as puppeteers, dancers, singers, and storytellers. Regional fairs and festivals figured in it. Artisan culture was also a component. So too was popular literature, art, and poetry. But the main element was popular Buddhism because it ministered to the peasants' and townsmen's material and spiritual needs. The Jōdō, Shin, Nichiren, and Sōtō Zen sects all played important roles in communicating to believers common conceptions of life and legends of all sorts. Next came countless local Shinto deities and, particularly in eastern Japan, remnants of pre-Buddhist fetishism.

This Tokugawa peasant culture, despite local differences fostered by the fief system, was remarkably homogeneous. Dialect differences were not such as to prevent the Japanese language from being understood, more or less, nearly everywhere. Homogeneity was also promoted by centuries of internal migration and a well-developed transportation system.

But it was at the local level, in the culture and folk beliefs of the village community, that peasant consciousness received its strongest impressions. Here beliefs and symbols of medieval provenance operated from within to limit the growth of peasant class consciousness, just as feudal repression acted on peasants from without.

Consider the ikki. Of all the customary ideas that peasants in extremis mobilized to strengthen their unity, none was more important than the ideas associated with *ikki*. That word, originally of Chinese derivation, was used in Japan since Heian times to mean identity, identical, or the same, as in "This and that are identical." By the late Kamakura period at the end of the thirteenth century, and especially after the conclusion of the succession dispute surrounding the imperial court at the end of the fourteenth century, the term became linked to the notion of a solidarity band (*ichimi dōshin*).[9] The solidarity band was formed expressly to make a decision that was just and unswayed by special interests because it was based on the will of heaven—an impersonal standard—rather than on consanguineous ties. But probing deeper, we see the ancient Japanese belief in the oneness of men through and with the gods. In the words of Katsumata Shizuo, "The consciousness that the decision of the solidarity band and the actions of the *ikki* carried the will of the gods was handed down to posterity among people who formed *ikki*. Even in the Edo period, when that idea had generally weakened, it can be found running through peasant revolts." Indeed, he argues, the consciousness of man's oneness with the gods shapes many of the characteristic features of the *ikki*: its belief in justice beyond consanguineous ties, initiative among participants in the solidarity band, and their strong independence and freedom from the ruling powers (whether of the fief or in the village).[10]

So the ikki was not only a habit, a defense, and a right to be exercised by peasants in times of acute crisis. It was also a ritual for keeping alive prefeudal ideas of impartial justice, equality, and equity in a society dominated by kinship, hierarchy, and fixed statuses. On the other hand, as the most extreme manifestation of the basic class conflict between peasants and lords, the ikki connoted an impulsive and constrictive style of politics. It was goal and issue oriented to be sure. But it was also the politics of anger, which disposed people to seek justice in revenge. Admittedly, the punishment of wrongdoers during an ikki underscored the close relationship between revenge and justice. Rather than being sharply antithetical notions, revenge has been, both historically and psychologically, the origin of justice. In that sense, the politics of anger was highly effective in assigning responsibility and punishing unjust men and unjust actions.[11]

But the consciousness of people who participated in ikki was undeniably backward looking, even if their historical role was progressive. All too often their anger dissipated itself without winning broad-based emotional support outside of rural areas for the standard of justice they sought to uphold. In short, the ikki was best suited to rural villages and the defense of their cultural values. There the cultural supports for protest were strongest and the teachings and values of the dominant ideology were more easily stretched and even discarded. By contrast, the ikki was least suited to castle towns and large cities, which were the main stronghold of *chōnin* culture and samurai values. In cities, the prohibitions of the dominant ideology had their greatest impact, especially on the ruling class which propagated the ban on ikki in the first place.

Another aspect of the ikki that captures its suitability to rural communities is the distinctive concept of discipline it manifested. The self-discipline of peasants in revolt was essentially communitarian in nature. Such discipline derived from the practice of joint agricultural labor in villages organized for production and was based on the mores of the community. Because the discipline of the ikki was the actualization of a specific, stagelike process of community mobilization, organization, and deployment in punitive action, it tended to last only as long as the punitive actions themselves lasted. Such disciplined self-control from below must be distinguished from modern forms of individualistic discipline, including the work discipline of the corporation and the discipline of subordinates to superiors within modern military organizations. The latter are techniques for the control of people from above which rest, ultimately, on material structures of power and punishment.[12]

Finally, when mobilized for an ikki, people assumed a new identity, even donned a new outfit to symbolize thier sharp break with the routine of daily life. At such times, consumption of alcohol for sacral purposes increased and its intoxicating effects were enlisted in the service of the demonstration.[13] And all the while episodes accumulated of the rules of feudal civility turned, momentarily, upside down.

So much for the ikki. Another important term, reflective of both the ideological terrain on which peasant struggles were frequently waged and their meaning, is *yonaoshi*. Addressing the question of its etymology, Miyata Noboru writes that in ancient Japan "*yo* meant a cycle starting from the beginning to the end of the rice growing. This was repeated every year and the breaking of the new *yo* or plant-growing cycle was *yonaori*. If the cultivator encountered obstacles or unfortunate circumstances impeding the growth cycle, he removed them and this removal of adversities in any form was then termed *yonaoshi*."[14] That was the basic meaning. But by the start of the nineteenth century, it had begun to acquire a more general sense of a world cleansed of evil and renewed for further growth. From there was but a short step to using *yonaoshi* to imply a millenarian renewal or a catastrophic event heralding the arrival of a new world.

Another scholar, Hayashi Motoi, in his researches on peasant revolts, found a number of early (albeit weak) eighteenth-century foreshadowings of this catastrophic sense of *yonaoshi*. It appears, for example, in a line in a satirical verse of 1708: "Wish to renovate [*yonaoshi*] the bent world." In ballad dramas of 1712 and 1718 the famous playwright Chikamatsu Monzaemon used the word in a spell that went: "Here, earthquake, thunderbolt, renovation! Heaven forbid!" A passive rendering of *yonaoshi* occurred in connection with the "rising for 3 *gō* of millet" in Hachinohe fief, northeastern Japan, in January 1834. This incident featured a gray-haired old man who allegedly emerged from the clouds and urged peasants to rise up, saying "I am the deity of renovation [*yonaoshi daimyōjin*] .... The time has come. Until now I have had a role to play. Hereafter there will be those who succeed to it." [15]

Whatever millenarian connotations *yonaoshi* may have had, they were not, even at the very end of the Tokugawa period, the dominant ones. Most often *yonaoshi* denoted a world-affirming experience. One engaged in such actions to exorcise the evils of local society, thereby preventing the world from coming to an end. But this concept, deriving from the Japanese agricultural community, seldom if ever implied any sort of a religious transcendence or negation of the temporal world in the Western sense.

Moreover, *yonaoshi* was based ultimately on a traditional idea of time as cyclical change. Agricultural life with its cycles of growth and of birth, life and death, confirmed such an outlook. But peasants had eventually to overcome that cyclic notion and embrace a new view of time in order to grasp the notion of progress or the modern principle of dynamic, unbounded change. [16]

In sum: ideas of solidarity, impartial justice, world renewal or renovation, unity of man with nature, unity of man with the gods of Buddhism and Shinto, and a cyclical view of life—all these beliefs found their expression in different senses of the key terms: *ikki*, *ichimi dōshin*, and *yonaoshi*.

THE LANDHOLDING CONSCIOUSNESS OF PEASANTS

We must now consider another aspect of peasant life related to rebellion. Class struggle episodes of the eighteenth and nineteenth centuries reveal a deeply rooted peasant feeling of oneness or unity between the cultivator and the land he worked. Such a belief lay behind the Tokugawa peasants' repeated assertion of an inextinguishable right to repurchase pawned land. Often they asserted that right even after the land in question had been forfeited for over a century because some ancestor, the original owner, had failed to redeem the loan on it within the originally specified time period. [17] Tokugawa peasants refused ever to recognize any sale, in fact, of an object as implying its complete and irrevocable alienation.

In this they were hardly unique. A similar kind of resistance to being separated from a customary land tenure has been reported in the agrarian history of many other societies. The *droit de marché* [right of the land], which Marc Bloch discovered in his study of medieval French agrarian life, was also "a reversion to the old notions of perpetuity and hereditability, which in the past had secured the [French peasants'] customary permanence of tenure." Bloch adds that "when a lease expired [a landlord] was in for trouble if he refused to renew it in favour of the former tenant, and on almost the same conditions. Even worse trouble was in store for the new tenant, if such could be found. . . . Both landlord and tenant were likely to pay dearly for their infringement of what the peasant community regarded as their rights. . . . no punishment was considered too great." [18]

In the Japanese case, the roots of this customary attitude toward landholding are difficult to establish. It seems, in part, to have been a historical legacy of the long superseded equal-field land regime of antiquity. It took clear shape, however, only during the sixteenth and seventeenth centuries, when the acquisition of land served to confirm, legally, the individual's personal independence and status as a small cultivator. The feudal landholding consciousness of Tokugawa peasants was not totally hostile to private property as such, in all of its many attributes. But it did indicate two distinct prior beliefs. One was a belief in the village community as an ultimate value for the sake of which the peasants' landholding right existed. An equally important though more submerged belief was in the need to preserve the person, and thereby the family, as an object of value.

So, we may say first that Japanese peasants put limits on the private accumulation of wealth within villages by condemning the covetousness and selfishness to which such accumulation gave rise. Second, they acted that way because they recognized that wealth, although not in itself bad, became an evil once it harmed poor people, who had just as much right to preserve themselves as did the rich. Since the unlimited accumulation of landed wealth destroyed the village community, the demand for the return of pawned or forfeited land was always a demand for its rehabilitation.

Furthermore, as the landholding right developed in Tokugawa times, it became, potentially, a source of equal human rights. For every assertion of a right to forfeited land entailed the prior claim that the individual person—as such, and not simply as a member of the family—was an object of value within the confines of the village community. The Tokugawa class struggle tradition kept alive this inherently humanistic implication of the property consciousness of Japanese peasants during most of the nineteenth century. Having few economic resources but expecting generosity, benevolence, and assistance from their rulers, Japanese peasants, like their counterparts in other lands, fought stubbornly to preserve a customary economic subsistence. In effect, they would not tolerate any transgression of the most important constituent of their livelihood—their multiple and direct entitlements to land.[19]

Just where their ideas of moral economy took them could be seen especially clearly during the last decade of the bakuhan state, following the commencement in 1860 of foreign trade. When the Western powers began having an impact on Japan in a thousand different ways, entire regions, where silk, tea, and cotton were grown, experienced the disintegrating effects of foreign trade. The indigenous advance of landlordism also quickened. Merchants and rich peasants then attempted to move in a capitalist direction by unilaterally accumulating large amounts of tiny land parcels. Immediately, they ran up against all the ideas around which small peasant cultivators, for centuries, had built their sense of land possession and human worth. The dominant forms of class struggle became the village disturbance (*murakata sōdō*) and the yonaoshi struggle, in which the poor compelled the rich to return pawned land and articles and to give rice and money to the sick and bankrupt so as to rehabilitate the village community. In so far as these struggle forms of poor people expressed (and sought to counter) the growing class polarization in Japanese society, they were far more progressive than is ever admitted by the conventional historiography, with its focus on the rising bourgeoisie of landlords and wealthy merchants.

As we shall see in the next three chapters, however, the risings of the 1830s and the years 1866 to 1873 did not, as a rule, take a direct antifeudal form. Nor did they call openly for land reform or the stabilization of ownership. Under the circumstances, the establishment of private, exclusive, bourgeois landownership could benefit only the rural rich. But the bearers of resistance to exploitation did reveal elements of a full-circle return to the eve of the founding stage of the Tokugawa system. Regeneration and renewal were themes that ran through many of the mid-nineteenth-century risings. As the bakufu visibly weakened, many peasants imagined they were experiencing a genuine historical turnabout, a true conversion to a new era. They became obsessed with the idea of inflicting punitive justice against their immediate oppressors, of destroying all the property and possessions of the exploiting rich, of eradicating everything material that was ill-gotten. The theme of local community regeneration, on the basis of peasant-type landownership and through the very process of property destruction itself, was the most widely shared of peasant beliefs in the last stages of the bakuhan state.

But the underlying limitation of the yonaoshi rhetoric of the bakufu's last years must also not be overlooked, since it relates to what happened after the Restoration. As Sasaki Junnosuke noted, even after the framework of the last Japanese feudal state had been enlarged into a nationally integrated unit and then thoroughly reorganized at the top, there continued to exist in peasant minds the sense of a "public authority," higher than the individual fiefs to which they belonged.[20] The institutions of the bakuhan state collapsed and disappeared, one by one; but that popular consciousness of belonging to a larger, transcendent entity remained. It persisted because peasants had not been able to produce an alternative conception of a state, though the emotional basis for such a consciousness may have been there in the longing for a yonaoshi renewal. Since yonaoshi feelings never developed so as to deny and supplant the old public-authority consciousness, Japan's ruling class was able to reorganize and perpetuate itself into the new era as the leadership of an emperor-centered state. Meanwhile, rich landlords and merchants retained command in the countryside. There, they preserved as much of the old feudal system as they could manage, including many forms of extraeconomic surplus extraction, just as the landlord-nobility did in tsarist Russia after Alexander's emancipation of the serfs in 1861.

CHAPTER THIRTEEN

Conflict and Social Change, 1800–1873

HAVING traced the struggle movement of peasants and other ruled classes through the seventeenth and eighteenth centuries, our task in the remainder of this study will be threefold. First, we shall shift the focus from peasant protest actions per se to the various background factors that paved the way for the risings of the nineteenth century. Second, we shall portray very briefly two instances of struggle that illuminated the broad range of urban and rural opposition to the bakuhan state during the last stages of its political decay. The Osaka insurrection of 1837 showed the joining of peasant and samurai ideological currents and the start of disaffection from the state by low-level bakufu officials. The Bushū rising of 1866 swept through the bakufu's main power base of Musashi province, straddling the Kantō Plain region. The ideology informing this action, the demands it raised, and the manner of its repression by peasant conscripts sheds light on peasant politics in a critical transition period.

Finally, in chapters 14 and 15, we shall take up two struggles in which both middle-strata peasants and that anonymous class called (for want of a better term) the Japanese semiproletariat figured prominently. The first incident, known as the Kaisei rising, occurred in Tsuyama fief in 1866–1867, on the eve of the bakufu's overthrow. The second protest, which takes us back to Ueda fief, unfolded in Shinshū province in 1869–1870, the early years of the construction of the Meiji state machine. Feudal administrative structures were being rapidly reorganized but village administration remained intact. Rice tribute continued to be collected from the villages in most regions and marketed by fiefs and newly established imperial prefectures. The modern apparatuses of a centralized, unified state had not yet fully emerged. In this context, some peasants, driven by antifeudal motives,

149

made one last appeal to a radical notion of property and livelihood as natural rights.

But on the horizon could be seen the outlines of a new epoch of Japanese social history, in which the rise of capitalism would force the class struggle into new forms. The intention of the last two chapters is not to show the country aflame with peasant revolts, though there were certainly plenty of them. Rather it is, first, to focus on different strata of the rural population as they became actively involved in conflicts and were militarily suppressed during a period of political confusion, extreme price inflation, and suffering. Second, the aim is to describe key moral and economic consequences of the triumph of capitalism and state centralization in Japan, and in that way to indicate exactly how those new forms of class struggle emerged.

To understand nineteenth-century protest struggles in Japan and to relate them to stages in the collapse of the bakuhan state, a general outline is needed of the main historical trends, landmarks, and episodes in the process leading to the Restoration. Accordingly, the last period of feudal political disintegration, culminating in the Meiji Restoration, may be divided roughly, for convenience of exposition, into three phases: 1800 to 1830, 1830 to 1859, and 1860 to 1873.

The first phase was a thirty-year period of outward social calm and demographic stagnation in which feudal society changed strictly in accordance with its own internal dialectic. The second phase, 1830 to 1859, began with a great national famine and ended with the signing of the unequal treaties. This was the prologue to the Restoration, when signs appeared of a quickening of economic growth and population increase. The third phase began in 1860, when foreign trade under the unequal treaties commenced in earnest. This thirteen-year period, ending with the land-tax reform and conscription in 1872–1873, is usefully viewed in terms of the spread of diverse conflicts at three different levels.

First, the relationship between Tokugawa society and the bakuhan state was influenced by imperialist political and economic pressures. These took such direct forms as the British shelling of Satsuma in July 1863 and the British-Dutch-French-U.S. naval bombardment of Chōshū to open the Shimonoseki Straits in August 1864. External pressure also included indirect and steadily mounting involvement in the Restoration process itself by the British, French, and American diplomatic corps. Imperialist pressures grew in tandem with the deepening power struggle within the samurai ruling class.

This second, far more important, level of conflict involved the Kyōto imperial court, Satsuma and Chōshū fiefs, and various pro-emperor activists. The complex military and political movement of articulate actors occupied, at all times, the historical foreground. But its true nature and full significance cannot be appreciated without grasping the protest struggles of the overwhelming majority that unfolded beneath, around, and finally, in opposition to it.

Thus, class struggles in villages, towns, and cities constituted the third level of conflict, which is the one we are interested in. Many of the material factors in response to which they developed had their starting point in the unequal treaties. The measures taken by the bakufu to cope with problems arising from foreign trade while, at the same time, preserving intact its trimetallic currency system, also precipitated rural unrest.[1] In judging the causes of the peasant risings of the 1860s, not only must the moral atmosphere of the times be treated but so too must a wide range of such relevant material antecedents. Consideration has to be given to rampant price inflation and currency disorders stemming partly from the currency clauses under article 5 of the Japan-U.S. Treaty of Commerce and its annex provisions. The fluctuating exchange rate between the Mexican dollar, which was the unit of trade in nineteenth-century Asia, and the Japanese silver and gold coin was a second material factor leading to popular unrest. Another factor was the bakufu's own currency "reform" of 1860, which reduced the gold content of the ryō, thereby restoring Japan's international currency parity at the expense of its domestic parity. Subsequently, the indiscriminate minting and forced circulation of devalued notes and debased coins by the bakufu and daimyo governments, and later by the new Meiji regime, also promoted widespread suffering. Foreign trade played its part by generating disturbances in the structure of incomes and of commodity distribution in agricultural export–producing regions. Nor is it possible to overlook the role of increased tenant rents and military and civil reforms, which were financed by stepped-up exploitation of peasants in the form of rice tributes and corvées. At different times and in different places over the period 1860 to 1873, one or more of these factors contributed directly to the impoverishment and misery of large numbers of people. In so doing, they stimulated their participation in antifeudal ikki, yonaoshi protests, rice riots, urban riots, and legal village disputes against the actions of local officials. To see how these came about, we shall have to look more closely at each period.

THE FIRST PHASE: 1800–1830

When the nineteenth century opened in East Asia, Japan's seclusion policy and its feudal mode of production were still intact politically. The opposition of classes and groups within the bakuhan state continued to be shaped by an internal dialectic of change undetermined by the world market and world politics. Most violent social struggles had ended. By the 1800s, bakufu and daimyo reformers could congratulate themselves in having secured at least outward compliance with feudal laws. They had also learned to be more calculating in the pursuit of such mundane goals as collecting tributes, levying enterprise taxes on peasant commodity production, and promoting the development of special products in the interests of their particular domains.

But in pursuit of these objectives, which aimed ultimately at stemming their own fiscal decline as a ruling class, they were forced, almost involuntarily, to increase their dependence on rich peasants and privileged merchants. Henceforth, every successful political defense they made of their own position was matched by a corresponding social advance by the top stratum of the peasant and merchant classes. Domanial rulers had no choice but to tolerate the growth of a commoner culture, which ended irrevocably their own monopoly on learning. They had to lean harder on their own retainers by cutting their stipends whenever economic difficulties became acute, which in turn spread discontent and demoralization within their own ranks. In this situation—and with Western ships beginning to ply the coasts of Japan—the daimyo and their fief elders reemphasized neo-Confucianism, an ideology that reaffirmed the traditional view of peasants as stupid, lowly creatures and of merchants as unclean, crafty money-grubbers. From the start of the nineteenth century, therefore, ruling-class ideology, with its emphasis on the strict separation and hierarchical subordination of occupational classes, functioned to aggravate structural tensions within the Tokugawa polity.

Meanwhile, structural changes that had started earlier, in the middle and last decades of the eighteenth century, continued. For example, regional markets, centering on Osaka, Nagoya, the Inland Sea region, and the Kantō Plain, specialized in different agricultural commodities and became more clearly defined. As they broadened their geographical spheres, they developed at a faster rate in all parts of the country. Also, within villages quantitative economic divisions deepened between upper-, middle-, and lower-stratum peasant households. Simultaneously, qualitative differences increased between the upper stratum of landlord peasants who served as village officials and all others in the village. Despite feudal laws and customary restraints on the full alienation of land, more and more peasants found themselves forced into tenancy relations to landlords and merchants. In commercially developed regions, such as the three Kinki provinces of Settsu, Kawachi, and Izumi, rich peasants and rural merchants joined more frequently in lawsuits against privileged castle town merchants and the powerful produce wholesalers of Osaka.

At the same time, educational institutions proliferated and literacy spread to even the most remote mountain villages. New knowledge of agricultural techniques and of social organization led to new activities. Increasingly, peasants and rural merchants gained new capabilities for moral and cultural growth that they had previously lacked. The growth of village culture also furnished new ideological mediums through which the struggle of classes could be waged.

But here the cultural orientations of upper-stratum peasants need to be distinguished from those of poor peasants. Sugi Hitoshi examined the cultural activities of peasants living in the commercially developed Kantō Plain villages along the upper reaches of the Tama River, between the Oume and Kōshū highways (present-day Tama district, Tokyo), during the period 1805–1830. He found that the daily activities and pastime pursuits of the upper stratum covered all fields: haiku poetry and linked verse, satirical verse, novels, floral art, tea ceremony, divination, book acquisition, and nationalist learning.[2] Rural village culture, he argued, was producing a small army of village officials, landlords, and merchants of outstanding capabilities. While accumulating wealth from farming, landlord operations, household industry, and especially grain brokering, they were also intent on finding new forms of cultural and ideological expression and new strategies for dealing with the problems of an increasingly restrictive system of feudal controls. For such peasants, this was a period of legal struggles to expand their scope of freedom for commercial activity. The period also saw the formation of regional cultural associations and the beginnings of the cultivation of the martial arts, nationwide, as a specifically landlord countermeasure against threats from the village poor.[3]

Earlier, in 1784, "some tens of thousands of peasants from about 37 villages of Tama district" rose up and destroyed the homes of local merchants.[4] Afterward, social calm returned to the Tama district. From the 1790s onward, the village poor in the Tama district shied away from collective actions. Instead, they turned increasingly to religion, hoping to find in different deities security for their villages and personal salvation from a world of hunger and the constant threat of famine. Sugi termed the 1800–1830 period an age of "deities in fashion" for the poor. Entire regions experienced waves of religious ferment during which new cults sprang up centering on local deities of Shintoist, Buddhist, and miscellaneous provenance. Through such shrine deities, the poor expressed their longing for a transformation of their own deadlocked situations. Their religious movements in these decades usually remained under firm village-official control and did not become overly political. But in the Tama district, by the late 1830s, religious movements sometimes did elude control by the rural elite. When that happened, threats or actual attacks were made by the heads of poor households against the property of the village rich.[5] In response, the latter strengthened their own defense setups by building upon their already existing cultural associations formed before 1830. Long before the Bushū yonaoshi rising (June 1866) engulfed the Tama district, the village elite had organized themselves militarily to protect their property.

Two points should be kept in mind from this discussion. The cultural activities of the poor and middle-strata peasants of the Tama district, even when they expressed themselves in religious form, were as much a motive force for change during the long calm of the early nineteenth century as the activities of the village elite. Second, as the gap widened between the elite and the rest of the village, the poor, feeling themselves unprotected both physically and morally, turned to new religions. These gave expression to their deep longing for economic equality and security, but without helping most of them to achieve it.

THE SECOND PHASE: 1830–1859

In the second period these trends became more pronounced. The number of poor peasants living in villages impoverished by feudal tributes and merchant usurers increased, though at a rate that is not easily measured. At the same time, there developed among many chronically indebted peasants new religions that preached the virtues of self-help, such as Tenri, Konkō, Kurozumi, Maruyama, and Fuji-ko. Harootunian suggests that these new religions represented the first step of a secession by the poor from the bakuhan state. They expressed, he says, more than a "heightened awareness of the necessity for relief and assistance." Ultimately, they were "an active enunciation of the ideal of world renewal in the form of universal relief and assistance." [6]

But he may be too quick to see in the new religions, and the type of moralism they fostered, an outlet for antifeudal feeling and thought. It seems more plausible that these religions impeded rational understanding of social structure and the real causes of social contradictions. Essentially, the new religions taught poor peasants to do their best within the limits of the status quo by overcoming their own personal weaknesses. What they fostered was thus not world renewal but self-renewal and reconciliation. In directing the struggle effort inward, moreover, they dampened rather than promoted class conflict, just as salvationist cults (which elevate personal salvation over justice) have done throughout history. On the other hand, the new religions helped some poor peasants to help themselves by taking a stand against, rather than fatalistically resigning themselves to, immediate circumstances, as they had been doing. [7] No doubt, too, they paved the way for a peculiar bourgeois morality among poor peasants.

Along with a problem of mass poverty, and the phenomenon of new religions as a direct response to it, the second three decades of the nineteenth century were dominated by a rising level of political dissent. This trend became noticeable during the famine years of Tenpō (1830–1844), when Japan registered a total of 1,012 struggle incidents nationwide. These included 455 ikki, 102 urban riots, and

465 village disturbances. The peak years were 1837 and 1838, after which the annual number of violent episodes declined over the remainder of the period from 1844 to 1859.[8] Another numerical analysis puts the figure at 365 ikki in the decade 1831 to 1841, 131 cases between 1842 and 1850, and 136 cases between 1851 and 1859.[9]

These collective actions were, generally speaking, highly organized (often by village associations acting in concert), carefully targeted against the property rather than the persons of the rich, and preceded by a long period during which the peasant leaders attempted unsuccessfully to negotiate their grievances. In these respects they were traditional. Where they differed most from eighteenth-century protests was in having a more prominent yonaoshi character. Also, occurring in a period when the possibilities for material improvement were greater than ever before, they revealed a scale of class consciousness that was gradually becoming regional and national rather than merely fief-bound. One of the most interesting signs of this progress in struggle over the course of the period was the joining of the peasant class paradigm of world renovation with the radical elements within the paradigmatic samurai ideology of neo-Confucianism. When the ruler lacked benevolence, the Wang Yang-ming (Ōyōmei) school of neo-Confucianism justified punitive revolt against the state. The bloody, armed Osaka insurrection of 1837 planned and led by Ōshio Heihachirō, to which we now turn, shows vividly how an ikki movement led by wealthy peasants could link up with samurai dissent.

Ōshio's Insurrection

Ōshio was a locally resident police official of the bakufu, attached to the office of the Osaka eastern town magistrate. As an hereditary police bureaucrat (yoriki), his occupational position was higher and more secure than that of the bailiffs who were his subordinates. More important, the social stratum he represented was intimately involved in investigating and suppressing peasant risings and in hearing lawsuits. In 1823 and 1824, for example, peasant representatives from 1,460 villages in the provinces around Osaka brought suit against three privileged Osaka cotton wholesalers, seeking to stop their interference in the sale of raw cotton. The case was brought to the magistrate's office where Ōshio worked. Among the peasant representatives at that time were two who later became Ōshio's supporters. Interestingly, the second lawsuit pertaining to cotton ended in victory for the peasants.[10]

By the 1830s, police officials like Ōshio were showing signs of increasing discontent with the bakuhan state. Ōshio had once taken temporary leave from his official duties to open his own school of Wang Yang-ming neo-Confucian studies.

Now, in 1830, his superior, the eastern town magistrate, retired and Ōshio, at age thirty-eight, followed suit in order to devote himself entirely to scholarship. Still, his interest in peasants remained even after his retirement. In the mid-1830s, Osaka began to feel the effects of the Tenpō famine, as scores of thousands of desperately poor people, many of them dying of hunger, poured into the city. At about the same time, over seven thousand peasants rose up in the vicinity of the Kako River in Harima province. They raised aloft a flag saying "Abandon life for the sake of the people" and a banner inscribed with the words "World renewal by the Long-Nosed Demon Matahachi." [11] Because his former police colleagues and subordinates were dispatched to investigate this rising and arrest the leaders, Ōshio had personal knowledge of it. Later he wrote, "In the vicinity of Harima the rice price per *koku* soared and this disturbance resulted. It was suppressed somehow but it is really a deplorable situation. There will be many casualties. For a benevolent person it is a matter of deep regret." [12]

Moved by traditional Confucian and ruling-class paternalism for the poor, Ōshio began to counsel his former superiors on how to organize relief for them. But his advice and appeals on behalf of the "humble people" went unheeded. The magistrates, aware of Edo's continued dependence on Osaka for key commodities, persisted in giving the shogun's capital priority in the shipment of rice rather than organizing poor relief for Osaka.

In early 1837, with peasant ikki occurring throughout the country, Ōshio felt he could wait no longer and began preparations for punishing the ruler in order to change "heaven's mandate." "On February 2 he sold off his entire library of fifty thousand volumes and, with the one thousand ryō obtained from the sale, donated one *shu* [1/6 of a ryō] to each of ten thousand houses of poor peasants and city poor. Then he divorced his wife, disowned his children, procured arms and ammunition and began to have his manifesto printed." [13]

The summons Ōshio drew up on behalf of the peasants clearly identified three adversaries: the Osaka town magistrates and their subordinates, the rich merchants of Osaka, and the shogun and his highest officials. It also declared, in the course of identifying their crimes, that "we can no longer stand the situation. . . . In the interests of the whole country . . . we punish the ruler and execute heaven's punitive will." He signed the summons: "Upholding heaven's mandate, we will execute heaven's punishment. Villages of Settsu, Kawachi, Izumi and Harima. To all village chiefs, elders, peasants and minor peasants." [14]

Ōshio chose to attack the regime in Osaka castle on February 19, 1837, the day on which the two magistrates were scheduled to tour the city. But his preparations were incomplete and his timing off. By February, the town magistrates had begun preparations for distributing rice within the city; rich merchants were distributing cash to the poor in order to counter rumors that they were cornering the market and sending rice prices soaring; and in the month of February the rice price itself had by no means reached its peak.[15] But owing to the treachery of a few samurai disciples, who leaked his plans to the city officials, Ōshio felt compelled to strike even though he knew conditions were not ripe.

In this first armed insurrection of peasants in alliance with samurai against the bakufu, about three hundred heavily armed volunteers joined Ōshio. They included a small group of disciples from his own school, a much larger number of rich peasants, some of whom were village officials and big landlords, and ordinary peasants and outcasts from nearby villages. His mainstay leadership group numbered about thirty. Eleven of them were low-status bakufu officials of police bureaucrat and bailiff rank. Twelve were wealthy peasants. Of this latter group, Hashimoto Chūbei, the headman of Hannyadera village, who raised money for the project, was thought to be Ōshio's most trusted follower and related to him by marriage. Most of the other peasant leaders were large landlords and money lenders. Other members of the core group of thirty were two doctors, two Shintō priests, two men of unknown occupation, and only one masterless samurai.[16]

Interestingly, the low-status samurai officials joined Ōshio as individuals, but the majority of his followers were commoners of rich peasant background who participated en masse, involving many others from their home villages.[17] Further, although Ōshio and his trusted followers organized in town districts and in villages on the outskirts of Osaka and along the left bank of the Yodo River (which runs through Osaka), they did not try to win the hearts and minds of the peasant masses. Instead they organized mainly other rich peasants, expecting them to join spontaneously with the rural and urban poor when the moment came for action. But when that time arrived, Ōshio's samurai-style military preparations and behavior did not commend themselves to poor peasants whose values were diametrically opposed to redemptive killing.[18] When the rising began, the landlords who led it did not link up with the city poor, nor did they obtain the participation even of their own direct tenants. Ōshio's fatally mistaken political strategy and tactics, together with his strong sense of samurai elitism, cut him off from the poorest strata of peasants who, at that very moment, were rising up in rural areas throughout western Japan. Thus, as Terao Gorō noted, his insurrection was in the nature of a commoners' struggle led by a samurai who had transformed himself from "a fighting arm of feudal power" into a champion of peasants.[19]

Several other historically significant features of this incident should be noted. First, before Ōshio's forces were decimated in their attempt to advance toward Osaka castle, they set afire about one-fifth of the city; estimates range from eighteen thousand to twenty thousand houses in the business centers. During the ensuing street fighting and confusion caused by the fire, Ōshio himself disappeared. For nearly forty days his whereabouts remained unknown to the authorities, while news of his deed spread far and wide. When his burned corpse was finally discovered, Ōshio had been transformed by the peasants into a martyr. The symbolic diffusion effects of his action proved far more important, and successful, than the action itself. For though it came upon them like a thunderbolt, the people immediately welcomed it. In Osaka, many commoners including even merchants who had been burned out, credited "the blessings of Ōshio-sama" with the official aid that afterward came into the city and with the increase in construction jobs. In Edo, officials reported that "all the people sympathize with and favor Ōshio," and "everyone took comfort in his action." [20]

Further, from around the time of Ōshio's insurrection, a few low-status bakufu officials began to participate in peasant risings. In June 1837, Ikuta Yorozu, a scholar of National Learning, under the influence of "Ōshio's great example" staged an armed uprising with fifteen followers in Kashiwazaki, Echigo province. The next month Yamadaya Daisuke, an Osaka pharmacologist rather than a bakufu official, led a rising of about fifteen hundred peasants in northern Settsu province. But also participating in this action was a discontented constable, one Motohashi Mitsujirō, who had been enticed to lend his support by the prospect of a new job.[21] These few instances of discontent among low-level bakufu officials should not be exaggerated. But coming in the wake of Ōshio's action, they probably increased the sense of crisis among many daimyo at the time. For the historian, however, the more interesting phenomenon is the widening sphere of matrimonial relations among rich peasants, which these incidents reveal. By way of matrimony and through ties of local origin, samurai families of low status were uniting with families of rich peasants who had risen to positions of economic prominence in their villages.[22]

Another noteworthy point is the coming together of samurai, rich peasants, and commoners in an armed revolt against the bakufu. Having been influenced by the ikki struggles of the time, Ōshio gave expression to those influences in his political practice. Najita, in his study of Ōshio, stresses that "Ōshio's radicalism did not provide a basis for coordinating his potential followers into a unified structure." [23] Although that is certainly true, the importance Najita places on "unified structure" misleadingly implies that a strong leadership organization is necessary if a coalition of social groups is to achieve its aims. But under certain conditions of political crisis, in certain historical periods, spontaneous popular revolts can effectively contribute to the toppling of states. And mass movements of poor people can succeed in winning their demands without a central organization's imposing itself upon and making choices for them.[24]

Moreover, the absence of a "unified structure" should not lead us to minimize the great moral and symbolic consequences of the insurrection Ōshio led. In this case, the problem of the individual and his ideology is less important than the sociology of the alliance that he momentarily forged with upward-striving peasants who were acquiring samurai status through marriage or in other ways. Within twenty years of Ōshio's action, disaffected sections of the ruling class, pondering the overthrow of either the bakufu or a particular domanial clique government, would not fail to consider ways of incorporating peasant grievances and slogans into their plans, just as Ōshio had done.

Finally, Ōshio's revolt is an example of how, under the dual stimulus of peasant suffering and Wang Yang-ming thought, a conservative intellectual of the ruling class came to furnish a Confucian moral sanction for justifying yonaoshi-type popular feelings. As such, it is a convenient point from which to mark the start of disaffections from the bakuhan system by samurai intellectuals, administrators, and lowly constables who were strategically situated at its very base, sharing the concerns of the village communities they supervised. But the growth of a dissident stratum within official ruling-class ranks was still at an early stage and did not presuppose any intention on the part of samurai to found a different, nonfeudal type of state.

During the 1840s, despite the dual shocks of the Ōshio insurrection and China's defeat in the Opium War, Japan's feudal ruling class as a whole still did not feel threatened internationally; and the weight of the domestic threat they did feel was not sufficient to justify any structural departures from the types of reform they had been accustomed to pursue in times of acute financial crisis.

Most fief and bakufu reforms of the 1830s and 1840s were reactionary in nature and undertaken in response to intense pressure from below. As seen in the generally unsuccessful bakufu reforms of 1841–1843, directed by the chief councillor Mizuno Tadakuni, their aims were, first of all, to demobilize and depoliticize the peasantry in areas where ikki had occurred. Through sumptuary regulations and moral exhortations, they sought to impose a stricter discipline on all ruled classes. In bakufu domains the reforms increased feudal levies on the peasantry, restrained commerce, and checked urban growth. Aiming to bring down commodity prices, Mizuno disbanded urban guilds, a move that favored rural merchants and artisans. But this measure succeeded only at the cost of further disrupting the market economy in the shogun's domains. It did mark, however, a step in the direction of implementing an expanded market control system that included rural merchants.[25]

Of course, no terse and partial listing such as this could possibly exhaust the range of reforms undertaken in the Tenpō period. But it is enough to show that, as far as the bakufu was concerned, they entailed no drastic structural departures from the previous shogunal reform tradition. Ultimately, the Tenpō Reforms could not succeed in controlling a market system that was being constantly undermined by new commodity exchange through regional markets and by the strengthening of fief autonomy.

The Unequal Treaties

The last of the major developments of the 1830–1859 period was the abrupt, forced opening of feudally backward Japan to Western-style diplomatic, trade, and commercial relations. Although Western ships had been encroaching on Japan's seclusion ever since the late eighteenth century, the opening process began suddenly when the Perry expedition arrived in 1853. Subjected to Perry's threats and gunboat diplomacy, the bakufu signed a navigation treaty with the United States the next year. Four years later, in 1858, the bakufu signed unequal economic treaties with the United States, Holland, Russia, Britain, and France.

Significantly, these treaties of peace, friendship, and commerce preceded the opening of the ports and created the essential legal and material conditions for Japan's subsequent incorporation into an expanded worldwide market, dominated at the time by Britain. Further, the treaties were highly unequal in that they deprived the bakufu of its fiscal, tariff, and currency autonomy. They also specified the opening of treaty ports and later, starting in 1863, served as pretext for allowing English and French troops to be stationed on Japanese soil until they were withdrawn in 1875. At the same time, the treaties granted to foreign powers most-favored-nation treatment, without requiring reciprocal treatment for Japan, and also granted to foreign nationals rights of extraterritoriality in visiting or residing in Japan. However, the one thing they did not grant, though Western diplomats insisted on it, was the right for foreign merchants to travel and conduct business in the interior. This important omission effectively confined them to a few treaty-port settlements on the coast, where Japanese merchants quickly gathered to act as their conduits and middlemen in trade. Thus, the implantation and subsequent "advance of capitalism in Japan" would take place entirely under indigenous auspices; and the result would be a distinctive type of capitalism. Here we have not only one of the earliest examples of how the fact of political independence determined the form of economic dependency. We also have a salutary reminder that in the nineteenth century different Western bourgeoisies were making an impact on very different types of non-Western societies. The result would be a multiplicity of paths of interdependent social transformation.[26]

In 1859 the treaty ports of Yokohama, Nagasaki, and Hakodate were opened and Japan received its first experience of "free trade." But it was not until the following year, 1860, that actual trade in the treaty ports got fully underway. The start of foreign trade was now to have profoundly dislocating effects on the

Tokugawa currency system and eventually on the entire, no longer autonomous, structure of the Japanese economy.

THE THIRD PHASE: 1860–1873

The opening up of Japan in the decade of the 1860s was, of course, a global rather than an isolated phenomenon. It marked the definite ending of the long historical epoch in which the non-Western peoples in Asia, Africa, Latin America, and Oceania could exist and develop in isolation from the world capitalist market system and its cycles of long and short duration.[27] Increasingly, from the third quarter of the nineteenth century onward, the bourgeoisies of Europe and North America acquired the power to change (or to leave unchanged) to their own advantage, the economic structures of countries all over the globe. It then became impossible for non-Western societies and states to avoid entering into some kind of subordinate relationship to the capitalist market system dominated by the leading Western nations.

In treating the process of historical change in Japan during the 1860s and early 1870s from the viewpoint of its dominated classes, three important characteristics stand out. One has already been noted: even during the very last stage of its collapse, the bakuhan state was able to actively mediate and transform the power of imperialism to change and disrupt the domestic economy. On the other hand, precisely because the bakufu and fief governments feudally controlled supply and demand relations through monopoly regulations and structures, the disruptive effects of foreign trade on the price structure were perceived by the ruled as an "internal factor" for which the bakufu and the various daimyo regimes were blamed, in spite of all their efforts to turn popular discontent outward.[28]

The second characteristic of the 1860s is the coincidence of deepening imperialist penetration with stages of Japanese political mobilization. Through the concrete mechanisms of unequal treaties and trade, imperialism may be said to have stimulated in countless ways the successive political mobilization of different classes and strata. The mobilization process started with the most politically advanced and favorably situated groups and ended with the least politically advantaged and situated. In the course of it, partly as a result of centuries of xenophobic indoctrination, all classes and strata were open to manipulation on the divisive racial and ethnic issue of the foreign presence in Japan. But in their cultural and ideological capacities for responding to the rapidly changing circumstances in which they found themselves, peasants, merchants, samurai, and lords differed greatly.

The emperor and the Kyoto court nobles were the first to be precipitated into open opposition to the bakufu by the signing of the unequal treaties in 1858. Their activities inaugurated the Restoration process within the samurai class, where many powerful daimyo and educated samurai (activists and thinkers) had the capacity for conceptualizing a different form of state to meet the dual threat to their class rule from within and without. But for two years, until the assassination in 1860 of the shogun's chief councillor, Ii Naosuke, the bakufu managed to control and contain dissent within ruling circles.

Then, between 1860 and 1863, the dislocating effects of foreign trade on supply and demand relationships helped to spread political conflicts outside ruling circles and downward to other classes. In these years, as the volume of exports and imports shot up, rich peasants, landlords, and rural merchants responded politically both to its antifeudal effects and to its opportunities for expanded domestic trade. Agitated also by peasant demands pertaining to land and rent, they began to participate in the Restoration process in a dependent alliance with different samurai factions.

Thus the effects of foreign trade on the domestic economy, as mediated by bakufu and fief administrators, together with growing class conflict in villages, set the educated rural elite into ferment. As that happened, vast numbers of peasant cultivators spawned from the poor and middle strata of the villages, together with the urban poor who were situated below them, moved into action. They were responsive less to the symbolic politics of the samurai and court than to the crop-growing cycle, the rice price, the weather, and their own tradition of protest. Usually, too, their struggles unfolded independently of the different samurai political coalitions and groupings forming and re-forming around them. But without their participation in large numbers, the success of the samurai-led military movement to sweep away the outmoded political and judicial structures erected by the bakufu is inconceivable.[29]

The third characteristic of the historical process in the 1860s and early 1870s was the appearance on the political stage of this mass of peasants, with the middle and lower strata in the vanguard and behind them, participating in a follower capacity, propertyless, indebted semiproletarians. However, we need to pause briefly before examining this third mobilization. For just as the ideological limitations of peasant protesters should not be obscured or exaggerated, so the polarity between samurai and peasants during the final decade of the bakuhan state should also not be exaggerated. Here a brief digression, in the form of a comparison with the mid-nineteenth-century peasant movement in tsarist Russia and its larger institutional context, may serve to put in perspective the issue of class polarization. Such a comparison may also help to suggest the difficulty of estimating its level.

The Japanese people never experienced a peasant war such as Russia's bloody Pugachev Rebellion of 1773–1775. But the agrarian movement in Japan displayed some common features with the Russian movement while also raising certain historic demands that were not unlike those articulated by Russian peasants both before and after Alexander II's Act of Emancipation of 1861. What separated the two peasantries, not only in their relations with their rulers but in the types of class solidarities they exhibited, were historical, ideological, and contextual differences.

To begin with, the mid-nineteenth-century tsarist state was not feudal and, despite its military debacle in the Crimean War, it was far stronger as an absolutist regime than the weakened, semicentralized bakuhan state. For that very reason, however, it was also more directly threatening to Russian peasants. Before 1861, the latter had the legal status of serfs but were locked into various forms, conditions, and degrees of servitude. Since the development of a commodity-money economy gradually penetrated agricultural production relations in Russia just as it did in Japan, the actual content of Russian serf status around the time of the reforms remains to be determined empirically. It may not have been too different from Japanese hereditary peasant status. However, the normative and physical contexts, as well as the communal structure within which Russian peasants lived out their lives, were certainly different; and illiteracy among Russian peasants was incomparably higher than in Japan. (In 1897 the national male illiteracy rate for the Russian peasant estate was officially estimated at 72 percent.)[30]

Second, as a result of the tsar's agricultural reforms of the 1860s, most peasants were left with about 85 percent of their original lands, while 15 percent was lost to them. Over a decade before limited bourgeois landownership rights began to be established in Japan, ownership of the land in Russia was granted to nominally free peasants under specific conditions. They had to pay a land tax and also make fairly large redemption payments in forty annual installments. These were payments to the state, if they had been serfs on state lands, and to nobles, if they had labored on private estates. So, the agricultural reforms gave peasants their personal freedom from serfdom. But they were implemented in such a way as to shift control over peasants from nobles to the state, while simultaneously leaving unresolved the concrete conditions of peasant freedom. Thereafter the land issue in Russia centered on those conditions. Politically, the tsar's reforms deepened the cleavage between the villages and the state. Economically, they failed to offer inducements to either peasants or nobles to use their accumulated savings for improving agricultural production. After 1861, as before, extreme poverty remained the lot of Russia's villages.[31]

Third, the differences between Russian and Japanese landlords must be noted. Unlike typical Japanese landlords, who were bound to their status as peasants and often shared common burdens with ordinary peasants, landlords in Russia were isolated nobilities living far from their estates. They were also firmly subordinated to the centralized state. Nobles served in the tsar's bureaucracy and army and left many of their estates in the hands of a hierarchy of administrators. Quite often their estate managers were Germans and Jews or other outsiders to the village who were hostile to peasants and loyal to noblemen. A chasm that was social, physical, structural, and even ethnic in nature thus separated Russian nobles from their peasants. Cultural differences widened that chasm even further.[32]

Another point of difference that must be emphasized is that Russian peasants believed the land belonged ultimately to God on whose account the tsar exercised supreme power.[33] In times of distress, they appealed to the tsar for deliverance. It has been said that the "myth of the Tsar-Deliverer" represented their "vision of justice, which was the cultural property of the peasantry as a class."[34] While that is undoubtedly true, the myth was also based on two real occurrences. Before the nineteenth century, when the peasants of European Russia suffered from Mongol (or Tartar) groups who raided their villages to take slaves, their only real defender was the tsar's army, which fought to stamp out the slave trade. And in 1861, when the nobility opposed the granting of land to peasants to go along with their personal freedom, Tsar Alexander II "delivered" for the peasants in opposition to his own nobles. Aware of this historical background, Russian peasants clung tenaciously to their belief in the tsar as deliverer and protector into the early twentieth century.[35]

Just when the myth of the Tsar-Deliverer and the symbolism of tsardom was decisively shattered is a vexed question. Most likely it was destroyed in stages. Moshe Lewin has speculated that from the 1860s onward "demographic and socioeconomic factors" were at work hastening the breakup of "big rural families into smaller 'nuclear' units, a process known as the 'nuclearization' of the family." As a result, "rural patriarchalism" also weakened, and along with it peasant "reliance on the magnified patriarchal figure of the top *khozyain* ["owner and chief"]. It also meant that a certain laicization of peasant political conceptions was setting in."[36] Political change accelerated such structural trends. Above all, the tsarist suppression of the great peasant rebellion and rural strikes of the years 1905–1907 was the decisive event. During that period tsarist troops and police invaded the villages. With whips, guns, and executions they brought peasants to the realization that the tsar would never grant their wish for the confiscation of nobles' land. Later, World War I brought an even more drastic situation to the villages. The mood of peasants who remembered how the army had once "put the fear of God and the Tsar" into them in 1905–1907 changed even more.[37]

But in the interval between their emancipation and the revolution of 1905–1907, Russian peasants held firmly to their belief in a monarchical savior.

They were also convinced that landlords had no right of use even to the land. In peasant eyes the real life mission of noble landlords was to be officers in the army and bureaucracy. And since the land belonged to god—that is, no one—Russian peasants fought to abolish outright all remaining landlord ownership per se. But their demands regarding land do not appear to have grown steadily more detailed over time. During the period 1861–1905, while they were struggling to make redemption payments and meet taxes and rent obligations, there was no apparent incremental increase in the concreteness of their demands. Only in 1905–1907 did they suddenly make a quantum leap in consciousness and grasp how much land they wanted and on what terms.[38]

Next, in Russia where most land was owned communally rather than by individual families, peasants had in the commune (*mir, obschina*) a much more independent and autonomous basis for resisting autocracy than the Japanese village. (Significantly, the Russian word *mir* has moral connotations, whereas the Japanese word for village, *mura*, has only neutral, administrative ones.) In the commune, Russian peasants made their own decisions concerning how and where to market their produce. They also elected their own part-time commune officials, headed by an elder, the *starosta*. The most important duty of the starosta and his assistants was to periodically reapportion obligations and land so as to avoid the impoverishment of households while maximizing economic efficiency.[39]

In this connection Shanin notes that "an assembly of heads of households ran the commune, deciding about services, electing officers, and collecting informal taxes or dues. Except for some areas in the west . . . the assembly also redivided the arable lands once in a while in accordance with egalitarian principles, usually to adjust for the changing size of families." [40] To this description Moore adds the important observation that the periodic redivision of property in land worked "to generalize land hunger" and "to align the richer peasants with the poorer ones." [41] The strong solidarity resulting from communal property arrangements Moore terms "radical," in contrast to the equally strong "conservative solidarity" found in Japanese villages.

Kolchin furnishes an interesting glimpse of this powerful tradition of radical communal solidarity as it operated in the year 1856:

The officials chosen [by the assembly of household heads] were consequently seen by the other serfs as their true representatives, who could deal with the outside world . . . on their behalf. When serfs were dissatisfied with their treatment and felt the need for redress, they turned instinctively to the commune. . . . communal leaders who refused to represent the villagers' interests often found themselves ignored or even replaced by more cooperative leaders. In 1856, when some serfs in Riazan province found themselves in a major dispute with their owner, Maj. Gen. P. E. Zavaritskii, their first act was to choose a new *starosta*, who announced to the owner and to the local police, "that he, elected *starosta* by the *mir*, would not recognize any authority except by the will of the *mir*." Reproached by Zavaritskii for his disobedience, the peasant leader replied, "I am just as much a general as you, since the *mir* elected me."[42]

Let us turn now from the Russian commune—a formation whose prototype and survivals can be found in many different historical settings—and consider the Japanese village.[43]

In contrast to peasants in Russia, Japanese peasants enjoyed a less harsh physical environment but a more tightly regulated social and economic one. Where Russian peasants practiced egalitarian inheritance. Tokugawa peasants (who did not experience the intact rural commune and thus lacked such a leveling mechanism) practiced nonegalitarian inheritance. In short, peasant property in the two countries evolved along different historical lines and was different in kind. The samurai ruling class recognized peasants as the agents of land possession. Law and local custom, on the other hand, prevented them from freely and openly selling it. Over many centuries Japanese peasants had grown accustomed to a structure of multi-tiered, conditional land possession. Within that framework, fief lords were, in principle, nonresident owners who guaranteed the cultivation rights of peasants in order to secure their own right of tribute from the same land. Lords were always the main beneficiaries of this form of landed property. By the middle of the nineteenth century, however, many Japanese peasants—perhaps one-third of all peasant households—were also surrendering part of their surplus to landlords as well as lords. But even when such landlords were village officials, they were not, as in Russia, intruding nobility. Rather, Japanese landlords were simply wealthier peasants residing in villages and cooperating with the fief administration. During yonaoshi-type risings, landlords and village officials became primary objects of punitive sanctions.

According to Moore's static definition, Japanese villages displayed a "conservative solidarity" based on "a division of labor that has behind it strong sanctions while at the same time it provides a recognized if humble niche for those with little property."[44] But it is more realistic to see the social cohesion in Japanese villages as the product of a dynamic situation in which the samurai ruling class was constantly imposing its will on the village. When samurai efforts became too threatening, peasants joined together (using the mechanism of ad hoc village associations) and displayed true solidarity. Their solidarity was conditioned, first, by how much land each household possessed and, second, by status consciousness and the sort of discipline that went along with it. If any political consequence can be derived from a Japanese type of village solidarity, then it was probably to direct attention *inward* to the system of exploitation *within* villages.

This was especially true in times of distress like the 1860s, when large numbers of small-scale, full-status peasants were being forced into landlessness and tenancy or becoming day laborers in rural towns. The conservative solidarity of Japanese villages thus reflected a particularly advanced phase in the breakdown of the hereditary status system and in the expropriation of minute-scale cultivators by landlords and rural merchants. By contrast, the radical solidarity of the Russian commune directed peasants' attention *outward* to the village's relationship with the state. This Russian externalization of conflict occurred on two levels. Communal villages contended against nobles who held land and represented the state; at the same time, they fought with the state power directly in the form of its army and police. (After 1906 they no longer distinguished the two.) In addition, Russian communal solidarity presupposed high social mobility within villages and a less advanced stage in the decomposition of the peasantry as a class than was the case in Japan.

Finally, Japanese peasants of the Tokugawa and early Meiji periods had a different religious mentality and were not yet staunch monarchists. Starting in the late nineteenth century, Japan's oligarchic rulers would succeed in inculcating emperor-worship as a way of forging a national community and deflecting class tensions outward against foreign enemies.[45] But that was definitely not the case at mid-century. In addition, Japanese peasants differed from Russian peasants in more or less eschewing the savior concept. They believed that the land belonged to the cultivator rather than to God. The cultivator established his possession partly by a sort of natural law and partly by means of early Tokugawa land policy, which, over a long period of time, had once sought to create full-status smallholders. The memory of that earlier Tokugawa policy conveniently served peasants as a weapon against the bakuhan state throughout the 1850s and 1860s.

Returning now to the Japanese popular movement, we find that what the antibakufu campaign of the samurai dared not touch between 1866 and 1873 the independent mobilization of Japan's rural population attacked directly: namely, the very pillars on which rested the entire feudal order. That is to say, the third or commoner mobilization (mentioned earlier in this chapter) targeted the system of class exploitation in villages. It also attacked two key features of the late feudal state: the system of domanial exploitation through tributes and corvées, and political controls on production and the circulation of commodities. Let us summarize the course followed by the Japanese popular movement down to 1873. By then political unification was achieved, fiefs and feudal stipends were abolished, prefectures were established, and the land-tax reform was in the process of being implemented.

In July 1866, bakufu forces failed in their second campaign to crush Chōshū fief and reassert the shogun's authority over Kyoto and the great lords of the southwest. That military defeat effectively destroyed its hegemonial pretensions to speak as the country's supreme public authority whose commands had, at all costs, to be obeyed. With its legitimacy in the eyes of the powerful daimyo and their officials ended and with many of its vassal fiefs, like itself, virtually bankrupt, the bakufu disengaged from the Chōshū front and tried to carry on with military and civil reforms in the Kantō region. Meanwhile a strange mood settled over the country as the rest of the daimyo balked at letting Satsuma and Chōshū lead the Restoration. Some daimyo simply withdrew their support from Edo and waited for events to take their course. Others were torn between rival probakufu and anti-bakufu factions. Precisely in this context of factional strife and political paralysis at the center of national affairs, a fierce wave of urban and rural disturbances spread over widely separated regions of Japan, further weakening the morale of pro-bakufu forces.

The Bushū Rising

The two such risings of greatest extent and destructive intensity occurred within days of each other in June 1866. Militarily and politically, the attention of the bakufu was diverted. For at that moment it was in the midst of its second campaign against Chōshū fief and its own military forces plus those of the Kantō area fudai daimyo were deployed in western Japan. Economically, the sericultural and the traditional cotton manufacturing regions of the country had been disrupted by the combined effects of Western capitalism and intensified exploitation by the rural rich. Specifically, the sericultural provinces of Kōzuke, Iwashiro, Musashi, and Shinshū had become tied to the world market through the treaty port of Yokohama. Despite bakufu efforts to discourage it, the volume of raw silk shipped through Yokohama had more than doubled in just five years, going from 7,703 piculs (65.6 percent of Japan's total foreign trade) in 1860 to 16,232 piculs (nearly 84 percent of total trade) in 1865. During that same period raw silk prices registered an over fivefold increase.[46]

Largely as a result, traditional price structures and commodity circulation routes were thoroughly disrupted, while the power of rural merchants was further strengthened at the expense of the urban guild merchants of Edo. In addition, the free trade regime had stimulated the formation of a new, more complex trading network, linking Japanese retail merchants with branch stores in Yokohama, via various intermediaries, to direct producers in the farming villages. Although some benefited from the silk trade, many more borrowed regularly to expand production and had their subsistences endangered by sharply rising prices for general commodities. The rice price alone rose nearly ninefold between 1857 and 1866.[47] This was the economic context in which the bakufu, in May 1866, put into effect new restrictions designed to reestablish its control over the silk export trade.

Disturbances in Fukushima and Bushū began a few weeks later. On June 14, in the Shinobu and Date districts of Fukushima fief in the northwest, there began to unfold a yonaoshi-type rising, which, before it ended, involved an estimated 170,000 peasants. The day before, peasants in Bushū (Musashi) province began a parallel rising, which soon spread through fifteen districts in Bushū and two districts in Jōshū, including part of Chichibu district and the Kantō Plain villages in the Tama district along the Tama River.

The Bushū disturbance lasted for only seven days, from June 13 to 19, and apparently involved little advance preparations. Nevertheless, peasants in vast numbers managed to organize themselves quickly into three types of groups. First came leader-organizer groups. Eyewitness reports describe them wearing head coverings made of silk wadding, fastened about with colorful headbands of white, dark red, and dark blue cotton. The leader-organizer groups decided strategy and tactics. Many leaders rode horses as they went from village to village recruiting by the usual coercive methods. Unconfirmed reports even speak of some being carried about in palanquins.[48]

Next came scouting companies of from two or three up to ten persons each. The scouts also wore headbands and operated directly under the leader groups. The third component consisted of house-smashing forces of from two thousand to three thousand each. Many wore traditional straw coats tied with colored cords. Though there must have been exceptions to the rule, the most recent study of the tools used in the Bushū rising concludes that, by and large, they carried with them only agricultural implements. These they christened "the tools of house-smashing."[49]

Using this three-division structure, not carrying military weapons, and avoiding clashes with samurai military forces, the peasant demonstrators focused their destructive fury on the property and possessions of local officials such as village headmen and their assistants, moneylenders, pawnshop operators, large landlords, and rural merchants. Merchants who engaged in foreign trade at Yokohama were especially assailed.

The first characteristic of the Bushū rising was the amazing discipline and solidarity of its participants. As many of the leaders stated at the time, their main aim was only "to save impoverished people" by bringing down grain prices and effecting the return of pawned land and goods. "The peasants, acting on their own thinking, are only to chastise the unjust and give the public an object lesson. [The party] does not dare to bring arms for harming human life."[50] In commenting on this aspect, Sippel writes that "military weapons were strictly prohibited by the leaders . . . and the sickles, axes, poles and other everyday implements used to break down houses rarely caused injury to the occupants. Victims, shocked at the violence of the attack on their property, were equally amazed at the absence of personal injury."[51]

Equally significant is the prominent role played by local peasant militia (nōhei) in the suppression of the Bushū rising. In Bushū the militia were recruited mainly from the top and middle strata of the villages. Many of them were officeholding merchants and large landowners. In this instance, they may be thought of as the repressive arm of the rich peasant class. Mobilized largely from within that class, they were also far more beholden to it (and to their own villages) than they were to the shogunal authorities who ordered them to fire on protesting peasants. In short, the militia seem to have obeyed the public authority not so much because they identified politically with it as because they feared the property destruction of the poor.

The first decisive clash of peasant militia, representing the interests of the village elite, and ikki forces, representing the poor, occurred on June 16 along the Tama River at Yagikubo, Tsukijigawara, and Irino villages. A second series of clashes took place two days later, on June 18, at Shinmichi, Honjō, and Fukaya in the northern Kantō Plain area. The last battle was fought the next day, June 19, with troops from the Shinobu fief and self-defense units composed of commoners from Ōmiya town.[52] With minor exceptions, which occurred during the clashes at Yagikubo village and Honjō, the ikki forces deliberately eschewed arming themselves with weapons of war. By adhering to their own ethical principle of bringing along only agricultural implements, they made their own defeat and punishment a foregone conclusion.[53] The colorful Bushū episode thus leaves the impression of a mass festival of property destruction, in which the ikki participants and the suppression forces knew in advance the inevitable outcome.

After the risings of 1866 were suppressed, the long crisis of feudal bakuhan rule entered its last stage. Early in 1867, a fourteen-year-old boy acceded to the throne in Kyōto as the new Meiji emperor. Then, in October 1867, the last shogun accepted an imperial court decree calling for the return of the Tokugawa domains to the emperor. Two months later, in December, another decree abolished the office of shogun and proclaimed a return to direct imperial rule.

Ee jya nai ka

In the interim between the January accession of the Meiji emperor and the December 1867 decree announcing the restoration of ancient imperial rule, the bakufu as a state regime collapsed and many small fiefs lost their power to maintain social order. As the tempo of political change rose to fever pitch, an ominous calm spread throughout the country. Then, suddenly, starting in July 1867 in Mikawa province, scene of earlier yonaoshi risings, a new social movement erupted. This one appeared to signal a renewal of the great mass pilgrimages that had appeared at intervals of about sixty years over the course of the Tokugawa period.

But unlike previous such movements, it showed greater experimentation with new modes of behavior. It was more exuberant, sexually open, and premeditated than those in the past. While it unfolded, the ethical idea of world renewal revealed itself in a new guise. Dancing movements broke out among the people and spread in frenzied fits and starts all along the eastern seaboard highway right up to the environs of Edo. From there the public dancing and street demonstrations moved into the interior provinces and westward to Ōsaka and Kyōto. In the excitement of the dancing, acts previously considered immoral were extolled as something good. Songs were sung with political overtones in the form of riddles. One couplet went: "Proposed: a good omen of *okage mairi*. I resolve that it is a great earthquake because the land of Japan moves." [54] Another song captured the dancers' happy mood and their idea of yonaoshi:

One—Unseen by others, everybody strives to be first in paying homage at Ise, just for world renewal.
Two—If couples get along well together, holy amulets will come raining down, just for world renewal.
Three—We decorate holy shrines beautifully with evergreen leaves, just for world renewal.
Four—Celebrating day and night, the stages play happy music with flutes and drums, just for world renewal.
Five—All too soon enormous numbers of people make rice cakes and celebrate, just for world renewal. . . .
Ten—Old people and children without exception fill up with rice cakes and sake, just for world renewal.[55]

One who has followed in detail this movement called *ee jya nai ka* ("who cares what happens," or "isn't it good"), Sasaki Junnosuke, concludes by extrapolating four distinguishing features.

First, it was composed mainly of the urban poor (men, women, and children) living in cities and towns and in villages near major post stations. Second, the main direct demand of the participants was for charity from the wealthy. But when charity was not given freely, they resorted to the "dance-in" (*odorikomi*)—a coercive technique whereby the dancers entered homes with their footwear on, wreaking destruction. Third, unfolding through definite stages, the ee jya nai ka movement shed its features of a tumultuous mass hysteria and at each stage gradually became more selectively violent, political, and antibakufu. Last, it was through the ee jya nai ka movement in its last stage that urban Japan, during late 1867, registered its response to the liquidation of the bakufu and gave expression to its hope for a more benevolent successor regime.[56] Ee jya nai ka, with its moral permissiveness and yearning for openness and equality, was precisely the right kind of movement to usher out the old regime.

The Intensification of Exploitation under the Meiji Regime

In January 1868, the combined forces of Satsuma and Chōshū launched their civil war against the bakufu in the Kyōto-Ōsaka region. After a few brief skirmishes the imperial forces defeated the ex-shogun's army and went on to eliminate the last vestiges of bakufu power in the Kantō region by April and in all of Honshū by November. Then, operating from their newly renamed capital, Tokyo, but with their power still based on their own fief organizations, the new Sat-Chō leaders set about constructing a temporary coalition regime against a background of mounting rural unrest. It was composed of court elements and representatives of most southwestern fiefs, and the loan money on which it depended during its first year came chiefly from powerful city bankers and merchants and, to a much lesser extent, from rural merchants and landlords, the very groups against whom the yona-oshi were directed. For the next four years the Meiji government ruled through the old fief system, retaining most daimyo in place as virtual civil servants. Village structures generally remained intact for purposes of social control.

The years 1868 and early 1869, the period of the Boshin civil war, brought more rampant inflation and acute suffering. In towns and villages, where people were mostly preoccupied with sheer survival, high hopes had been pinned on the renovation regime after the bakufu fell. But little changed. Decrees from the new Council of State in Tokyo merely confirmed that the shogunate was gone and that the ban on ikki and on the making of political parties still held. Everywhere in the countryside popular expectations were cruelly betrayed. Feudal levies and corvées remained and grew more onerous. Temple registers remained, as did the system of three important village officials. When it became clear that the new regime intended to raise taxes while keeping wants below the level of production, the number of peasant risings shot up dramatically.

During the first decade of Meiji, 1868 to 1878, there were, nationwide, at least 508 peasant risings. Over half of them (261) occurred during the first three years alone, with nearly three times the national average occurring in Shinshū province, where many small and medium-sized fiefs existed alongside the first directly administered prefectures established by the Meiji government.[57] Peasants who participated in these struggles usually demanded cash reductions in rice tributes, the lowering of rice prices, the dismissal of unjust village and district officials, the election of new ones, the reduction or elimination of feudal levies, reductions in tenant rent, and the return of pawned land and articles. Not surprisingly, they stopped short of demanding full land reform since that would have meant the abolition of the very system of multiple ownership that sustained them and the establishment of its direct opposite: exclusive, landlord-type ownership. Nevertheless, during 1869 and again in 1871, many poor peasants were excited by rumors and gossip of an impending equal land distribution in the form of an "equalization of fields between rich and poor" and an "edict of equalization."[58] But, partly because it conflicted with their own immediate interests and partly out of political ignorance, they themselves never raised it to the level of a political demand.

The new Meiji regime, which in 1869 and 1870 was still only a superstructure, had powerful reasons for not allowing this mounting peasant unrest, with its portent of increased power for peasants, to continue too long. Not only did it undermine the already weakened system of social control through village and fief officials; it also posed the danger of an alliance between peasant ikki and discontented samurai. Under these circumstances, the government moved swiftly to abolish the fief system altogether. In its most revolutionary series of reforms, it divided the entire country into prefectures controlled from Tokyo. Then, by force and legal deceit, it established a national land tax and a conscription system. Finally, it proceeded to strengthen the court and the emperor as the new axis for an absolutist centralized state.

The reforms of 1871–1873 definitely ended Japan's long feudal epoch. But it must also be stressed that they preserved aspects of feudalism in the countryside and, equally important, did not succeed either in immediately establishing modern bourgeois landownership. Bourgeois landownership rights, including the all-important right of landlords to confer jointly with their former feudal masters on tax matters, were established only in the course of a lengthy and bloody dual process. That process consisted of populist struggles during the 1870s and 1880s on the one hand and the economic collapse of traditional peasant-type landownership on the other.[59] Out of it was born the emperor-system state of late nineteenth-century Japan.

CHAPTER FOURTEEN

The Kaisei Rising in Tsuyama, 1866–1867

THE PROBLEM OF NAMING

FIVE months after the great yonaoshi risings in Fukushima and Bushū were suppressed by locally recruited and locally deployed peasant militia, another series of attacks occurred in various fiefs in the eastern Chūgoku region. They lasted over a two-month period, from mid-November 1866 to mid-January 1867, and are known to historians today as the "Kaisei" rising or ikki. That name, however, stems in part from a contemporary account allegedly written by one Kobayashi Sōsuke, a samurai doctor who viewed the episode from the perspective of the samurai factional struggle then underway in Tsuyama castle. According to Kobayashi's account, *Kaisei ichiranki*, the failure of Tsuyama fief's probakufu government to make needed reforms resulted in a "disturbance" (*ichiran*), which led finally to a "great political reform" (*kaisei*).[1]

Another contemporary text, anonymously authored but fairly sympathetic to peasants, titles it simply the *hinin sōdō*, meaning "poor people's disturbance."[2] From the viewpoint of the peasant participants, the whole affair was no doubt seen as a traditional ikki. The naming of this particular incident thus registers a historical problem. If one believes (as did historian Nagamitsu Norikazu, who excavated and annotated most of the relevant documents) that a yonaoshi vision, and yonaoshi-type demands concerning land and rent, gave these scattered attacks their full unity, then the contemporary naming, kaisei ikki—which also revealed Kobayashi Sōsuke's political affiliation—was entirely appropriate. However, *ikki* implies pluralistic participation by peasants representing not just the village poor but a wide range of socioeconomic strata within villages.

The title *hinin sōdō*, by contrast, implies a narrower social range of partici-

pation. It also highlights the ambiguous class nature of many who participated in
the episode. For *hinin* not only means "poor people" and "poor souls" but can also
mean "beggars" and "outcasts" standing at the bottom of the feudal class structure
and, in a sense, outside the state's formal technical classification. By deliberately
designating themselves hinin and hinindomo, many poor peasants may have intended a moral criticism of Tsuyama's samurai bureaucracy. But the very existence
of a large social stratum that no longer considered itself classified by fixed hereditary status meant that the status system itself had broken down and no longer functioned effectively as a mechanism of social control. This new self-image of the poor
is also suggestive of another point. Whether seen as a rising caused by a failure to
make necessary political reforms or caused by bad political reforms, or simply as
a "poor people's disturbance," the Kaisei rising registered an unintended "future
thrust." For the poor peasants and day laborers who furnished most of the energy
for it were precursors of Japan's industrial proletariat of the future. In that respect,
the Kaisei rising was similar to the other great peasant disturbances of the climactic
year 1866.

Finally, the main body of the Kaisei participants was indicative of Japan's future in a deeper sense. This was, first, because they were people who were slowly
losing control of their means of production or who had already done so. Second,
the political and ideological superstructure of the bakuhan state was changing
rapidly at this time, and as it changed, so too did the feudal class structure it partly
determined. The hinindomo of late Tokugawa–early Meiji Japan were thus a
component part of a rapidly changing class structure. By looking closely at a complex rising that combined strong ikki features and weaker yonaoshi elements,
we may now gain knowledge of how class relations changed during the initial
phase of Japan's transition to capitalism and how that change effected people's
consciousness.

CAUSES AND COURSE OF THE RISING

The Kaisei rising occurred when price inflation was at a record high, yonaoshi disturbances and ikki were flaring up across the country in unprecedented numbers,
and the start of civil war had dramatically weakened the shogun's power. In these
circumstances, an anonymous but sympathetic eyewitness, perhaps a village official, authored an account of the rising in 1868 that attributed it to a combination
of three factors.

According to the "Sakushū hinin sōdōki," blame fell first on Tsuyama fief's
"New Laws," or reforms, first introduced in 1861, and its merciless tax squeezes, in

effect since 1863. In that year, the fief government established a strict grain inspection system to ensure that only top-grade rice was paid in as tribute. Despite repeated winnowing of the rice,

the officials would find fault, saying this is good quality but that is not. Three bales out of every ten would be rejected and later four or five bales would be returned. Thus, out of ten bales, only two or three would pass without trouble.

At the rice inspection site, the fief employed inspection women. For every bale of rice they charged a commission of 0.25 sho for making up the bale. At the measuring site, they measured 33 sho and then charged, in the name of "actual measurement" (*ikemasu*), an additional 1.75 sho per 33 sho to make a regular bale. But according to the so-called Sakushū province tradition, the peasants put in to each bale as much as 36 sho. Even so, many bales were still designated as deficient. No matter how many bales of quality rice the peasants made up, there was a lot of returned rice, so that they suffered greatly.

Under these circumstances, though the peasants repeatedly petitioned in writing asking for merciful reductions in rice tribute, no sign of pity was ever shown them. Thus not only peasants but village officials were always in distress.[3]

The twin issues of rice tribute inspection and actual measurement were to figure prominently in peasant demands in the winter of 1866.

A second cause of the rising was the successive disruptions of local village life arising from political developments at the national level. Beginning in February 1863, Tsuyama's lord stationed himself in Kyōto, the new locus of national political activities. Around the same time, the alternate attendance system came to an end. This further complicated the political situation in the fief, since the retired lord, who had been living in Edo, and the incumbent lord's wife both returned to Tsuyama castle. Then in June 1865, the fief issued a military mobilization order to villages, which affected the sons of rich peasants. Finally, on top of these departures from custom, the shogun ordered two costly military campaigns against Chōshū fief which directly affected the entire Chūgoku region. Mounted on the backs of peasant laborers who were conscripted from villages to carry supplies, these military preparations further disrupted normal agricultural life and local society in general. Conversely, however, the cumulative effect of all these disruptions enabled some peasants to sense that extraordinary changes were in the offing and that they might well seize the moment to act in their own interests against the probakufu clique then in power in Tsuyama castle.

The third causal factor described in detail in the "Sakushū hinin sōdōki" was crop disasters in the summer and fall of 1866.

In May, after the plants took root, it rained fairly heavily and there were unseasonably cold temperatures. However, everybody was pleased because there was no crop destruction from insects. But in the middle of July, following the early crops which turned out badly—and just when the middle and late crops were about to ripen—unusually cold weather arrived, causing anxiety and perplexity. Then from early afternoon on August 7, a northern wind began to blow. By 8 o'clock that evening, it had become a huge north wind and by next morning all the rice plants, and even small huts, had been blown away. Heavy rains after the crops took root, cold weather from the middle of July and great winds in August—these three great disasters reduced crops to 40 percent of the normal harvest.[4]

As the winter of 1866 approached, peasants throughout Mimasaka province faced one of the harshest periods in their memory. They had been driven to the limit of their physical endurance. Many were hungry and impoverished. When their feudal masters refused to show them any mercy as tax time approached, they rose in revolt.

Before glancing at the course of the rising, the circumstances and character of its leaders require clarification. The Kaisei rising began when six peasants of middling status from the western branch of Yukishige and surrounding villages in Tsuyama's Tōhokujō region formed a solidarity band. The original six were Naokichi (age fifty-six), Miyozō (age twenty-nine), Heikichi (age sixty), Genkichi (age thirty-nine), Heiroku (age thirty-eight), and Den'emon (age forty-eight). A short time later, two others—Kojirō and Masanojō—joined Naokichi. The holdings of this core group of peasant cultivators (see table 2) ranged from 4.5 koku in the case of Genkichi to 10.6 koku for Naokichi and 13.8 for Masanojō; many of them also owned draft animals. In terms then of the distribution of holdings in the tiny (24 households) branch village of Yukishige (see table 3), the initial leaders of the rising were definitely property holders of middle rank.[5]

But to rank in terms of landholdings, without taking family size into account, is deceptive. The actual existential situation of these leaders, most of whom had large families to support, was far more precarious than village landholding figures would seem to indicate. Moreover, their middle-range class location may have been precisely why Naokichi and his compatriots felt most keenly the social forces bearing upon the mass of poorer peasants whom they helped organize.

We do not know exactly what happened on the night of November 24, but it appears that Naokichi and the others probably addressed large numbers of peasants gathered for a rally in an open field some distance from Yukishige village. With pine torches lighting up the scene, they seem to have decided on a peaceful demonstration in force within Tsuyama castle town. To ensure the broadest possible participation, they sent around to neighboring villages the usual circular notice threatening abstainers with house destruction. Their main professed objectives were typical of peasant ikki for centuries: to press demands for reduction in tribute and corvée duties (in the form of requisitions for horses and men) and for deliveries of relief rice in a bad crop year. But as they proceeded with their night march to the castle town, whatever order there was to begin with broke down. The homes of

TABLE 2. Leaders of the Kaisei Rising in Tsuyama

Leader's Name	Age	Landholdings (koku)	Family Size	Cows	Reason for Arrest	Punishment
Tsuyama						
1. Naokichi	56	10.6	8	1		Life imprisonment
2. Kojirō	?	10.3	5	1		?
3. Masanojō	?	13.8	4	1		?
4. Miyozō	29	10.9	8	1		Life imprisonment
5. Heikichi	60	7.9	4	0		”
6. Genkichi	39	4.5	6	?		”
7. Heiroku (also called Heizō)	38	12+	6	?		”
8. Den'emon	48	6+	6	?		”
9. Uhei	36	5+	8		Stealing	”
10. Hamazō	45	6+	3		”	Banishment from village
11. Kajurō	22	1+	5		”	”
12. Yōsuke	38	3+	8		”	”
13. Namiji	42	7+	9		”	”
14. Shinsaku	47	0.85 (tenant)	10		Rowdyism	”
Shōdo Island						
15. Chōbei	50	0.1	8			?
16. Jirokichi	49	0.13	9			”
17. Kisaku	55	0.085	4			”
18. Gonpachi	43	0.8	3			”
19. Tomozaemon	46	0.6	5			”
20. Kichizō	45	0	5			”
21. Han'emon	46	4.5	7			”

Sources: Kurushima Hiroshi, Review of "Sasaki Junnosuke, *Yonaoshi*," *Rekishigaku kenkyū*, no. 429 (May 1981): 27; and "Kōshō narabi ni mōshiwatashi ukagaisho" (Oral depositions recorded by gundai), *Nihon kinsei shomin seikatsu shiryō shūsei* 13 (1970) pp. 348–372.

intermediate-level officials, such as district headmen and deputy district headmen) as well as merchant moneylenders living in the vicinity, came under attack.

Very soon another phenomenon common to ikki since the mid-eighteenth century appeared. As the armed demonstration proceeded, beggars, outcasts, peddlers, migrant domestic servants hired out to towns, and large numbers of marginalized, impoverished peasants who referred to themselves as hinin flocked to join in. Then, as these dispossessed peasants swelled the ranks of the marchers, the

TABLE 3. Class Composition in Terms of Landholdings in the Western Branch of Yukishige Village, Tōhokujō District

Holdings in Koku	1864			1870		
	Number of Households	Percentage of Total Households	Percentage of Total Holdings	Number of Households	Percentage of Total Households	Percentage of Total Holdings
30–40	2	8.3%	21.9%	2	8.3%	23.3%
20–30	1	4.2	6.9	2	8.4	15.8
10–20	13	54.1	51.7	10	41.7	45.0
5–10	6	25.0	18.1	5	20.8	11.6
1–5	1	4.2	1.4	4	16.6	4.3
0–1	0	0	0	0	0	0
0	1	4.2	0	1	4.2	0
Total Households		24			24	
Total Koku		318.804			306.236	

Source: Compiled by Kurushima Hiroshi, Review of "Sasaki Junnosuke, Yonaoshi," Rekishigaku kenkyū, no. 429 (May 1981): 28.

original leadership under Naokichi was eclipsed by others of apparently lower class status. However, this shift in leaders did not, at this point, connote any dissimilarities in action, aims, and discipline of the participants.[6]

At some point during the night of November 24, and into the early morning hours of the next day, the marchers divided into two or three armed forces of about three thousand each, which then attacked the two biggest towns. One motley force, dressed in traditional ikki garb of matted straw raincoats and sedge hats, marched off in the direction of Kurashiki, then the primary center of rice and cotton culture in eastern Tsuyama. The other rushed headlong for the seat of domanial power: Tsuyama castle town. There, according to the "sōdōki," the first bloody encounter occurred.

The first wave massed before the Ōhashi barrier gate, where Satō Gōzaemon dismounted to meet them. He told them "Peasants, above all, must be quiet and submit in writing their petitions of any sort. I will then transmit them." Thereupon the peasants replied, "We don't need your kind to look after us. It is because of you people that we applied winnowing baskets repeatedly and worked day and night to make up rice bales. When we came to pay tributes, we were told that the bales were unacceptable and many were rejected. You people ought to know how the peasants suffered for the past four years ever since 1863. We will never ask you to be our mediator. We ourselves will ask the lord directly."[7]

The vanguard of the march thereupon approached and made ready to cross the road barriers. The samurai gate guards then fired rifles and artillery at them, killing four and wounding many more. Enraged by the slaughter of their comrades, the peasants began throwing stones and by sheer pressure of numbers managed to outflank the outnumbered Matsudaira troops and send them fleeing.

The first peasant force entered Tsuyama town from all directions on the morning of November 25. Thereupon a partial breakdown of discipline occurred, a display of behavior that was usually not sanctioned by the norms of peasant protest as displayed elsewhere in the year 1866. Migrant servants, temporary room renters who earned their living as day laborers, and lumpen-proletarian elements joined the demonstration. These

poor tenant-house residents of the back alleys mixed with the peasants and rioted and plundered throughout the towns. They stole not only money but clothing and footwear. And they smashed properties, including . . . a Chinese goods store named Suzukaya in Kyō district, where they threw twenty or thirty rooftiles from the front door. They also smashed everything inside and the noise was truly unprecedented. When the morning of the 25th dawned, the raging peasants on the Oimawashi riverbank rushed back to their villages.[8]

This image of peasants and free-riding "residents of the back alleys" at their worst, engaged in collective acts of rioting and theft, depends partly on unconfirmed reports and may therefore be exaggerated. But even if it could be fully documented, the fact remains that peasants were quite discriminating in their choice of targets for house destruction. For two nights in a row, huge crowds of peasants joined in destroying only the homes of town rice merchants and moneylenders. These were the very people with whom they had the most experience because they usually encountered them in relations of exploitation. This is not to deny, of course, that drunkenness was an incidental factor during the opening days and nights of protest; nor is it to claim that no innocent people were assailed by "the raging peasants."

Returning to the narrative of events, we find that the fief authorities did not strike back immediately. Instead, with the merchant quarters of the castle town in a state of near anarchy, they met late into the night of the twenty-fifth and decided to avoid armed suppression as much as possible. They also arranged for the immediate distribution, by villages, of fifteen thousand bales of relief rice.

A document circulated to villages and recorded in the official fief history gives us a glimpse of the Confucian thinking at work when the situation was out of control and the decision had been made to grant relief to the poor. Dated November 30, 1866, and signed by two high officials, Shinano (Ebihara) and Omi (Okuma), it ordered peasants to

make it your primary concern to be pious to your parents, compose your minds, reflect on your behavior and support your wives and children. Without these considerations you will deviate from heaven's reason. However, under the conditions this year, some can hardly support themselves. But the lord will not fail to help them. Therefore you may feel relieved and return to your places forthwith. Those who violate the lord's will shall certainly encounter stern measures.[9]

Around the same time as it issued this order to villages, the fief sent into the countryside, in an effort to persuade peasants to cease rioting and negotiate their demands, the thirty-two-year-old Confucian scholar and proemperor activist, Kurakake Torajirō, together with four other negotiators, company commanders, and armed escorts.[10] Their mission was to convince peasants to set their grievances down in writing and then return home and wait for the authorities to act. In December, these samurai negotiators received the assistance of Buddhist priests, who often played a leading role in preaching obscurantism and in persuading peasants to compromise their demands.[11]

Meanwhile, with Tsuyama town occupied, other demonstrators entered Kurashiki, destroyed merchant property, and attacked the fief's grain storage warehouse. According to the "Sakushū hinin sōdōki":

At Kurashiki, conscripted peasant soldiers [nōhei], in charge of guarding the fief's warehouse, fired on the peasants and killed one. The peasants then were encouraged to take a hard hand to the enemy. Their spirits rose and they felled one official with a stone. He was sent to Tsuyama in a palanquin on the verge of death. The other officials fled to the bakufu district magistrate's office in nearby Miuchi [Toki] fief.[12]

This small confrontation at Kurashiki—repeated under similar circumstances elsewhere in Japan until the peasant soldiers were abolished in early 1868—was a foretaste of their reliability, especially if deployed locally, in putting down disturbances by poor peasants.

The second stage of the rising began as soon as news reached the countryside of the successful invasion of Tsuyama and Kurashiki. On November 26, about 850 peasants from six villages near Ichinomiya reportedly "rioted." Another 900 rose up two days later on November 28 in the vicinity of Komi and Meki villages in Ōba district, the Sanchū region. From that point forward there was no stopping the peasant drive to punish their oppressors. District headmen and their deputies, privileged merchants, landlords, and moneylenders—all felt the wrath of poor peasant wreckers. Village officials who had been spared at the outset also received harsh criticism now for their unjust actions and special privileges.

At the very end of November, the struggle spread beyond Tsuyama into the neighboring fiefs of Katsuyama and Toki (also called Miuchi). In the small (fifteen-thousand-koku) fudai domain of Toki, two thousand peasants rallied en masse at the Miuchi magistrate's office, destroying merchant property in the course of their appeal. Sporadic rioting in Toki lasted for two weeks. Then, on December 26, the disturbances spread across the Inland Sea to Shōdo Island, which since 1838 had been a detached territory of Tsuyama fief. On Shōdo Island, the troubles began with a petition for a reduction of annual tributes and calls for an end to the system of military conscription of peasants. Rioting and destruction of landlord property began on January 13 and lasted for nearly a week, after which negotiations continued for another month before the disorders subsided.[13]

A combination of force and persuasion finally brought the rising to an end. At first, Tsuyama fief used armed force but then immediately compromised. Kurakake and his negotiators dealt separately, on an individual basis, with different peasant bands. Everywhere the fief ended up accepting the peasants' demands and feeding the rioters. Although approximately eight hundred people were imprisoned in connection with the struggle between late November 1866 and March 1867, almost all of them were quickly released and even the leaders were soon pardoned.

ANATOMY OF A RISING: ROLE REVERSALS, LAND TRANSFERS, AND MORAL RIGHTEOUSNESS

Let us now sum up and then try to discern the self-consciousness of the peasant demonstrators. Unfolding rapidly, in waves, and without any apparent coordinating body, fierce village demonstrations engulfed all administrative regions of Tsuyama and the Sanchū region. Then, like a chain reaction, they spread into the neighboring fiefs of Katsuyama and Toki. Finally, after reaching Shōdo Island in the Inland Sea, the disorders came to an end in late February 1867.

Throughout the Kaisei rising, the Tsuyama participants sought to abrogate the fief's rice inspection system, drive down tribute payments in kind and cash, interdict corvée duties, control galloping rice prices, replace village officials, and remove the fief's ban on grain imports and exports. These key demands registered the structural persistence of the two-tiered surplus extraction process. Feudal controls over production and distribution had remained intact, and for most peasants, living conditions in a time of crop failures were as bad in the late 1860s as they had been in the 1720s. Precisely because society retained its essentially feudal form, with all of its original contradictions unresolved, the Kaisei disturbances had to reproduce many of the same demands as the Sanchū revolt of 1726–1727.

But, as we know, a great deal had changed and conditions within Tokugawa feudalism were obviously not the same at the very end of the Tokugawa epoch as in the middle of it. Thus the short (two-day) urban-centered first stage led on to a longer, more complicated, and rural-centered second stage. Opposition to fief reforms and tax increases continued. In addition, many new demands characteristic of a yonaoshi disturbance appeared. Once outlying areas learned of the successful penetration of Tsuyama castle town and of Kurashiki, conflicts between rich and poor within villages erupted almost immediately. And no village, regional, or even fief boundary seemed able to contain the growing solidarity of the poor.

This second stage had three distinguishing features, which need to be discussed separately. These were role reversals, demands pertaining to tenancy, and expressions of a keen sense of moral righteousness.

The phenomenon of role reversal occurred whenever the poor and powerless momentarily took the roles of the rich and powerful. For centuries symbolic role reversals have been an integral, though fleeting, element in movements of mass social protest. De Ste. Croix cites the example of the militant wing of the fanatic anti-Catholic Donatist movement in fifth-century North Africa—the "Circumellions." They attacked Roman landowners but "were anything but a terror to the poor, for we hear of them threatening to punish moneylenders . . . and forcing landlords to dismount from their carriages and run before them while their slaves drove, or to do slaves' work at the mill." [14] Ladurie, in his history of the popular uprising at the time of the Mardi Gras Carnival in late sixteenth-century Romans, called role reversals the "Carnival's ultimate spasm." [15] During the radical phase of the French Revolution, two centuries later, role reversal was one of the more common, pleasurable ways in which small shopkeepers, journeymen, petty traders, and the urban poor demonstrated a new order of things. R. C. Cobb writes that, at the height of the French popular (sansculotte) movement in 1792–1793,

the *commissaires* would get their victims to cook them copious meals, which they then had to serve standing up, while the *commissaires* themselves sat down with the local *gendarmes* and the artisan members of the local comité—a Passion Play in food egalitarianism that was performed over and over again in the areas subjected to ultrarevolutionism. [16]

In Japan, role reversals appeared almost everywhere that local officials and the rich confronted peasant demonstrators. The "sōdōki" gives us a brief glimpse of it when describing how the powerful district headman, Yasuguro of Ozasa village, "came to the gate wearing a straw raincoat and politely greeted" the armed peasant raiding party. "He offered them wine and food. The peasants ate to their full and then asked the district headman to guide them to the home of Yamaguchi Kōhei of that village. He said that he had urgent business and would have someone else show them the way." [17] Quite often, in encounters with yonaoshi bands, the hierarchically superior would be made to kneel down and prostrate themselves before the humble poor. Here Yasuguro got off merely with assuming the traditional peasant protest garb and hosting the raiders to wine and food.

The second, ultimately more important, feature of the Kaisei rising concerns the limited, inherently reformist, and yonaoshi nature of many of the peasants' demands, especially those pertaining to land, Everywhere during the second stage of the rising, common peasants told fief officials to reduce tributes and corvées. But they also told wealthy peasants and their own village officials (the fief's tax-collecting agents) to return to their original owners "without payment, all cultivated lands forfeited fifty years ago." Landlords were asked to issue documents certifying that the ownership of fields would remain as of the previous year. Other common peasant demands were for the replacement of village headmen and, in some areas, the abolition of the offices of both village headman and caretaker. Most significant of all were the demands for the reduction, by half, of that year's tenant fees in rice and the fixing of a ten-year period for the return of pawned land. Since the issue of pawned land tenancy has often appeared in the course of this study, a brief consideration that pulls together some of the main points about it is now in order.

Just as Marx termed the secret history of the Roman republic "the history of its landed property," so we may say that the secret history of the bakuhan state concerned its arrangements for land transfers.[18] These went on between peasants all the time, were highly complex in origin, and eventually gave rise to different forms of lender–debtor or landlord–tenant relationships. It is difficult to generalize about these patterns because they differed remarkably from one region to another and have not been adequately studied. But it seems that out of fief and merchant investments in land reclamation projects came one form of tenancy and out of the extended family another. The most widespread type of tenancy, however, was found especially in the commercially developed regions around Ōsaka and Kyōto as well as in one-crop rice field areas of the northeast. Its roots lay in the practice whereby hard-pressed cultivators pawned their land and were then allowed to continue occupying it as tenants. Such pawned land tenancy centered on village headmen and middle-level intermediaries who made fixed-term tax loans to poor peasants in money or grain, receiving as security their plots of land.[19]

The legal framework within which pawned land tenancy developed can be stated directly. It began with the bakufu's land edicts of 1643. These prohibited the permanent sale of cultivated fields and the hiding of reclaimed fields, while at the same time specifying harsh punishments for violators. In 1673 Edo placed additional restrictions on the subdivision of cultivated fields. But high tribute rates invariably forced some peasants to transfer land among themselves in order to fulfill their main duty of taxpaying. Under such circumstances, tenancy developed during the second half of the seventeenth century, and by its end the bakufu was forced to give its attention to the problem of land forfeitures. As noted in the first part of this study, an important component of Yoshimune's Kyōhō reforms was a 1722 "ban on the forfeiture of land," which aimed unsuccessfully at reconstructing small-scale farming as the traditional foundation of shogunal rule.

After the withdrawal of that ban in 1723, tenancy continued to increase for the remainder of the eighteenth century. In 1744 the magistrates of the shogun's high court lightened the punishments for those persons caught conducting the permanent sale of fields. Their action officially justified the accumulation of landholdings by the method of concentrating forfeited plots of pawned land. But still the bakufu refused to withdraw its original prohibition on the sale of cultivated fields, together with punishments for violators. While these remained in effect, land could not be freely sold and transfers had to take the form of pawning, with the standard pawn period set at ten years.

When the bakuhan system became self-negating—around the end of the eighteenth century and the beginning of the nineteenth century—landlord-tenant relations entered a stage in which fief policy gave clearer preference to landlord interests over tenant interests. The distinction between forfeiture and permanent sale became blurred, though landlord ownership was by no means secure. In addition, tenant contracts in some parts of the country began to register shorter time periods for the return of the original money loan on which land served as security.

The outlines of the late nineteenth-century Meiji landlord system could already be discerned by the third and fourth decades of that century. Large-scale landlords, who had accumulated and concentrated tiny plots of pawned land from large numbers of impoverished peasants, aimed at making profits from their tenant fees. They entrusted the management of their holdings to a hierarchy of rent collectors in a system that paralleled the village administrative hierarchy. Tenant fees continued to be fixed by contract and regulated by local customs. Peasants called them, meaningfully, "rice interest" or "tribute" (nengu). Usually, the tenant fee did not change because both parties considered it to be a fixed interest payment on a loan for which the guarantee was the land itself.

During the 1850s and 1860s a more advanced form of disguised landlord-tenant relations seems to have emerged in Kōzuke province (present-day Gumma prefecture). There the accumulation of land by landlords and the borrowing of money by peasants with land as security grew further apart. In Uzen province (present-day Yamagata prefecture), the largest landlord family in pre-1945 Japan had already emerged at the very beginning of the nineteenth century. This was the Honma family, whose annual income from hundreds of pawned land tenants in the year 1801 was 14,830.7 bales of rice. By 1866, the Honma's holdings had grown to where they were receiving annually twice that amount in tenant fees, or 30,823.4 bales of rice.[20]

When we turn at last to the Chūgoku region during the 1860s, we find that peasant landholdings were generally small compared to other regions that have been better studied such as the northeast. But here too tenancy was widespread and straddled village borders. Exactly how many peasants were involved in tenant relations is not known, but two examples are suggestive. The first concerns the Tokuyama family of landlords and iron mine owners in Ōba district, Tsuyama. They began accumulating the pawned land of tenants in the late eighteenth century and by 1822 were receiving annually rents of about 102 koku from tenants in over seven villages. By 1844 the Tokuyama had 113 tenants and received from them over 315 bales of rice, 2.190 grams of silver, and tobacco worth 2.028 grams of silver. The second example concerns the powerful Yabuki family of Yukishige village in Katsunan district, where the Kaisei rising originated. Yabuki Yakurō was the village headman and Namba Kōroku, the assistant headman, was a tenant presumably dependent on the Yabuki family. In 1868—about a year after the peasants' demands for the return of pawned land had been rejected, thereby confirming landlord ownership—Yabuki Yakurō had tenant lands in eighteen different villages and was collecting annually 1,090 bales of tenant rice (about 382 koku) from more than 150 tenants. Clearly, landlords like the Tokuyama and the Yabuki would have good reason not to return pawned lands.[21]

As for the demands raised by peasants during the Kaisei disturbances, none was unique to Tsuyama fief, let alone the Chūgoku region. With the exception of those pertaining to tribute, all were quintessential yonaoshi demands of the sort which marked Japan's path into the capitalist world. In Musashi province as in Mimasaka, yonaoshi forces at the close of the feudal epoch tried to compel wealthy peasants and local officials to return pawned land so that the families of distressed peasants—in this case the self-designated hinin—could be preserved and village communities restored. Japan by this time was headed in a capitalist direction. But the laws and customs governing its agricultural production and distribution were still feudal, not even semifeudal. The forces at the bottom of Japanese society, exposed to meteoric price rises and locked into an agricultural economy that was being buffeted by capitalist market forces, were compelled to challenge their future. By opposing the land accumulation of the wealthy, with its damaging effects on communal life, and by insisting on their own inclusive right to land, these hinin were helping to preserve for the distant future the ancient idea of man's natural right to the means of production. Seen in just this light, the consciousness their yonaoshi struggles represented was more forward looking than we realized— and certainly more forward looking than what one normally encounters in a typical ikki.

The third major feature of the Kaisei rising was this keen sense of moral justice and the basic integrity of the poor, which the mob-drunkenness of the first phase had obscured. Hard-pressed tenant farmers, agricultural day laborers, castle town tenement residents, house renters, the homeless and unregistered—all who composed the rural and urban poor—became the driving force during the second stage. In many cases of house-smashing, they demanded money or relief rice. But that was not their chief objective. Mainly, they wanted to punish "evil," defined as commercial profiteering and lack of sympathy for the poor. Some pertinent examples, which reveal this aspect of their consciousness, are offered by historian Sasaki Junnosuke in his provocative book *Yonaoshi* (1979). When the mob that invaded Tsuyama castle town was about to attack the home of one Ikegami Sahei, this exchange took place:

Sahei: I for one have no reason for inviting a grudge. If the money I lent is no good, then I'll return these documents to everyone of you individually.
Rioters: You're stupid, Sahei. We came from far away and none of us will borrow your money.[22]

A few days later in Toki fief, a crowd is about to destroy the property of two notorious rice merchants. To one they say:

You've risen from a lowly status, saved a little money and everyday you take advantage of us, willfully setting cheap prices for the rice, tea and wood charcoal we sell. Not only that, recently you've not hesitated to corner the market in rice and refuse to sell to us. In recent years you were allowed to have a surname through contributing money to the authorities. Don't all these things mean that you've risen in the world by sucking money gathered from our blood and sweat? But hiding all these facts you looked down upon us as lowly mountain rustics. What a serious crime you've committed!

And to the other merchant, Tanaka Yaichiemon, the headman of Iguchi village:

You are the representative of the caretakers and the head of officials with many subordinates under you. Yet simply out of your selfish desires, without any feeling whatsoever for saving the impoverished people, you lent money, taking away our fields and forests as security. You are driving the peasants to ruin.

A loud shout then went up—"Today you have been censured by heaven for these crimes!"—and the wrecking began.[23]

As we have noted already, the main thrust of the Kaisei rising was directed squarely against Tsuyama fief itself. On Shōdo Island, the peasants also registered fierce opposition to the fief's military mobilization order of June 1865, which allowed the second and third sons of rich peasants to serve as peasant soldiers in units commanded by the sons of district headmen.[24] But the rising had a dual structure and embraced many other diverse aims. Thus, in villages where property destruction occurred, the main demands were for a 50 percent reduction in tenant rents and the return, without payment, of forfeited fields to their original owners. Stressing this aspect, Sasaki suggested that the Kaisei rising be read, at one level, as a fight by nominally independent, self-cultivating peasants who felt themselves falling into a condition of proletarianization and misery. Bondage to landlords had become, by this time, as onerous as subordination to feudal lords. So, hard-pressed proprietors and, even more remarkable, one tenant were in the forefront of the action.

This thesis, I think, contains much truth. In support of it, Sasaki cites a deposition that sheds light on the immediate context within which many nominally independent cultivators acted. It was given to the district magistrate of Tōhokujō by one Shinsaku of Misaki Kawara village. Shinsaku was a tenant. By virtue of that fact alone one would think that he was poorer, more economically dependent, and therefore less likely to take the part of leader for his neighbors and friends. Yet the authorities designated him as a leader in riots that began in Komi village on December 28, 1866. Later arrested and charged with the crime of "rowdyism," Shinsaku told the magistrate that

I have holdings of 8 to 5 sho and a family of ten to support. For a long time I've been in distress. So I increased the amount of land I work as a tenant and we narrowly managed to support ourselves. Recently, prices have risen and last year we had poor crops. I worried a lot about not being able to make full tribute payments. Around the 15th or 16th [of December], when I met with someone from Komi village [present-day Ochiai City, Okayama prefecture] and with Seisaku from my village, I suggested that, in view of the bad conditions in Kawahara village, we might join with Komi village to demand a reduction in tributes. To this they replied, "That's too risky to be good. First we might ask our respective landlords to reduce the tenant rice rent. If they should refuse to budge at all, we might as well destroy the homes of the district headmen and deputy district headmen. But this village alone can't do it." Well, on December 24, when the villagers all gathered at the tutelary shrine, they agreed that if just the tenants, acting individually, demanded that landlords reduce tenant rents it would be hopeless. We would have to get the village officials to represent them in negotiating with landlords. The village officials then entered into negotiations. But before we received their replies, we were called out in a mobilization which started from Shimo village. Thus we were led to participate in the troubles.[25]

All over Japan at the end of the 1860s the bulk of the protesting poor were people like Shinsaku and Naokichi—household heads and direct cultivators who were experiencing a drastic decline in their economic situations. They were also the "poor tenant-house residents of the back alleys" who mixed with them whenever the former were "called out in a mobilization." One of the unexplained problems of Japan's transition to capitalism is how to characterize such people. Did they constitute a clearly defined semiproletariat? If so, was that semiproletariat a class or a stratum?[26] Or is it more accurate, given the limitations of the documentary evidence pertaining to Tsuyama's poor, to see them primarily as minute agricultural producers, members of desperately poor households who were becoming true semiproletarians, but who still aspired to return to petty farming rather than to attain higher wages?

My own view is to see the semiproletariat as a recognizable class, consisting mainly of two types of people for whom ascribed hereditary status was no longer morally or economically meaningful, though it still had psychological value and could not be easily renounced. These people were the propertyless poor who worked for wages in cities, towns, and villages on the outskirts of castle town districts and certain landholding peasants whose own minute plots compelled them to earn part-time wages outside their villages in neighboring towns. The ambiguous class position of these people was still at a very early stage of being resolved by the policies of the late bakuhan state and the early Meiji state. However, the Restoration reforms of the 1870s, enforced by a new machinery of state power, would eventually turn them into full proletarians.

Our study of the Kaisei rising underlines, once again, the driving power of class struggles in the process of Japan's transition to capitalism. Growing economic inequality and exploitation, and unprecedented political change resulting from violent struggle rather than consensus, formed the background against which the social history of the late 1860s unfolded. Now, to complete our account, we shall compare the Kaisei events with the Sanchū rising studied earlier. Afterward we shall examine one last wave of yonaoshi disturbances. These were the mass protests that spread through Shinshū province in 1869–1870, helping to set the stage for the final abolition of fiefs and the emergence of a new form of state based on a distinctive fusion of old (semifeudal tenancy) and new ("free" wage-labor) methods of surplus extraction.

THE EVENTS OF 1726 AND 1866 COMPARED

First, differences in historical context, and in degree of social stratification based on the division of labor, help explain the contrasting natures of the two episodes and many of their demands.

The Sanchū rising of the late 1720s spread quickly from village to village until it involved the peasantry of the entire fief. But massive samurai military force, deployed with little restraint, easily defeated it in a matter of weeks. With their leaders gone and their spirit of resistance broken, the Sanchū peasants failed to effect any change whatever in Tsuyama fief's principles of rule or in its tax practices. In 1727, the weak forces of feudal disintegration were as nothing compared to the forces making for peasant acquiescence to oppression and to consensus within the ruling class. In short, the Sanchū rising of 1726–1727 is easily categorized as a trans-fief ikki typical of an early stage of a systemic feudal crisis: when to rebel seemed futile and rural protest was relatively unbuttressed by movements of urban and samurai protest occurring simultaneously.

The Kaisei rising, by contrast, had a more complex structure. Longer lasting and more intense, it involved all oppressed classes, both rural and urban. Its associations were less with images of futility and the distant past than with the revolutionary present. At every stage of its advance, processes of political and economic change not even on the horizon in 1727 shaped its path. In the late 1860s, Japan was being drawn into a new system of trade and diplomatic interrelationships characteristic of the capitalist era. All over Asia great peasant revolts were occurring: anti-imperialist struggles in Vietnam, peasant risings in Korea, the Taiping rebellion in China, the Sepoy rising in India, and innumerable peasant risings in Russia. Thus, externally, the struggle for reforms in Mimasaka occurred within a context of peasant disturbances and revolutionary movements throughout Asia.

Internally, too, it was a time of upheaval. The alternate attendance system, which required the daimyo to spend part of each year in Edo, had been discontinued. Rising military defense needs, reparations payments to Western nations, and, in certain areas, the withdrawal of peasants from the productive process in order to serve as soldiers—all these developments had dramatically increased the financial burdens on the peasantry. In addition, Edo was engaged in a civil war with Chōshū fief which signaled the end of the Tokugawa regime. And within Tsuyama fief a fierce struggle for power was underway between pro- and anti-bakufu forces.

In form, the Kaisei rising was primarily a peasant ikki. Its most insistent and general demands were directed at the foundations of the old regime. These were the village tribute-collecting system; the middle-level intermediaries and supervisors of tribute collection, together with their deputies, both of whom were closely connected with fief power; and the fief reforms predicated on increased tributes and corvée duties. But combined with these traditional features of an ikki struggle were the customary demands and characteristics of a yonaoshi disturbance or sōdō. Demands for rent reduction and the return of pawned land and articles denoted the yonaoshi dimension. So too did the refusal to make any demands, but simply to mete out property destruction against the covetous and greedy. That feature probably confused many observers who viewed events from the perspective of a traditional ikki protest. But when poor people become rebellious they do not have to present formal demands for their actions to be purposive and political within the normative framework that they themselves establish.

What had happened in the 140 years between the two risings was the growth

of rural commerce, the differentiation of the peasantry, the development of "rural
districts on the periphery of the castle town districts," the influx into them (and
into the castle town districts proper) of large numbers of unregistered homeless
people who could somehow make a living as day laborers, and the growth of de
facto landlord-tenant relations.[27] In the Chūgoku region by the middle of the
nineteenth century large numbers of peasants belonged to a distressed class of debtors. Rent had become institutionalized in various forms of loan contracts that
stipulated a permanently fixed rate of interest on a loan the collateral for which was
the cultivator's land or house. Many peasants—though how many we do not
know—pawned their land for a fixed period of time in return for a cash loan with
which to pay their taxes. The landlord then had the option of working the land
himself or letting it out to outsiders or to the original owner himself as a sort of
hired laborer. Usually in such cases, however, tenants claimed a right to have their
pawned land returned to them whenever the principal and the interest on their
original loan was repaid.[28]

   But during the 1860s landlords who accumulated the pawned land of poor
peasants were often unwilling to honor such traditional rights. The best evidence
we have of this is the frequency with which peasants, during uprisings, demanded
that landlords return to them their pawned land. We may conclude, therefore, that
Tsuyama fief in the 1860s was more economically developed than it had been in the
1720s; but it was also far more riven by internal class antagonisms. Moreover, debt
bondage in the form of tenancy was on its way to becoming a new and crucially
important mechanism of social control. Because of the two-tiered chain of landlord and fief oppression, public opinion in villages endorsed the destruction of the
property of middle-level officials, who had been overzealous in enforcing the fief's
reform measures. Village opinion also supported attacks on speculative rice merchants, moneylenders, and landlords. Both target groups interpenetrated. Both
represented the forces of a fettered and distorted commercial capitalism that had
never been allowed to come into its own, but grew up within the womb of feudal
society, depriving peasants of their land and trampling underfoot their customary
notion of inalienable possession.

   Inevitably, the Sanchū and Kaisei episodes yielded very different results. The
weakened condition of the bakuhan state after a century and a half of ever more
bitter class struggles helps explain some of the differences. The repressive power of
many fiefs had been irrevocably weakened, and the Tokugawa regime, having lost
its legitimacy in the eyes of many samurai, was on the verge of being overthrown.
During 1866 and 1867 peasants in fiefs throughout Japan were scoring small successes against their domanial bureaucracies, while losing out in contests with landlords. In Mimasaka province the Kaisei struggle yielded the quick release from jail

of hundreds of people arrested in connection with the rioting. By the end of 1867, even leaders who had been transported to Tsuyama castle and sentenced to life imprisonment were pardoned and released. In Tsuyama fief at least the disorders did not end, as in the past, with a public execution scene.

Economically, the peasants forced the Matsudaira clan to surrender one-sixth of its rice tribute income for the year (amounting to some twenty-four thousand koku). They also ended the fief's reform program, its extortionate tax practices, and its rice quality-control system for which peasants paid the bills.[29] Their one anomalous achievement for that particular time and region was the rehabilitation of distressed villages and households. They accomplished it by forcing landlords (who were often village officials and rice merchants) to accept restrictions on the accumulation of landed capital—something that peasants in other parts of the country were less successful in achieving.

But all these gains from months of violent mass protest were of limited temporary significance. The real impact of the Kaisei rising was indirect. Politically, as historian Nagamitsu Norikazu pointed out, the poor people's struggle in Tsuyama both hastened and shaped a separate political struggle already underway within ruling-class circles in Tsuyama castle. The disturbance revealed the inability of the probakufu clique, then in power, to govern the countryside. When it had subsided, an anti-Tokugawa group, led by Kurakake Torajirō, the loyalist who had been instrumental in pacifying peasants, replaced the Matsudaira officials who originally engineered the fief's reforms. By rising up in late 1866, the peasants of Tsuyama did the samurai loyalists of the fief a favor. Inadvertently, they brought to power, in March 1867, a new clique of samurai retainers committed to the overthrow of the bakufu.[30]

In this respect the actions of poor peasants illustrate an important general point that, as Piven and Cloward observe, most students of mass protest seldom acknowledge. Mass defiance often has a disruptive impact, which is *indirectly* felt; and protest "is more likely ... to evoke wider political reverberations when powerful groups have large stakes in the disrupted institution."[31] Spurred by the peasants' protest and with their own careers at stake in the outcome of Tsuyama fief's reforms, the dissident samurai took the initiative from the peasants and resumed their vanguard role in guiding Tsuyama into the new era.

A great many social forces contributed to the breakdown of the bakuhan state and to the political changes known as the Meiji Restoration. But peasant risings, such as occurred in the Chūgoku region in the winter of 1866–1867 in an institutional setting of severe samurai infighting and fief instability, furnished the energy from below that made those changes possible.

In the next chapter we shall see how foreign trade in the treaty ports created new relations of exploitation which gave to peasant struggles different dimensions and a heightened intensity. We shall also see how, after the shogun's overthrow, peasants and townsmen, without pausing, staged mass protests that fatally weakened the old state structure. Their actions served to accelerate the dismantling of the fief system and other remaining institutions of feudalism. Equally as important, the next round of disturbances allowed the poor to perceive that behind their familiar foe—the rural bourgeoisie—stood a new enemy, the Meiji government, rising up upon foundations laid by the old state power.

CHAPTER FIFTEEN

The Debased-Currency Risings in Shinshū, 1869–1870

THE analysis of peasant needs and aspirations, so central to understanding Tokugawa Japan, continued to be important for the history of the Meiji era (1868–1912). For the shogun's overthrow ushered in a period of socioeconomic revolution in which ex-samurai bureaucrats from the southwestern domains staked the success of their nation building upon a more effective exploitation of the countryside. Quickly, they set about constructing the power machinery and the legal institutions with which to extract massive economic surpluses from the peasantry. This strategy of continuity with the feudal past, which the Meiji leaders broke with in areas outside of agriculture, provoked an immediate response from peasants, making the 1870s and 1880s decades of extremely bitter class strife.

One of the stages on which the opposing forces made an early appearance was Shinshū province. There, in the year 1869, the traditional factors of bad weather, poor harvests, and worsening price inflation combined to stir unrest. As the Western system of "free trade" worked its destructive effects on Japanese domestic industry (still based on petty commodity production), prices soared. The dual burden of corvée duties and grain tributes was felt everywhere, but especially in prefectures under Tokyo's direct jurisdiction. The previous year, 1868, the Council of State initiated a policy of abolishing customary tribute reductions and, as summer 1869 approached, the issue of reductions was becoming more insistent.

Adding to the misery created by inflation and the recently concluded civil war was a deepening currency crisis. It affected even the most remote mountain villages. Like the inflation problem to which it was directly related, the currency crisis of 1869–1870 had a number of causes, most notably Japan's subordination to the West. Unequal treaties, indemnities, and loans perpetuated that subordination. What really deepened it, however, was the bakufu's earlier monetary reform of

1860 and its subsequent indiscriminate overissue of inconvertible notes and debased coins. When the new regime took over in Tokyo in early 1868, it continued past practices, issuing during its first two years alone 48 million ryō of new inconvertible gold notes (called *dajōkan-satsu*) and, during the first year of operation of its new Ōsaka mint, some 6 million ryō in coin. The debased ryō coins (*nibukin*, *ichibugin*, and *isshugin*) circulated chiefly among peasants.[1]

In addition, many fiefs and individual merchants, in defiance of new government prohibitions, secretly minted their own debased coins during 1868–1869. There were in 1869 "13 or 14 types of one-half ryō (*nibu*) gold coins coming in daily [to money exchanges in Tokyo, Ōsaka, and Kyōto] of which 70 to 80 percent were metallically debased."[2] By summer of that year, when nibu gold coins had ceased to circulate in many places, the monetary debacle had reached enormous proportions. A Meiji government report issued in early 1872 (after the entire Tokugawa monetary system had been abolished and the yen established in place of the ryō) uncovered 1,694 different types of inconvertible fief notes circulating in 244 fiefs, 14 ex-bakufu domains, and 9 direct retainer fiefs. Their total face value of 38,550,000 yen was comparable to Japan's total national revenue in 1872 of 50 million yen.[3] When a rejection of this devalued currency set in that summer, it generalized all the other grievances that had been building up against feudal burdens and touched off an explosive chain reaction of risings.

In the context of these developments, the large-scale peasant uprisings that occurred in Shinshū province take on particular significance. Four factors need to be considered. First, Japan's integration into the world market, and the development of commercial capitalism under the stimulus of foreign trade, brought to the surface contradictions, such as the need for currency reform. Its solution demanded the framework of a new political system. But in 1869 and 1870 such a framework had not yet sufficiently emerged.

Second, popular expectations of improved working conditions and a lessening of exploitation had been stirred. Yet, in the villages and towns, little changed. All signs pointed instead to the new regime's intention to increase rice tributes and continue feudal modes of operation.

Third, geographically and economically, the sericultural regions of Shinshū in which the risings unfolded had become linked to the world market through the export of silk yarn, shipped through Yokohama. Considerable tenancy had also developed, placing Shinshū in an intermediate position between the northeast and the Chūgoku regions, both of which had higher tenancy rates. However, within Shinshū there were areas, such as Ina (later changed to Chikuma) prefecture where the tenancy rate was much higher than in the ex-bakufu domains that surrounded it.[4]

Last, in April 1868 the new regime established the first imperial court domains.

The continued existence of fiefs alongside these first prefectures created space within which the rural poor as well as the propertied middle and upper strata of the villages could, at last, act successfully to weaken the fetters of the tribute system.

Keeping the above points in mind, we shall proceed to do two things. First, we shall look at how the process of social change at the very start of the Meiji Restoration was reflected in a series of scattered risings in Shinshū province. These disturbances began in Iida fief, crossed over to Ueda and then to four districts in Ina prefecture, and finally spread in succession through Matsushiro, Susaka, and Nakano in northern Shinshū. Next, after surveying the currency-debasement disturbances, we shall look briefly at the changed situation in the early 1880s. By then, the focus of peasant protest in the sericultural prefectures had shifted from inflationary grain prices and currency issues to debt refundment and taxes; and popular protest had forged an ideological base that was both traditional and new.

IIDA, JULY 2–4, 1869

The first disturbance broke out in the south of Shinshū in tiny Iida fief, shortly after rice prices peaked in June. That month, merchants from Gōshu province (Shiga prefecture), intent on purchasing silk thread, brought over 10,000 ryō of debased gold coins into Iida.[5] The actual amount of bad currency in circulation at the time, however, may have been over five times that amount since Iida fief eventually converted 57,613 ryō in dajōkan notes.[6] In early July, the duped peasants of Iida discovered that their hard-earned petty income from the sale of silk would not convert to rice or any other daily necessity, that it consisted, in fact, of utterly worthless fief notes and debased coins whose metallic worth was far below their face value at par.

In this situation, the paper-cord makers who depended on cheap rice for making paste were the first to act. They had taken the lead in earlier rice riots in 1838 and 1865 and, ever since, had been predisposed to tangle with silk wholesalers and yarn merchants. Led by these relatively independent workers with their own organization,[7] approximately thirteen thousands peasants from villages through-out Iida answered different musters and formed armed bands which proceeded to smash the homes of landlords, merchants, and moneylenders.

UEDA, AUGUST 16–21, 1869

About one hundred kilometers to the north of Iida, along the main mountain roads, lay Ueda fief. Here, where nearly sixty thousands ryō of metallically de-based coins had circulated, news of the Iida rioting needed little propagation.[8]

Ueda had long been the center and leader of Shinshū's entire sericulture industry—
a preeminence it was to lose during the 1870s and 1880s as more modern machine-
reeling shifted to neighboring regions. But in 1869 Ueda was still known as "the
Yokohama of Shinshū," outproducing other surrounding fiefs and prefectures in
the manufacture of silk thread. Before looking at the riots in Ueda, which eclipsed
in fury and destructiveness all previous risings in that fief's long history, three
aspects of its development since the late eighteenth century should be noted.

First, after the Hōreki rising of 1761–1763, petty-commodity production
centering on traditional hand-reeled silk registered steady gains. During the late
1800s and again in the 1850s, the peasant households of the fief made the switch to
improved reeling instruments, and by the late 1860s, they were producing nearly
35 percent of all the silk thread in Shinshū, far ahead of their nearest competitor,
Matsushiro fief.[9] But the form of silk-reeling operations in Ueda remained a side
work of agricultural households, employing the labor of wives and daughters.
There is no documentary evidence to indicate even the existence of a putting-out
system. Silk wholesale merchants, who made no contribution to production,
merely bought up the finished product from peasants and shipped it to Yokohama.
Peasants dealt with, and were completely at the mercy of, these middlemen who
actually placed the silk on the market. The biggest of them—Nagaoka Manpei,
Tanaka Chūshichi, and Yoshiike Sadanosuke—took their orders from the Matsudaira officials.[10]

Second, since Hōreki the conflict between town and countryside had continued to deepen as peasant cultivators and small-scale rural merchants spread their
commercial activities broadly through all districts of Ueda. Already by the 1790s
the stage was set for the breakdown of the feudal division of labor based on occupational specialization and organized as a division of labor between town and
countryside. During the 1830s and 1840s, Ueda's castle town merchants demanded
a drastic tightening up of restrictive controls over all commercial operations
within the rural districts. In answering this challenge, the peasants deployed the
argument that "in the matter of making a living, peasants cannot maintain their
hereditary family occupation unless, at the same time, they do business, just as
townsmen cultivate land while working in their own occupations." A related
argument was that "we do not think it is the case that we began recently to hinder
the townsmen's business. For it has been the common trend that peasants do
business while townsmen cultivate the land. So we are bothered by the appeal the
townsmen made to the authorities."[11] Given the persistence of feudal economic
and political restrictions in a context of growing antifeudal consciousness, the
hostility between town and countryside could only continue to grow.

The third point concerns growing poverty in Ueda as reflected in the growth of tenancy. Unfortunately, here information is scanty and all that can be said is, first, following bakufu precedent, Ueda fief gradually relaxed its legal restrictions on the selling of land.[12] Starting in the late eighteenth century, the number of tenants working pawned land steadily increased. At the same time, village head- men and district headmen, some of whom had even joined with peasants in the Hōreki rising, accumulated land and deepened their ties with the castle authorities. By the middle of the nineteenth century, the tendency for land to become broken into ever smaller units was quite pronounced. Yet, as Yokoyama Toshio pointed out, mountain villages like Irinaramoto and its surrounding hamlets in Urano district, where the 1869 rising originated, had the largest number of peasants cultivating their own minute plots and the fewest number of tenants and destitute poor.[13] It was not semiproletarians who had nothing to lose but desperately poor and frustrated petty cultivators who initiated the Ueda rising.

Turning now to the details of the rioting and conflagration, we find that peasants from Urano district—estimates of their number range widely from four to five and twenty to thirty—began it on the evening of August 16. In the words of one anonymous contemporary account, with "Kurōemon, Umanojō, Kōno- suke, Moichi, and Tamazō" as their leaders, they "made a religious association in honor of the mountain gods."[14] To defend themselves against fake one-half-ryō gold coins, the abuses of local officials and the rich, and the general economic dis- location of the times, they decided to call out all the villages for an appeal at the castle. They then commenced the usual mobilization operation. Bands of militants went around the villages throughout the night and into the early morning hours of the next day threatening house destruction to those who refused to participate.

On the morning of August 17 the roads and bypaths leading to Ueda castle town were jammed with thousands of demonstrators. Few of them bothered even to carry flags; fewer still had any clear idea of the demands they were going to make. Most were looking simply for revenge and their mood was angry and threatening. Since fief power supported the system of exploitation in which they were trapped, it was only natural for them to aim first at the fief government in Ueda castle. At different points into the town, high officials tried to persuade the different vanguards to desist, but they kept coming.

They marched from the Ueda embankment and began by totally destroying the house of the wine merchant Yamaura Sasuke; from there they went to Gosho village where they totally destroyed the pawnshop of Yokozeki Senzaemon. Meanwhile everyone from Shioda district rushed out. Around noon on August 17 the vanguard reached the grain inspection guard post at Konya in Ueda castle town, where they spent much time. They spent a little over an hour inside the town. After 4 P.M. they forced their way into the main gate of the castle and advanced fearlessly into the main garden where the officials in charge of rural affairs were waiting.[15]

After they had violated the sanctity of the inner castle garden and milled about hurling insults at, but not molesting, the gathered officials, the demonstrators quieted down somewhat when confronted by the governor. They denied having any hostility to the fief government but, at the same time, refused to present their demands in writing. They were suffering, they claimed, because of high prices and the fact that the petty profits they had earned from silkworm culture were worthless one-half-ryō coins that would not circulate. Finally, they committed their demands to writing, and over the next few days district officials managed to respond affirmatively to over twenty of them.[16] Most concerned the issues of debased currency, high prices, excessive feudal levies, and the abuses of district tribute officers and village headmen, and demanded a one-year rotation in office of all village headmen and the abolition of the office of district tribute officer. On almost all demands, Ueda fief yielded to the peasants' wishes.

The confrontation in the castle garden wound up toward evening. Although the peasants had not initially presented demands, their protest actions were purposeful and, in general, targeted carefully against specific individuals. But with the entire town occupied, there developed toward evening an atmosphere of general drunkenness and a breakdown in self-restraint, which was not in keeping with the rest of the disturbance. In these circumstances, a fire erupted and quickly got out of control. It

started in the official inn in Unno and turned into a great conflagration. In the east the fire swept the town as far as Gangyōji temple in Yoko. In the west it stopped near the Produce Office in Hara. Meanwhile the people destroyed every single house and even the sealed clay warehouses and records warehouses. They took out and trampled upon clothing and drapes.[17]

By the time the last rioters departed Ueda castle town, on August 18, 214 homes and other properties had been destroyed by arson. Merchants, of whom 87 were totally burned out, suffered the most damage. But, as fire spread out of control into the pauper sections, the poor also suffered, Then, for another three days, bands of rioters went from village to village destroying the property of village officials, landlords, and the rich. By August 21, 269 homes of district headmen, village headmen, and rich merchants had suffered partial or complete destruction. When all the rioting and arson had ended, the Ueda government again revealed its powerlessness by arresting only six rioters. Five of them were known organizers of the demonstration: sixty-five-year-old Kurōemon and four other peasants said to have been his gambling associates. The sixth man was executed for thievery.

In three respects the Ueda yonaoshi rising of 1869 resembled the Hōreki ikki of 1761–1763. First, ideology and organization provided direct links with the past. The rising began with a nocturnal meeting (or meetings) in the mountains at which time peasants made a religious association (*kō*) in honor of the mountain gods. This invocation of the gods who watched over agriculture and who, when angry, punished evildoers was entirely archaic. So too was the solidarity band formed by Kuroemon with his fellow "gamblers" (or day laborers?) as the nucleus.

Second, the same villages in Urano district that were centers of antifeudal unrest in 1761–1763 continued to be bastions of militancy 107 years later in 1869. But whether this was true in the other riotous areas of northern Shinshū the following year remains to be studied.

Third, the very same rural chain of command as in the Hōreki period, with district tribute officers (wariban) in charge at the intermediate level, still existed in 1869. In attacking this familiar component of domanial power and of the rich peasant stratum, Ueda's petty producers and homeless poor were trying, once again, to gain control of the local system of feudal rule in the countryside.

However, in most other important respects, the two episodes were entirely different. A chief characteristic of the Hōreki rising was the detailed, protracted negotiations between villages and castle authorities that started just after the peasants displayed their utmost power and then continued all the while they retreated from their initial line. By contrast, 1869 was a short, violent explosion of fury and revenge, directed more at landlords, the rich, and the local representatives of fief power than at the highest levels of fief officialdom. By 1869 the daimyo were no longer fundamental to Japanese feudalism as they had been in the eighteenth century. They were merely "governors" drawing a household stipend fixed at 10 percent of the assessed value of their respective fiefs, enjoying no guarantee of hereditary office and—as events in Matsushiro fief the following year would show—subject to immediate punishment if they ignored government directives or policies. That is why villagers brought no written demands when they invaded Ueda castle and why they committed their grievances to writing only after repeated pressing by fief officials.

Significantly, too, Ueda castle in 1761–1763 was fairly generous to peasants because it feared the bakufu. In 1869 it was generous to peasants because it feared them in their own right. For these poor people may have really believed that their lands would be returned and their poverty abolished by the new Restoration government. Now they knew better and were inwardly enraged.

Also, despite their tribute-bearing character, the stratum of minute-scale peasant cultivators was significantly different from what it had been a century earlier. Thus the Ueda Hōreki was begun and concluded as a local fief affair. It could be studied meaningfully as a single episode illuminating an important stage in the decline of Tokugawa feudalism. But the 1869 rising in Ueda cannot be studied in isolation from either the larger peasant movement that flowed around it or from the far-reaching political changes of the Restoration period.

From the outset, it was part of an immense movement of petty landholding cultivators, tenants, and destitute poor laborers. Poverty and household indebtedness seem to have been on the increase in all the areas through which it spread. And those areas were also particularly vulnerable to such unrest because of the complex structure of adminstrative jurisdictions throughout Shinshū. That yonaoshi disturbances spilled over village, district, and fief boundaries and expanded regionally was also related to Shinshū's position as a sericulture region, producing a product for the international market and therefore subject to sharp fluctuations in prices. Finally, as unrest became the normal state of affairs in the countryside, the yonaoshi risings, such as occurred first in Iida and Ueda, began to show signs of reversion to the more traditional type of ikki rising. This feature of the Shinshū risings, however, did not emerge until the winter of the following year. Meanwhile, riots continued in areas inundated with debased coins and paper money.

AIDA, AUGUST 25–26, 1869

When Ueda's frenzied rioting tapered off, news of what had happened there spread quickly along post-station routes to about seventy villages and towns in four (ex-bakufu) districts—Aida, Kawate, Sakakita, and Asazumi—which were under the administrative jurisdiction of newly created Ina (later Chikuma) prefecture. The district where the rioting began, Aida, was a mountain-ridge region of sloping fields traversed by post roads and post-station villages. Its rural population engaged mainly in the cultivation of rice, raw silk, mulberry, tobacco, soba, and millet.

The rising apparently began in Aida village around August 25 when a small group of peasants fixed a time, drew up a list of grievances, and then, on a rainy night, rang fire bells to call out their neighbors for a traditional protest action. Further mobilizations occurred under different leadership the next day, August 26, in Midarebashi village. Also on that same day, there appeared on village notice boards throughout Sakakita and Asazumi districts a list of seven grievances justifying the protest. These included high rice prices, the noncirculation of one-half-ryō coins, excessively high tributes, the exorbitant interest rates being charged by the village rich, and the existence of the system of three important village officials.

The wave of yonaoshi and village disturbances in Aida and its neighboring districts was, like the Ueda rising, short-lived, lasting for only three days. But, for reasons that are not clear, it involved only some three thousand to five thousand peasants. Yet these smaller numbers managed to attack the property (but not the persons) of virtually the entire political and economic elite of all four districts: sake dealers, grain merchants, village officials, moneylenders, and landlords. Significantly, many who suffered property destruction had been accumulating land at the expense of their neighbors ever since 1865.

The Aida disturbances ended shortly after troops (including many outcasts) were ordered into the region from nearby Matsumoto fief. At different places and times the troops confronted the rioting peasants in brief skirmishes. In one encounter in the vicinity of Yabara village, they shot and killed an unknown number of peasants, caused others who were crossing a river to drown, and ended up arresting large numbers. A second encounter at Tohara village ended peacefully, with the peasants promising to disperse if their demands were conveyed to higher authorities. By September 4, a total of 184 peasants in Aida and Kawate districts, and 38 to 41 others in Asazumi district, had been arrested. Arrest records revealed that most of the participants, including four leaders later executed, were holders either of from ten to six koku or of less than three koku. This suggests participation by a broad cross section of the village, including many respectable, middle-strata peasants. The participants shared in common a general condition of economic insecurity, heavy indebtedness, and a recent history of steady land losses to moneylenders and landlords.[18]

Neither Ueda nor Aida district returned to normal even after all arrests had been made. For tenants in both places continued to approach landlords in border villages, demanding rent reductions and the return of pawned land. Unrest was becoming steadily more generalized even when it did not lead to attacks on property. After Aida, the center of action shifted to nearby Komoro fief, where about two thousand peasants, demanding the redemption of worthless currency, rioted more tamely on August 28. Timely action by fief officials may have headed off more trouble there.

As the path of risings moved slowly northward through the mountains and valleys of Shinshū, the energy for them continued to be furnished by the poorest strata of minute-cultivating peasants and the propertyless poor, who demanded an end to all the excessive burdens that were bankrupting their lives. Nearly everywhere their demands were the same: they called for abolition of the old village official system, reductions in the tribute rice price, continuation of customary tribute reductions on fields unsuited for rice production, and the return of pawned land and articles. But, at the same time, new elements entered the picture. The policies of the Meiji government and the fiefs had begun to endanger the prosperity of the upper strata of well-to-do peasants, forcing them to involve themselves with the poor. With their return to the scene the demands and the leadership of the peasant struggle movement gradually changed.

During the spring and summer of 1870, government officials and the rural elite concentrated their efforts on financial reform and the establishment and operation of commercial firms to redeem the holders of bad currency. The momentum of the movement then slowed. But by winter, acute economic distress had returned, causing the movement to pick up and attain its peak. Different class strata and groups that had earlier been opposed to the struggles of the village poor now joined up with them. In some places rich peasants and village officials merely extended their sympathy to demonstrators; in other places they took the lead in making legal appeals on their behalf; and in still other places they actually joined in demonstrations against government policies. In short, by November 1870 the protest movement in Shinshū had taken on the character of an all-inclusive mass struggle of entire villages united against the highly unpopular tax and economic policies of the fiefs, the Meiji government, and its prefectural officials.[19] This progression can be seen in the fierce rioting and tumult that occurred in Matsushiro fief between November 25 and 27, and then spread during December to nearby Susaka fief and Nakano prefecture.

MATSUSHIRO, SUSAKA, AND NAKANO, NOVEMBER – DECEMBER 1870

Between November 25 and 27, tens of thousands of peasants in Matsushiro rose up against the fief government. Three weeks later, starting on December 17, the unrest spread to nearby Susaka (a fifteen-thousand-koku fief) and Nakano prefecture, where it finally ended. In Matsushiro the rising involved a commercial firm established the previous year with the dual function of engaging in the silk trade and aiding impoverished peasants by collecting and redeeming their bad currency. Most of the capital for the firm was furnished by village officials, landlords, and silk merchants, including one Ōtani Kōzō of Haneo village. Ōtani's contribution allowed the new firm to issue over 200,000 ryō of notes, much of which he himself used to corner the entire silkworm egg-card crop in the region. But the export trade at Yokohama suffered a severe slump during 1870 and the value of the commercial notes collapsed, causing heavy losses to many noteholders.

Then, with worthless commercial notes circulating in Matsushiro alongside debased one-half-ryō coins and devalued fief notes, the officials of Matsushiro decided, unwisely though at the urging of the Meiji government, to increase tribute exactions. As explained in an essay by Ochiai Nobutaka:

The [Meiji] government had already prohibited the printing and circulation of fief notes and obligated them to be returned. However, since Matsushiro fief delayed redeeming the notes, the Council of State urged it to redeem them by means of the tax collection. The deputy councillor, Takano [Hiroma], on the order of the Meiji government, then changed the price of tribute rice paid in kind, which had already been promulgated. He ordered that in converting the notes issued by the Council of State into commercial firm notes, a discount be made of 25 percent. He also fixed the price of tribute rice paid in kind at 4.5 bales of unhulled rice for 10 ryō. Within the fief government there was strong opposition but Takano beat down his critics by saying "Which is more important, the imperial court or the villages under the fief?"[20]

Sparked by Takano's trick, a series of disturbances began simultaneously in several places. One of them was Kamiyamado village, Sarashina district, where nearly 86 percent of the inhabitants possessed less than five koku each and were either poor tenants who worked for absent landlords or semiproletarians, that is, landless and impoverished poor people working in miscellaneous occupations.[21] Here, on the night of November 25, bands of peasants, carrying pine torches, burned down Ōtani's home in Haneo village along with the homes of two other large merchants in the employ of the fief. Their main demands, at this point, were a fairer conversion rate for fief notes and cash reductions in tribute.

Afterward, three areas within Matsushiro became the main centers of punitive actions by peasants. These were Zenkōji town, a commercial center on the Hokkoku highway, Matsushiro castle town, the fief's administrative hub, and the Kamigo sericulture area on the border with Ueda. The core group of protesters, who marched into Zenkōji through the peripheral villages on its outskirts, was composed chiefly of peasants, miscellaneous artisans who had dropped out of the restrictive guild system, petty former retainers, and day laborers. Their main targets in and around Zenkōji were merchants specializing in silk thread, grain, and oil, pawnshop and cake-shop proprietors, moneylenders, sake brewers, textile merchants, and high-ranking fief officials. Altogether, the protesters managed to burn to the ground about eighty homes belonging to such people.[22]

While Zenkōji was under assault, other mixed groups struck at merchants, village headmen, sake brewers, and landlords living in semiurbanized villages along the Hokkoku highway in the Kamigo area. But what may have been the largest protest action occurred within the castle town itself. A large group of undetermined numbers marched into the town and fired the homes and offices of 24 ex-samurai officials. They also inflicted varying degrees of damage on 115 homes belonging to merchants. A key happening was the complete destruction of the building housing the commercial firm established the previous year by Matsushiro fief. In another incident within the town, demonstrators surrounded the ex-lord, their new governor, demanding both a five-year moratorium on all back tributes and a new tribute price of ten ryō for ten bales.[23] Eventually, they ended up winning a discount set at seven bales for ten ryō. After promises of tribute reductions and a fairer currency exchange rate had been secured, the mobs in Matsushiro castle town finally dispersed. But disturbances in the countryside continued a while longer as tenants pressed demands for rent reductions.

Historian Matsuda Yukitoshi, in a detailed study of these Matsushiro disturbances, divided the targets of property destruction into three categories: (1) the top
echelon of the fief bureaucracy, (2) locally prominent landlords and privileged
merchants, both of whom were closely allied with the fief bureaucrats, and (3) the
rural and urban merchant strata in general. He argued that the first two groups
suffered the most destruction because the Matsushiro events mainly expressed a
fusion of two struggles: one against fief power, the other against landlords and
usurious moneylenders who controlled peasants in the course of their day-to-day
activities.[24]

By looking closer at the targets of looting and property destruction, we may
perceive a crucial political dimension to the struggle. Many protesters were producers of silkworm cocoons, egg cards, seeds, and silk thread, which they sold to
the big urban merchants through fief-licensed brokers. The latter lived in the villages and were also small producers like themselves. During the disturbances, peasants carefully distinguished between these small licensed middlemen and more
powerful silk merchants living in the castle town—Matsushiro's growing bourgeoisie. The latter were hated because they worked with the fief in exploiting and
controlling the smaller silk producers and brokers.

Thus the class struggle in Matsushiro was directed primarily against the predatory combination of fief officials and local bourgeois who were seeking control
over the sericulture industry. By contrast, small rural merchants, not closely connected with them, became secondary targets of attack. But in some areas of the fief,
such as Kamiyamada village in Kamigo, the struggle pitted tenants on newly reclaimed lands against landlord developers and grain merchants. In this analysis of
the targets of popular wrath and the reasons behind it, one general point is particularly important. The multisided conflicts in northern Shinshū during 1870
were fought out on a very practical terrain in which local political and economic
aspects of domination were inseparably fused, just as these two dimensions—the
economic and the political—had been inseparably fused in peasant demands at the
start of the feudal era. Most of the struggles examined throughout this study have
borne out precisely that point.

Turning next to the participants in the Matsushiro disturbances, Matsuda
Yukitoshi presents some evidence, based on incomplete official arrest records,
which suggests that the demonstrators represented a cross section of the fief's ruled
population. Over four hundred people were eventually arrested and punished in
Matsushiro, but initially arrests occurred on a small scale. The available evidence
indicates that poor peasants (many with large families and holdings of less than
three koku), from villages around Matsushiro castle town and the Kamigo area,
participated in large numbers. In Zenkōji and its environs, on the other hand, the

overwhelming majority consisted of nonguild artisans and manual laborers—the urban poor—whom the authorities all too quickly labeled as "outlaws," "scoundrels," and "gamblers" (see table 4). In addition, some of the arrested demonstrators, such as the cotton dealer Komasuya Yahei, the silk yarn merchant Takamatsuya Chihei, and the dyer Eitarō, were fairly respectable rural merchants—Chihei had earlier lent two hundred ryō to the fief—and one of the ringleaders, Goemon, was a village official.[25]

So much for the Matsushiro rising. All told, the social forces that made their appearance in it anticipated the lineup of antagonists in Shinshū for the remainder of the decade. The new Meiji government was going to be perceived as the main enemy of the poor, and the growing prefectural bourgeoisie was going to become, after a long period of bitter political strife, the staunch ally of the government.

After Matsushiro, outbreaks of rioting and incendiarism on a relatively larger scale occurred in neighboring Susaka fief. There many poor villagers had appealed through their village headmen for a tax freeze. When news of the Matsushiro events suddenly spread through the fief, it obviated their need to wait for the government's reply. "Bearing hatchets and saws, the peasants rallied others along the highway and set fire to the property of sake merchants and village headmen."[26] Twice, on December 16 and 17, a mob of about fifteen hundred peasants swept into Susaka castle town, where they confronted fief soldiers who initially fired nonlethal bean pellets at them. When that failed to stop them, the troops switched to live ammunition, killing two protesters and wounding eight others. It was to no avail. Before the rioting in Susaka was put down, peasants allegedly succeeded in destroying the properties of many privileged wholesale merchants involved in fief-sponsored projects. They also demanded tribute reductions and sought to exploit the difference in the imperial court price for tribute (the price charged in neighboring prefectures administered by imperial officials) and the fief price. They also boldly demanded lifetime indemnity payments to the families of peasants killed by fief soldiers and smaller indemnities to the families of those who had suffered wounds. And as in Matsushiro, Susaka officials promised to lower their tribute rates and abolish the advance payment portion for the following year.[27]

The wave of disturbances in northern Shinshū climaxed finally in massive demonstrations and riots in Nakano prefecture between December 19 and 21. These events have not been as well studied as the Matsushiro incident, but it is known that the pattern in Nakano was similar to what had occurred in Matsushiro and Susaka, though on a far larger scale. Here village headmen had forwarded appeals for a reduction in tributes only to see the new prefectural government reject them and issue orders for additional taxes. When the villages learned of what had happened

TABLE 4. Holdings and Occupations of People Who Were Arrested after the First Wave of Rioting Subsided in the Matsushiro Rising, 1870

From Matsushiro Castle Town and Its Environs

Name	Holdings in to*	Occupation
Kei	o	water mill worker
Taki	o	mat maker
Nagasawa Keisaku	3.3	(7 family members took part)
Koyama Nakagorō	30.	(6 family members took part)
Narita Haruji	4.3	(3 family members took part)
Kobayashi Kyūsaku	14.	(4 family members took part)
Kitamura Tomozō	4.	(5 family members took part)
Kitamura Hassaku	18.	(3 family members took part)
Kitamura Yosuke	20.	(3 family members took part)
Nakamura Mosuke	14.	(5 family members took part)
Goemon	?	ring leader [upper–stratum peasant]
Kondō Yasaji	3.0	(4 family members took part)
Miyamoto Chū'emon	o	landless, destitute bonded servant
Zenroku	10.	(5 family members took part)
Miyaguchi Tōsaku	?	(6 family members took part)
Sukesaburō	o	firewood carrier

From Kamigō Area: A Sericultural Area in Matsushiro Fief near the Border with Ueda

Name	Holdings in to*	Occupation
Kodama Seinosuke	5.	(4 family members took part)
Ōi Matsuhei	14.	(6 family members took part)
Miyazaki Heizō	7.	(4 family members took part)
Hanbei	o	servant
Magosaku	o	servant
Fujimoto Kinosuke	30.	(7 family members took part)
Nishizawa Jūkichi	7.	(4 family members took part)
Kigenta	5.	(5 family members took part)
Kichiemon		⎫
Sasuke		contract laborers engaged in Miyamoto
Tarobei		Kiemon's mountain development
Chūta		
Miyazaka Daijirō	26.	⎭ (6 family members took part)

in Matsushiro and Susaka, they immediately rose up. Although the entire prefecture was affected, the main rioting and property destruction occurred within Nakano town itself, when peasants were joined by the urban poor in attacks on the property of merchants and officials. According to one unconfirmed report, at the height of the disturbance thousands of demonstrators surrounded the official re-

TABLE 4. *(cont.)*

From Zenkōji Town and Its Environs

Name	Holdings in to*	Occupation
Kazunosuke	o	cooper
Heihachi	o	outlaw
Tsurukichi	o	outlaw
Zenshichi	o	outlaw
Sankaku	o	outlaw
Hatsutarō	o	formerly engaged in robbery
Yasubēe	o	on the surface, a fireman, actually a gambler
Takamatsuya Chihēe	o	silk yarn and cotton merchant
Umekichi	o	woodcutter
Yohēe	o	tinsmith
Shinsuke	o	fireman
Hanaya Denshichi	o	provides accommodation for gamblers
Kasuke	o	gardener
Eitarō	o	dyer
Teikichi	o	professional gambler
Mitsugorō	o	manservant for Kisōta
Kasuke	o	resident of rented house
Shōryū	o	gambler
Shinkichi	o	tavernkeeper
Teikichi	o	draper
Gunji	o	brothelkeeper
Kumekichi	o	matmaker
Umeta	o	gambler
Taichi	o	gambler
Kihei	o	gambler
Eisaku	o	gambler
Fukujirō	o	gambler
Sakichi	o	gambler
Yahēe	o	gambler
Daigorō	o	bird dealer
Komasuya Yahei	o	cotton dealer
Tokuji	o	nail maker
Nakamuraya Jisuke	o	gambler
Sōzō	o	gambler
Katsusaburō	o	homeless
Mansaku	o	pack horse driver
Naoemon	o	carpenter
Eikichi	o	Village Headman's son
Zenkichi	o	clerk
Uchida Risaku	33	(3 family members took part)
Uchida Yachōji	20	(3 family members took part)
Zenji	o	homeless

* 1 *to* = 1/10 of a koku or 4.65 U.S. gallons; 1 *sho* = 1/10 of a *to* or 0.477 U.S. gallons.
Source: Charts compiled by Matsuda Yukitoshi, "Meiji shonen no kaikyū tōsō—Shinshū Matsushiro 'gosatsu sōdō' no baai" (Class Struggle in Early Meiji: On the "Disturbances in Connection with Currencies Issued in 1870" in Matsushiro Fief, Shinshū), *Rekishigaku kenkyū*, no. 359 (April 1970): 36–37.

sidence of the governor, screaming, "We will never go back until we can see the chief councillor beheaded and we want all the other officials killed." [28] This certainly fits the image of plebeian bloody-mindedness, but whether it is true or not is another question. There is no doubt, however, that the peasants burned down the governor's residence, forcing him to flee for his life. In the confusion, a prefectural official was killed trying to stop the protesters. Other peasant bands were later rumored to have gathered at the borders of Nakano prefecture to prevent imperial officials from returning to Nakano town. The protesters apparently managed to hold Nakano town and the surrounding area for three days, during which time they inflicted a great deal of punitive property destruction.

Meanwhile, by late December 1870, it was clear to officials in Tokyo that no single fief or prefecture in Shinshū province, acting on its own, was capable of suppressing a determined peasant disturbance. Altogether the Meiji government ordered in a total of three companies of conscripts in order to reinforce fief soldiers who were trying to stamp out the risings in Matsushiro, Susaka, and Nakano. Tokyo also sent out directives to another nineteen fiefs ordering them to furnish aid to the riot-affected areas.[29] But when reinforcements arrived in northern Shinshū, the fury of poor peasants and townsmen had already spent itself against the property of their traditional enemies.

CONCLUSION: THE END OF MORAL ECONOMY CONSIDERATIONS AND THE CHICHIBU REBELLION

The debased-currency disturbances in Shinshū may be situated along the same line of development as earlier yonaoshi and ikki incidents of the 1860s. Their rhetoric and method of mobilization by village units was thoroughly traditional. Their demands too ran the familiar gamut of issues: from the return of pawned land and articles, the removal of hated fief and village officials, and the open conduct of village affairs, on the one hand, to tribute reductions, lower grain prices, and charity for the poor, on the other. But other aspects of these scattered incidents could also be interpreted as forerunners of a new era. For at that juncture, 1869–1870, the relationship between state and society was undergoing fundamental revision. What the peasants demanded most of all—the redemption of debased currency— was something that no fief government on its own could resolve. Moreover, they showed signs of developing an all-inclusive mass movement against the biases of Meiji tax and fiscal policies.

Yet, in the early years of the Restoration, such aspects of newness in social struggles were sharply limited. For Japan's period of primitive capital accumulation had only just begun and the state itself still lacked the capability to greatly expand its role in reorganizing the economy on behalf of the dominant economic classes and groups. Stated differently, the complex historical processes leading to the formation of proletarians and capitalists, and to a specifically capitalist type of everyday economic life, were still at an early stage. Consequently, moral considerations that mitigated harshness in the collection of debts continued to govern relations between lenders and borrowers at the local level. And not only did the force of custom and traditional morality shape business operations and property relations in villages. Institutionally, a tax revision and a legal system leading to the establishment of capitalist private property in land had yet to be created. Lacking, in addition, a modern army to enforce its commands, the new government had to respect peasant traditions and, on occasion, even yield to their demands.

So rapid was the pace of change, however, that it took but a single decade to turn that situation completely around. By the early 1880s drastic changes were occurring in the historical process. These related partly to capitalism's arrival in the countryside and partly to modifications in the character and behavior of the state. Backed by its new conscript army of peasants, the Meiji government was at an advanced stage in implementing a nationwide land tax reform, which carried with it profound long-term consequences. Simultaneously, it was also crushing out dissent and asserting a more formidable power at the village level.

For many peasants and town laborers, suffering and misery increased as rural-centered light industrialization proceeded. The decade of the 1880s was characterized in rural areas by the restructuring effects of the government's deflationary measures and its heavy tax policies. Together they caused soaring household indebtedness, bankruptcies, and land forfeitures. Earlier, in the late 1870s, laws were rewritten to encourage high-interest usury. Within a few years there appeared on the local scene new institutions of social control: modern banks, local courts, police stations, and village offices where debts were registered with land certificates pledged as security. Because the state, via its new court and police system, ranged itself unequivocally on the side of rural creditors, the scales tilted more sharply than they ever had before in favor of landlords and rural capitalists. In the eyes of small cultivators and tenants, the moral legitimacy of the state plummeted.

Under such conditions, relations between lenders and borrowers in villages, as exemplified in the traditional pawnshop financing system, could not help but become impersonal and highly antagonistic. This was especially true in districts where sericultural production was most advanced and modern banks and financial institutions had made significant inroads. Saitama, Gumma, Kanagawa, Nagano, Yamanashi, and Shizuoka prefectures all witnessed the introduction of modern methods of calculating interest on loans and a more single-minded pursuit of debts by creditors. Creditors could now lodge legal suits against debt defaulters and get the Meiji state, via the local courts, to collect not only the collateral and, later, any unredeemed portion of whatever was still owed them but also the interest on it plus the court fees. Such a relationship of the dominant economic class to the state already implies a degree of "transfer of political power to private property" that would have been impossible under Tokugawa feudalism.[30]

Thus, during the 1880s, many new elements of the capitalist transformation process combined to destroy what remained of the old paternalism in village affairs. The form of the state also changed, its repressive power growing to where, once again, it seemed intolerably despotic to middle- and lower-strata peasants alike. Bearing these circumstances in mind, let us look briefly at what turned out to be the very last yonaoshi ikki in Japanese history as well as the largest armed peasant revolt of the Meiji era.[31]

The Chichibu incident of 1884 was a violent response by silk-growing peasants to precisely those changes in the character of the economy and the state that we have been discussing. The overwhelming majority of those who participated in it were self-cultivating owners of dry fields who paid land taxes and supplemented their income from sericultural production. The Chichibu district of Saitama prefecture, where most of them lived, had become tied by its exported silk to Lyons, France. When international economic relations turned unfavorable and an agricultural crisis struck Japan in 1883, the mountain villages of Chichibu, already suffering acutely from the imperial government's deflationary policies, were profoundly affected.

In these circumstances, sometime between spring and fall of 1883, small groups of heavily indebted peasants began to petition the civil authorities and local moneylenders. They asked for reductions in state, prefectural, and local village taxes as well as for deferral of their debts. The next year, 1884, the crisis to rural life and subsistence in Chichibu and other sericultural districts worsened, whereupon various "poor people's parties" sprang up in many parts of the Kanto Plain, including the villages of Chichibu. Their members followed the ex-samurai and landlord-led opposition to the Meiji regime by taking the label "party" and appropriating for their own, more egalitarian purposes, the rhetoric, vocabulary, and even some of the topics of Liberal party debate. When the gentlemen of the Liberal party convened a general meeting in Tokyo in March 1884, with representatives from around the country in attendance, five Chichibu peasant leaders participated.

There should be no mistake about this, however. Many leaders of the poor people's party (such as the wealthy peasants from the Saku district of Shinshū, Ide Tamekichi and Kikuchi Kanbei) were saturated with modern Western political ideas and did join the Liberal party. But the branches of their own poor people's party, in which nearly all peasant activists coalesced, were far more akin to secret solidarity bands than to the Liberal party, which mainly attracted the village rulers. And even if indebted peasants operated now more openly than in the past, within an expanded organizational form, most of them still drew their inspiration from a thoroughly premodern tradition of protest. The important points then are these. First, there was a dimension of close interaction between the emerging bourgeois politics of the ex-samurai and landlords and local peasant politics. But most peasants acted inside a distinctive cultural arena. Here Western ideas were not as important in shaping their moral consciousness and conduct as was a deep-rooted native (Shintoist) ideology of equality and brotherhood and sisterhood, known as "purification religion" (*misogikyō*). Furthermore, peasants acted within village communities that had carefully preserved memories of Sakura Sōgorō and of the Bushū yonaoshi uprising that had swept through their region eighteen years earlier.

So, the Chichibu poor people's party commenced quite peacefully, seeking only to press a lawful campaign for debt relief. But after several months of unsuccessful negotiations with the civil authorities, its members discovered that the state sustained private economic power in ways that closed off all peaceful public paths to the redress of their economic grievances. For the Meiji state proclaimed its neutrality and noninterference in "private" lender-borrower relations, while all the time creating laws that threatened peasants with arrest and punishment for engaging in collective negotiations with their creditors. During the spring and summer of 1884, at the height of the deflation, household bankruptcies in Chichibu increased weekly, and bad weather struck, ruining the summer silk crop. Feeling themselves driven into a desperate predicament, the leaders of the debt deferral campaign abruptly escalated their protest. Overnight it became an armed insurrection.

In this second, insurrectionary stage, as described by Inada Masahirō, the initial economic goals remained, but a drastic change in consciousness occurred. The leaders came to feel that their salvation lay not simply in inflicting punitive sanctions on the property of their opponents, as in the past, but in actually overthrowing them and setting up in their place a new government of social justice. At the highest level, that meant waging "yonaoshi warfare" against the Saitama prefectural government and its judicial, police, and village officials. Thus we might say that the Chichibu rebels now grasped, in their own concrete terminology, a point that was seen only dimly by the Shinshū peasants in 1870: in the shift to capitalism on the political plane, the intermediate level of government becomes the vital link in maintaining repressive state power at the local level. Second, peasants also sought the punishment of bankers and usurious moneylenders, who were the very embodiment of their antagonism with the state. Above all, they meant to destroy debtor-creditor relations by burning the official notary book of seals in which village office clerks had registered peasant debts with land certificates as collateral. How the insurrection unfolded is worth outlining.

On October 31, 1884, the Fuppu village branch of the poor people's party rose up in an armed rebellion and headed off to Shimo Yoshida village where, by prearrangement, other armed contingents were also gathering. The leader of the rebellion was Tashiro Eisuke, a silk farmer, unlicensed "people's advocate," and famous "fixer" with a large clientele in his hometown, the district capital of Ōmiya. In order to dispense justice on behalf of poor people, "commander" Tashiro Eisuke, his "vice commander," the pawnshop operator and merchant Katō Orihei, their "chief of staff" Kikuchi Kanbei, and other leaders proceeded to turn the poor people's party into a "poor people's army." On the night of November 1, an estimated three hundred to three thousand peasants, wearing white headbands (the symbol of purity) and carrying swords, spears, and flintlock rifles, assembled in the courtyard of Muku Shrine in Shimo Yoshida village. There they formed into large and small-sized combat units, and were given a military code of conduct and short speeches by their leaders. The entire scene at the crucial moment of escalation enacted a series of military rituals in defense of the people that symbolically counterpointed the more powerful militarism of the Meiji state, which was exercised on behalf of the rich and propertied.

Next day the main unit marched into Ōmiya (present-day Chichibu City), occupied the district office, and turned it into a "revolutionary headquarters." For two days and nights the poor people's army, estimated at from five thousand to ten thousand strong, controlled the Chichibu countryside. Then, on November 4, Tokyo mobilized sufficient military and police power to begin crushing the uprising. After several pitched battles were fought, it ended formally on November 9 at the base of Mt. Yatsuga in Saku district, Nagano prefecture, Shinshū province. Eventually, over 3,000 people, including many who surrendered themselves to the police, were tried and convicted for participating in the struggle.

To resume: the Chichibu rebellion occurred (a) in a region made vulnerable by its deepening linkages to the world economy, (b) in the period of the dissolution of the freedom and people's rights movement, and (c) at a time when modern capitalist methods of exploitation had made deep inroads. Not surprisingly, it displayed a unique combination of elements old and new. From beginning to end, ikki and yonaoshi traditions of protest pervaded this rebellion and were its main source of ideological strength. Drawing upon beliefs and practices stemming from their own regional political culture, the peasants of Chichibu and its surrounding districts attempted to restore vital aspects of a dying moral economy. In the end, they succeeded in envisioning, as peasants (and workers) so often do, a more just form of government than the one that their modernizing elites were forcibly imposing upon them.

But perhaps because many of the cooperative social relationships that sustained peasant uprisings in the past had broken down at this stage, there may appear to be grounds for arguing that the organizers were forced to rely to an unusual degree on threats and coercion in mobilizing peasants to participate. Such an interpretation is possible but unlikely, for even at this late date peasant practice did not support it. In respect to motivation, the use of coercive recruitment techniques was not a symptom of any sort of desperation felt by the organizers; nor can it be taken to imply, as the judicial authorities at the time maintained, that the majority of the Chichibu rebels blindly followed their leaders. Peasants were not unaware of the inherent ambiguity of such techniques. That coercion had been used in the initial stage of the rising could later be turned around by peasants: in the moment of defeat and interrogation by the authorities many could plead extenuating circumstances as a defense against harsh punishment.

In two other respects as well, the Chichibu rising followed late Tokugawa precedent. Its participants were stimulated by the idea of yonaoshi, which they raised to the level of a universal but still politically shallow principle and justification for action. And the top leaders, the popular Tashiro Eisuke and Katō Orihei, were figures straight from the world of the legends of exemplary martyrs rather than politicians of people's rights.

This picture of a traditional peasant uprising changes, however, once we consider the connection between the Chichibu poor people's party and the Liberal party and the form that the struggle took. At those levels the description of the rising conveys a transitional if not modern image. Not only was it more disciplined and carefully planned than most risings that preceded it; it also differed from them in the high degree of political consciousness shown by its leaders, who directly took the Meiji state as their target and were willing to confront it militarily at the prefectural level. Above all, Chichibu was distinctive insofar as its mode of organization was thoroughly military and hierarchical, and its participants were no longer hesitant to steal money and supplies for their campaign or even to destroy human life in self-defense. When the totality of its characteristics are accounted for, the Chichibu rebellion, which started off as a debt-deferral movement, no longer fits the historical category of a peasant uprising (ikki) with which we began our study. As Inada Masahirō suggested, its intermixed elements or contents had burst the feudal form. Historical understanding of class struggles in Japan requires that we think hereafter in terms of different concepts. Less than twenty years divide the Chichibu incident from the yonaoshi risings in Bushū, the western Chūgoku region, and Shinshū; yet it is not improper to speak of 1884 as the end of an epoch.

CHAPTER SIXTEEN

Results and Conclusion

W E have completed a reconstruction of Japanese social history in terms of recurring instances of peasant and commoner revolt. Our presentation depended on giving careful attention to the relationship between particular class struggle events and the local, regional, and "national" circumstances, as well as the periods in which they occurred.[1] It turned also on showing the changing forms of struggle and how each incident contained within itself moments of a larger evolution of feudal society and state through specific stages of growth and decay. All four parts of the study emphasized the dynamics of the class struggle process, first under the premises of a feudal system, later under the transition to early capitalism. In pursuit of these concerns, we have had to address the precipitating causes of rebellion, the sequence of events whenever peasants appeared on the political stage, the contents of their demands, their underlying goals and values, and the consequences of their actions. Last, we tackled the relationship between the unfolding of risings and successive stages of, and turning points in, economic development.

In thinking about the connection between class struggles and economic stages, we did not assume that economic development automatically implied continuous political progress over time in the unfolding of risings. That is to say, wherever the empirical evidence allowed, we related the risings to historically specific stages of economic development. In terms of the larger story of Japan's transformation from a feudal to a capitalist society, those stages were progressive in nature. Yet we did not infer from that that in the risings themselves, the ascent of peasant political consciousness was reflected through ever higher levels of development. For the maturation of political consciousness is never a direct function of time: it does not unfold upward in unilinear stages, from one historical epoch to another; nor can there be anything at all mechanistic in its explanation.

That observation, however, is perfectly compatible with what E. H. Carr termed belief in "the progressive development of human potentialities" in the course of historical change. During two and a half centuries of Tokugawa rule and through the early decades of Meiji, measurable political progress was occurring in peak periods of class conflict. At such times the objective circumstances—famines, political crises, imperialist intervention, acute inflation and deflation, and so on— fostered environments that aided rebellious peasants and townspeople in making demands and calling their oppressors to justice. The political advances we were concerned with involved large numbers of people in situations where they remembered and drew strength from their own past experiences of resistance to authority, or where they succeeded in utilizing selected elements of the dominant ideology in order to achieve their own ends. Their protests continually engaged the moral, political, military, and economic energies of the bakuhan (and Meiji) state, and acted as restraints on its excesses. At the same time, the historical record of the protests revealed to us some degree of conceptual advance over time for peasants in their understanding and practical assertion of rights, as in their rational pursuit of aims. The inherent dynamism of class relationships within the Tokugawa type of feudal polity made advances possible. Progress was also possible because peasants could draw on their own organizational, cultural, and religious resources, part of which always remained beyond the control of the state. The following chronological review, which takes up the remainder of this chapter, bears out these claims once again.

We started off by describing the circumstances that Japan passed through during the first half of the seventeenth century, when the shoguns organized the bakuhan state and Tsuyama took shape as a western fief. A key concern was to register at the outset certain continuities between medieval and early modern Japan as reflected in peasant strategies for forging unity and resisting excessive exploitation. Moving into the second half of the seventeenth century, Mori tax policy in Tsuyama began to promote full-status peasants who exploited their own independent family labor and paid tributes in kind and cash. The tribute rate was set so high, however, that it kept a large part of the peasantry in perpetual debt while also furthering the intermediate exploitation of peasants by local merchants. In 1697 Edo confiscated Tsuyama fief, removed the Mori family of daimyo, and appointed Matsudaira Naganori as the new lord of a geographically reduced Tsuyama. Following this shogunal action, which deliberately weakened fief power, Matsudaira Nagonori in 1698 opted to continue Mori tax policy and the Mori system of rural control through district, deputy district, and village headmen.

At that point, the antagonisms that had been building in village society exploded in a violent but unsuccessful peasant appeal, mediated by a sympathetic district headman and village headman. Then, twenty-eight years later, with memories of this 1698 incident still fresh in many minds, peasants rose up throughout the entire fief and, for the first time, registered in their own voices the full range of their grievances against the fief.

To understand the hierarchy of causes that led to the Sanchū rising, account had to be taken of a combination of political and economic factors. These included the Matsudaira's bureaucratic reforms, led by Kubo Shimbei and undertaken in parallel with Shogun Yoshimune's Kyōhō reforms. Changes in fief political economy and in village-level context had also to be noted. That meant addressing the degree of market activity and of social stratification that obtained at the time, together with the persistence in village social relations of bonded labor as a remnant of earlier centuries. Most peasants in Tsuyama engaged in market activities primarily in order to meet tax payments in kind. But as the local village economy developed and became more diversified, they found themselves forced into increasing competition with the fief for scarce land and forestry resources. Many also found themselves locked into localized subsystems of indebtedness to rural merchants, store operators, mine owners, and village officials.

The Sanchū rising lasted ten weeks and unfolded in two stages. Throughout both stages, peasants in Sanchū displayed a keen desire to secure administrative control of their villages by stripping all power from local officials, many of whom were also their creditors and employers in the iron mines. Their acutely felt need to control their own villages through popularly chosen message receivers is precisely what gave the Sanchū rising its past orientation.

In Tsuyama fief in 1726–1727, the peasants challenged and tried to reform a rural status hierarchy inherited from the founding stage of the bakuhan state. At the time of their rising, the samurai still displayed undiminished enthusiasm for their calling, while the social order still allowed a minority of full-status, privileged "peasants," many from old warrior lineages, to exercise by hereditary right all power over various types of unfree serflike laborers. In fighting to replace their existing system of village government with the message receiver system, Tsuyama's peasants signaled their own existential awakening to the problems of an antiquated and highly repressive control structure. They also showed sharp awareness of the fact that control over their production process depended on the mechanism of appointing and dismissing peasant officials at the village and district levels. That key political issue, which pitted peasants directly against the fief, was joined once the peasants acted on their belief that if a lord died, or had been dismissed from office, his officials had no right physically to remove tribute from a district.

The Sanchū rising ended in the total defeat of the peasants once outside forces had been mobilized and brought to bear against them. Increased repression in villages and heightened contradictions in the fief economy were the main results of the Sanchū rising. Yet its real historical significance lay elsewhere, for this incident signaled the arrival of material conditions—stagnant population growth, landlord-tenant relations, declining rice prices, and so on—marking a new stage in a systemic crisis of feudalism. Under these conditions, the rising spirit of dissent and rebelliousness, which the Sanchū peasants displayed during the 1720s, would continue to characterize the peasantry in many areas of Japan right through the remainder of the feudal epoch, and beyond that to the end of the landlord system.

We made our second deep cut into the body of feudal society in Ueda fief in central Japan, thirty-five years after the Sanchū rising. By the sixth decade of the eighteenth century, fief financial difficulties had increased, commercial activities had spread more broadly, and village structure was noticeably more advanced than in Tsuyama. Here rebellion was motivated by antipathy to new and excessive tributes and corvées, illegal fief manipulation of the rice-cash conversion rate, a desire for local political reform, and a growing rift between countryside and castle town. Horizontal conflicts within the top stratum of the peasant class preceded the rising and helped to produce leaders against the fief. Rejecting Ueda fief's efforts to increase tributes and strip them of the fruits of their developing market activities, Ueda's peasants drew on an even longer tradition of past resistance to feudal misrule and displayed a greater sense of irreverence toward samurai.

Unlike Tsuyama, all strata of Ueda's peasants, as well as its merchants, artisans, and even outcasts rose en masse over long-standing grievances. Their numerous detailed demands covered both economic and political issues. The Ueda rising also lasted longer than that in Tsuyama and succeeded ultimately in realizing many of its demands. Significantly, at the start of the armed demonstration before Ueda castle, many peasants took umbrage at being called hinindomo. Later, through all stages of their struggle, they displayed a keen sense of status consciousness which reinforced their unity against the fief.

In many respects the Ueda rising was unlike what had gone before. By this time, peasant solidarity based on an ideology of fixed hereditary status had reached its furthest limit and would begin to disintegrate. Originally, status was a political instrument of class domination. The bakuhan authorities had revitalized and applied it to peasants and townsmen in order to tie them to their public, occupational functions. But economic advance complicated and blurred those functions. Over the course of the next century, class and income stratification advanced further within villages and towns, land tenure became more insecure, and different class strata in villages relied increasingly for protection on their own organizations. In the process, many awakened to the political, inherently fictitious nature of status ideology. They then sought to develop ideological grounds for resistance that were more in accord with their true life situations.

Ueda was transitional in four other senses as well. First, the Ueda trans-fief ikki developed into a series of village house-smashings on a noticeably larger scale than in Tsuyama. Village disputes characterized its middle and later stages, and these prefigured the growing importance of village-level struggles over the headmen's abuse of power and the landlords' injustices.

Second, Ueda showed indications of the urban rice riots that became the main form of urban disturbance from the 1760s onward. Its townsmen and town-peasants were at the hub of the fief economy. They could see, more clearly perhaps than peasants in villages, whose vision was ordinarily more restricted, how the fief authorities criminally overtaxed and overregulated them at every turn. Not surprisingly, when fief tax practices provoked peasants into intense conflict, townsmen wasted little time in making their own public protests, for some of the same reasons. But Ueda's urban riot, and the demands it raised, may also be seen as harbingers of two other late eighteenth-century phenomena. One was the increase in the number of urban poor as a result of growing class differentiation in villages; another was the rising importance of rural merchants and their success in monopolizing rural markets outside the control of privileged town merchants.

Third, as the Ueda struggle unfolded, serious splits appeared within the samurai retainer band, brought on by the stipend-cutting policies of senior officials. We could also glimpse, in the official record of this incident, the aging process in a feudal form of administrative organization. Once challenged by a united peasantry, the fief's joint council system of rule quickly collapsed, a frequent occurrence thereafter in other fiefs rocked by disturbances.

Finally, the Ueda rising of 1761–1763 foreshadowed the growing importance of cash payment as the key nexus of man with man. While peasants demanded restrictions on the number of servants sent out from villages, thereby testifying to a growing problem of labor shortage, merchants and artisans demanded payments from Ueda's samurai for work that had previously been compulsory.

In the half-century after the Ueda Hōreki incident, many peasants continued to assert their intrinsic worth as producers upon whom the samurai were economically dependent. But all the while peasant horizons, particularly in the more commercially developed regions of the country, were being widened by the development of market mechanisms, the proliferation of rural commerce, and rural-urban competition. After steadily building up production from the mid-seventeenth century, rich peasants and merchants in the second half of the eighteenth century began to transform fiefwide market economies into regional markets. As their work advanced, subdivisions and lines between peasant strata multiplied and hardened. Under conditions of growing economic complexity, hereditary status began to seem an insufficient basis on which to sustain unity between rich and poor within villages. One of the earliest indications that peasants were seeking a new basis for class unity was the religious symbolism embodied in the god of purification (Bonten), which appeared for the first time during the gigantic Tenma disturbance of 1764–1765. By the early 1760s, the word *yonarashi* was being used by peasants to describe and justify the act of punishing the rich and unjust by destroying their property.[2]

Thus many changes had already come over the scene when the first truly great, countrywide wave of trans-fief risings and urban riots occurred in the late 1780s. The struggle of 1786–1787 in Fukuyama fief, Bingo province, had to be situated both in terms of the famine conditions prevailing nationally during the early 1780s and in connection with the growth of agricultural-commodity production, tenancy, merchant financial power, and the formation of regional market areas transcending fief borders. Historically, the stormy events of the short Tenmei famine period (1781–1788) marked a new stage of crisis for the bakuhan state. In these years, peasants, rural merchants, and low-status samurai alike all began openly to chafe under the burden of the fief as an apparatus of social control and ground-rent extraction. Morally, the crisis took the form of a loss of respect and credibility for the shogun's top advisers, led by Tanuma Okitsugu. Hereafter, how could the gaps be narrowed between the nascent bourgeoisie of merchants, artisans, and rich peasants, an impoverished class of very low-status samurai, and a peasantry increasingly divided between rich and poor within villages?

In Fukuyama fief, the Abe family's finances had worsened, placing onerous burdens on all classes, but particularly on peasants and low-status samurai. Meanwhile, rich peasants, de facto landlords, merchants, and moneylenders from villages and towns all gained increased control over the fief's new agricultural production. In this context, Fukuyama's peasants raised the demand for freedom of trade and the lowering of tenant rents and surcharges on commodity production. The fact that these issues were now on a par with tribute extortion, forced labor, and abuses by local officials meant that the ikki form of struggle was entering a new stage.

Significantly, no exemplary martyrs appeared in the Fukuyama rising. Instead of gimin, the people's heroes were whole village units which shut out the village headman stratum and acted in concert. The Ohira band and the less-celebrated Munehira and Shizuka bands furnished the leadership throughout the struggle. The Fukuyama episode thus pointed toward the increased possibilities for autonomous action by village organizations, which could be turned into strike organizations, and also the peasants' growing ability to develop new forms of association between villages. In this sense, the fading out of the gimin portended a new era in which society would be stronger, and the state weaker, than ever before.

How did the daimyo class as a whole respond to these multiple challenges from below, raised by insolent peasants and townspeople during the 1780s? Having reached the peak of their power, the daimyo usually dug in, made needed reforms, and asserted "the proper way of government," which meant hereditary, autocratic rule according to neo-Confucian norms. Abe Masatomo, lord of Fukuyama, yielded to his peasants on rice tribute matters. But he could not afford to abstain from taxing the production of cotton and controlling its circulation. Neither could he contemplate "giving peasants a free hand in the rule of the domain" by allowing them to choose their own local officials. After returning to Fukuyama from Edo, he initiated a series of reforms that combined large doses of coercion and intimidation with persuasion. For a while, Masatomo's Kansei-era reforms succeeded in rejuvenating feudal rule. But they also furthered the power and influence of the upper strata of rich peasant landlords and merchants, thereby undermining, in the long run, Fukuyama fief's economic base of minute tribute-paying proprietors. Henceforth, the growth of de facto landlordism (or "hidden" tenancy) in late Tokugawa Japan served the social function of extending and diversifying the feudal form of control over the majority population.

Following the Tenmei risings, social quiet returned rather quickly to Japan and lasted from the 1790s through the 1820s. Backed by strong bakufu leadership, many daimyo in this period tried to resolve their peasant conflicts by reorganizing the system of tribute collection. They also strengthened paternalistic ideological controls and shifted more of the burdens of public relief onto the rural elite. The latter, as a form of insurance protection and of profit making, accommodated the poor by funding public welfare institutions for which they received feudal privileges of various sorts. However, this support of the rural elite for the bakuhan state was not structured from above into an independent organizational form. Even if it had been, landlord and rural merchant cooperation could not have meliorated the deepening class conflict between lords and peasants within a politically fragmented feudal system that was in decline.

Throughout the first three decades of the nineteenth century, Japan's social structure continued to evolve in ways destructive of the bakuhan system. All classes went on accumulating knowledge, skills, and cultural competences of various kinds. Landlords and village officials, who were of the peasants but increasingly above them, continued to amass the pawned land of minute cultivators. In Kantō

Plain villages along the upper reaches of the Tama River, they formed regionwide cultural associations and began movements of legal appeal to expand the scope of their commercial activities. In the Ōsaka region, they took the lead in organizing legal protests and protracted public demonstrations against shogunal efforts to control the circulation of cotton and rapeseed through the agency of merchant financiers. Meanwhile, poor peasants increasingly read the world in terms of religious "deities in fashion" that offered them personal salvation. It is debatable, however, whether this turning inward by poor and often physically ill people, in search of salvation, helped them to prepare later on for the practical resolution of contradictions in yonaoshi-type struggles. Religious asceticism in general played down political activity.

By the early 1830s, the bakufu, like most fief governments, was in deep financial trouble, and famine once again stalked the land. In 1837, Ōshio Heihachirō rose up in a wild, violent attempt to punish the bakufu and the merchants of Ōsaka for their crimes against the people. The urban insurrection he led showed how the gap between samurai intellectuals and at least the top stratum of peasants could be bridged, releasing forces of discontent that had built up below. But it also showed (by its violent tactics, mistaken recruitment strategy, paternalistic ideology, and eventual betrayal by some of Ōshio's samurai followers) just how unreliable samurai actually were as allies in furthering peasant aims. During the 1840s, the bakufu undertook its third major reform effort. But by this time Edo had lost the power to rotate the daimyo at will, irrespective of the wishes of the peasants in their domains. With increasing frequency over the 1850s, whole villages joined in protest organizations that transcended the framework of domanial control.

Middle-strata peasants especially had begun to see themselves differently. They were no longer mere people of the fief for whom land was the source of all value. Rather, some of them could perceive clearly the possibilities of acquiring wealth through hard labor and immersion in the market. For such people, at this particular time, the main obstacle to advancement was a fief system which retarded economic development. They were well along in the process of mobilizing their material and normative resources against it when Perry arrived in 1853–1854. At that point imperialism entered into the explanation of peasant class struggles. It did so not as an exogenous factor but as the expression of new, geographically distant class relations. These relations were mediated by a global system of international trade, by foreign diplomats, and by the offshore naval forces they had at their command.

Where before 1853 peasant risings had served to expose the daimyo's declining powers of social control, the signing of unequal treaties by the bakufu which followed over the next six years revealed the bakufu's military weakness vis-á-vis the foreigners. Starting in 1860, the invasion of "free trade" in the treaty ports began to have significant corrosive effects on the bakuhan state. Foreign trade and new urban development accelerated the internal political breakdown of Tokugawa feudalism while simultaneously introducing new conditions for the growth of capitalism. Over the period from 1860 to 1866 the bakufu and many fief governments concentrated on modernizing. But imperialist pressure on Japan mounted, and price inflation worsened. Finally, civil conflict between pro- and antibakufu forces broke into the open. In areas strongly affected by foreign trade at Yokohama and by the growth of tenancy and civil war, the bottom began to fall out of the peasant world.

After 1860 two distinct but overlapping class forces dominated Japan's mass struggle movement for social change. One consisted of the actual organizers of militant populist protest: the middle-strata peasants who were being ruined by inflation and feudal tax pillaging. They were activated by economic insecurity rather than poverty per se. The other force consisted of lower situated, more atomized and heterogeneous semiproletarians of villages and towns, who composed the bulk of their followers. Both groups championed the cause of yonaoshi: of remaking the local community on principles of justice and equality. But because of the diverse local economic conditions under which they developed, their relationship varied depending on the region. In the Kantō plain, for example, they were sometimes more antagonistic than cooperative toward one another.

In 1866, in the Bushū, Fukushima, and Chūgoku regions, middle-strata peasants and semiproletarians came onto the scene in vast numbers, only to be defeated nearly everywhere by samurai military forces acting in concert with the much larger military forces recruited from, and officered by, the land-amassing rich peasant class. Thus, having used the commercial and moneylending capacities of the nascent rural bourgeoisie to sustain their rule into the mid-nineteenth century, the samurai had ultimately to rely on them also for military support in putting down peasant risings. Clearly, the defeat of the large-scale yonaoshi risings during 1866 strengthened the rural ascendancy of landlords, district headmen, and village officials. But it did not, even at this late stage, secure for them any new institutional powers. Attacks from below on the system of class exploitation in villages and towns continued.

In this context, the successes scored by Tsuyama fief's peasants against landlords and local officials in early 1867 were exceptional, though in most other respects the Kaisei rising was quite typical. Typicality meant that this incident reflected the heightened rhythm of agricultural work and commercial life throughout Japan during the 1860s, and the growing acuteness of the tenancy problem. It also meant that samurai contenders for power were manipulating behind the scenes, using the peasants' autonomous mobilization against fief tax practices for their own advantage.

The Kaisei events, in addition, revealed the hardships inflicted on the peasantry by the shogun's war against Chōshū fief and by the increasing militarization of society. Structurally, the Kaisei incident showed the complex fusion of an ikki rising against feudal oppression with a yonaoshi disturbance against wealthy landlords and local officials, with a view to saving poor people from destruction. The features of popular consciousness glimpsed during this two-month episode could also be seen throughout the 1866–1871 period, when populist yonaoshi disturbances were at their height. Poor people living in villages and towns did not surrender meekly to acts of the marketplace that stripped them of rights of distributive justice. On the contrary, they fought every emerging trend toward private (exclusive) land ownership and bourgeois social relations in agriculture.

Like other risings of the late 1860s, the debased-currency disturbances in Shinshū province (1869–1870) occurred in an environment in which foreign trade affected continually market and price structures. But further along in time than the Kaisei events, they also reflected better the emergence of new economic problems. The Shinshū protests spread through villages and towns in the same period that saw the incorporation of the first joint stock company in Japan (1869) and the establishment of the first Ministry of Industry (1870), signifying the formal start of industrialization from above. Shinshū afforded us a glimpse of the dismantling of the feudal state system—a process that culminated in 1871 in the total abolition of fiefs and the establishment of prefectures. Foreign trade in the treaty ports conditioned the Shinshū risings as did the massive-scale metallic debasement of nonconvertible coins and the overissuance of paper money. Not until the 1880s would the problem of depreciated paper currency be brought under control. In following the course of the Shinshū protests, we also encountered, in the collapse of the semiofficial silk trading firm in Matsushiro, the first signs of the short-term capitalist business cycle, which individual fiefs and prefectural governments were totally unable to handle.

Finally, fourteen years after the Shinshū disturbances—with the infrastructure for a future industrial capitalist form of society being rapidly constructed and the modern political party form of struggle, based on voluntary association, becoming possible for propertied males—the peasants of Chichibu rose up in an armed revolt that marked the end of the age of ikki and yonaoshi.

Let us now take just the period 1866 to 1884, shift our focus a bit, and review the role of peasant struggles in the transformation and restructuring of political power in Japan. To begin with, certain general features stand out. Real power in the bakuhan and early Meiji state was dispersed and subject to check from below. In the course of struggles, peasant protesters usually displayed exemplary discipline and integrity along with a keen sense of justice and righteousness. They maintained these characteristics in the face of mounting state violence that was increasingly thrust upon them. Their dominant tendency was to be dispersed, local, one following after the other, and usually lacking (or seeming to lack) any strong political coordinating center. Both the Bushū yonaoshi rising of June 1866 and, later, the Chichibu debt deferral struggle of 1884, however, showed strong central coordination. Second, the sheer number of peasants, semiproletarians, and others who participated in these movements for social justice, or were affected by them, was tremendous. Even though they ended in defeat, these local peasant actions were at all times a constraint and a shaping influence on the Meiji state and its various apparatuses. Third, when the protest incidents are placed on the broad canvas of Japanese social history, they can be seen as constituting a specific populist stage in the long, bloody process of establishing modern land ownership in Japan.

More specifically, a massive wave of struggles by peasants and townspeople began in 1866, continued into the early 1870s, ebbed on the eve of the land tax revision in 1873, and then resumed against that law and the conscription law. The more revolutionary peasant protests of the early 1880s followed basically along that same path. But as seen in the Chichibu incident, they also reflected changes in the economy, the state, and the political system that had accumulated in the interim. At each stage of their unfolding, the risings examined here were able to accomplish more than their participants ever consciously aimed at or intended. Whenever militant protest actions resulted in a temporary reduction in feudal levies and tenant rents, the giving of charity in rice or cash, or the return of pawned and forfeited land, they directly improved the economic situation of some impoverished people for short periods of time. Whenever, as also sometimes happened, they forced out of office corrupt or unjust hereditary officials, they strengthened village autonomy and successfully asserted the principle of social justice. But, apart from these immediate positive results, the peasant battles at each stage had more lasting indirect effects on power holders at higher levels.

By building on experiences gained during previous centuries of struggle, by rising up repeatedly against the abuses of a corrupt feudal system, by connecting in their feelings as well as in their actions with yonaoshi movements which looked toward a coming great transformation of the world, the peasants and townspeople of the 1860s decisively undermined fief and shogunal power. In that way, they helped topple the bakuhan system from below. Equally important, as these peasant movements continued into the 1870s and early 1880s, they served on the coalition of Restoration leaders a prophetic warning. At a practical level, they made the new rulers contemplate the very real possibilities for political upheaval inherent in a continuation of the existing situation. At a more abstract level, popular struggles could also be read as saying that the true purpose of government was not to oppress powerless people but to help them by removing the causes of inequality and injustice in their lives. From either perspective, the conclusion was inescapable: a different form of state, capable of securing widespread legitimation, had to be constructed in order to replace the historically obsolete bakuhan state.

For a short period of about three years after the Boshin war of 1868, collective actions by peasants and townsmen helped accelerate the process of dismantling the still lingering feudal institutions and practices. In the absence of a cohesive power system at the national level, rural unrest and rebelliousness prevailed in the countryside and, in some areas, even went so far as to undermine the village tribute collection system.[3] In Shinshū province, for example, peasants made ground-rent collection impossible in many areas by forcibly removing village officials and destroying cadastral survey records, temple registers, and village account books. Their militant direct actions also strengthened the self-governing character of village organizations.

Partly to counter these tendencies toward administrative independence at the village level and the undermining of extra-economic coercion in areas such as Shinshū, the Meiji government abolished the remaining fiefs in 1871 after less than a year of planning. This action completed the process of state centralization which the Tokugawa house had begun in the early seventeenth century. There followed, among other reforms, the assumption of the fief debts, the pensioning off of the nonproductive daimyo and samurai, currency reform, and the adoption of the Gregorian calendar. Significantly, the new calendar represented a framework of orientation in time suitable for a people who were now participating in the stream of world history.

Once the basic contradiction between peasants and lords had been abolished, the new government set about strengthening the state power and creating a uniform legal framework for shifting onto the backs of peasants its increased financial burdens, including indemnity payments to approximately 370,000 samurai and daimyo. This project, occurring against a background of peasant attacks on the traditional means for collecting ground rent, set the stage for land settlement and military conscription: the two most repressive of all Meiji Restoration reforms.

During the 1870s, land became freely alienable, and new administrative units were created from above to control peasants by usurping power from their village governing organizations. Beginning with an edict of January 1873, the land tax revision went into effect and continued for wet and dry fields until 1880 and for village common land until 1889. Under the principles of the new system, the tax ceased to be based on the size of the harvest and became a tax on the value of land. And, rather than having all direct producers pay it to feudal lords and shogun, the new land tax was to be paid, by landowners and in money only, to a centralized unitary state.[4]

Ultimately, the Meiji land tax revision stabilized the position of landlords at the expense of small owners and tenants. It also made possible the later petit bourgeois development and increased prosperity of Japanese agriculture. But more important politically, it ushered in another long era of rural agitation and suffering by the poor. For the land settlement as a whole tied to the Meiji state the majority of landlords who (until the very start of the twentieth century) had a greater interest in amassing tenant rents than in investing in capitalist industrialization.

During the early 1880s, there appeared on the local scene in eastern Japan transitional forms of rural protest, such as poor people's parties and debtors' parties. This development followed a decade of educational work by the freedom and people's rights activists and a few years of intense propaganda activities by Japan's first national political party, the Liberal party, formed in October 1881. Although the poor people's parties were not modern political associations, they nevertheless reflected changes in the political language, perceptions, and capacities of their members. After their suppression in 1884–1885, Japanese society moved quickly into an era dominated by imperialism and the industrial capitalist mode of production. Politics soon acquired a different doctrinal language and a new structural location: the prefectural, city, town, and village assemblies at one pole and the national Diet at the other. The popular struggle forms of the 1890s and after, together with many of the constraints that acted upon those forms, were specific to that more dynamic political terrain and not to feudalism.

Yet in the world of early Japanese capitalism, the feudal past (embodied in institutions and cultural legacies) was not easily transcended. It lived on as a negative material presence exacting a price that later generations would have to pay. Japan's political disasters of the 1930s are not fully explicable without taking account of how the leaders of the Meiji era preserved the structural foundations of the Tokugawa past in the form of village communities and the landlord system: a set of labor-repressive institutions for extracting a surplus from peasants. In the course of the Meiji leaders' efforts to deny the popular demand for people's rights, some of the worst features of Japan's authoritarian political heritage were resurrected and strengthened. These could be seen in the 1889 Meji Constitution, the 1891 Imperial Rescript on Education, certain features of the Civil Code, and the whole ambiguous framework of emperor-centered, Shinto-infused nationalism that loosely structured Japanese political life down to 1945.

On the other hand, from the viewpoint of the present, more positive legacies may also be discerned. There can be no doubt that the last great wave of peasant protests, with its many twists and turns from 1866 to 1884, prepared rich soil for the freedom and people's rights movement. Led by ex-samurai and landlords, the people's rights movement took as its principal slogans the early convening of a national assembly, enactment of a constitution, treaty revision, and state tax reduction. Today it is remembered mainly for having introduced the liberal political thought of Europe to Japan and for having attempted to limit the growth of prewar imperial despotism by forcing the Meiji oligarchs to grant a constitution. Yet this first constitutional movement in Japanese history is intelligible only if we think in terms of what powered it: the larger context of peasant class struggles fed by entirely indigenous Japanese beliefs.

For not just harsh objective conditions alone but subjective assessments of those conditions molded by ideas, values, and characteristics deriving from the Tokugawa peasant struggle tradition fueled nearly all the popular movements of Japan's period of primitive capital accumulation. Both the longing for status equality and the criticism and denial of feudal tax practices were direct legacies of the yonaoshi risings. The late-nineteenth-century quest of minute cultivators for economic equality and security was a Tokugawa legacy; so too was the popular belief in the importance of autonomous local communities in which property was regulated to prevent abuses from arising. Another vital Tokugawa legacy was the use of religious ideas, symbols, and values (all grounded in the practices of agricultural production) to justify reform and to strengthen individuals in their personal struggles against economic misery and unjust authority. Where these very general dimensions of resistance and human aspiration are concerned, we should see the popular protesters of late nineteenth- and early twentieth-century Japan at one with their Tokugawa forebears. They were indeed the heirs to the peasant traditions of protest.

Notes

INTRODUCTION

1. Borton's book is badly written and out of date. For a qualitative evaluation of it, see Donald W. Burton, "Peasant Struggle in Japan, 1590–1760," Journal of Peasant Studies 5, no. 2 (January 1978), and Jon Halliday's comments in *A Political History of Japanese Capitalism* (New York: Pantheon Books, 1975), p. 317n51. Donald Burton's work stands apart from the revisionist current in American Japan studies, while Halliday's book is the first Marxist history of Japan in English in the postwar period.

2. On modernization scholarship and trends in American Japan studies during the 1970s, see H. P. Bix, "Kiro ni tatsu Amerika no Nihon kenkyū" (American Japan Studies at the Crossroads: Some Thoughts on Rereading E. H. Norman), *Shisō* (Thought) no. 634 (April 1977), pp. 140–150.

3. Thomas C. Smith, *The Agrarian Origins of Modern Japan* (Stanford: Stanford University Press, 1959), p. 172.

4. Irwin Scheiner, "Benevolent Lords and Honorable Peasants: Rebellion and Peasant Consciousness in Tokugawa Japan," in *Japanese Thought in the Tokugawa Period: Methods and Metaphors*, ed. Tetsuo Najita and Irwin Scheiner (Chicago: University of Chicago Press, 1978), pp. 39–62; Najita Tetsuo and J. Victor Koschman, eds., *Conflict in Modern Japanese History: The Neglected Tradition* (Princeton: Princeton University Press, 1982).

5. A good model of such scholarly practice is G. E. M. de Ste. Croix, *The Class Struggle in the Ancient Greek World: From the Archaic Age to the Arab Conquests* (London: Duckworth and Co., 1981), pt. 1, pp. 31–275. I learned much from this very rich work.

6. My discussion of class draws on Ste. Croix, ibid., pp. 41–43; Teodor Shanin, "Class, State and Revolution: Substitutes and Realities," in *Introduction to the Sociology of "Developing Societies"*, ed. Hamza Alavi and Teodor Shanin (New York: Monthly Review Press, 1982), pp. 320–325.

7. Perry Anderson, *Arguments within English Marxism* (London: NLB & Verso Editions, 1980), p. 40.

8. See the *Encyclopaedia of the Social Sciences*, vol. 6, *Expatriation-Gosplan* (New York: Macmillan Co., 1935, 1959), p. 16.

9. For a theoretical discussion of "categories of exploitation," see Geoff Hodgson, *Capitalism, Value and Exploitation: A Radical Theory* (Oxford: Martin Robertson & Co., 1982), pp. 202–216. James C. Scott links exploitation to feelings of oppression and argues that for both poor and "middle" peasants, the main criterion "in judging the exactions that are an inevitable part of . . . life is whether they increase or reduce the chance of a disaster." The peasant notion of exploitation may also be seen, he notes, as "a form of false consciousness." For the peasant "asks how much is left before he asks how much is taken; he asks whether the agrarian system respects his basic needs as a consumer." Scott's outstanding work is *The Moral Economy of the Peasant: Rebellion and Subsistence in Southeast Asia* (New Haven: Yale University Press, 1976), pp. 25, 31.

10. For an illuminating discussion of tribute, see Hal Draper, *Karl Marx's Theory of Revolution*, vol. 1, *State and Bureaucracy* (New York: Monthly Review Press, 1977), pp. 550–553. Also worth consulting, though less satisfactory, is the discussion of tribute in the *Encyclopaedia of the Social Sciences*, vol. 15, *Trade Unions-Zwingli* (New York: Macmillan Co., 1935, 1959), pp. 102–104.

11. For information on razobran, I am indebted to a work by Teodor Shanin, *Russia 1905–7: Revolution As a Moment of Truth*, chap. 3, "The Revolution from Below: Land and Liberty!" forthcoming in 1986 from Macmillan Press.

12. See J. Craig Jenkins, "Why Do Peasants Rebel? Structural and Historical Theories of Modern Peasant Rebellions," *American Journal of Sociology* 88, no. 3 (November 1982): 502.

13. A noteworthy but unsuccessful attempt to reinterpret Japanese economic history from an anti-Marxist perspective, using quantitative methods and a simple two-region model, is Susan B. Hanley and Kozo Yamamura, *Economic and Demographic Change in Preindustrial Japan 1600–1868* (Princeton: Princeton University Press, 1977). The authors present much information on the documents of village population and on demographic changes. But their work is based on a faulty methodology and unreliable, incomplete quantitative data. It gives an untrue picture of Tokugawa village society as (in the words of one reviewer) "an eastern Arcady where rosy-cheeked peasants merrily drown their offspring for the sake of conspicuous consumption, or where farmers always abandon their farms in hope, never in desperation. The idea that there might be exploitation in Tokugawa Japan is discounted—the very word, when introduced in page 3, is imprisoned within inverted commas." See Harold Bolitho's review in *Harvard Journal of Asiatic Studies* 39, no. 2 (December 1979). Dana Morris examined the authors' use of quantitative data and found that they mishandled village population data and drew faulty conclusions: "Given the nature of the evidence available, the writing of Tokugawa economic history cannot be divorced from social history." See Morris's long review in *Journal of Asian Studies* 39, no. 2 (February 1980): 361–368.

14. Aoki Kōji, *Hyakushō ikki sōgō nenpyō* (Comprehensive Historical Chronology of Peasant Uprisings) (Tokyo: San'ichi Shobō, 1975); Yokoyama Toshio, *Hyakushō ikki to gimin denshō* (Peasant Uprisings and Legends of Exemplary Martyrs) (Tokyo: Kyōikusha, Rekishi Shinsho 85, 1977).

15. See Yamanaka Kiyotaka, "Hyakushō ikki no jidaisei to chiikisei" (The Chronology and Regional Distribution of Peasant Uprisings), *Rekishi Kōron*, [Historical Forum] (June 1978, p. 58; also Yokoyama Toshio, ibid., p. 156. According to Yokoyama, four provinces in the southeastern Kantō plain—Kazusa, Shimōsa, Hitachi, and Shimotsuke—constituted a fourth region of relatively few risings.

16. See Douglas C. North, *Structure and Change in Economic History* (New York: W. W. Norton Co., 1981), pp. 20–32; and Göran Therborn, *What Does the Ruling Class Do When It Rules?* (London: New Left Books, 1978).

17. See Sasaki Junnosuke, "Bakuhansei kokka to higashi Ajia" (The Bakuhan State and East Asia) in *Nihonshi o manabu 3, kinsei* (The Study of Japanese History, Volume 3, The Early Modern Period) ed. Yoshida Akira, Nagahara Keiji, et al. (Tokyo: Yūhikaku, 1976), pp. 1–15. Also Minegishi Kentarō, "Sakoku" (Seclusion), in ibid., pp. 49–60. After the imposition of seclusion, Japan's trade with Holland and China increased and relations were maintained with Korea via Tsushima fief and with China via the Ryūkyū Islands. For short discussions in English of the bakuhan state, see John W. Hall, *Japan—From Prehistory to Modern Times* (New York: Delacorte Press, 1970), and Conrad Totman, *Politics in the tokugawa Bakufu, 1600–1843* (Cambridge, Mass.: Harvard University Press, 1967). For helpful Marxist discussions, see Halliday, *Political History of Japanese Capitalism*, and Perry Anderson's chapter on "Japanese Feudalism" in *Lineages of the Absolutist State* (London: New Left Books, 1974). Less satisfactory but worth consulting is Reinhard Bendix, *Kings or People—Power and the Mandate to Rule* (Berkeley: University of California Press, 1978).

18. Sasaki Junnosuke, "Bakuhansei kokka to higashi Ajia," ibid., p. 9, and Minegishi Kentarō, "Bakuhansei shakai no mibun kōsei" (The Status Structure in Bakuhan Society), in (eds.), Kōza Nihon Kinseishi 3, *Bakuhansei shakai no kōzō* (Lectures on the History of Early Modern Japanese Society; The Structure of Bakuhan Society, Volume 3), ed. Fukaya Katsumi and Matsumoto Shirō (Tokyo: Yūhikaku, 1980), pp. 32, 37.

19. Katsumata Shizuo, *Ikki* (Risings) (Tokyo: Iwanami Shinsho, 194, 1982), pp. 179–180.

20. For the standard portrayal of the Tokugawa village, see Kurt Steiner, *Local Government in Japan* (Stanford: Stanford University Press, 1965), pp. 9–18. On the state-village relationship in general, see Harumi Befu, "The Political Relation of the Village to the State," *World Politics* 19, no. 4 (July 1967), and Joel Migdal, *Peasants, Poltics and Revolution: Pressures toward Political and Social Change in the Third World* (Princeton: Princeton University Press, 1974), pp. 47–56. The village autonomy issue has confused a number of writers who have otherwise written insightfully on Japan. Specifically, Ellen Kay Trimberger's account of Tokugawa feudalism is fatally weakened by her uncritical acceptance of the village autonomy thesis. See Trimberger, "State Power and Modes of Production: Implications of the Japanese Transition to Capitalism," *Insurgent Sociologist* 7, no. 2 (Spring 1977): 85–98.

21. Quoted in Minegishi Kentarō, "Bakuhansei shakai no mibun kōsei," pp. 262, 264.

22. Quoted in Kashiwabara Yūsen, "Edoki minshū to Bukkyō no fukyū" (The People of the Edo Period and the Diffusion of Buddhism), *Nihongaku* (The Quarterly of Japanology), no. 3 (December 1983), p. 81.

23. For European feudalism, see Nicholas Abercrombie, Stephen Hill, and Bryan S. Turner, *The Dominant Ideology Thesis* (London: George Allen & Unwin, 1980), pp. 69–70. Drawing on evidence from English and French history, the authors argue that the peasantry

in medieval society "remained incorrigible. . . . They were largely untouched by the civilising role of the church throughout the Middle Ages and they remained the main vehicle of magical, irrational practices up to the Counter–Reformation and the era of the Protestant evangelical movements of the nineteenth century when the peasantry as a class was transformed into urban wage labourers. . . . The cultural dominance of the religion of the ruling class was limited by the weakness of the apparatus of ideological communication and transmission."

24. On peasants as negotiators, see Stewart Gordon's comment in "Recovery from Adversity in 18th Century India: Rethinking 'Villages,' 'Peasants' and Politics in Pre–Modern Kingdoms," *Peasant Studies* 8, no. 4 (Fall 1979): 78. This same issue also contains Teodor Shanin's important essay, "Defining Peasants: Conceptualizations and De-conceptualizations: Old and New in a Marxist Debate," pp. 38–60.

25. The Japanese concept of "blood-tie group" (*Ketsuen-dan*) is not synonymous with biological blood group but includes members who, in order to preserve the household as an active production unit and constituent member of the village, are brought in and often elevated to its head.

26. Presumably, if most peasants had been fully independent proprietors, the power of domanial lords vis-à-vis the bakufu would have been stronger than it actually was. Shoguns would not then have been able to dispossess their vassals' fiefs so easily or relocate them so frequently to other fiefs. See Nagahara Keiji, "Hōken shakai no Ajia-teki tokushitsu" (The Asian Characteristics of Feudal Society), in *Kōza shiteki yuibutsuron to gendai* (Lectures on Historical Materialism and the Present), ed. Nagahara Keiji and Bandō Hiroshi vol. 3 (Tokyo: Aoki Shoten, 1978), pp. 293–295.

27. Harumi Befu, "The Political Relation of the Village to the State," *World Politics* 19, no. 4 (July 1967): 613.

28. James I. Nakamura, "Human Capital Accumulation in Premodern Rural Japan," *Journal of Economic History* 41, no. 2 (June 1981): 279, and Kurt Steiner, *Local Government in Japan* (Stanford: Stanford University Press, 1965), pp. 3–18.

29. See Kurushima Hiroshi, "Mura to mura no kankei—kumiai mura (mura rengō) kenkyū nōto" (Relations between Villages—Notes on the Study of Village Federations), *Rekishi kōron* (Historical Forum), no. 106 (September 1984), pp. 67–69.

30. Steiner, p. 16. A further consideration in discussing the autonomy issue is that (as Lenin once observed) the only truly autonomous political entities are those that have the ability to secede from the political associations to which they belong.

31. James C. Scott, "Protest and Profanation: Agrarian Revolt and the Little Tradition, Part 2," *Theory and Society* 4, no. 2 (1977): 277. This is an important essay.

32. Yokoyama Toshio, *Gimin: hyakushō ikki no shidōshatachi* (Exemplary Martyrs: Leaders of Peasant Risings) (Tokyo: Sanseidō, 1973), pp. 10–19.

33. Although it takes no account of Japanese experience, a useful theoretical perspective on some of the issues discussed here is J. H. M. Beattie, "On Understanding Sacrifice," in *Sacrifice*, ed. M. F. C. Bourdillon and Myer Fortes (London and New York: Academic Press, 1980), pp. 38–43.

34. Moriyama Gunjirō, "Chichibu jiken no hyōka o megutte—Irokawa Daikichi shi no hihan ni kotaenagara" (Historical Evaluation of the Chichibu Incident: Comments on the Criticism of Mr. Irokawa Daikichi), *Rekishigaku kenkyū*, [Journal of Historical Studies] no. 535 (November 1984), p. 70.

35. Quoted from the famous firsthand account of the incident by Shinto priest Tanaka Sen'ya in Inada Masahirō, "Chichibu jikenzō saikōsei no tame no shiron" (Preliminary Sketch for the Reconstruction of the Chichibu Incident), *Rekishi hyōron*, November 1984, p. 42.

36. James C. Scott, "Protest and Profanation: Agrarian Revolt and the Little Tradition, Part 1," *Theory and Society* 4, no. 1 (Spring 1977): 5.

CHAPTER 1

1. The first scholarly accounts of the Sanchū rising appeared at the end of World War I in works by Takimoto Seiichi and Kokusho Iwao. But historical understanding of the incident made little further advance until 1957 when Mori Kiyoshi and other local scholars in Okayama prefecture formed the Sanchū Rebellion Memorial Society (*Sanchū ikki gimin kenshōkai*). Thanks to the efforts of this group, the available documentation on the rising was gathered and carefully analyzed, and important studies were written by Kamei Masao, Nagamitsu Norikazu, and, most recently, Nakano Michiko. My own study is based largely on the original work of these three scholars.

Of documentary collections dealing with the Sanchū events, the most important is Nagamitsu Norikazu, ed., *Bizen, Bitchū, Mimasaka hyakushō ikki shiryō, dai ikkan* (Historical Materials on Peasant Uprisings, vol. 1: Bizen, Bitchū, Mimasaka) (Tokyo: Kokusho Kankōkai, 1978), pp. 55–227. This work contains fourteen contemporary documents on the Sanchū rising, together with Nagamitsu's notes and critical summaries. A basic document crucial to my own analysis—the "Mikoku shimin ranpōki" (An Account of the People's Revolt in the Province of Mimasaka)—appears here and also in Yasumaru Yoshio et al., *Nihon shisō taikei 58, minshū undō no shisō* (Compendium of Japanese Thought, vol. 58, The Thought of the People's Movements) (Tokyo: Iwanami Shoten, 1970), pp. 186–206. My own translation of the "Mikoku shimin ranpōki" is based on this latter source. About a year after completing it, in September 1981, I toured the Sanchū region in the company of local historians belonging to the Sanchū Rebellion Memorial Society, gathering information on the rising and the terrain in which it occurred.

Kamei Masao's "Mimasaka no kuni Sanchū ikki no rekishiteki haigo" (The Historical Background to the Sanchū Rising in Mimasaka Province) proved helpful, though it must now be supplemented by the authoritative *Kawakami sonshi* (History of Kawakami Village) (Okayama-shi: Sanyō Insatsu Kabushikigaisha, 1980), prepared by the Editorial Committee for the History of Kawakami Village. This massive local history contains Nakano Michiko's very fine essay, "Kyōhō no Sanchū ikki" (The Sanchū Rising of the Kyōhō Era), as well as helpful discussions of rural class structure by Takatani kuniko. A clear concise introduction to the Sanchū rising is Yokoyama Toshio, *Gimin—hyakushō ikki no shidōshatachi* (Exemplary Martyrs—Leaders of Peasant Rebellions) (Tokyo: Sanseidō Shinsho 118, 1973), pp. 138–162.

2. *Kawakami sonshi* (History of Kawakami Village), Kawakami Village History Editorial Committee (Kawakami sonshi henshū iinkai) (Okayama: Sanyō Insatsu Kabushikigaisha, 1980), pp. 113, 116, 186–188.

3. Kamei Masao, "Mimasaka no kuni Sanchū ikki no rekishiteki haigo" (The Historical Background of the Sanchū Rising in Mimasaka Province), *Okayama shigaku*, no. 3 (1958), p. 51.

4. *Kawakami sonshi*, p. 185. Merchants who stayed over two nights in a village had to be reported to the headman. Wanderers and gamblers were barred altogether from lodging in villages.

5. For a contemporary functional equivalent in advanced capitalist societies to this Tokugawa system of hereditary statuses, one might cite the dual system of wage-income inequality and occupational hierarchy within corporate organizations.

6. *Tsuyama shishi daisankan, kinsei 1, Morihan jidai* (The History of Tsuyama City, vol. 3, Early Modern Times 1, The Age of the Mori Fief) (Tsuyama–shi: Tsuyama Shiyakusho, 1973), pp. 208–209.

7. Ibid., p. 202

8. See Morimoto Kiyoshi, "Sanchū ikki oboegaki" (Memorandum on the Sanchū Rising) (No place or date), p. 14.

9. *Yubara chōshi zenpan* (History of Yubara Town, vol. 1) Taniguchi Sumio and Morimoto Kiyoshi, eds., (Okayama: Ōba-gun, Yubara-machi, 1953), p. 63.

10. *Tsuyama shishi*, vol. 3, pp. 90–91, 134.

11. Yamada Tadao, "Bakuhansei kokka to ikki" (The Bakuhan State and Peasant Risings), in *Ikki—ikki to kokka 5* (Uprisings, vol. 5, Uprisings and the State) (Tokyo: Tokyo Daigaku Shuppankai, 1981), pp. 204–210.

12. *Tsuyama shishi*, vol. 3, p. 86.

13. Nishida Masaki, "Ikki no tenkai" (The Development of Peasant Uprisings), in *Ikki—ikki no rekishi 2* (Uprisings, vol. 2, The History of Uprisings) (Tokyo: Tokyo Daigaku Shuppankai, 1981), pp. 177–179.

14. On Shimabara, see Fukaya Katsumi, "Bakuhansei shakiai to ikki" (Bakuhan Society and Peasant Uprisings), in *Ikki—ikkishi nyūmon 1* (Uprisings—Introduction to the History of Uprisings, vol. 1) (Tokyo: Tokyo Daigaku Shuppankai, 1981), p. 119. For discussion of ikki and religious belief, see Nakura Tetsuzō, "Kinsei no shinkō to ikki" (Early Modern Religious Beliefs and Peasant Uprisings), in *Ikki 4—seikatsu, bunka, shisō* (Uprisings—Life, Culture and Thought, vol. 4) (Tokyo: Tokyo Daigaku Shuppankai, 1981), p. 302.

15. G. E. M. de Ste. Croix, *The Class Struggle in the Ancient Greek World: From the Archaic Age to the Arab Conquests* (London: Duckworth & Co., 1981), p. 215.

16. Katsumata Shizuo, *Ikki* (Uprisings) (Tokyo: Iwanami Shinsho 194, 1982), pp. 143–144.

17. For details, see H. P. Bix, "Miura Meisuke, or Peasant Rebellion under the Banner of 'Distress,'" *Bulletin of Concerned Asian Scholars* 10, no. 2 (April–June 1978): 18–26.

18. Nakano Michiko, "Kyōhō no Sanchū ikki" (The Sanchū Rising of the Kyōhō Era), in *Kawakami sonshi*, p. 312.

19. *Tsuyama shishi*, vol. 3, p. 220; Nakano, ibid., p. 299.

20. *Kawakami sonshi*, p. 187.

21. Kamei Masao, p. 46.

22. Ibid., p. 13.

23. Ibid., p. 14.

24. Nakano Michiko, p. 297.

25. Kamei Masao, pp. 15–16.

26. *Kawakami sonshi*, p. 289.

27. For development of this theme, see Oliver Thomson, *Mass Persuasion in History: A*

Historical Analysis of the Development of Propaganda Techniques (New York: Crane, Russak & Co., 1977).

28. *Tsuyama shishi*, vol. 3, pp. 112–114, 138.

29. According to one estimate, at the time of the Mori's removal in 1697, the castle town of Tsuyama had a population of 16,445 townspeople (*chōnin*) and approximately 8,000 samurai retainers and their families. After the Mori departed and the fief was cut in half, the castle town experienced a drastic decline, particularly as many chōnin, parasitic on samurai, migrated elsewhere in Mimasaka or relocated to more prosperous castle towns. When the 1726–1727 rising erupted, the town of Tsuyama was down to only 9,981 chōnin and probably, at most, about 4,000 samurai. Source: *Tsuyama shishi, dai ikkan, genshi, kodai* (The History of Tsuyama City, vol. 1, Prehistory and Antiquity) (Tsuyama: Tsuyama Shiyakusho, 1972). p. 10; also see Nakano, "Kyōhō," p. 298.

30. Nakano, pp. 295, 297, 300.

31. "Sakuyō chihō kyūki" (Official Record of the Sakuyō Region), in *Mimasaka shiryō, dai isshū* (Historical Materials of Mimasaka, vol. 1), ed. Mimasaka Region Historical Studies Association (Tsuyama: Tsuyama Local History Museum, 1956), p. 2. This document was kindly furnished by the Okayama-ken Sōgō Bunka Senta (Okayama Prefecture General Culture Center, Okayama City).

32. Nakano, pp. 309–310.

33. Ibid., p. 298. She notes that the intendants in 1697 granted complete exemptions from rice tribute to five villages in Yumoto district, Ōba region.

34. Matsudaira Naganori was a descendant of the senior branch of the Matsudaira Echizen family, which issued from Tokugawa Ieyasu's second son, Hideyasu. Source: E. Papinot, *Historical and Geographical Dictionary of Japan* (Tokyo: Charles E. Tuttle Co., 1912, 1973), p. 356.

35. Nakano, pp. 299–300; by 1717 the number of Tsuyama villages had increased by 5 to 259; also see Nagamitsu Norikazu's comments in Shoji Kichinosuke, Hayashi Motoi, and Yasumaru Yoshio, eds., *Nihon shisō taikei 58, minshū undō no shisō* (Compendium of Japanese Thought, vol. 58, The Thought of the People's Movements) (Tokyo: Iwanami Shoten, 1970), p. 467.

36. According to Nakano (pp. 309–310), at the end of the seventeenth century, each circular district in Tsuyama averaged ten to twenty villages apiece.

37. Ibid., pp. 306–307, 311.

38. Ibid., pp. 301, 312.

CHAPTER 2

1. On taxation in early modern Europe, see Gabriel Ardant, "Financial Policy and Economic Infrastructure of Modern States and Nations," in *The Formation of National States in Western Europe* ed. Charles Tilly (Princeton: Princeton University Press, 1975), pp. 164–242.

2. *Kawakami sonshi*, pp. 152–153. One mountain village in the western part of the fief, Kasagiwake, had a tribute rate in 1719 that was nearly 40 percent of the net yield of the village after deductions had been made for *okuhikimai*. That term specifically meant fees for village headmen, deputy district headmen, and district headmen, together with relief rice set aside for the village sick and impoverished. Generally, during the Kyōhō era (1716–1735),

the *okuhikimai* rate for each village in the fief averaged about 3 to 4 percent, much less than what was needed to meet the needs of a mushrooming population of hungry, destitute peasants.

3. Otaniya Heibei, an iron mine owner who appears in some accounts as the merchant Heibei of Hijiya, lent his house as the headquarters of the ikki leaders. "From the beginning of the uprising, Otaniya's place was the message center for communications between eastern and western regions. He even allowed his seal to be used on letters to the east." Another merchant and townsman, who held the post of warehouse keeper in Takada village and operated many branch stores in neighboring villages, one Tsukataniya Ichirōemon (surname Kaneda), is also identified in documents as an active sympathizer with the rebel forces. Source: "Mikoku shimin ranpōki," p. 193 jōdan.

4. Miyoshi Motoyuki and the Sanchū ikki kenkyūkai, "Sanchū ikki kenkyūjō no mondaiten" (Issues in the Study of the Sanchū Rising) (No place or date), p. 26.

5. *Kawakami sonshi*, p. 289.

6. Quoted in Nakano, p. 339.

7. Ibid., p. 321. Although the site of one of Tsuyama fief's warehouses, Takada had been under direct bakufu jurisdiction ever since 1697.

8. Nakano, pp. 337, 339.

9. Ibid., p. 319.

10. Namba Nobuo, "Bakuhansei kaikaku no tenkai to kaikyū tōsō" (The Development of Bakuhan Reforms and Class Struggle), in *Taikei Nihon kokka-shi 3, kinsei* (Outline Series on the History of the Japanese State, vol. 3, The Early Modern Period), ed. Sasaki Junnosuke et al. (Tokyo: Tokyo Daigaku Shuppankai, 1975), p. 265.

11. Katsumata Shizuo, pp. 181–183.

12. See Niwa Hiroshi, *Jinushisei no keisei to kōzō—Minojima chitai ni okeru jisshōteki bunseki* (The Formation and Structure of the Landlord System: An Empirical Analysis of the Mino Striped-Textile Producing Area) (Tokyo: Ochanomizu Shobō 1982), p. 143.

13. Ishii Kanji, *Nihon keizai-shi* (Japanese Economic History) (Tokyo: Tokyo Daigaku Shuppankai, 1976), p. 24. This is a very useful short survey of Japan's economic evolution from the earliest times to 1945.

14. Conrad D. Totman, *Politics in the Tokugawa Bakufu 1600–1843* (Cambridge, Mass.: Harvard University Press, 1967), p. 87.

15. Fujii Masao, *Bingo Fukuyama shakai keizai-shi* (A Socio-economic History of Bingo Fukuyama) (Fukuyama City: Kojima Shoten, 1974), p. 242.

16. Ishii Kanji, p. 23.

17. For the higher figure, see Ishii Kanji, p. 23, and for the lower one, see Tsuji Tatsuya, *Kyōhō kaikaku no kenkyū* (A Study of the Kyōhō Reforms) (Tokyo: Sobunsha, 1963), p. 288.

18. See Futakawa sonshi kankōkai, ed., *Futakawa sonshi* (History of Futakawa Village) (Okayama-ken: Nōkyō Insatsu Kabushiki-gaisha 1965), p. 115; Nakano Michiko, p. 315.

19. See Nagamitsu Norikazu's discussion of Kubo in *Bizen, Bitchū, Mimasaka hyakushō ikki shiryō, dai ikkan* (Historical materials on Peasant Uprisings, vol. 1, Bizen, Bitchū, Mimasaka) (Tokyo: Kokusho Kankōkai, 1978), p. 90, and in Yasumaru Yoshio et al., *Nihon shisō taikei 58, minshū undō no shisō* (Tokyo: Iwanami Shoten, 1970), p. 467; also Nakano, pp. 315–316.

20. Quoted in Sanchū ikki gimin kenshōkai, ed., "Gairyaku Sanchū ikki" (Outline of the Sanchū Rising) (n. p., April 1965), p. 1.

CHAPTER 3

1. See his introduction to the "Mikoku shimin ranpōki" in Yasumaru Yoshio et al., *Nihon shisō taikei 58, minshū undō* (Tokyo: Iwanami Shoten, 1970), p. 471. Takada is part of present-day Katsuyama City. On the *Taiheiki*, see the very partial translation by Helen Craig McGullough, *The Taiheiki—A Chronicle of Medieval Japan* (Rutland, Vt., and Tokyo, Japan: Charles E. Tuttle Co., 1979). She has translated twelve out of a possible forty chapters.

2. "Mikoku shimin ranpōki," p. 188 gedan.

3. Ibid., p. 188 gedan.

4. For the daikan text used here (dated January 15, 1727), see Hayashi Motoi, ed., and Nagamitsu Norikazu, reviser, *Mimasaka no kuni Sanchū ikki shiryō* (Historical Materials on the Sanchū Rising in Mimasaka Province), published in 1957 by the Sanchū Rebellion Memorial Society, pp. 13–22. The quoted lines appear on p. 13. A similar though longer document, with slight discrepancies in the dating of events, appears in *Bizen, Bitchū, Mimasaka hyakushō ikki shiryō, dai ikkan* ed. by Nagamitsu Norikazu, pp. 84–90, where it is titled "Sanchū hyakushō sōdōki" instead of "Mimasaka no kuni hyakushō sōdōki."

5. Quoted in Sanchū ikki gimin kenshōkai, ed., "Gairyaku Sanchū ikki" (Outline of the Sanchū Rising), p. 2.

6. Tokuemon's origins and his exact burial place are disputed. Apart from the fact that he was a peasant and had a younger brother, little else is known about him. A short essay on "Tokuemon" appears in *Setouchi no senkakusha—shisō no nagare* (Pioneers of the Inland Sea Area: The Flow of Thought) (Okayama City: Sanyō Shimbunsha, 1977), pp. 202–209.

7. "Mikoku shimin ranpōki," p. 189 jōdan and gedan. I deleted from the translation village names contained in the original as they were not pertinent here.

8. See "Mimasaka no kuni hyakushō sōdōki," pp. 14–15, in Hayashi Motoi, ed., and Nagamitsu Norikazu, reviser, *Mimasaka no kuni Sanchū ikki shiryōshū*. Published by the Sanchū Rebellion Memorial Society, 1957.

9. Nakano, p. 321.

10. "Gairyaku Sanchū ikki," p. 3.

11. "Mikoku shimin ranpōki," pp. 190–191.

12. "Mimasaka no kuni hyakushō sōdōki," p. 14.

13. On the message receivers—termed variously *jōsashi, jōtsuki, jōyado*—see Nakano, p. 332.

14. "Sakuyō chihō kyūki" (Official Record of the Sakuyō Region), p. 5, and Nakano, p. 332.

15. "Furebure sōbyakushō gansho" (Appeal of All Peasants in All the Villages), in Hayashi Motoi and Nagamitsu Norikazu, eds., *Mimasaka no kuni Sanchū ikki shiryō*, pp. 18–19.

16. Nakano, p. 368.

17. Ibid., p. 331.

18. Ibid., pp. 331–332.

19. For an overly abstract account of ruling class or great tradition conceptions of heaven, see Sannosuke Matsumoto, "The Idea of Heaven: A Tokugawa Foundation for Natural Rights Theory," in *Japanese Thought in the Tokugawa Period*, ed. Tetsuo Najita and Irwin Scheiner (Chicago: University of Chicago Press, 1978), pp. 186–199. There remains a need for a detailed study of heaven in the thought of popular protest.

20. "Mikoku shimin ranpōki," pp. 194 jōdan, and 202–203. The next line reads: "'You are a people's commander and will regret being caught alive out of consideration for your mother. Forget about me and have it out with the generals from Tsuyama. Make your name known throughout the country. How regrettable it is that lord Amano [Tokisada] was taken alive so easily,' said the old mother grinding her teeth and wiping her tears with a sleeve."

21. "Mikoku shimin ranpōki," p. 193 jōdan.

22. Ibid., p. 193 gedan.

23. Nakano, p. 338.

24. "Mikoku shimin ranpōki," p. 194 jōdan.

25. Ibid., p. 195 jōdan.

26. Ibid., p. 196 gedan.

27. See Yokoyama Toshio, Gimin, p. 138, and Yasumaru Yoshio, Nihon no kindaika to minshū shisō (Japan's Modernization and Popular Thought) (Tokyo: Aoki Shoten, 1974), p. 208; also Yubara chōshi kohan (History of Yubara Town, vol. 2), ed. Taniguchi Sumio and Morimoto Kiyoshi (Okayama: Yubara-machi, 1953), p. 794.

28. Nakano, p. 357.

29. "Mimasaka no kuni hyakushō sōdōki," pp. 15–16.

30. "Mikoku shimin ranpōki," p. 186 jōdan.

31. Ibid., pp. 200–201.

32. By the side of a highway in Tsuyama City, six small gravestones mark the spot, across from the riverbed, where the leaders were executed. Tokuemon also has his own memorial stone in the Sanchū: on a mountain slope about two kilometers from present-day Doi village.

33. "Mikoku shimin ranpōki," p. 206 jōdan.

34. The second version, favorable to officials, is quoted without source in the "Gairy-aku Sanchū ikki," p. 13.

35. "Mikoku shimin ranpōki," p. 206 gedan.

36. Nakano, p. 368.

CHAPTER 4

1. See James I. Nakamura, "Human Capital Accumulation in Premodern Rural Japan," Journal of Economic History no. 2 (June 1981): 263–281. Nakamura's approach fails to shed any light on the precocious development of Japanese capitalism over the past century, and his claims about Tokugawa peasant involvement in the "democratic resolution of vil-lage problems" are exaggerated.

2. Nakano, pp. 369–370.

3. A brief rundown of such incidents can be found in Taniguchi Sumio and Mori-moto Kiyoshi, eds., Yubara chōshi, kōhan (Yubara-machi, Okayama, 1957), pp. 795, 820, 854, 856, 870.

4. Ichii Saburō and Fukawa Kiyoshi, Dentōteki kakushin shisōron (Essays on Traditional Reformist Thought) (Tokyo: Heibonsha, 1972), p. 139.

5. James C. Scott develops this theme of "conflict within hegemony" with great sub-tlety in "Hegemony and Consciousness: Everyday Forms of Ideological Struggle," the concluding chapter to his forthcoming book.

CHAPTER 5

1. I based the preceding analysis partly on official sources and partly on translations made from contemporary nonofficial accounts by unknown authors who utilized official documents and letters (*kōkiroku*) in writing their own interpretations. I also used in the text information about geography and terrain gained from visiting the remains of Ueda castle in August 1978 and retracing, together with Yokoyama Toshio and Ōkubo Genji, the 1761 march of the Ueda peasants. Parallel versions of the Ueda Hōreki uprising, both of official and nonofficial provenance, exist in abundance. But most Japanese scholars regard the "Ueda Sōdō Jikki" (referred to hereafter as "Sōdō jikki") and the "Uedajima Kuzuregōshi" (referred to hereafter as "Kuzuregōshi") as the most interesting and informative of all extant texts dealing directly with the uprising. Both documents can be found in their entirety in *Nihon shomin seikatsu shiryō shūsei dai rokkan, ikki* (A Collection of Historical Materials on the Life of the Japanese Common People, vol. 6, Peasant Uprisings). The collection was edited by Aoki Kōji, Ikeda Hiroshi, Takakura Shinichirō, Mori Kahei, et al. and published in 1968 by San'ichi Shobō. Yokoyama Toshio discovered, elucidated, and footnoted the "Sōdō jikki." He also prepared the notes for the "Kuzuregōshi." The latter was first published in modern characters in 1948 by the Ueda Chiisagata Publishing Society. It covers, in a manner highly sympathetic to peasants, one month of the uprising, beginning on December 12, 1761, and ending on December 31. By contrast, the "Sōdō jikki" spans the entire fifteen months of the struggle from December 1761 to March 2, 1763. And, unlike the "Kuzuregōshi," it contains sufficient internal evidence to suggest authorship by someone who sympathized with peasants yet was even more indulgent to samurai. Perhaps the author was a member of the village headman stratum. Or perhaps he was a priest or even a lower-status samurai. There is no way of knowing for sure.

To help locate quoted lines in the San'ichi Shobō version of the "Sōdō jikki" and "Kuzuregōshi," *jōdan* hereafter means upper half of page, *gedan* the lower half. The interested reader can find a modern Japanese language version of part of the "Sōdō jikki" in the original 1968 edition of Yokoyama Toshio's *Uedahan nōmin sōdōshi*, pp. 114–141. It proved useful as an aid in translation. My own English version of the "Sōdō jikki" appears, together with an introduction, in the 1981 revised and expanded edition of Professor Yokoyama's book.

Finally, no documents exist that record the unmediated thoughts of the ikki leaders or explain the Hōreki upheaval from the viewpoint of the people.

2. Yokoyama Toshio, *Ueda han nōmin sōdōshi* (The History of Peasant Uprisings in Ueda Fief) (Ueda City: Ueda Chiisagata shiryō kankōkai, 1968), p. 67. A revised and expanded version of this book, containing new historical materials on the Hōreki rising, was published in 1981 under the same title by Heirindō Shoten, Ueda City, Nagano prefecture. I used the 1968 edition unless otherwise indicated.

3. Shimizu Toshio, ed., *Chiisagata Ueda rekishi nenpyō* (Historical Chronology of Chiisagata Ueda) (No place: Chiisagata, Ueda kyōdo kenkyūkai [Chiisagata Ueda Local History Study Group], 1955), p. 31.

4. Yokoyama Toshio, p. 66. On the Edo rice exchange in the year 1706 one koku was worth 1.100 ryō. See the chart in Yamazaki Ryūzō, *Kinsei bukka shi kenkyū* (A Study of the History of Prices in the Early Modern Era) (Tokyo: Hanawa Shobō, 1983), p. 106.

5. Ibid., p. 59.

6. The real historical nature of the medieval kandaka system remains obscure. Standard sources assert that it developed naturally in the centuries before Oda Nobunaga and Toyotomi Hideyoshi's cadastral surveys. Under the kandaka system the tax on land, based on the price of crops, was converted into a monetary unit called the kanmon. The kanmon then indicated indirectly, in a very rough way, the taxable land area. By contrast, the samurai warriors of early Tokugawa times imposed the kokudaka system by military force throughout Japan in the wake of Nobunaga and Hideyoshi's unification campaigns. That system expressed directly the amount of output or produce from the land, as well as the amount of land itself. But, conceivably, by the Hōreki period (1751–1763), Ueda fief's kandaka system may have been unlike the kandaka system of medieval times and similar to the kokudaka system. A terse definition of kandaka can be found in Takeuchi Rizō and Takayanagi Mitsutoshi, eds., *Nihonshi jiten* (Dictionary of Japanese History) (Tokyo: Kadokawa Shoten, 1978), p. 234; for a fuller discussion, see Yokoyama Toshio, pp. 289–290. For the kokudaka system, see Iinuma Jirō, *Kokudakasei no kenkyū* (A Study of the Kokudaka System) (Tokyo: Mineruva Shobō, 1974–75); also, for an English-language discussion, Nagahara Keiji, "The Sengoku Daimyo and the 'Kandaka' System," in *Japan before Tokugawa: Political Consolidation and Economic Growth, 1500–1650*, ed. John W. Hall et al. (Princeton: Princeton University Press, 1981), pp. 27–63.

7. Yokoyama Toshio, p. 67.

8. Ibid., p. 70.

9. Ibid., p. 68.

10. *Ueda shishi* (The History of Ueda City), vol. 1, ed. Fujisawa Naoe and Itō Denbei (Nagano City: Shinano Mainichi Shimbunsha, 1940; reprinted 1974), p. 621.

11. Yokoyama Toshio, p. 58.

12. Yokoyama Toshio, p. 70. Also Amamiya Yuki, "Shinshū Uedahan Hōreki sōdō no kōsatsu" (A Study of the Uprising in Shinshū Ueda Fief during the Hōreki Era), *Ochanomizu shigaku* (Ochanomizu Historical Studies), no. 8 (1965): 77.

13. Yokoyama Toshio, pp. 72–73.

14. Amamiya, p. 76.

15. *Ueda shishi*, vol. 1, p. 620.

16. Amamiya, p. 76.

CHAPTER 6

1. Amamiya Yuki, "Shinshū Ueda han Hōreki sōdō no kōsatsu" (A Study of the Uprising in Shinshū Ueda Fief during the Hōreki Era), *Ochanomizu shigaku* (Ochanomizu Historical Studies), no. 8 (1965): 74.

2. *Ueda shishi*, vol. 1, pp. 423–440.

3. Amamiya, p. 75.

4. Ibid., p. 67.

5. Ibid., p. 81n1.

6. Yokoyama Toshio, *Ueda han nōmin sōdōshi* (The History of Peasant Uprisings in Ueda Fief) (Ueda City: Ueda Chiisagata shiryō kankōkai, 1968), pp. 83–86.

7. Ibid., p. 87.

8. Ibid., pp. 93–100; also Yokoyama Toshio, *Hyakushō ikki to gimin denshō* (Peasant Uprisings and Legends of Exemplary Martyrs) (Tokyo: Kyōikusha, Rekishi Shinsho 85, 1977), pp. 226–227.

9. Ibid., pp. 101–102; *Hyakushō ikki to gimin denshō*, pp. 229–230.

10. Ibid., pp. 99–102.

11. For interesting reflections along these lines, see Barrington Moore, Jr., *Injustice: The Social Bases of Obedience and Revolt* (New York: MacMillan Press, 1978), especially chap. 3, "The Rejection of Suffering and Oppression," pp. 81–125. Until the 1970s, a less realistic view of peasant revolts in precapitalist society was prevalent in Japanese academic circles. This view focused on the inertial forces at work when peasants are engaged in recurring tasks. It also exaggerated the suddenness of the movement from peasant submissiveness and belief to disbelief and anger, thereby implicitly overvaluing the role of ideology and ruling-class control mechanisms. These tendencies can be seen, to some extent, in this long quotation from historian Tōyama Shigeki. Tōyama was writing in 1947 at a time when there was a strong need in Japan to establish the argument for an indigenous revolutionary tradition against despotic rule. He began by observing that peasant serfs rose in rebellion only as a last resort: "Unlike a slave which was a material possession, a serf was supposed to have been recognized as a human being. However, in relations with the feudal lord, the peasants' identity, as illuminated by blood relations in the closed society of the village, was submerged and he could not but fall into a spontaneous attitude of submission toward the ruling power. Indeed, such submissiveness was the state of mind appropriate to agricultural production in which people were obliged to be meekly obedient to the power of nature. Class, an individualistic, *gesellschaftliche* concept, presupposes opposition, whereas caste is a concept of communal *gemeinschaft* in which such opposition is unknown. A caste system, with people's positions determined by birth and their social roles fixed for life, is brought into the life of the village. There, people are confined to a narrow world, shun non-kin strangers, and are content with the unchanging consciousness of kinship and with a homogeneity that excludes occupational differentiation. Once caste enters into that world, rigid custom and traditionalized authority come to have predominant control over peasant psychology. Without reflecting on the grounds and significance of custom and authority, the peasants take it as something natural and self-evident. Thus even the illegal oppression of the ruling caste is submitted to spontaneously, as a traditional custom of long standing. But as soon as authority exceeds its traditional form and degree, employs new methods or increases its cruelty, the peasant's sense of identity is shocked; and for the first time he reacts spontaneously [*taijiteki ni*]." See Tōyama Shigeki, "Hyakushō ikki no kakumeisei ni tsuite" (On the Revolutionary Nature of Peasant Uprisings), *Hyōron* (Criticism), May 1947, reprinted in Rekishi kagaku kyōgikai, ed., *Rekishi kagaku taikei, dainijūnikan, nōmin tōsōshi* (Historical Science Series, vol. 22, History of Peasant Struggles) (Tokyo: Azekura Shobō, 1973), p. 72.

12. Amamiya, p. 72.

13. Perhaps eighteenth-century Tokugawa Japan could be described, not too unrealistically, as a zero-sum society in which famines occurred periodically because of social and political causes as well as natural ones.

14. Amamiya, p. 72.

15. Ibid.

16. *Nihon shomin seikatsu shiryō shūsei, dairokkan, ikki* (A Collection of Historical Materials on the Life of the Japanese Common People, vol. 6, Uprisings) (Tokyo: Sanichi Shobō, 1968), p. 183n2, written by Yokoyama Toshio.

17. For discussion of the general idea of moral ceilings on the claims that ruling classes can make on peasants, see James C. Scott, "Protest and Profanation: Agrarian Revolt and the Little Tradition, Part I," *Theory and Society* 4, no. 1 (Spring 1977): 12–16. For exploita-

tion in the Greek and Roman world, the definitive study is G. E. M. De Ste. Croix, *The Class Struggle in the Ancient World: From the Archaic Age to the Arab Conquest* (London: Duckworth & Co., 1981). Among his many examples of merciless treatment of peasants by church officials (and private landowners) are these two (from p. 225): "In A.D. 603 we find Pope Gregory writing to a notary, Pantaleo, of his indignation at the discovery that certain *coloni Ecclesiae* [peasants on ecclesiastical lands in Sicily] had been obliged to hand over their produce according to a *modius*-measure containing no fewer than 25 *sextarii* instead of the proper 16: he expresses his pleasure at the news that Pantaleo has now broken up the iniquitous measure." and "Again, the charming life of St. Theodore of Sykeon (an almost exact contemporary of Pope Gregory) describes how the peasants of the estates of the Church of Anastasiopolis in Galatia were constantly harried by Theodosius, a leading man of the city who had been appointed chief administrator of the Church lands, to the point at which they were driven to resist him by force."

18. Amamiya, p. 73, citing the *Ueda Chiisagata shishi*, vol. 2, p. 288. Four shō, two gō, seven shaku, five sai per bale of commissariat rice (jōmai) was about enough to support at least two persons for seven days. The distance from Ueda castle town to Komoro was approximately thirty-six kilometers.

19. Amamiya, p. 78.

20. Amamiya, p. 74.

21. *Furushima Toshio chosakushū, dai ikkan, fueki rōdōsei no hōkai katei* (The Collected Works of Furushima Toshio, vol. 1, The Process of Disintegration of the Corvée Labor System) (Tokyo: Tokyo Daigaku Shuppankai, 1974), p. 27.

22. "Sōdō jikki," p. 173 gedan.

23. Amamiya, p. 76.

24. *Ueda shishi*, vol. 2, p. 452.

25. The term *gundai* can mean "superintendent or head of local officials and their affairs." But in Ueda at this time *gundai* connoted the samurai official in charge of the entire fief during the lord's absence. He was a very high-ranking person who could be likened, in effect, to a viceroy sent out to govern a colony. In this respect, he was quite unlike the *gundai* of Tsuyama fief.

26. Amamiya, p. 67.

CHAPTER 7

1. Katsura Kakuemon, *"Shigi seijiroku"* (A Personal Account of Fief Administration), January 1762, in Yokoyama Toshio, *Ueda han nōmin sōdōshi (zōho shinpan)* (Uedashi, Naganoken: Heirindō Shoten, 1981), p. 474.

2. "Sōdō jikki," p. 175 jōdan.

3. Amamiya, p. 81n1. She cites no source for this fact.

4. "Sōdō jikki," p. 173 gedan.

5. Ibid., p. 173 gedan.

6. *Ueda Chiisagata shishi, yohen*, ed. Chiisagatagōri Yakusho (n.p.: Chiisagata Jihōsha, 1923), p. 784.

7. Ibid., p. 784.

8. "Sōdō jikki," p. 174 jōdan.

9. *Ueda Chiisagata shishi, yohen*, p. 784.

10. "Sōdō jikki," p. 174 jōdan.

11. *Ueda shishi*, vol. 2, pp. 136–137.

12. *Ueda Chiisagata shishi*, p. 789.

13. *Ueda shishi*, vol. 2, p. 137.

14. Amamiya, pp. 72 ff.

15. "Uedajima Kuzuregōshi," p. 190 jōdan.

16. *Ueda shishi*, vol. 2, pp. 235–236. The officially registered population at this time was 2,609 or 413 "households." The castle town itself, centering on the castle built by Sanada Masayuki in the 1580s, was divided into seven town-districts or *machi* (Unno, Yoko, Kaji, Hara, Ta, Yanagi, Konya) and a subordinate entity called Jishamonzen. Unno and Hara contained the largest concentration of merchants, and Kaji and Konya were centers for artisans and craftsmen apprentices.

17. "Sōdō jikki," p. 174 jōdan.

18. "Sōdō jikki," p. 174 gedan.

19. *Ueda Chiisagata shishi*, p. 789.

20. "Sōdō jikki," p. 174 gedan; also see *Ueda Chisagata shishi*, p. 789, which states that Okabe left for Edo on the night of the thirteenth.

21. "Kuzuregōshi," p. 193 jōdan.

22. *Ueda shishi*, vol. 2, p. 141; "Kuzuregōshi," p. 191 jōdan.

23. "Sōdō jikki," p. 175 jōdan.

24. *Ueda Chiisagata shishi*, p. 792.

25. Katsura Kakuemon, "Shōhiroku" (A Short Elaboration), January 1762, in Yokoyama Toshio (1981), p. 464.

26. "Sōdō jikki," p. 175 gedan.

27. Yokoyama Toshio suggests this interpretation in his comments in *Uedahan nōmin sōdōshi*, pp. 110–113.

28. "Kuzuregōshi," p. 196 jōdan.

29. "Sōdō jikki," p. 175 gedan; Amamiya, p. 70.

30. *Ueda shishi*, vol. 2, p. 149, and vol. 1, p. 623. Ueda's town officials beneath the level of magistrate were all appointed from the highest stratum of the merchant and artisan classes. These were the town *tonya* (equivalent to the tribute officers of the rural districts) and their assistants, called town elders (*machidoshiyori*). Source: Ōishi Shinzaburō, *Nihon kinsei shakai no shijō kōzō* (Market Structure in Early Modern Japanese Society) (Tokyo: Iwanami Shoten, 1975), p. 50. It was not always the case in all fiefs, however, that town elders were ranked below tonya. In some castle towns a reversed ranking may have obtained or the two posts could be held concurrently by the same person. But that was not the arrangement in Ueda at this time.

31. Francis Fox Piven and Richard A. Cloward, *The New Class War: Reagan's Attack on the Welfare State and Its Consequences* (New York: Pantheon Books, 1982), p. 142.

32. "Sōdō jikki," p. 176 jōdan, gives December 22 as the day of Okabe's return to Ueda castle; the "Kuzuregōshi" states that it was December 24. Neither figure may be correct. Equally difficult to establish is the exact number of townsmen's demands. The "Sōdō jikki" claims eleven while the *Ueda shishi*, vol. 2, pp. 146–148, gives the figure of fourteen that I have used here. Also see Amamiya, p. 70.

33. Oishi Shinzaburō, pp. 43–51. Pongee is a silk fabric woven of relatively untwisted waste filaments, which give it a slightly uneven, rough texture.

34. Ibid., pp. 53–54, 69; also see Fukai Jinzō, "Kinsei toshi no hattatsu" (The Development of Early Modern Cities) in Matsumoto Shirō and Yamada Tadao, eds., *Genroku Kyō-*

hōki no seiji to shakai, kōza Nihon kinseishi 4 (Politics and Society from Genroku to Kyōhō, Lectures on Early Modern Japanese History) (Tokyo: Yūhikaku, 1980), p. 191n39.

35. Iijima Shiaki, "Jōkamachi to shūhen nōson—bunseki shikaku to kadai no teiji" (Castle Towns and Surrounding Villages), *Chihōshi kenkyū 166* 30, no. 4 (August 1980): 19. The *machi byakushō* may be likened to the "ploughmen" of sixteenth-century Romans, described by Emmanuel Le Roy Ladurie, *Carnival in Romans: A People's Uprising at Romans 1579–1580* (New York: Penguin Books, 1981), pp. 25–26.

36. *Ueda ₋hishi*, vol. 2, pp. 146–147.

37. "Sōdō jikki," p. 176 jōdan.

38. "Kuzuregōshi," p. 196 gedan.

39. *Ueda Chiisagatashi*, p. 793.

40. "Kuzuregōshi," p. 196 gedan.

41. Ibid., p. 196 gedan.

42. Ibid., p. 197 jōdan.

43. "Hōreki juisai kanoto sōdō hikae." A "Record of the Disturbances in December of the 11th year of the Hōreki Era" by Kanae Kamenosuke, a village headman of Kokubunji district.

44. "Sōdō jikki," p. 178 gedan.

45. Ibid., p. 178 jōdan.

46. Ibid., p. 176 jōdan and gedan.

47. Barrington Moore, Jr., *Injustice: The Social Bases of Obedience and Revolt* (London: MacMillan Press, 1978), pp. 369, 370. Drawing on the work of French historian Marc Ferro, Moore goes on to say, however, that "in the characteristic euphoria of a revolution's first phase, when everything suddenly seems within reach and the aura of inevitability has suddenly evaporated, the Russian workers were hardly in a mood to wait. Their demands were limited and concrete. But they had to be met, completely and without delay. In the prevailing circumstances of chaos and destruction, disappointment and further radicalization were more than likely" (p. 370).

48. "Sōdō jikki", p. 179 jōdan.

49. Ibid., p. 178 gedan.

50. Ibid., p. 178 jōdan.

51. Ibid., p. 178 gedan.

52. Ibid., p. 178 gedan. This interrogation of peasant prisoners by the mighty Okabe Kurobei may be compared with the more famous dialogue between Alexander the Great and a captured pirate, which St. Augustine cites in his *City of God*: "Elegant and excellent was that pirate's answer to the great Macedonian Alexander, who had taken him: the king asking him how he durst molest the seas so, he replied with a free spirit: 'How darest thou molest the whole world? But because I do it with a little ship only, I am called a thief: thou, doing it with a great navy, art called an emperor.'" In other words, rulers should govern justly (St. Augustine, *The City of God [De Civitate Dei]*. Trans. John Healey [London: J. M. Dent & Sons, 1945], bk. 4, chap. 4, p. 115). I owe this example to Geoffrey de Ste. Croix, *The Class Struggle in the Ancient World*, p. 477.

53. James C. Scott, quoting Irving Goffman, writes: "We must be very careful . . . not to infer the values of the oppressed from their behavior. Much of what passes as deference 'is ritualized and habitual' or even calculating: 'a great deal of this deferential behavior can be understood solely in terms of the constraints surrounding the actor that sanction any other form of behavior.' There may in fact be a large disparity between this constrained behavior

and the behavior that would occur if constraints were lifted. The degree of this disparity would be some index of the disingenuousness of deferential acts." See Scott, *The Moral Economy of the Peasant: Rebellion and Subsistence in Southeast Asia* (New Haven: Yale University Press, 1976), p. 232.

54. "Sōdō jikki," p. 178 gedan.

55. Ibid., p. 179 gedan.

56. *Ueda shishi*, vol. 2, p. 85.

57. Hayashi Motoi, "Hōreki-Tenmeiki no shakai jōsei" (The Social Circumstances in the Hōreki and Tenmei Eras), in *Iwanami kōza, Nihon rekishi 12, kinsei 4* (Tokyo: Iwanami Shoten, 1967), p. 149.

58. Ibid., pp. 147–148.

59. Ibid., p. 149.

60. Ibid., p. 151.

61. "Sōdō jikki," p. 179 gedan and p. 180 all.

62. All quotations from the execution scene given in this section come from the "Sōdō jikki," pp. 180–181.

63. Shimizu Toshio, ed., *Chiisagata Ueda rekishi nenpyō*, p. 39.

CHAPTER 8

1. See Francis Fox Piven and Richard A. Cloward, *Poor People's Movements: Why They Succeed, How They Fail* (New York: Vintage Books, 1977, 1979), p. xi. On the division between blacks and whites within the American working class, they comment: "If ever there were sectors of the working class that should have been 'the closest of allies' . . . it was the black and white poor. But the institutional development of the United States had determined otherwise, as witness the history of failed efforts to produce multiracial class-based protest movements. And so, when massive socioeconomic and political changes finally made an independent black struggle possible, black eruptions provoked the violent opposition of southern white working-class people and later the opposition of northern working-class people as well. No course of action available to blacks could have prevented the worsening of antagonisms so deeply embedded in the experience of the white working class. If blacks were to mobilize at all in the United States in the 1950s and 1960s, working-class divisions would inevitably be widened" (pp. xi–xii). Significantly, they add that ultimately "the black movement . . . may have improved the possibilities for more broad-based working-class struggles in the future."

2. See Yokoyama Toshio, (1968), pp. 277–286.

3. Shimizu Toshio, pp. 39–40.

4. Katsura Kakuemon, "Shigi seijiroku" (A Personal Account of Fief Administration), January 1762, in Yokoyama Toshio, (1981), pp. 472–473. My translation is based on Professor Yokoyama's own "transliterated excerpts" of this document, written originally in the old-style calligraphy.

CHAPTER 9

1. Hayashi Motoi, "Hōreki-Tenmeiki no shakai jōsei" (The Social Situation in the Hōreki and Tenmei Eras), in *Iwanami kōza, Nihon rekishi 12, kinsei 4* (Tokyo: Iwanami Shoten, 1967), p. 150.

2. Ibid., pp. 150–151.

3. Takehiko Ohkura and Hiroshi Shimbo, "The Tokugawa Monetary Policy in the Eighteenth and Nineteenth Centuries," *Explorations in Economic History* 15, no. 1 (January 1978): 106–107.

4. John Whitney Hall, *Tanuma Okitsugu, 1719–1788: Forerunner of Modern Japan* (Cambridge, Mass.: Harvard University Press, 1955) contains rich material on this period. But Hall minimizes the importance of class conflict and exaggerates Tanuma's personal role. By interpreting everything in terms of a single individual, he distorts the nature of bakufu politics in the Meiwa-Tenmei eras.

5. Herman Ooms, *Charismatic Bureaucrat: A Political Biography of Matsudaira Sadanobu 1758–1829* (New Haven: Yale University Press, 1974), p. 75. He adds that the Edo "rioters believed they were being led by a sturdy and fierce-looking samurai (possibly suggesting Sano) and by a handsome young man who rode in front of them in the skies—a symbol of their hopes represented by the twenty-eight-year-old lord of Shirakawa? From the *bakufu*'s viewpoint the situation looked frightening. After two days of turmoil a militia totaling three thousand men was sent into the city to restore order" (pp. 75–76).

6. Ibid., p. 9.

7. Ibid., p. 10.

8. See the discussion in Yamada Tadao, "Hōreki-Tenmeiki bakusei no tenkai" (The Development of Bakufu Politics in the Hōreki and Tenmei Eras), in Ōishi Shinzaburō, ed., *Nihonshi 5, kinsei 2* (Japanese History 5, The Early Modern Era, vol. 2) (Tokyo: Yūhikaku Shinsho 560, 1978), pp. 94–95; and Takeuchi Makoto, "Kansei kaikaku" (The Kansei Reforms), in *Iwanami kōza, Nihon rekishi 12, kinsei 4* (Iwanami Lectures, Japanese History 12, The Early Modern Era, vol. 4) (Tokyo: Iwanami Shoten, 1976), p. 5.

CHAPTER 10

1. Harold Bolitho, citing the *Fukuyama shishi, chūkan*, describes the Abe family thusly: "This particular branch of the Abe was descended from Abe Shigetsugu, the Bakufu official of the early seventeenth century. From the mid-eighteenth century onward, his descendants compiled a record of Bakufu office-holding unsurpassed among *fudai* families. From Abe Masatomi (1700–1769) onward, not one of the Fukuyama Abe daimyo failed to hold Bakufu office at some stage of his career. If there was ever any Bakufu hostility to *tozama* daimyō and suspicion of contacts with them, one would expect to see it reflected in a discriminating approach to the pedigrees of those who sought and obtained Bakufu office. There most surely can have been no such antipathy. Of the six successive daimyō of Fukuyama who ruled between the Abe entry into Fukuyama in 1710 and the incumbency of Masahiro (the Bakufu official to whom fell the duty of negotiating with Commodore Perry in 1853), no fewer than five found brides from among the daughters of *tozama* daimyō" (*Treasures among Men, The Fudai Daimyo in Tokugawa Japan* [New Haven: Yale University Press, 1974], pp. 98–99).

2. Michishige Tetsuo, "Fukuyama-han Tenmei roku-shichinen ikki no shiryō ni tsuite—hanshu Abe Masatomo shokan o chūshin toshite" (Historical Materials on the Tenmei Rising of 1786–87 in Fukuyama Fief: Lord Abe Masatomo's Correspondence), *Geibi chihōshi kenkyū*, no. 58 (August 1965), pp. 19–26. All quotations from Abe Masatomo come from the letters reproduced in this article, to which my own analysis is deeply indebted.

3. "Abeno dojimon" (Account of the Boy From Abeno), in *Nihon shomin seikatsu shiryō shūsei dai rokkan, ikki* (A Collection of Historical Materials on the Life of the Japanese Common People, vol. 6, Peasant Uprisings) (Tokyo: San'ichi Shobō, 1968), p. 343 gedan. The document is footnoted (pp. 382–386) and introduced (pp. 341–342) by Michishige Tetsuo.

4. From the Author's Introduction to the "Abeno dōjimon," p. 343 gedan.

5. *Hiroshima kenshi, kinsei 1* (History of Hiroshima Prefecture, vol. 1, The Early Modern Period) (Hiroshima Prefecture, 1981), p. 447.

6. *Fukuyama shishi, chūkan* (History of Fukuyama City, vol. 2) (Fukuyama City: Editorial Committee for the History of Fukuyama City, 1968), p. 470.

7. Katsumata Shizuo, *Ikki* (Uprisings) (Tokyo: Iwanami Shinsho 194, 1982) p. 110.

8. See *Fukuyama shishi, chūkan*, pp. 956–959.

9. On "righteous government debt-cancelation edicts" (*tokusei*), see Katsumata Shizuo, pp. 152–178. He argues that the debt-cancelation ikki of the fifteenth and early sixteenth centuries may be seen as a peasant response to the unsettled situation produced by the breakdown of the medieval manorial system (*shōen*), the spread of money economy in the Kinki region, and the emergence of a more dynamic agrarian economy. The tokusei ikki presupposed a definite peasant consciousness of land ownership.

10. *Fukuyama shishi, chūkan*, p. 962; Fujii Masao, *Bingo Fukuyama shakai keizai shi* (A Socio-economic History of Bingo Fukuyama) (Fukuyama City, Kojima Shoten 1973), p. 247. This is an important source to which I am much indebted.

11. Fujii Masao, pp. 250–252.

12. Ibid., p. 265; *Fukuyama shishi, chūkan*, p. 971, gives slightly smaller figures.

13. "Abeno dōjimon," p. 343 gedan.

14. "Abeno dōjimon," p. 384–35; *Fukuyama shishi, chūkan*, p. 963.

15. Michishige Tetsuo, p. 20; Herman Ooms, p. 7. Ooms notes that during the Tenmei famines the price of rice "soared to unprecedented heights: 98.3 in 1783, 111.2 in 1784, and 167.9 in 1787" (p. 7).

16. "Abeno dōjimon," p. 349 gedan; pp. 383–384n25; Fujii Masao, p. 262.

17. *Fukuyama shishi, chūkan*, p. 946.

18. Ibid., p. 965.

19. "Abeno dōjimon," p. 343 gedan.

20. *Fukuyama shishi, chūkan*, p. 968.

21. Michishige Tetsuo, pp. 21–22.

22. "Abeno dōjimon," pp. 376 and 386n72.

23. Michishige Tetsuo, p. 24.

24. Ibid., pp. 24–25.

25. "Abeno dōjimon," p. 386n74; *Fukuyama shishi, chūkan*, p. 975.

26. Fujii Masao, pp. 263–264.

CHAPTER 11

1. My summary of the economic side of the Kansei Reforms draws chiefly on Herman Ooms, pp. 86–104; Ishii Kanji, *Nihon keizai-shi* (Japanese Economic History) (Tokyo: Tokyo Daigaku Shuppankai, 1976, 1980), pp. 25–26; and especially Namba Nobuo, "Bakuhansei kaikaku no tenkai to kaikyū tōsō" (The Development of Bakuhan System

Reforms and Class Struggle), in Sasaki Junnosuke et al., eds., *Taikei Nihon kokkashi 3, kinsei* (Outline Series on the History of the Japanese State, Volume 3, The Early Modern Era) (Tokyo: Tokyo Daigaku Shuppankai, 1975), pp. 283–286.

2. See Ooms, p. 87.

3. Namba Nobuo, p. 285; Ishii Kanji, p. 27.

4. Fujii Masao, pp. 268–269. An alternative but much less satisfactory rendering of *seidō* is "the path of righteousness." Also see *Fukuyama shishi, chūkan*, pp. 543–545.

5. Fujii Masao, p. 270.

6. Ibid.

7. Ibid., p. 271

8. Ibid., p. 273.

9. Ibid., pp. 275–276; *Fukuyama shishi, chūkan*, pp. 898–899.

10. Fujii Masao, pp. 271–272; *Fukuyama shishi, chūkan*, pp. 1009, 1012.

11. Fujii Masao, p. 266.

12. *Fukuyama shishi, chūkan*, pp. 1021–1022.

13. Ibid., p. 1023.

14. On this point, see James C. Scott, "Hegemony and Consciousness: Everyday Forms of Ideological Struggle," unpublished manuscript, 1984.

CHAPTER 12

1. Shintani Masamichi, "Andō Shōeki no rōdōkan" (Andō Shōeki's View of Labor), *Kikan kuraishisu* (The Crisis Quarterly), no. 14 (Winter 1983), pp. 129–138.

2. Ichii Saburō and Fukawa Kiyoshi, *Dentōteki kakushin shisōron* (Essays on Traditional Reformist Thought) (Tokyo: Heibonsha 1972), p. 139.

3. I am indebted for this insight to James C. Scott, "Hegemony and Consciousness: Everyday Forms of Ideological Struggle."

4. Ibid.

5. Kitazawa Fumitake, *Meiwa no dai ikki* (The Great Uprising of the Meiwa Era) (Tokyo: Hatano Mori Shoten, 1973), pp. 8, 16. Honjō was the tenth post station from Nihonbashi in Edo.

6. Ibid., pp. 167–183.

7. Ibid., p. 75.

8. "Kamo no sawagitachi" (The Disturbance in Kamo District), in *Nihon shisō taikei 58, minshū undō no shisō* (Compendium of Japanese Thought, Vol. 58,—The Thought of the People's Movement), ed. Shōji Yoshinosuke, Hayashi Motoi, and Yasumaru Yoshio (Tokyo: Iwanami Shoten, 1970), pp. 254, 267.

9. Katsumata Shizuo, *Ikki* (Uprisings) (Tokyo: Iwanami Shinsho No. 194, 1982), pp. 61–62.

10. Ibid., pp. 23–24, 34.

11. On the phenomenology of anger and political anger, see Peter Lyman, "The Politics of Anger: On Silence, Resentment and Political Speech," *Socialist Review*, no. 57 (May–June 1981), p. 67ff. On the close relationship between revenge and justice, see Freud's remarks on violence and right in "Why War?" (1932), in *Collected Papers*, vol. 26, p. 275.

12. See Sune Sunesson, "Organizing and Discipline," *Acta Sociologica— The Journal of the Scandinavian Sociological Association* 27, no. 3 (1984): 199–213.

13. See Klaus Mäkelä, "The Uses of Alcohol and Their Cultural Regulation," *Acta Sociologica—The Journal of the Scandinavian Sociological Association* 26, no. 1 (1983): 21–31.

14. Miyata Noboru, "Nōson no fukkō undō to minshū shūkyō no tenkai" (The Restoration Movement in Agricultural Villages and the Development of Popular Religion), in *Iwanami kōza, Nihon rekishi 13, kinsei 5* (Iwanami Lectures, Japanese History, vol. 13, The early Modern Period, vol. 5) (Tokyo: Iwanami Shoten, 1977), p. 230.

15. All the quotations in this paragraph are from Ichii Saburō and Fukaya Kiyoshi, pp. 264–265.

16. Miyata Noboru, p. 231. Also see the interesting "Historical Afterword" in John Berger, *Pig Earth* (London: Writers and Readers Publishing Cooperative, 1979), pp. 200–209.

17. Ochiai Nobutaka, "Yonaoshi to sonraku kyōdōtai" (World Renewal and the Village Community), in Rekishigaku kenkyūkai henshū, *Minshū no seikatsu, bunka to henkaku shutai* (The Life and Culture of the People and the Main Body of Reform) (Tokyo: Aoki Shoten, November 1982), p. 99.

18. Marc Bloch, *French Rural History—An Essay on Its Basic Characteristics*. Trans. Janet Sondheimer (London: Routledge & Kegan Paul, 1966), pp. 179–180.

19. On this, James C. Scott's reflections are invaluable. See *The Moral Economy of the Peasant: Rebellion and Subsistence in Southeast Asia* (New Haven: Yale University Press, 1976), chap. 6.

20. Sasaki Junnosuke, *Yonaoshi* (World Renewal) (Tokyo: Iwanami Shinsho 90, 1979), pp. 204–205.

CHAPTER 13

1. On the currency crisis, see Shibahara Takuji, *Nihon kindaika no sekaishiteki ichi— sono hōhōronteki kenkyū* (The World Historical Position of Japan's Modernization) (Tokyo: Iwanami Shoten, 1981), pp. 173–178. The traditional currency system consisted of gold, silver by weight, and copper coins, plus fief paper notes (*hansatsu*), private bills of credit, and promissory notes (*tegata*).

2. Sugi Hitoshi, "Ka-seiki no shakai to bunka—zaison bunka no tenkai to kinseiteki bunka kōzō no kaitai" (Society and Culture in the Bunka-Bunsei Period [1804–1829]: On the Development of Rural Village Culture and the Disintegration of the Early Modern Structure of Culture), in *Tenpōki no seiji to shakai* (Politics and Society in the Tenpō Period), ed. Aoki Michio and Yamada Tadao (Tokyo: Yūhikaku, 1981), p. 28.

3. Ibid., pp. 37, 52.

4. Patricia Sippel, "Popular Protest in Early Modern Japan: The Bushū Outburst," *Harvard Journal of Asiatic Studies* 37, no. 2 (December 1979): 280. A good discussion marred only by its gross mischaracterization of the Bushū incident as an "outburst."

5. Sugi Hitoshi, pp. 44–46.

6. Harry Harootunian, "Ideology As Conflict," in *Conflict in Modern Japanese History: The Neglected Tradition*, ed. Tetsuo Najita and J. Victor Koschmann (Princeton: Princeton University Press, 1982), pp. 55, 57.

7. Yasumaru Yoshio, *Nihon no kindaika to minshū shisō* (The Modernization of Japan and Popular Thought) (Tokyo: Aoki Shoten, 1974), p. 45.

8. Aoki Michio, "Tenpō ikkiron" (Risings of the Tenpō Era) in Aoki Michio and Yamada Tadao, eds., pp. 114–115.

9. Sasaki Junnosuke, *Yonaoshi* (World Renewal) (Tokyo: Iwanami Shinsho 90, 1979), p. 22.

10. Terao Gorō, *Sōmō no ishinshi* (A Restoration History of the Commoners) (Tokyo: Tokuma Shoten, 1980), pp. 117–118. On the provincial lawsuits brought by rural merchants, landlords, and village officials, see Tsuda Hideo, *Nihon no rekishi 22, Tenpō kaikaku* (The Tenpō Reforms) (Tokyo: Shōgakukan, 1975), pp. 88–94.

11. Terao Goro, p. 118.

12. Ibid., p. 118.

13. Ibid., p. 120.

14. Ibid., pp. 121–123. These pages contain Ōshio's complete manifesto.

15. Sakai Hajime, "Ōshio no ran to kinai nōson" (The Ōshio Insurrection and Agricultural Villages in the Ōsaka-Kōbe-Kyōto Area), in Aoki Michio and Yamada Tadao, eds., *Tenpōki no seiji to shakai*, pp. 228, 231, 233.

16. Sakai Hajime, pp. 191–193; Terao Gorō, p. 127.

17. Sakai Hajime, p. 193; Terao Gorō, p. 126.

18. On the general theme of violence and its practitioners, Moore writes realistically that "enthusiasm for the act of violence as somehow redeeming and therapeutic for the victim as well as for the victimized society does not appear to be a prominent current among ordinary members of subordinate or oppressed groups. For one thing it is often just too dangerous. In the second place it can bring reprisals on the whole group" (Barrington Moore, Jr., *Injustice—The Social Bases of Obedience and Revolt* [London and New York: Macmillan Press, 1978], p. 429). These reasons apply with particular force to Japanese peasants. Forbidden upon pain of death to bear weapons of war, they usually directed violence against property rather than persons and spared rather than killed their opponents. Their convention of relative pacifism represented the conversion of a disadvantage into a virtue. But the virtue weakened with the increased militarization of Japanese society during the closing years of the bakufu and the early years of the Meiji regime.

19. Terao Gorō, p. 128.

20. Aoki Michio, "Tatakau nōmin shimintachi" (Fighting Peasants and Townsmen), in *Nihonshi 5, Kinsei 2* (Japanese History, vol. 5, The Early Modern Period, vol. 2), ed. Ōishi Shinzaburō (Tokyo: Yūhikaku 1978), pp. 168–169.

21. Tsuda Hideo, pp. 228–229.

22. Sakai Hajime, p. 191.

23. Tetsuo Najita, "Ōshio Heihachirō," in *Personality in Japanese History*, ed. Albert M. Craig and Donald H. Shively (Berkeley: University of California Press, 1970), p. 178.

24. For further argumentation and evidence, see Francis Fox Piven and Richard A. Cloward, *Poor People's Movements: Why They Succeed, How They Fail* (New York: Vintage Books, 1979), and Moore, pts. 2 and 3.

25. On the Tenpō reforms, see Mikio Sumiya and Kōji Taira, eds., *An Outline of Japanese Economic History 1603–1940: Major Works and Research Findings* (Tokyo: University of Tokyo Press, 1979), pp. 112–129.

26. A key source on this whole question is Teodor Shanin, ed., *Late Marx and the Russian Road: Marx and "the peripheries of capitalism"* (New York: Monthly Review Press, 1983), especially the introductory essay by Shanin, pp. 3–39.

27. See Nakamura Satoru, "Kaikokugo no bōeki to sekai shijō" (Trade and the World Market after the Opening of the Ports), in *Iwanami Kōza, Nihon rekishi 13, kinsei 5* (Tokyo: Iwanami Shoten, 1977), pp. 118–119. Significantly, Perry's opening of Japan occurred at about the same time as the United States began intervening militarily in Latin America. And the same impulse to accumulate capital on a global scale lay behind it as motivated the other Western bourgeoisies in their respective drives to expand abroad in the future by first creating the requisite conditions for such expansion in the present.

28. Sasaki Junnosuke, p. 53.

29. E. H. Norman notes that "the Imperial armies were aided by numerous peasant uprisings directed against bakufu forces which so paralyzed the latter, by compelling them to keep troops immobilized in remote far-flung parts of the country, that it was quite easy for the regular troops of the Imperial army to deal a death blow at the nerve centers of Tokugawa control in the vital key areas. In a very real sense the peasant risings ... particularly as they became most frequent and violent in the last decade, played a noteworthy part in overthrowing the Bakufu. Thus the Restoration, to a large degree, can be justly called the harvest of peasant revolt" (*Soldier and Peasant in Japan: The Origins of Conscription* [New York: Institute of Pacific Relations, 1943], p. 37).

30. See Teodor Shanin, *Russia as a "Developing Society"—The Roots of Otherness: Russia's Turn of Century*, vol. 1 (London: Macmillan Press, 1985), pp. 59–61. On degrees of servitude, see also Marc Raeff's comments in "Review of Slavery in Russia 1450–1725. By Richard Hellie," *Labor History* 24, no. 3 (Summer 1983).

31. Shanin, *Russia as a "Developing Society,"* pp. 132–149.

32. See J. Craig Jenkins, "Why Do Peasants Rebel? Structural and Historical Theories of Modern Peasant Rebellions," *American Journal of Sociology* 88, no. 3 (November 1982): 511.

33. On this point and on the mid-nineteenth-century peasant struggles in Russia, see Hayashi Motoi, "Soren ni okeru kaikyū tōsōshi kenkyū: hōken shakai makki no nōmin undōshi o chūshin ni" (Studies in the History of Class Struggle in the Soviet Union: On the History of the Peasant Movement in Late Feudal Society), in Hayashi Motoi, Kaikyū tōsōshi kenkyūkai (ed.), *Kaikyū tōsō no rekishi to riron, ikkan* (The History and Theory of Class Struggle, vol. 1) (Tokyo: Aoki Shoten, 1981), p. 203.

34. James C. Scott, "Protest and Profanation: Agrarian Revolt and the Little Tradition, Part II," *Theory and Society* 4, no. 2 (1977). This essay yields many new insights into the complex relationship between popular religion (the little tradition) and class struggle.

35. I owe these points to discussion with Professor Teodor Shanin and to chapter 3 ("Revolution from Below: Land and Liberty") of his forthcoming book, *Russia 1905–7: Revolution As a Moment of Truth* (London: Macmillan Press).

36. Moshe Lewin, *The Making of the Soviet System: Essays in the Social History of Interwar Russla* (New York: Pantheon Books, 1985), p. 15; also Shanin, Ibid., chap. 3.

37. Shanin, chap. 3.

38. Ibid.

39. See Peter Kolchin, "Reevaluating the Antebellum Slave Community: A Comparative Perspective," *Journal of American History* 70, no. 3 (December 1983): 593–594.

40. See Teodor Shanin, "Late Marx and the Russian Periphery of Capitalism," *Monthly Review* 35 (June 1983): 13. Also worth consulting are the essays in Wayne S. Vucinich, ed., *The Peasant in Nineteenth-Century Russia* (Stanford: Stanford University Press, 1968).

41. Barrington Moore, Jr., *Social Origins of Dictatorship and Democracy—Lord and Peasant in the Making of the Modern World* (Boston: Beacon Press, 1966), p. 476.

42. Kolchin, p. 595.

43. On communes in history, see Karl Marx's "Drafts of a Reply to Vera Zasulich" (1881) in Shanin, ed., *Late Marx and the Russian Road*, espec. pp. 105–117.

44. Moore, p. 476.

45. See H. P. Bix, "Rethinking 'Emperor-System Fascism': Ruptures and Continuities in Modern Japanese History," *Bulletin of Concerned Asian Scholars* 14, no. 2 (April–June 1982): 3–5.

46. See the charts in "Bakumatsu no shakai hendō to 'yonaoshi'" (Social Change and "Yonaoshi" in the Last Years of the Bakufu), *Rekishigaku kenkyū*, no. 458 (July 1978), pp. 15–16. This is a special issue on the Bushū rising introduced by Sasaki Junnosuke and prepared by the Association for the Study of Early Modern Village History.

47. Ibid., p. 17.

48. For the organizational structure of the Bushū ikki, see Mori Yasuhiko, "'Yonaoshi' ikki no tenkai to minshū ishiki" (The Development of a "Yonaoshi" Rising and Popular Consciousness), *Rekishigaku kenkyū*, no. 458 (July 1978), p. 21. For a good description of clothing worn during this episode, see Saitō Yōichi, "Bushū yonaoshi ikki no idetachi to emono" (Clothing and Tools in the World Renewal Rising in Musashi Province), *Gakushūin daigaku shiryōkan kiyō* (Bulletin of the Gakushūin University Archives Museum), no. 1 (March 1983), pp. 3–8.

49. Saitō Yōichi, Ibid., p. 36.

50. Sasaki Junnosuke, *Yonaoshi*, p. 79; also Mori Yasuhiko, p. 21.

51. Sippel, p. 293.

52. Mori Yasuhiko, p. 30. Also, on the composition of the peasant militia at the time of the Bushū rising, see Mogi Yōichi, "Bakumatsuki bakuryō nōhei soshiki no seiritsu to tenkai" (The Formation and Development of Peasant Militia in the Last Decade of the Bakufu), *Rekishigaku kenkyū* [Journal of Historical Studies], no. 464 (January 1979), pp. 22–23.

53. See Saitō Yōichi, pp. 40–44.

54. Ichii Saburō and Fukawa Kiyoshi, *Dentōteki kakushin shisōron* (Essays on Traditional Reformist Thought) (Tokyo: Heibonsha, 1972), p. 267.

55. *Shimada shishi shiryō, dai rokkan* (Historical Materials on the History of Shimada City, vol. 6) (Shimada City: Shimada Shiyakusho, 1970), pp. 10–11. I am indebted to Sasaki Junnosuke for this source.

56. Sasaki Junnosuke, *Yonaoshi*, pp. 96–98, 103. Two other interpretations of the ee jya nai ka movement, though somewhat dated, are also worth reading. The best is E. H. Norman's richly documented and insightful discussion in "Feudal Background of Japanese Politics," in *Origins of the Modern Japanese State: Selected Writings of E. H. Norman*, ed. (New York: Pantheon Books, 1975), pp. 343–349. The other account is Paul Akamatsu, *Meiji 1868* (New York: Harper & Row, 1972), p. 215. Akamatsu writes: "On about September 20 (1867), the rumour suddenly sprang up at Nagoya that amulets from the great Shinto temple of Ise had fallen from heaven. The townspeople—particularly the young folk—massed in the street, dancing and singing, men dressed up as women and women as men. They were drinking *sake*, breaking into the houses of the rich, and seizing whatever objects they could lay their hands on. It was all going on in a spirit of celebration, both the pillagers and the inhabitants of dwellings they invaded, exchanging couplets of songs punctuated by the

chorus: 'What is the good of that?' The intoxicated demonstrators were lying down and sleeping anywhere and getting up again to dance and sing anew. Everyone seemed to be celebrating a change for the better in the times, which had not yet taken place but which was augured for the near future.

By degrees, these mad escapades contaminated the neighboring towns, Osaka, Kyoto, then Shizuoka, Yokohama, Yedo, and went on until the winter.

This popular rejoicing presaged serious trials for the great of the land. A change was necessary to calm the unleashed crowd: above all, the countryside had to be prevented from rising up" (p. 215).

57. Yokochi Jōji, "Ina-ken ni okeru nōmin tōsō no tenkai (1)" (The Development of Peasant Struggles in Ina Prefecture, Part 1), *Shinano* 22, no. 6 (June 1970): 435–436.

58. Sasaki Junnosuke, p. 188.

59. See Makihara Norio, "'Kindaiteki tochi shoyū' gainen no saikentō" (A Reconsideration of the Concept of "Modern Land Ownership"), *Rekishigaku kenkyū*, no. 502 (March 1982), pp. 50–51.

CHAPTER 14

1. The first of two key documentary sources for the Kaisei rising is Nagamitsu Norikazu, ed., *Bizen, Bitchū, Mimasaka hyakushō ikki shiryō, daisankan* (Historical Materials on Peasant Uprisings in Mimasaka, Bitchū and Bizen, vol. 3) (Tokyo: Kokusho Kankōkai 1978), pp. 759–1042. This work contains Professor Nagamitsu's explanatory notes and footnotes for twenty-one Kaisei documents. The "Kaisei ichiranki," which Kobaysahi Sōsuke probably wrote between mid-November 1867 and March 1868, can also be found, along with several other related documents, in *Nihon shomin seikatsu shiryō shūsei* (A Collection of Historical Materials on the Life of the Japanese Common People), vol. 13 (Tokyo: San'ichi Shobō, 1970).

2. The document is the "Sakushū hinin sōdōki." The full text is in Nagamitsu, *Bizen, Bitchū, Mimasaka*, vol. 3, pp. 808–818, and in *Nihon shomin seikatsu shiryō shūsei*, vol. 13, pp. 316–321. Although the two texts are identical, all my quotations from the "Sōdōki" will be from the latter collection.

3. "Sōdōki," p. 318 jōdan.

4. Ibid., p. 318 *gedan*.

5. Personal data on the original leaders have been collected in charts by Kurushima Hiroshi in his critical review of "Sasaki Junnosuke, *Yonaoshi*," in *Rekishigaku kenkyū*, no. 492 (May 1981), pp. 27–28. Additional facts are contained in *Nihon kinsei shomin seikatsu shiryō shūsei*, vol. 13, pp. 348–372.

6. Both Sasaki Junnosuke, *Yonaoshi* (Tokyo: Iwanami Shinsho No. 90, 1979), pp. 86–87, and Nagamitsu Norikazu emphasize sharp differences in aims and actions once the original leaders were displaced. The composition and the character of the rising underwent change as it unfolded. The class practices of different strata also showed differences. But this did not mean that the rising underwent drastic political degeneration simply because urban poor and lumpen-proletarian elements corrupted the peasants whom Naokichi and his band originally organized and led. Many poor peasants were hard-drinking to begin with and the desire to get even and punish the rich was a constant theme from beginning to end.

7. "Sōdōki," p. 320 jōdan.

8. "Sōdōki," p. 320 gedan. At the time of the Kaisei rising, Tsuyama castle town had an official population of about 8,000. This represented an increase of approximately 2,000 since the 1790s. The stratum of house renters living within the castle town districts had also increased slowly since the late eighteenth century. Registered houses tenants numbered 1,063 persons living in 2,351 houses in 1788. By 1830 such house tenants composed about 40 percent of the registered town district population. This percentage remained unchanged in 1866. Homeless and unregistered people, however, would not be reflected in official statistics. A recent study by Andō Osamu indicates that during the first half of the nineteenth century there was, in fact, a steady influx of such people into villages along the main roads adjacent to the castle town districts. Facts such as these throw into question the thesis of urban stagnation in early nineteenth-century Japan. See Andō Osamu, "Mimasaka chiiki ni okeru zaikata shōgyō no hatten to jōkamachi Tsuyama no henshitsu" (The Development of Rural Commerce in the Mimasaka Region and the Transformation of Tsuyama Castle Town), in *Okayama no rekishi to bunka* (The History and Culture of Okayama). Prepared by the Editorial Committee to Celebrate the Seventy-seventh Birthday of Professor Fujii Takashi (Okayama-shi: Fukutake Shoten, 1983), pp. 443, 447, 457.

9. *Tsuyama shishi, dai gokan, kinsei III, bakumatsu-ishin* (The History of Tsuyama City, vol. 5, Early Modern Period 3, the Bakumatsu-Restoration Period) (Tsuyama-shi: Tsuyama City Office 1974), p. 43.

10. Ibid., p. 41. Also see Nagamitsu, ed., *Bizen, Bitchū, Mimasaka hyakushō ikki shiryō*, vol. 3, p. 796.

11. For evidence on this point, see Nagamitsu's commentary on "Gōso nikki" (Record of the Violent Appeal, in Nagamitsu, ed., *Bizen, Bitchū, Mimasaka hyakushō ikki shiryō*, vol. 3, p. 765.

12. "Sōdōki," p. 321 jōdan.

13. For the details of the disturbance on Shōdo Island in which some village headmen also participated, see "Ranbō gojitsu banashi no koto" (The Story of the Violence and Its Aftermath), in *Nihon shomin seikatsu shiryō shūsei*, vol. 13, pp. 336–346.

14. G. E. M. De Ste. Croix, *The Class Struggle in the Ancient Greek World: From the Archaic Age to the Arab Conquests* (London: Duckworth & Co., 1981), p. 482.

15. Emmanuel Le Roy Ladurie, *Carnival in Romans: A People's Uprising at Romans 1579–1580* (Harmondsworth, England: Penguin Books, 1981), p. 297.

16. R. C. Cobb, *The Police and the People: French Popular Protest 1789–1820* (Oxford: Oxford University Press, 1970), pp. 174–175.

17. "Sōdōki," p. 320 gedan.

18. Karl Marx, *Capital—A Critique of Political Economy* (New York: Modern Library Edition, no date), bk. 1, pt. 1, chap. 1, p. 94n2.

19. My discussion of Tokugawa tenancy in the next four paragraphs is based on Ochiai Nobutaka, "Yonaoshi to sonraku kyōdōtai" (World Renovation and the Village Community), in *Minshū no seikatsu, bunka to henkaku shutai* (Popular Culture and Its Bearers of Change), ed. Rekishigaku Kenkyūkai (Tokyo: Aoki Shoten, November 1982), pp. 97–107; Nakayama Kiyoshi, "Beisaku tansaku chitai ni okeru jinushiteki tochi shoyū no tenkai" (The Development of Landlord Ownership in One-Crop Rice-Growing Regions), in *Bakuhansei kokka kaitai katei no kenkyū* (Studies in the Disintegration Process of the Bakuhan State), ed. Kitajima Masamoto (Tokyo: Yoshikawa Kōbunkan, 1978); and Niwa Hiroshi, *Jinushisei no keisei to kōzō: Minojima chitai ni okeru jisshōteki bunseki* (The Formation

and Structure of the Landlord System: An Empirical Analysis of the Mino Striped-Textile-Producting Area) (Tokyo: Ochanomizu Shobō, 1982), pp. 147–158.

20. Kanno Noriko, "Kawariyuku muramura" (The Changing Villages), in *Nihon minshū no rekishi 5, Yonaoshi* (History of the Japanese people, vol. 5, World Renewal), ed. Sasaki Junnosuke (Tokyo: Sanseidō, 1974), p. 187.

21. For the Tokuyama family, see *Kawakami sonshi* (History of Kawakami Village), Editorial Committee for the History of Kawakami Village (Okayama: Sanyō Printing Company, 1980), pp. 286–287; for the Yabuki, see the Yabuki family documents quoted in Ochiai Nobutaka, pp. 102–103.

22. Quoted by Sasaki Junnosuke, p. 87, from the "Kaisei ichiranki" in Nagamitsu, ed., *Bizen, Bitchū, Mimasaka hyakushō ikki shiryō*, vol. 3, p. 776.

23. Sasaki Junnosuke, p. 88. Both quotations are taken from the "Gōso nikki" in Nagamitsu, vol. 3, pp. 972–973.

24. See Nagamitsu, p. 373 gedan.

25. Quoted in Sasaki Junnosuke, p. 90. Shinsaku's full deposition is contained in "Kōsho narabi ni mōshiwatashi ukagaisho," in *Nihon shomin seikatsu shiryō shūsei*, vol. 13, pp. 358–359.

26. For a discussion of these matters, see Kurushima Hiroshi, pp. 26–27.

27. Andō Osamu, pp. 442–462.

28. See Shirakawabe Tatsuo, "Murakata sōdō to yonaoshi" (Village Disturbances and World Renewal), *Rekishi kōron* (Historical Forum), 4, no. 6 (June 1978): 84–94; also Ochiai Nobutaka, pp. 97–107.

29. Nagamitsu Norikazu, "Mimasaka Tsuyama han kaisei ikki" (The Kaisei Rising in Tsuyama Fief, Mimasaka Province), in *Nihon shomin seikatsu shiryō shūsei*, vol. 13, p. 294.

30. Ibid., p. 294.

31. Francis Fox Piven and Richard A. Cloward, *Poor People's Movements: Why They Succeed, How They Fail* (New York: Vintage Books, 1979), p. 24.

CHAPTER 15

1. Shibahara Takuji, *Nihon kindaika no sekaishiteki ichi—sono hōhōronteki kenkyū* [The World Historical Position of Japan's Modernization] (Tokyo: Iwanami Shoten, 1981), pp. 174, 176.

2. Ibid., p. 175.

3. Ibid., p. 174. A feudal or parcelized political-economy, to paraphrase Marx, is supported by a heterogeneous monetary system. Once it is incorporated into the world market, it requires a unified currency system. The unequal treaties and the opening of trade ports brought to the surface Japan's need for currency reform.

4. Hashizume Yōji, "Meiji ninen no jōsei to Aida ikki" (The Situation in 1869 and the Aida Rising), *Shinano* 27, no. 5 (May 1975): 414.

5. Hirasawa Kiyoto, *Hyakushō ikki no tenkai* (The Development of Peasant Risings) (Tokyo: Azekura Shobō, 1972), p. 236.

6. Matsuda Yukitoshi, "'Goisshin' to minshū" (The Restoration and the People), in *Nihon minshū no rekishi 5, yonaoshi*, ed. Sasaki Junnosuke (Tokyo: Sanseido, 1974), p. 346.

7. Hirasawa Kiyoto, pp. 261–263.

8. Matsuda Yukitoshi, p. 346.

9. Machida Shōzō, "Meiji zenki ni okeru Nagano-ken Ueda chiiki seishigyō no re-

kishi chirigakuteki kenkyū" (An Historical-Geographical Study of the Silk-Reeling Industry in the Ueda Region of Nagano Prefecture in the Early Meiji Period), *Shinano* 22, no. 10 (October 1970): 2.

10. Ibid., pp. 4, 15. Large-scale silk mills equipped with modern reeling machinery did not come into Ueda until the late 1880s.

11. Quoted in Iijima Chiaki, "Jōkamachi to shūhen nōson—bunseki shikaku to kadai no teiji" (Castle Towns and Surrounding Villages), *Chihōshi kenkyū, 166* 30, no. 4 (August 1980): 19, 20.

12. See Shimizu Toshio, ed., *Chiisagata Ueda rekishi nenpyō* (Historical Chronology of Chiisagata Ueda), published by the Chiisagata Ueda Local History Study Group 1955, pp. 39–40.

13. Yokoyama Toshio, *Uedahan nōmin sōdōshi* (The History of Peasant Uprisings in Ueda Fief) (Ueda: Heirindo Shoten, 1981), p. 435. Ueda fief's officially registered population in 1868 was 57,250. Three years later, in 1871, it had increased to 62,230. Source: *Ueda shishi*, vol. 2, pp. 235–236, 238, 481.

14. "Meiji ninen tsuchinoto-mi Uedajima motsure gōshi" (The Ueda Entanglement of 1869), in ibid., p. 420.

15. Ibid., pp. 420–421.

16. Yokoyama Toshio, p. 353. Professor Yokoyama has collected over fifty demands from different villages and classified them in fourteen categories.

17. Ibid., pp. 350, 355.

18. Information on the Aida rising comes from Hashizume Yōji, "Meiji ninen no jōsei to Aida ikki" (The Political and Economic Situation in 1869 and the Aida Rising), *Shinano* 27, no. 5 (May 1975). Also see Yokochi Jōji, "Ina-ken ni okeru nōmin tōsō no tenkai I" (The Development of the Peasant Struggle in Ina Prefecture, Part I), *Shinano* 22, no. 6 (June 1970): 435–449; and Nakamura Bun, "Meiji ninen nōmin tōsō no rekishiteki zentei: Shinano-kuni Chikuma-gun Midarebashi mura," (Historical Premises of the Peasant Struggles of 1869: Midarebashi Village in Chikuma District, Shinano Province) *Shinano* 32, no. 2 (February 1980): 164–168.

19. Yokochi Jōji, *Shinano* 22, no. 7 (July 1970): 21, 25.

20. Ochiai Nobutaka, "Yonaoshi," (World Renewal) in *Ikki 2, ikki no rekishi* (Uprisings, Vol. 2—The History of Uprisings) (Tokyo: Tokyo Daigaku Shuppankai, 1982), p. 322.

21. Sasaki Junnosuke, p. 166.

22. Matsuda Yukitoshi, "Meiji shonen no kaikyū tōsō—Shinshū Matsushiro 'gosatsu sōdō' no baai" (Class Struggle in Early Meiji: On the 'Disturbances in Connection with Currencies Issued in 1870' in Matsushiro Fief, Shinshū), *Rekishigaku kenkyū*, no. 359 (April 1970), pp. 33–35.

23. Ochiai Nobutaka, p. 328.

24. Matsuda Yukitoshi, p. 35.

25. Ibid., pp. 37–38.

26. Naitō Masanaka, "Meiji shonen Hokushin no nōmin sōdō" (The Peasant Disturbances in Northern Shinshū during the Early Meiji Years), *Rekishi hyōron* (Historical Review), no. 45 (May 1953), p. 32.

27. Ibid.

28. Quoted in ibid., p. 39, and Ochiai Nobutaka, p. 323.

29. Ochiai Nobutaka, p. 324; Matsuda Yukitoshi, p. 41; Sasaki Junnosuke, p. 167.

30. See the fine discussion of the new indebtedness and the collapse of moral economy considerations in Yasumaru Yoshio, "Konmintō no ishiki katei" (Developing the Thought of the Poor People's Party), *Shisō* (Thought), December 1984, pp. 80–83.

31. My discussion of the Chichibu insurrection is based on Yasumaru Yoshio, ibid.; Inada Masahirō, "Chichibu jikenzō saikōsei no tame no shiron" (Preliminary Sketch for the Reconstruction of the Chichibu Incident), *Rekishi hyōron*, November 1984, pp. 39–52; and Emura Eiichi, "Jiyū minken to Chichibu jiken" (Freedom and People's Rights and the Chichibu Incident), *Bungei Chichibu*, no. 30 (1980), pp. 1–13.

CHAPTER 16

1. For discussion of such an approach, see Sasaki Junnosuke, "Ikki, sōdō–shi no hōhō ni tsuite" (On Methodology for the History of Risings and Disturbances), *Rekishi hyōron* (Historical Review), No. 396 April 1983, pp. 2–30.

2. Shōji Kichinosuke, *Yonaoshi ikki no kenkyū* (A Study of Yonaoshi Risings) (Tokyo: Azekura Shobō, 1970), p. 347.

3. The percentage of the total tribute actually interdicted by peasants was probably small.

4. The social meaning of the Meiji tax principles emerged during the bitter rural strife of the 1870s and early 1880s. Intent on promoting capitalism from above, the Meiji government from the outset followed a path that steadily widened the gap between industry and agriculture. It began by fixing the land tax at a high, uniform rate of 3 percent of the assessed land value. Peasant protests between 1873 and 1877 then forced it to revise the land tax downward in 1877 to 2.5 percent of the land price. But in 1899 it again raised the land tax to 3.3 percent in order to finance a major arms buildup. In effect, the Meiji government through its tax and finance policies, increased the number of small, independent proprietors who, on pain of bankruptcy, were forced to supplement their household budgets with cash earnings outside of agriculture. Simultaneously, the whole manner in which it terminated feudal land ownership also furthered the growth of tenancy and perpetuated various economic and psychological aspects of the de facto landlord–tenant relations of the late Tokugawa period.

Nationally, in 1873, at least 30 percent of all farmland in Japan was tenant land, though in some prefectures and districts the percentage was either much higher or lower than the national average. The Instructions to Local Officials, promulgated together with the Land Tax Revision Edicts, assumed the continuation of feudal tenant rents. The tenant, in other words, would continue paying in kind to the landlord as much as 68 percent of the total harvest. This meant that no matter how much the rice price rose, the tenant cultivator always paid the same amount in kind to the landlord, who alone could profit from the price rise. It also meant that the tenant was left with a small amount of the harvest (32 percent) from which he had to meet his own costs of reproduction including living expenses, surcharges, and local taxes. Thereafter, the main distinguishing feature of prewar Japanese agrarian relations was the economic subordination and rent–gouging of millions of poor tenants at the hands of landlords who had originally grown rich by amassing the pawned land of countless small cultivators.

Interestingly, when the Meiji government in the early 1870s redefined some of the people in their relationship to the state as property owners and taxpayers, it also created a nonfeudal, but thoroughly repressive, relationship toward the whole adult male population through its military conscription system. Earlier, in the 1850s and 1860s, imperialist pressure and intensified class strife forced the ruling class to expand the concept of the military. Building on that initial limited militarization process, the Meiji government went on to create a modern army and navy by recombining the very categories that the bakuhan state had originally separated: namely, soldier and farmer. In this way, conscription furthered Japan's transition to a unified state, which then paved the way to industrial capitalism. The opening of the door to popular participation in military activities was accompanied, after the Sino–Japanese War of 1894–1895, by the diffusion of militarism throughout all levels of Japanese society. This process was as integral to the creation of the modern capitalist state in Japan as, nearly three centuries earlier, the demilitarization and disarming of commoner society had been to the creation of the feudal bakuhan state.

Era Names

1573– Tenshō 天正
1592– Bunroku 文禄
1596– Keichō 慶長
1615– Genna 元和
1624– Kan-ei 寛永
1644– Shōhō 正保
1648– Keian 慶安
1652– Jōō 承應
1655– Meireki 明暦
1658– Manji 萬治
1661– Kanbun 寛文
1673– Enpō 延寶
1681– Tenna 天和
1684– Jōkyō 貞享
1688– Genroku 元禄
1704– Hōei 寶永
1711– Shōtoku 正德
1716– Kyōhō 享保
1736– Genbun 元文
1741– Kanpō 寛保

1744– Enkyō 延享
1748– Kan-en 寛延
1751– Hōreki 寶暦
1764– Meiwa 明和
1772– An-ei 安永
1781– Temmei 天明
1789– Kansei 寛政
1801– Kyōwa 享和
1804– Bunka 文化
1818– Bunsei 文政
1830– Tenpō 天保
1844– Kōka 弘化
1848– Kaei 嘉永
1854– Ansei 安政
1860– Man-en 萬延
1861– Bunkyū 文久
1864– Genji 元治
1865– Keiō 慶應
1868– Meiji 明治

Glossary

PERSONAL NAMES

Abe Masakiyo 安部正精
Abe Masatomo 安部正倫
Amakusa Shirō 天草四郎
Amano Shirōno Saemonnosuke Fujiwara
    Tokisada 天ノ四郎ノ左衛門佐藤原
    時貞
Amida Nyorai 阿弥陀如来
Andō Motome 安藤主馬
Andō Shōeki 安藤昌益
Arakawa Tadaemon 荒川唯右衛門
Asagorō 浅五郎
Asanojō 浅え丞
Ashikaga Tadayoshi 足利直義

Benzō 弁蔵

Chikahira 親平
Chikamatsu Monzaemon 近松門左衛門
Chōbei 長兵衛
Chūemon 忠右衛門
Chūjirō 忠次郎
Chūta 仲太
Chūzaemon 忠左衛門

Daigorō 大五郎
Dangoemon 団古衛門
Date-ke 伊達家
Den'emon 傳右衛門

Echizen Matsudaira 越前松平
Eikichi 栄吉
Eisaku 栄作
Eitarō 栄太郎
Endō Benzō 遠藤弁蔵

Fuchinobe Yoshihiro 渕辺義博
Fujimoto Kinosuke 藤本喜え助
Fujiwara Tokihira 藤原時平
Fukujirō 福治郎
Fukushima Zenbei 福島善兵衛
Funakoshi Ban'emon 船越伴右衛門

Genkichi 源吉
Genzaemon 源左衛門
Godaigo (Tennō) 御醍醐 (天皇)
Goemon 五右衛門
Gonpachi 権八
Gunji 軍治

Hamazō 濱蔵
Hanaya Denshichi 花屋伝七
Hanbei 半兵衛
Han'emon 半右衛門
Hanpei 半兵
Hanroku 半六
Hara Zendayū 原善太夫
Hashimoto Chūbei 橋本忠兵衛

261

Hatsutarō 初太郎
Hattori Jūrōbei 服部十郎兵衛
Hayakawa Rinpei 早川林平
Hayashi Hachirōji 林八郎治
Hayashi Tokuemon 林徳右衛門
Hayashi Tōshirō 林藤四郎
Heiemon 平右衛門
Heijirō 平次郎
Heihachi 平八
Hei-ke 平家
Heikichi 平吉
Heiroku 平六
Higuchi Shichirōbei 樋口七郎兵衛
Higuchi Yajirō 樋口弥次郎
Hirabayashi Shinshichi 平林新七
Hisamatsu Shume (Motome) 久松主馬
Honma-ke 本間家

Ide Kudayū 出九太夫
Ieharu 家治
Iemitsu 家光
Ieshige 家重
Ieyasu 家康
Iganokami Tadayori 伊賀守忠順
Ii Naosuke 井伊直弼
Ikegami Sahei 池上佐兵衛
Itakura Sadonokami 板倉佐渡守
Iwasaki Kichirōji 岩崎吉郎次

Jirōkichi 次郎吉
Jūzō 重蔵
Jūzō 十蔵
Jūrōzaemon 重郎左衛門

Kajūrō 嘉十郎
Kannoshōkō 菅乃相公
Kasuke 嘉助
Katō Orihei 加藤織平
Katō Sachū 加藤佐仲
Katsura Kakuemon 桂覚右衛門
Katsusaburō 勝三郎
Kazunosuke 数え助
Kei 慶
Kichiemon 吉右衛門
Kichizō 吉蔵
Kigenta 喜源太
Kihei 喜兵衛
Kiheiji 喜平次
Kimura Kageyu 木村勘解由
Kinjirō 金次郎
Kisaku 喜作
Kitamura Tomozō 北村友蔵

Kitamura Yasaku 北村八作
Kitamura Yosuke 北村与助
Kobayashi Kyūsaku 小林久作
Kobayashi Sōsuke 小林曽助
Kodama Seinosuke 児玉清え助
Kōjirō 光次郎
Komasuya Yahei 小増屋弥兵衛
Kōmei 孔明
Kondō Chūzaemon 近藤忠左衛門
Kondō Yasaji 近藤弥作治
Kōnosuke 幸え助
Koyama Kyūsuke 小山久介
Koyama Nakagorō 小山仲五郎
Kozaemon 小左衛門
Kubo Shimbei (Shinpei) 久保新平
Kumekichi 久米吉
Kurakake Torajirō 鞍懸寅二郎
Kurōemon 九郎右衛門
Kurushima Hiroshi 久留島浩
Kusunoki Masashige 楠木正成
Kyūzaburō 久三郎

Magoemon 孫右衛門
Magosaku 孫作
Maki Tōsuke 牧藤助
Mansaku 万作
Masuda Yohei 増田与兵衛
Matagorō 又五郎
Matsudaira Asagorō 松平浅五郎
Matsudaira Naganori 松平長矩
Matsudaira Sadanobu 松平定信
Matsudaira Tadachika 松平忠周
Matsudaira Tadazane 松平忠愛
Matsukura Katsuie 松倉勝家
Miki Jinzaemon 三木甚左衛門
Mitsugorō 三津五郎
Miyaguchi Tōsaku 宮口東作
Miyamoto Chōemon 宮本長右衛門
Miyazaka Daijirō 宮坂代次郎
Miyazaki Heizō 宮崎兵蔵
Mizuno Tadakuni 水野忠邦
Morinaga 護良
Mori Nagatsugu 森長継
Mori Tadamasa 森忠政
Morooka Kahei 師岡嘉兵衛
Murakami Sahei 村上佐兵衛

Nagasawa Kesaku 長沢毛作
Nakamura Mosuke 中村茂助
Nakamura Seidayū 中村清太夫
Nakamura Yazaemon 中村弥左衛門
Nakamuraya Jisuke 中村屋治助

Namiji 波治
Naniwa Jōnan inshi 浪華城南隠士
Nanba Kōroku 難波幸六
Naoemon 直右衛門
Naokichi 直吉
Nichiren 日蓮
Nishizawa Jūkichi 西沢重吉
Nobutomi 宜富
Noma Koemon 野間小右衛門

Oda Nobunaga 織田信長
Ōi Matsuhei 大井松平
Okabe Kurobei 岡部九郎兵衛
Ōshio Heihachirō 大塩平八郎
Otaniya Heibei 小谷屋平兵衛

Saburobei 三郎兵衛
Saburōemon 三郎右衛門
Shakamuni 釈迦牟尼
Saji Ichiemon 佐治市右衛門
Saji Hachiemon 佐治八右衛門
Sakichi 佐吉
Sakura Sōgorō 佐倉惣五郎
Sanada 真田
Sankaku 山鶴
Sasuke 佐助
Satō Gōzaemon 佐藤郷左衛門
Satō Shinshirō 佐藤新四郎
Seisaku 清作
Shichizaemon 七左衛門
Shimpūken Chikuō 神風軒竹翁
Shinkichi 新吉
Shinsaku 新作
Shinsuke 新助
Shōryū 症竜
Sōzō 荘蔵
Sugawara Michizane 菅原道真
Sukesaburō 助三郎
Sumiya Sōjirō 隅屋宗次郎
Suzukaya 鈴鹿屋
Suzuki Sukenoshin 鈴木助え進

Tadazane 忠愛
Taichi 多一
Takamatsuya Chihei 高松屋治兵衛
Taki 滝
Tamazō 玉蔵

Tanaka Yaichiemon 田中弥一右衛門
Tanuma Okitsugu 田沼意次
Tarobei 太郎兵衛
Tashiro Eisuke 田代栄助
Teikichi 定吉
Tokuemon 徳右衛門
Tokugawa Ieyasu 徳川家康
Tokuji 徳治
Tokuyama-ke 徳山家
Tomozaemon 友左衛門
Tōsuke 藤助
Toyotomi Hideyoshi 豊臣秀吉
Tsukatani Ichirōemon (Tsukataniya)
　　塚谷市郎右衛門 (塚谷屋)
Tsurukichi 鶴吉

Uchida Risaku 内田利作
Uchida Yachōji 内田弥長治
Uhei 卯兵衛
Umanojō 午え丞
Umedo Yozōemon 梅戸与惣右衛門
Umekichi 梅吉
Umeta 梅太

Yabuki Yakurō 矢吹弥九郎
Yahei 弥兵衛
Yamada Bumpachi 山田文八
Yamada Heinai 山田兵内
Yamadaya Daisuke 山田屋大助
Yamagata Daini 山県大弐
Yamaguchi Kōhei 山口幸平
Yamamoto Bensuke 山本弁助
Yamane Gorōemon 山根五郎右衛門
Yamaura Sasuke 山浦佐助
Yasubei 安兵衛
Yasuhara Tarō 安原太郎
Yohei 与兵衛
Yokozeki Senzaemon 横関仙左衛門
Yoshimune 吉宗
Yōsuke 要助

Zen'emon 善右衛門
Zenji 善治
Zenkichi 善吉
Zenroku 善六
Zenshichi 善七

VILLAGES

Aida 会田
Akano 赤野

Amari 余里
Asazumi 麻績

Ayabe 綾部

Daikanaya 台金谷
Doi 土居

Ebihara 海老原

Fumiiri 踏入

Hijiya 小童谷
Hinata 日名田
Hiraide 平井出

Ichinomiya 一宮
Iguchi 井口
Ikushima 生嶋
Inaba 稲葉
Ippō 一方
Irinaramoto 入奈良本

Kagami 香々美
Kamigō 上郷
Kamigōchi 上河内
Kamishimo 上下
Kawabe 川辺
Kawate 川手
Kazawa 加沢
Koizumi 小泉
Komaki 小牧
Komi 古見
Konakahara 小中原
Koshido 越戸
Kuginuki 針貫
Kuse 久世

Meki 目木
Mikamo 美甘
Mio 美尾
Misaka 三坂
Mitsue 三家
Miyauchi 宮内
Moriwaki 森脇

Nakabasami 中挾
Nakajima 中嶋
Nakama 仲間
Narita 成田

Ninomiya 二宮
Nishihara 西原
Nishikayabe 西茅部
Nokedai 野介代

Ochiai 落合
Ogami 夫神
Ogawa 小川
Ōhashi 大橋
Ōhira 大平
Ōkuma 大熊
Ōmori 大森
Oshiire 押入
Ōzasa 大篠

Sakakita 坂北
Seba 洗馬
Shimomi 下見
Shimonaramoto 下奈良本
Shinjō 新庄
Shinobu 信夫
Shioda 塩田
Shirakawa 白河
Suwabe 諏訪部

Tabe 田辺
Tōgō 当郷
Takada 高田
Takakura 高倉
Takeishi (Takeshi) 武石
Takizawa 滝沢
Tanaka 田中
Tanomura 田邑
Tazawa 田沢
Tōhara 塔原
Toki 土岐
Tokuda 徳田
Tsukatani 塚谷

Uedabara 上田原
Uedamura 上田邑
Umagōshi 馬越
Urano 浦野

Yubara 湯原
Yukishige 行重
Yumoto 湯本

TOWNS

Chiyoda 千代田

Dazaifu 大宰府

Fuchū 府中

Hara 原
Honjō 本庄

Iida 飯田
Innoshō 院庄
Ise 伊勢

Kaji 鍛治
Kokubunji 国分寺
Komoro 小諸
Konya 紺屋
Kyō 京

Maruyama 丸山
Matsushiro 松代
Mikawa 三河

Susaka 須坂

Tsuyama 津山

Ueda 上田
Unno 海野

Yanagi 柳
Yoko 横
Yoshiwara 吉原

CITIES AND DISTRICTS

Anna (Yasuna) 安那
Ashida (Ashita) 葦田

Chichibu 秩父
Chiisagata 小県
Chiyoda 千代田

Dejima 出島

Fukatsu 深津
Fukuyama 福山

Hakata 博多
Hakodate 函館
Hiruzen 蒜山

Ina 伊那

Kamakura 鎌倉
Karatsu 唐津
Katsunan (Shōnan) 勝南
Katsuyama 勝山
Kawanakajima 川中島
Kumenanjō 久米南条
Kurashiki 倉敷
Kurume 久留米
Kyōto 京都

Majima 真嶋

Matsuida 松井田
Matsumoto 松本
Matsushiro 松代

Nagatō 長藤
Numakuma 沼隈

Ōba 大庭
Ōmiya 大宮

Seihokujō 西北条
Seiseijō 西々条
Sekigahara 関ヶ原
Shinaji (Honchi) 品治

Takakura 高倉
Tabe 田辺
Tōhokujō 東北条
Tomi 富
Tōnanjō 東南条
Tsukatani 塚谷
Tsuyama 津山

Ueda 上田

Wake 分

Yamakita 山北
Yokohama 横浜

REGIONS, PROVINCES, AND PREFECTURES

Amakusa 天草

Bingo 備後

Bitchū 備中
Bizen 備前
Bushū 武州

Chikugo 筑後
Chōshū 長州

Gōshū 江州

Hizen 肥前
Hōki 伯耆

Izumi 和泉
Izumo 出雲

Jōshū 上州

Kōshū 甲州

Mimasaka 美作
Musashi 武蔵

Nagano 長野
Nagasaki 長崎
Nanbu 南部

Ōmi 近江

Sado 佐渡
Sakushū 作州
Sanchū 山中
Sat-Chō 薩長
Shiga 滋賀
Shimabara 島原
Shimotsuke 下野
Shinano 信濃
Shinshū 信州
Shōdojima (Shōdoshima) 小豆島

RIVERS AND RIVERBANKS

Asahi 旭(川)
Chikuma 千曲(川)
Kako 加古(川)
Kamo 加茂(川)
Numeri 滑(川)

Ōdankoge 大段芝
Oimawashi 追廻し
Ubu 産(川)
Yodo 淀(川)
Yoshii 吉井(川)

TEMPLES AND SHRINES

Daihōji 大法寺
Daitō no Miya 大塔の宮
Gangyōji 願行寺
Hakusanji 白山寺

Hannyadera 般若寺
Ōmiya daimyōjin 大宮大明神
Zenkōji 善光寺
Zenzanji 前山寺

ROADS AND MOUNTAINS

Hofukuji kaidō 保福寺街道
Hōki (Ōrai) 伯耆(住来)
Hokkoku kaidō 北国街道
Kanjyadake 冠者岳
Nakasendō 中仙道

Oume (Ōme) kaidō 青梅街道
Ōyama kaidō 大山街道
Tōkaidō 東海道
Yatsugatake 八ヶ岳

RELIGIONS

Fujikō 富士講
Konkō 金光
Kurozumi 黒住
Maruyama 丸山
Misogikyō 禊教
Shingonshū 真言宗
Shinshū 真宗

Shintō 神道
Shugendō 修験道
Sōtō 曹洞
Tendaishū 天台宗
Tenri 天理
Zenshū 禅宗

PERIODS

Bakumatsu 幕朱   Heian 平安

OFFICES, INSTITUTIONS, GENERAL ADMINISTRATIVE DIVISIONS, AND STATUSES

ashigaru 足軽

bakufu 幕府
bakuhan 幕藩
busen 夫銭

chigyōchi 知行地
chōnin 町人
chōrigashira 長史頭
chūjōya 中庄屋

daikan 代官
daimyō 大名
dajōkan 太政官
dajō-kansatsu 太政官札
debito 出人
debito-moyaikin 出人催合金
dogō 土豪
dōshin 同心

eta 穢多

fudai 譜代
fudasashi 礼差
fure 触

gisō (gikura) 義倉
gō 合
gojōmoku 御條目
gokachū 御家中
goningumi 五人組
gōnō 豪農
gōshō 豪商
goshuin 御朱印
goyōkin 御用金
gōzamurai 郷侍
gozenmai 御膳米
gun 郡
gundai 郡代

han 藩
hanshu 藩主
hatake kanjōbugyō 畠勘定奉行
hatamonoza 織物座
hatamoto 旗本

heinō-bunri 兵農分離
hinin (domo) 非人（共）
hōkōnin 奉行人
honbyakushō 本百姓
hyakushōdai 百姓代
hyakushō sōdai 百姓惣代

ichibugin 一分銀
ikemasu 生升
iriaichi 入会地
isshugin 一朱銀

jitō 地頭
jōbiki 定引
jōmai 城米
jōmen 定免
jōmenhō 定免法

kabunakama 株仲間
kamisuki-unjōkin 紙漉運上金
kan 貫
kandaka 貫高
kanmon 貫文
karō 家老
kashira byakushō 頭百姓
kemi 検見
kemihō 検見法
kerai 家来
kijitonya 木地問屋
kimoiri 肝煎
kinnō no shishi 勤皇の志士
kō (kamae) 構
kōgi 公儀
koku 石
kokudaka 石高
kokujin 国人
komononari 小物成
kōribugyō 郡奉行
kumigashira 組頭
kunizamurai 国侍
kyūjin 給人

machi 町
machibyakushō 町百姓
machidoshiyori 町年寄

mizunomi byakushō 水呑百姓
mominō 籾納
momme 匁
murakata 村方
motokata 元方
myōgakin 冥加金

nago 名子
nanushi 名主
nanryō-nishu 南鐐二朱
nengu 年貢
nibukin 二分金
nishugin 二朱銀
nōhei 農兵

ofure 御触
okuhikimai 奥引米
ōjōya 大庄屋
ōmetsuke 大目付
omonogashira 御物頭
osabyakushō (otonabyakushō) 長百姓

ri 里
rōnin 浪人（牢人）
ryō 両
ryōshu 領主

sai 才
saikakukin 才覚金
sakoku 鎖国
samurai 侍
sankin kōtai 参勤交代
seidō 正道
seii taishōgun 征夷大将軍
sewayaku 世話役
seyo 施与

shaku 勺
shasō (shakura) 社倉
shimpan 親藩
shōen 荘園
shōgun 将軍
shoshidai 所司代
shōya 庄屋
shu 朱
sobayōnin 側用人
sukegō 助郷

taifu 大夫
taishō 大将
tanomoshi-kō 頼母子講
tedai 手代
tenma 伝馬
tenryō 天領
to 斗
Tokugawa bakufu 徳川幕府
tonya 問屋
toshiyori 年寄
tozama daimyō 外様大名

ukesho 請書
umadaikin 馬代金
unjōkin 運上金

wariban 割番

yakusho 役所
yamabataraki-nengu 山働年貢
yoriki 与力

zaichū sōnomikomi 在中惣吞込
zaikata shōnin 在方商人
zōzei 雑税

MISCELLANEOUS TERMS

bōdō 暴動
bonten 梵天
Boshin (no eki) 戊辰（の役）

chōsan 逃散

ebizeme 海老責め
eiya, eiya えいやえいや
ee ja naika ええじやないか

fuon 不穏

genmai 玄米
gimin 義民
gosho 御所
gōso 強訴

haiku 俳句
haori 羽織
hashigozeme 梯子責め
hōki 蜂起
Hōrei ikki 宝暦一揆

ichimi dōshin 一味同心
ikki 一揆

jikata kōsha 地方巧者
jōdan 上段

Kaisei (ikki) 改政（一揆）
ketsuen-dan 血縁団
kōsatsu 高札
kozura no wagamama 小面え我侭
Kyūsukekō え介講

mimochi 身持
miso 味噌
mochigome 糯米
mokubazeme 木馬責め
murakata sōdō 村方騒動

nenbutsu 念仏
ninokuruwa 二曲輪

odorikomi おどりこみ
Okagemairi お蔭参り
ōsei fukko 王政復古

osso 越訴
ōte 大手

Sanchū ikki 山中一揆
seidō tachimōsazusōrō 正道立不申候
seirōzeme 井楼責め
Shimabara (no ran) 島原（の乱）
shinsui 神水
shūso 愁訴
sōdō 騒動
sogan 訴願

tenma sōdō 伝馬騒動
toku 徳
Tokusei (ikki) 徳政（一揆）
totō 徒党

uchikowashi 打ちこわし
Ueda tsumugi 上田紬

yo 世
yonaori 世直り
yonaoshi 世直し
yonaoshi no kami 世直しの神

HISTORICAL MATERIALS

Abeno Dōji-mon 安部野童子問

gimin denshō 義民伝承
gonarika yosechō 御成箇寄帳
goryō goningumi kajōgaki 御料五人組箇条書
goshōmon 御証文

Hinin sōdōki 非人騒動記

ichiranki 一乱記

Keian ofuregaki 慶安御触書
kōkiroku 公記録
kuzuregōshi 崩格子

Mikoku shimin ranpōki 美国四民乱放記

minsei kyōsho 民生教書

Nihon shomin seikatsu shiryō shūsei
日本庶民生活資料集成

ōjō yōshū 往生要集

Sakushūki 作州記
sōdō jikki 騒動実記

Taiheiki 太平記
Tsuyama shishi 津山市史

Uedahan nōmin sōdōshi 上田藩農民騒動史
Uedajima kuzuregōshi 上田縞崩格子
Ueda shishi 上田市史
Ueda sōdōjikki 上田騒動実記

PREMODERN PROVINCES AND MODERN PREFECTURES

Province (kuni) 国	*Prefecture* (ken) 県		
Tohoku Region (東北地方)		Rikuchū 陸中	Iwate 岩手
		Rikuzen 陸前	Miyagi 宮城
		Uzen 羽前	Yamagata 山形
Mutsu 陸奥	Aomori 青森	Iwashiro 岩代	Fukushima 福島
Ugo 羽後	Akita 秋田	Iwaki 磐城	

Province (kuni) 国	*Prefecture* (ken) 県

Kantō Region (関東地方)

Hitachi 常陸	Ibaraki 茨城
Shimotsuke 下野	Tochigi 栃木
Kōzuke 上野	Gunma 群馬
Musashi 武蔵	Saitama 埼玉
	Tokyo To 東京都
Sagami 相模	Kanagawa 神奈川
Shimōsa 下総	Chiba 千葉
Kazusa 上総	
Awa 安房	

Chubu Region (中部地方)

Echigo 越後	Niigata 新潟
Sado 佐渡	(the island)
Etchū 越中	Toyama 富山
Kaga 加賀	Ishikawa 石川
Noto 能登	
Echizen 越前	Fukui 福井
Wakasa 若狭	
Suruga 駿河	Shizuoka 静岡
Izu 伊豆	
Kai 甲斐	Yamanshi 山梨
Shinano 信濃	Nagano 長野
Mikawa 三河	Aichi 愛知
Owari 尾張	
Mino 美濃	Gifu 岐阜
Hida 飛騨	

Kinki Region (近畿地方)

Ōmi 近江	Shiga 滋賀
Tanba 丹波	Kyōto Fu 京都府
Tango 丹後	
Kii 紀伊	
Ise 伊勢	Wakayama 和歌山
Iga 伊賀	Mie 三重
Tajima 但馬	
Tanba 丹波	Hyōgo 兵庫
Harima 播磨	
Awaji 淡略	

Kinai Region (畿内地方)

Yamashiro 山城	Kyōto Fu 京都府

Izumi 和泉	Ōsaka Fu 大阪府
Kawachi 河内	
Yamato 大和	Nara 奈良
Settsu 摂津	Hyōgo 兵庫

Chūgoku Region (中国地方)

Bizen 備前	Okayama 岡山
Bitchū 備中	
Mimasaka 美作	
Bingo 備後	Hiroshima 広島
Aki 安芸	
Nagato 長門	Yamaguchi 山口
Suō 周防	
Inaba 因幡	Tottori 鳥取
Hōki 伯耆	
Izumo 出雲	Shimane 島根
Iwami 石見	
Oki 隠岐	(the island)

Shikoku (四国)

Sanuki 讃岐	Kagawa 香川
Iyo 伊予	Ehime 愛媛
Awa 阿波	Tokushima 徳島
Tosa 土佐	Kōchi 高知

Kyushu (九州)

Chikuzen 筑前	Fukuoka 福岡
Buzen 豊前	
Bungo 豊後	Ōita 大分
Hyūga 日向	Miyazaki 宮崎
Chikugo 筑後	Saga 佐賀
Hizen 肥前	Nagasaki 長崎
Iki 壱岐	(the island)
Tsushima 対馬	(the island)
Higo 肥後	Kumamoto 熊本
Satsuma 薩摩	Kagoshima 鹿児島
Ōsumi 大隅	

Ryūkyū (琉球)

Ryūkyū 琉球	Okinawa 沖縄

Hokkaidō (北海道)

Matsumae 松前	Hakodate Shi 函館市

Bibliography

"Abeno dōjimon" (Account of the Boy from Abeno). *Nihon shomin seikatsu shiryō shūsei dai rokkan, ikki* (A Collection of Historical Materials on the Life of the Japanese Common People, vol. 6, Peasant Uprisings). Tokyo: San'ichi Shobō, 1968.

Abercrombie, Nicholas; Hill, Stephen; and Turner, Bryan S. *The Dominant Ideology Thesis.* London: George Allen & Unwin, 1980.

Alavi, Hamza, and Shanin, Teodor, eds. *Introduction to the Sociology of "Developing Societies"*. New York: Monthly Review Press, 1982.

Ardant, Gabriel. "Financial Policy and Economic Infrastructure of Modern States and Nations." In *The Formation of National States in Western Europe*. Edited by Charles Tilly. Princeton, Princeton, University Press, 1975.

Akamatsu, Paul. *Meiji 1868.* New York: Harper & Row, 1972.

Amamiya, Yuki. "Shinshū Uedahan Hōreki sōdō no kōsatsu" (A Study of the Uprising in Shinshū Ueda Fief during the Hōreki Era). *Ochanomizu shigaku* (Ochanomizu Historical Studies), no. 8 (1965).

Anderson, Perry. *Arguments Within English Marxism.* London, NLB and Verso Editions 1980.

————. *Lineages of the Absolutist State.* London, New Left Books 1974.

Andō, Osamu. "Mimasaka chiiki ni okeru zaikata shōgyō no hatten to jōkamachi Tsuyama no henshitsu" (The Development of Rural Commerce in the Mimasaka Region and the Transformation of Tsuyama Castle Town). In *Okayama no rekishi to bunka* (The History and Culture of Okayama). Prepared by the Editorial Committee to Celebrate the Seventy-seventh Birthday of Professor Fujii Takashi. Okayama-shi: Fukutake Shoten, 1983.

Aoki, Kōji. *Hyakushō ikki sōgō nenpyō* (Comprehensive Historical Chronology of Peasant Uprisings). Tokyo: San'ichi Shobō, 1975.

Aoki, Kōji, et al., eds. *Nihon shomin seikatsu shiryō shūsei, dai rokkan, ikki* (A Collection of Historical Materials on the Life of the Japanese Common People, vol. 6, Peasant Uprisings). Tokyo: San'ichi Shobō, 1968–1970.

Aoki, Michio. "Tatakau nōmin shimintachi" (Fighting Peasants and Townsmen). *Nihonshi 5, kinsei 2* (Japanese History, vol. 5, Early Modern Era II). Edited by Ōishi Shinzaburō Tokyo: Yūhikaku Shinsho 560, 1978.

Aoki, Michio, and Yamada, Tadao, eds. *Tenpōki no seiji to shakai* (Politics and Society in the Tenpō Period). Tokyo: Yūhikaku, 1981.

Asad, Talal. "Anthropological Conceptions of Religion: Reflections on Geertz". *Man: The Journal of the Royal Anthropological Institute* 18, no. 2 (June 1981).

"Bakumatsu no shakai hendō to minshū ishiki: Keiō 2 nen Bushū yonaoshi ikki no kōsatsu" (Social Change and Popular Consciousness in the Last Decades of the Bakufu: Studies of the Bushū Yonaoshi Uprising of 1866). In Special Issue of *Rekishigaku kenkyū* (Journal of Historical Studies), no. 458, (July 1978).

Beattie, J. H. M. "On Understanding Sacrifice." In *Sacrifice*. Edited by M. F. C. Bourdillon, and Myer Fortes. London and New York: Academic Press, 1980.

Bendix, Reinhard. *Kings or People—Power and the Mandate to Rule*. Berkeley: University of California Press, 1978.

Berger, John. *Pig Earth*. London: Writers and Readers Cooperative, 1979.

Bhaduri, Amit. "A Study in Agricultural Backwardness under Semi-Feudalism." *Economic Journal* 83, no. 329 (March 1973).

————. "On the Formation of Usurious Interest Rates in Backward Agriculture." *Cambridge Journal of Economics*, no. 1 (1977).

Bix, Herbert P. "Kiro ni tatsu Amerika no Nihon kenkyū" (American Japan Studies at the Crossroads: Some Thoughts on Rereading E. H. Norman). *Shisō* (Thought), no. 634 (April 1977).

————. "Miura Meisuke, or Peasant Rebellion under the Banner of 'Distress.'" *Bulletin of Concerned Asian Scholars*, 10, no. 2 (April-June 1978).

————. "Rethinking 'Emperor System Fascism': Ruptures and Continuities in Modern Japanese History." *Bulletin of Concerned Asian Scholars* 14, no. 2 (April-June 1982).

Bloch, Marc. *French Rural History: An Essay on Its Basic Characteristics*. Translated by Janet Sondheimer. London: Routledge & Kegan Paul, 1966.

Blum, Jerome. *Lord and Peasant in Russia, from the Ninth to the Nineteenth Century*. Princeton: Princeton University Press, 1961.

Bolitho, Harold. *Treasures among Men, the Fudai Daimyo in Tokugawa Japan*. New Haven: Yale University Press, 1974.

————. Review of *Economic and Demographic Change in Preindustrial Japan, 1600–1868* by Susan B. Hanley and Kozo Yamamura. *Harvard Journal of Asiatic Studies* 39, no. 2 (December 1979).

Borton, Hugh. *Peasant Uprisings in Japan of the Tokugawa Period*. Transactions of the Asiatic Society of Japan, vol. 16, 2nd ser., 1938. Reissued with a new introduction. New York, Paragon Books, 1968.

Bourdillon, M. F. C., and Fortes, Meyer, eds. *Sacrifice*. London and New York: Academic Press, 1980.

Brenner, Robert. "The Origins of Capitalist Development: A Critique of Neo-Smithian Marxism." *New Left Review*, no. 104 (July–August 1977).

Burton, W. Donald. "Peasant Struggle in Japan, 1590–1760." *Journal of Peasant Studies* 5, no. 2 (January 1978).

Carr, E. H. *What is History?* New York: Penguin Books, 1964.

Cobb, R. C. *The Police and the People: French Popular Protest 1789–1820*. Oxford: Oxford University Press, 1970.

De Ste. Croix, G. E. M. *The Class Struggle in the Ancient Greek World: From the Archaic Age to the Arab Conquests*. London: Duckworth & Co., 1981.

Draper, Hal. *Karl Marx's Theory of Revolution* Vol. 1, *State and Bureaucracy*. New York: Monthly Review Press, 1977.

Emura, Eiichi. "Jiyū minken to Chichibu jiken" (Freedom and People's Rights and the Chichibu Incident). *Bungei Chichibu*, no. 30 (1980).

Encyclopaedia of the Social Sciences, Vol. 6, *Expatriation-Gosplan*. New York: Macmillan Co., 1935, 1959.

Encyclopaedia of the Social Sciences, Vol. 15, *Trade Unions-Zwingli*. New York: Macmillan Co., 1935, 1959.

Engels, Friedrich. *The German Revolutions: "The Peasant War in Germany" and "Germany: Revolution and Counter-Revolution."* Chicago: University of Chicago Press, 1967.

Fujii, Masao. *Bingo Fukuyama shakai keizai-shi* (A Socioeconomic History of Bingo Fukuyama). Fukuyama City: Kojima Shoten, 1973.

Fukai, Jinzō. "Kinsei toshi no hattatsu" (The Development of Early Modern Cities). In *Genroku Kyōhōki no seiji to shakai, kōza Nihon kinseishi 4* (Politics and Society from Genroku to Kyōhō, Lectures on Early Modern Japanese History). Edited by Matsumoto Shirō and Yamada Tadao. Tokyo: Yūhikaku, 1980.

Fukaya, Katsumi. 'Bakuhansei shakai to ikki" (Bakuhan Society and Peasant Uprisings). In *Ikki—ikkishi nyūmon 1* (Uprisings—Introduction to the History of Uprisings, vol. 1). Tokyo: Tokyo Daigaku Shuppankai, 1981.

Fukuyama shishi chūkan (The History of Fukuyama City, vol. 2). Editorial Committee for the History of Fukuyama City. Fukuyama-Shi: Koyama Ofusetto Printing Co., 1968.

Furushima Toshio chosakushū, dai ikkan, fueki rōdōsei no hōkai katei (The Collected Works of Furushima Toshio, vol. 1, The Process of Disintegration of the Corvee Labor System). Tokyo: Tokyo Daigaku Shuppankai, 1974.

Futakawa sonshi kankōkai, ed. *Futakawa sonshi* (History of Futakawa Village). Okayama-ken: Nōkyō Insatsu Kabushikigaisha, 1965.

Gluck, Carol. "The People in History: Recent Trends in Japanese Historiography." *Journal of Asian Studies* 38, no. 1 (November 1978).

Halliday, Jon. *A Political History of Japanese Capitalism*. New York: Pantheon Books, 1975.

Hall, John W. *Japan: From Prehistory to Modern Times*. New York: Delacorte Press, 1970.

———. *Tanuma Okitsugu, 1719–1788: Forerunner of Modern Japan*. Cambridge, Mass.: Harvard University Press, 1955.

Hanley, Susan B., and Yamamura, Kozo. *Economic and Demographic Change in Preindustrial Japan 1600–1868*. Princeton: Princeton University Press, 1977.

Harootunian, Harry. "Ideology as Conflict." In *Conflict in Modern Japanese History: The Neglected Tradition*. Edited by Najita, Tetsuo, and J. Victor Koschman. Princeton: Princeton University Press, 1982.

Hashizume, Yōji. "Meiji ninen no jōsei to Aida ikki" (The Situation in 1869 and the Aida Rising). *Shinano* 27, no. 5 (May 1975).

Hayashi, Motoi. "Hōreki-Tenmeiki no shakai jōsei" (The Social Situation in the Hōreki and Tenmei Eras). In *Iwanami kōza, Nihon rekishi 12, kinsei 4* (Iwanami Lectures, Japanese History 12, The Early Modern Era, vol. 4). Tokyo: Iwanami Shoten, 1967.

———. "Soren ni okeru kaikyū tōsōshi kenkyū: hōken shakai makki no nōmin undōshi o chūshin ni" (Studies in the History of Class Struggle in the Soviet Union: On the History of the Peasant Movement in Late Feudal Society.) In *Kaikyū tōsō no rekishi to riron, ikkan* (The History and Theory of Class Struggle, vol. 1). Edited by Hayashi Motoi, Kaikyū tōsōshi kenkyū kai. Tokyo: Aoki Shoten, 1981.

Hayashi, Motoi, ed., and Nagamitsu Norikazu, reviser. *Mimasaka no kuni Sanchū ikki shiryōshū* (Historical Materials on the Sanchū Rising in Mimasaka Province). Published by the Sanchū ikki gimin kenshōkai, 1957.

Hill, Christopher. *The World Turned Upside Down: Radical Ideas during the English Revolution*. London: Penguin Books, 1982.

———. *The Century of Revolution 1603–1714*. London: Abacus Sphere Books, 1961, 1978.

Hirasawa, Kiyoto. *Hyakushō ikki no tenkai* (The Development of Peasant Risings). Tokyo: Azekura Shobō, 1972.

Hiroshima kenshi, kinsei 1 (History of Hiroshima Prefecture, vol. 1, The Early Modern Era). Hiroshima Prefecture, 1981.

Hodgson, Geoff. *Capitalism, Value and Exploitation: A Radical Theory*. Oxford: Martin Robertson & Co., 1982.

"Hōreki jūisai kanoto sōdō hikae" (A Record of the Disturbances in December of the 11th Year of the Hōreki Era) by Kanae Kamenosuke, village headman of Kokubunji district. Ueda City Historial Museum.

Ichii, Saburō, and Fukaya, Kiyoshi. *Dentōteki kakushin shisōron* (Essays on Traditional Reformist Thought). Tokyo: Heibonsha, 1972.

Iijima, Shiaki. "Jōkamachi to shūhen nōson—bunseki shikaku to kadai no teiji" (Castle Towns and Surrounding Villages). *Chihōshi kenkyū 166* 30, no. 4 (August 1980).

Iinuma, Jirō. *Kokudakasei no kenkyū* (A Study of the Kokudaka System). Tokyo:

Mineruva Shobō, 1974–75.

Inada, Masahiro. "Chichibu jikenzō saikōsei no tame no shiron" (Preliminary Sketch for the Reconstruction of the Chichibu Incident). *Rekishi hyōron*, November 1984.

Ishii, Kanji. *Nihon keizai-shi* (Japanese Economic History). Tokyo: Tokyo Daigaku Shuppankai, 1976, 1980.

Jenkins, J. Craig. "Why Do Peasants Rebel? Structural and Historical Theories of Modern Peasant Rebellions." *American Journal of Sociology* 88, no. 3 (November 1982).

Kamei, Masao. "Mimasaka no kuni Sanchū ikki no rekishiteki haigo" (The Historical Background of the Sanchū Rising in Mimasaka Province). *Okayama shigaku* (Okayama University Historical Journal), no. 3 (1958).

"Kamo no sawagitachi" (The Disturbance in Kamo District). In *Nihon shisō taikei 58, minshū undō no shisō* (Outline Series on Japanese Thought, vol. 58, The Thought of the People's Movements). Edited by Shōji Kichinosuke, Hayashi Motoi, and Yasumaru Yoshio. Tokyo: Iwanami Shoten 1970.

Kanno, Noriko. "Kawariyuku muramura" (The Changing Villages). In *Nihon minshū no rekishi 5, yonaoshi* (History of the Japanese People, vol. 5, World Renewal). Edited by Sasaki Junnosuke. Tokyo: Sanseidō, 1974, p. 187.

Kashiwabara, Yūsen. "Edoki minshū to Bukkyō no fukyū" (The People of the Edo Period and the Diffusion of Buddhism). *Nihongaku* (The Quarterly of Japanology). no. 3 (December 1983).

Katsumata, Shizuo. *Ikki* (Uprisings). Tokyo: Iwanami Shinsho 194, 1982.

Katsura, Kakuemon. "Shigi seijiroku" (A Personal Account of Fief Administration), January 1762, In Yokoyama Toshio, *Ueda han nōmin sōdō shi* (The History of Peasant Uprisings in Ueda Fief). Nagano-ken, Ueda-shi: Heirindō, 1981.

————. "Shōhiroku" (A Short Elaboration), January 1762, In Yokoyama Toshio, *Ueda han nōmin sōdō shi* (The History of Peasant Uprisings in Ueda Fief). Nagano-ken, Ueda-shi: Heirindō, 1981.

Kawakami sonshi (History of Kawakami Village). Kawakami sonshi henshū iinkai (Editorial Committee for the History of Kawakami Village). Okayame City: Okayama Sanyō Printing Co., 1980.

Kitajima, Masamoto. *Nihon no rekishi 18, bakuhansei no kumon* (Japanese History, vol. 18, The Anguish of the Bakuhan System). Tokyo: Chūkō Bunko, 1974.

Kitazawa, Fumitake. *Meiwa no dai ikki* (The Great Uprising of the Meiwa Era). Tokyo: Hatonomori Shoten, 1973.

Kodama, Kōta, et al., eds. *Kinseishi handobukku* (Handbook of Early Modern History). Tokyo: Kondō Shuppansha, 1972.

Kolchin, Peter. "Reevaluating the Antebellum Slave Community: A Comparative Perspective." *Journal of American History* 70, no. 3 (December 1983).

Kurushima, Hiroshi. Review of Sasaki Junnosuke, *Yonaoshi. Rekishigaku kenkuū*, no. 492 (May 1981).

————. "Mura to mura no kankei—kumiai mura (mura rengō) kenkyū nōto" (Relations between Villages—Notes on the Study of Village Federations). *Rekishi kōron* (Historical Forum), no. 106 (September 1984).

Ladurie, Emmanuel Le Roy. *Carnival in Romans: A People's Uprising at Romans 1579–1586.* London: Penguin Books, 1981.

Leiter, Samuel L. "The Depiction of Violence on the Kabuki Stage." *Educational Theater Journal* 26, no. 2 (May 1974).

Lewin, Moshe. *The Making of the Soviet System: Essays in the Social History of Interwar Russia.* New York: Pantheon Books, 1985.

Lyman, Peter. "The Politics of Anger: On Silence, Resentment and Political Speech." *Socialist Review*, no. 57 (May-June 1981).

Machida, Shōzō. "Meiji zenki ni okeru Nagano-ken Ueda chiiki seishigyō no rekishi chirigakuteki kenkyū" (A Historical-Geographical Study of the Silk-Reeling Industry in the Ueda Region of Nagano Prefecture in the Early Meiji Period). *Shinano* 22, no. 10 (October 1970).

Mäkelä, Klaus. "The Uses of Alcohol and Their Cultural Regulation." *Acta Sociologica—The Journal of the Scandinavian Sociological Association* 26, no. 1 (1983).

Makihara, Norio. "'Kindaiteki tochi shoyū' gainen no saikentō: saikin no Seiyō kindai jinushisei-shi kenkyū o tegakari ni" (A Reconsideration of the Concept of "Modern Land Ownership," with Reference to Recent Studies of Land Ownership in the West). *Rekishigaku kenkyū*, no. 502 (March 1982).

Maruyama, Masao. *Studies in the Intellectual History of Tokugawa Japan.* Tokyo: University of Tokyo Press, 1974.

Marx, Karl. *Capital—A Critique of Political Economy.* Translated from the 3d German edition by S. Moore and E. Aveling. Charles H. Kerr & Co., 1906; New York: Modern Library Edition, u. d.

Matsuda, Yukitoshi. "'Goisshin' to minshū" (The Restoration and the People). In *Nihon minshū no rekishi 5, yonaoshi* (History of the Japanese People, vol. 5, World Renewal). Edited by Sasaki Junnosuke. Tokyo: Sanseidō, 1974.

————. "Meiji shonen no kaikyū tōsō—Shinshū Matsushiro 'gosatsu sōdō' no baai" (Class Struggle in Early Meiji: On the "Disturbances in Connection with Currencies Issued in 1870" in Matsushiro Fief, Shinshū). *Rekishigaku kenkyū*, no. 359 (April 1970).

Matsumoto, Sannosuke. "The Idea of Heaven: A Tokugawa Foundation for Natural Rights Theory." In *Japanese Thought in the Tokugawa Period.* Edited by Tetsuo Najita and Irwin Scheiner. Chicago: University of Chicago Press, 1978.

Michishige, Tetsuo. "Fukuyama-han Tenmei roku shichinen ikki no shiryō ni tsuite—hanshu Abe Masatomo shoken o chūshin toshite" (Historical Materials on the Tenmei Rising of 1786–87 in Fukuyama Fief: Lord Abe Masatomo's Correspondence). *Geibi chihōshi kenkyū*, no. 58 (August 1965).

Migdal, Joel S. *Peasants, Politics, and Revolution: Pressures toward Political and Social*

Change in the Third World. Princeton: Princeton University Press, 1974.

"Mikoku shimin ranpōki." [An Account of the People's Revolt in the Province of Mimasaka] In *Bizen, Bitchū, Mimasaka hyakushō ikki shiryō 1–5* (The Documents of Peasant Risings, vols. 1–5, Bizen, Bitchū, Mimasaka). Edited by Norikazu Nagamitsu. Tokyo: Tosho Kankōkai, 1978.

Minegishi, Kentarō. "Bakuhansei shakai no mibun kōsei" (The Status Structure in Bakuhan Society) In *Kōza Nihon kinseishi 3, bakuhansei shakai no kōzō* (Lectures on Early Modern Japanese History, vol. 3, The Structure of Bakuhan Society). Edited by Fukaya Katsumi and Matsumoto Shirō. Tokyo: Yūhikaku, 1980.

Miyamoto, Tsuneichi, Yamamoto, Shūgorō, et al., eds. *Nihon zankoku monogatari* (Tales of Cruelty in Japan). Tokyo: Heibonsha, 1960.

Miyata, Noboru. "Nōson no fukkō undō to minshū shūkyō no tenkai" (The Restoration Movement in Agricultural Villages and the Development of Popular Religion). In *Iwanami kōza, Nihon rekishi 13, kinsei 5* (Iwanami Lectures, Japanese History 13, the Early Modern Era, vol. 5). Tokyo: Iwanami Shoten, 1977.

Miyoshi, Motoyuki and the Sanchū ikki kenkyūkai. "Sanchū ikki kenkyūjō no mondaiten" (Issues in the Study of the Sanchū Rising). No place or date.

Mogi, Yōichi. "Bakumatsuki bakuryō nōhei soshiki no seiritsu to tenkai" (The Formation and Development of Peasant Militia in the Last Decade of the Bakufu). *Rekishigaku kenkyū* (Journal of Historical Studies), no. 464 (January 1979).

Moore, Barrington, Jr. *Social Origins of Dictatorship and Democracy: Lord and Peasant in the Making of the Modern World*. Boston: Beacon Press, 1966.

————. *Injustice: The Social Bases of Obedience and Revolt*. London and New York: Macmillan Press, 1978.

Mori, Yasuhiko. "'Yonaoshi' ikki no tenkai to minshū ishiki" (The Development of a *Yonaoshi* Rising and Popular Consciousness). *Rekishigaku kenkyū* (Journal of Historical Studies), no. 458 (July 1978).

Morimoto, Kiyoshi. "Sanchū ikki oboegaki" (Memorandum on the Sanchū Rising). No place or date.

Moriyama, Gunjirō. "Chichibu jiken no hyōka o megutte—Irokawa Daikichi shi no hihan ni kotaenagara" (Historical Evaluation of the Chichibu Incident: Comments on the Criticism of Mr. Irokawa Daikichi). *Rekishigaku kenkyū* (Journal of Historical Studies), no. 535 (November 1984).

Morris, Dana. Review of *Economic and Demographic Change in Preindustrial Japan*, by Susan B. Hanley and Kozo Yamamura. *Journal of Asian Studies* 39, no. 2 (February 1980).

Nagahara, Keiji. "The Sengoku Daimyo and the 'Kandaka' System." In *Japan before Tokugawa: Political Consolidation and Economic Growth 1500–1650*. Edited by John W. Hall, Keiji Nagahara, and Yamamura Kozo. Princeton: Princeton

University Press, 1981.

Nagahara, Keiji, and Bandō, Hiroshi, eds. *Kōza shiteki yuibutsuron to gendai, 3 sekaishi ninshiki* (Lectures on Historical Materialism and the Present, vol. 3, The Understanding of World History). Tokyo: Aoki Shoten, 1978.

Nagamitsu, Norikazu, ed. *Bizen, Bitchū, Mimasaka hyakushō ikki shiryō, 1–5* (Historical Materials on Peasant Uprisings, vols. 1–5, Bizen, Bitchū, Mimasaka). Tokyo: Kokusho Kankōkai, 1978.

Nagamitsu, Norikazu. "Mimasaka Tsuyama han kaisei ikki" (The Kaisei Rising in Tsuyama Fief, Mimasaka Province). In *Nihon shomin seikatsu shiryō shūsei*, vol. 13. Tokyo: Son'ichi Shobō, 1970.

Naitō, Masanaka. "Meiji shonen Hokushin no nōmin sōjō" (The Peasant Disturbances in Northern Shinshū during the Early Meiji Years). *Rekishi hyōron* (Historical Review), no. 45 (May 1953).

Najita, Tetsuo. "Ōshio Heihachirō." In *Personality in Japanese History*. Edited by Albert M. Craig and Donald H. Shively. Berkeley: University of California Press, 1970.

Najita, Tetsuo, and Koschman, J. Victor, eds. *Conflict in Modern Japanese History: The Neglected Tradition*. Princeton: Princeton University Press, 1982.

Najita, Tetsuo, and Scheiner, Irwin, eds. *Japanese Thought in the Tokugawa Period*. Chicago: University of Chicago Press, 1978.

Nakamura, Bun. "Meiji ninen nōmin tōsō no rekishiteki zentei: Shinano-no-kuni, Chikuma-gun Midarebashi mura" (Historical Premises of the Peasant Struggles of 1869: Midarebashi Village in Chikuma District, Shinano Province). *Shinano*, 32, no. 2 (February 1980).

Nakamura, J. I. "Human Capital Accumulation in Premodern Rural Japan." *Journal of Economic History* 41, no. 2 (June 1981).

Nakamura, Masanori. *Nihon no rekishi 29, rōdōsha to nōmin* (The History of Japan, vol. 29, Workers and Peasants). Tokyo: Shogakukan, 1976.

Nakamura, Satoru. "Kaikokugo no bōeki to sekai shijō" (Trade and the World Market after the Opening of the Ports). In *Iwanami kōza, Nihon rekishi 13, kinsei 5* (Iwanami Lectures, Japanese History 13, the Early Modern Era, vol. 5). Tokyo: Iwanami Shoten, 1977.

Nakano, Michiko. "Kyōhō no Sanchū ikki" (The Sanchū Rising of the Kyōhō Era). In *Kawakami sonshi* (The History of Kawakami Village). Kawakami sonshi henshū iinkai (Kawakami Village History Editorial Committee). Okayama City: Okayama Sanyō Printing Co., 1980.

Nakayama, Tomihiro. "Keiō sannen Bingo-no-kuni, Eso-gun hyakshō ikki no kisoteki kenkyū" (A Basic Study of the Peasant Rising in Eso District, Bingo Province in 1867). *Shigaku kenkyū* (Review of Historical Studies) Hiroshima Daigaku, no. 156 (July 1982).

Nakura, Tetsuzō. "Kinsei no shinkō to ikki" (Early Modern Religions Beliefs and Peasant Risings). In *Ikki 4, seikatsu, bunka, shisō* (Uprisings, vol. 4, Life, Culture and Thought). Tokyo: Tokyo Daigaku Shuppankai, 1981.

Namba, Nobuo. "Bakuhansei kaikaku no tenkai to kaikyū tōsō" (The Development of Bakuhan Reforms and Class Struggle). In *Taikei Nihon kokkashi 3, kinsei* (Outline Series on the History of the Japanese State, vol. 3, the Early Modern Era). Edited by Sasaki Junnosuke et al. Tokyo: Tokyo Daigaku Shuppankai, 1975.

Naramoto, Tatsuya. *Nihon no rekishi 17, chōnin no jitsuryoku* (Japanese History, vol. 17, The Actual Power of Merchants). Tokyo: Chūkōbunko 1974.

Nihonshi jiten (Dictionary of Japanese History). Edited by Takeuchi Rizō and Takayanagi Mitsutoshi. Tokyo: Kadokawa Shoten, 1978.

Nihon shomin seikatsu shiryō shūsei (A Collection of Historical Materials on the Life of the Japanese Common People). Vol. 6, Tokyo: San'ichi Shobō, 1968; Vol. 13, Tokyo: San'ichi Shobō, 1970.

Nishida, Masaki. "Ikki no tenkai" (The Development of Peasant Uprisings). *Ikki 2, ikki no rekishi* (Uprisings, vol. 2, The History of Uprisings). Tokyo: Daigaku Shuppankai, 1981.

Niwa, Hiroshi. *Jinushisei no keisei to kōzō—Minojima chitai ni okeru jisshōteki bunseki* (The Formation and Structure of the Landlord System: An Empirical Analysis of the Mino Striped-Textile-Producing Area). Tokyo: Ochanomizu Shobō, 1982.

Norman, E. H. "Feudal Background of Japanese Politics." In *Origins of the Modern Japanese State: Selected Writings of E. H. Norman.* Edited by John W. Dower. New York: Pantheon Books, 1975.

———. *Soldier and Peasant in Japan: The Origins of Conscription.* New York: Institute of Pacific Relations, 1943.

North, Douglass C. *Structure and Change in Economic History.* New York: W. W. Norton & Co., 1981.

Ochiai, Nobutaka. "Yonaoshi" (World Renewal). In *Ikki 2, ikki no rekishi* (Uprisings, vol. 2, The History of Uprisings). Tokyo: Tokyo Daigaku Shuppankai, 1982.

———. "Yonaoshi to sonraku kyōdōtai" (World Renewal and the Village Community). In *Minshū no seikatsu, bunka to henkaku shūtai* (Popular Life and Culture and Its Bearers of Change). Edited by Rekishigaku Kenkyukai. Tokyo: Aoki Shoten, November 1982.

Ohkura, Takehiko, and Shimbo, Hiroshi. "The Tokugawa Monetary Policy in the Eighteenth and Nineteenth Centuries." *Explorations in Economic History* 15, no. 1 (January 1978).

Ōishi, Shinzaburō. *Nihon kinsei shakai no shijō kōzō* (Market Structure in Early Modern Japanese Society). Tokyo: Iwanami Shoten 1975.

Ooms, Herman. *Charismatic Bureaucrat: A Political Biography of Matsudaira Sadanobu 1758–1829.* New Haven: Yale University Press, 1974.

Papinot, E. *Historical and Geographical Dictionary of Japan.* Tokyo: Charles E. Tuttle Co., 1912, 1973.

"Peasant Strategies in Asian Societies: Moral and Rational Economic

Approaches—A Symposium." *Journal of Asian Studies* 42, no. 4 (August 1983).

Piven, Francis Fox, and Cloward, Richard A. *Poor People's Movements: Why They Succeed, How They Fail.* New York: Vintage Books, 1979.

———. *The New Class War: Reagan's Attack on the Welfare State and Its Consequences.* New York: Pantheon Books, 1982.

Poggi, Gianfranco. *The Development of the Modern State.* Stanford: Stanford University Press, 1978.

Popkin, Samuel L. *The Rational Peasant: The Political-Economy of Rural Society in Vietnam.* Berkeley, University of California Press, 1979.

Raeff, Marc. Review of *Slavery in Russia 1450–1725,* by Richard Hellie. *Labor History* 24, no. 3 (Summer 1983).

Saitō, Yōichi. "Bushū yonaoshi ikki no idetachi to emono" (Clothing and Tools in the World Renewal Rising in Musashi Province). *Gakushūin daigaku shiryōkan kiyō* (Bulletin of the Gakushūin University Archives Museum), no. 1 (March 1983).

Sakai, Hajime. "Ōshio no ran to Kinai nōson" (The Ōshio Insurrection and Agricultural Villages in the Osaka-Kobe-Kyoto Area). In *Tenpōki no seiji to shakai* (Politics and Society in the Tenpō Era). Edited by Aoki Michio and Yamada Tadao. Tokyo: Yūhikaku, 1981.

"Sakushū hinin sōdōki" (Account of the Poor People's Disturbance in Sakushū). In *Nihon shomin seikatsu shiryō shūsei, dai jūsankan* (A Collection of Historical Materials on the Life of the Japanese Common People, vol. 13). Tokyo: Sanichi Shobō, 1970.

"Sakuyō chihō kyūki" (Official Record of the Sakuyō Region). In *Mimasaka shiryō, dai isshū* (Historical Materials of Mimasaka, vol. 1). Edited by the Mimasaka Region Historical Studies Association. Tsuyama Local History Museum, 1956.

Sanchū ikki gimin kenshōkai, ed. "Gairyaku Sanchū ikki" (Outline of the Sanchū Rising). April 1956.

Sasaki, Junnosuke. "Bakuhansei kokka to higashi Ajia" (The Bakuhan State and East Asia) In *Nihonshi o manabu 3, kinsei* (The Study of Japanese History, vol. 3, The Early Modern Period). Edited by Yoshida Akira, Nagahara Keiji, et al. Tokyo: Yūhikaku, 1976.

———. "Ikki, sōdō-shi no hōhō ni tsuite" (On Methodology for the History of Risings and Disturbances). *Rekishi hyōron* (Historical Review), no. 396 (April 1983).

———. *Yonaoshi* (World Renewal). Tokyo: Iwanami Shinsho 90, 1979.

———. "Bakuhansei kokkaron" (On the Bakuhan State). *Taikei Nihon kokkashi 3, kinsei* (Outline Series on the History of the Japanese State, vol. 3, The Early Modern Period). Edited by Junnosuke Sasaki et al. Tokyo: Tokyo Daigaku Shuppankai, 1975.

Scheiner, Irwin. "Benevolent Lords and Honorable Peasants: Rebellion and Peasant Consciousness in Tokugawa Japan." In *Japanese Thought in the Tokugawa Period*. Edited by T. Najita and I. Scheiner. Chicago: University of Chicago Press, 1978.

Scott, James C. *The Moral Economy of the Peasant: Rebellion and Subsistence in Southeast Asia*. New Haven: Yale University Press, 1976.

————. "Protest and Profanation: Agrarian Revolt and the Little Tradition (Parts I and II)." *Theory and Society* 4, nos. 1–2 (1977).

————. *Everyday Forms of Peasant Resistance: Class Relations and the Green Revolution in Malaysia*. New Haven: Yale University Press, 1985.

Setouchi no senkakusha—shisō no nagare (Pioneers of the Inland Sea Area: The Flow of Thought). Okayama City: Sanyō Shimbunsha, 1977.

Shanin, Teodor. *Russia as a "Developing Society"—The Roots of Otherness: Russia's Turn of Century*. Vol. 1. London: Macmillan Press, 1985.

————. *Russia 1905–7: Revolution as a Moment of Truth*. London: Macmillan Press, forthcoming.

Shanin, Teodor, ed. *Late Marx and the Russian Road: Marx and "the peripheries of capitalism."* New York: Monthly Review Press, 1983.

Shibahara, Takuji. *Nihon kindaika no sekaishiteki ichi—sono hōhōronteki kenkyū* (The World Historical Position of Japan's Modernization). Tokyo: Iwanami Shoten, 1981.

Shimada shishi shiryō dai rokkan (Historical Materials on the history of Shimada City, Volume 6). Shimado City: Shimada Shiyakusho, 1970.

Shimizu, Toshio, ed. *Chiisagata Ueda rekishi nenpyō* (Historical Chronology of Chiisagata Ueda). Published by the Chiisagata, Ueda Local History Study Group, 1955.

Shintani, Masamichi. "Andō Shōeki no rōdōkan" (Andō Shōeki's View of Labor). *Kikan kuraishisu* (The Crisis Quarterly), no. 14 (Winter 1983).

Shirakawabe, Tatsuo. "Murakata sōdō to yonaoshi" (Village Disturbances and World Renewal). *Rekishi Kōron* (Historical Forum) 4, no. 6 (June 1978).

Shōji, Kichinosuke. *Yonaoshi ikki no kenkyū* (A Study of Yonaoshi Risings). Tokyo: Azekura Shobō, 1970.

————. Hayashi Motoi and Yasumaru Yoshio, eds. *Nihon shisō taikei 58, minshū-undō no shisō* (Compendium of Japanese Thought, vol. 58, The Thought of the People's Movements). Tokyo: Iwanami Shoten, 1970.

Sippel, Patricia. "Popular Protest in Early Modern Japan: The Bushū Outburst." *Harvard Journal of Asiatic Studies* 37, no. 2 (December 1977).

Smith, Thomas C. *The Agrarian Origins of Modern Japan*. Stanford: Stanford University Press, 1969.

Steiner, Kurt. *Local Government in Japan*. Stanford: Stanford University Press, 1965.

Sugi, Hitoshi. "Ka-seiki no shakai to bunka—zaison bunka no tenkai to kinseiteki bunka kōzō no kaitai" (Society and Culture in the Bunka-Bunsei Period

(1804–1829): On the Development of Rural Village Culture and the disintegration of the Early Modern Structure of Culture). In *Tenpōki no seiji to shakai* (Politics and Society in the Tenpō Period). Edited by Aoki Michio and Yamada Tadao. Tokyo: Yūhikaku, 1981.

Sugiura, Minpei. *Ishin zenya no bungaku* (Literature on the Eve of the Restoration). Tokyo: Iwanami Shoten, 1967.

Sumiya, Mikio, and Taira, Kōji, eds. *An Outline of Japanese Economic History 1603–1940: Major Works and Research Findings.* Tokyo: University of Tokyo Press, 1979.

Sunesson, Sune. "Organizing and Discipline." *Acta Sociologica—The Journal of the Scandinavian Sociological Association* 27, no. 3 (1984).

Takeuchi, Makoto. "Kansei kaikaku" (The Kansei Reforms). In *Iwanami Kōza, Nihon rekishi 12, kinsei 4* (Iwanami Lectures, Japanese History 12, The Early Modern Era, vol, 4). Tokyo: Iwanami Shoten, 1976.

Terao, Gorō. *Sōmō no ishinshi* (A Restoration History of the Commoners). Tokyo: Tokuma Shoten, 1980.

Therborn, Göran. *What Does the Ruling Class Do When It Rules? State Apparatuses and State Power under Feudalism, Capitalism and Socialism.* London: New Left Books, 1978.

The Taiheiki, A Chronicle of Medieval Japan. Translated with an introduction and notes by Helen Craig McCullough. Tokyo: Charles E. Tuttle Co., 1979.

The Transition from Feudalism to Capitalism. Introduction by Rodney Hilton. London: New Left Books, 1976.

Thomson, Oliver. *Mass Persuasion in History: A Historical Analysis of the Development of Propaganda Techniques.* New York: Crane, Russak & Co., 1977.

Tilly, Charles. "Do Communities Act?" *Sociological Inquiry* 43, no. 3–4 (1973).

Totman, Conrad. *Politics in the Tokugawa Bakufu 1600–1843.* Cambridge, Mass.: Harvard University Press, 1967.

Tōyama, Shigeki. "Hyakushō ikki no kakumeisei ni tsuite" (On the Revolutionary Nature of Peasant Uprisings). *Hyōron* (Criticism), May 1947. Reprinted in *Rekishi kagaku taikei, dai nijūnikan, nōmin tōsōshi* (Historical Science Series, vol. 22, History of Peasant Struggles). Edited by Rekishi kagaku kyōgikai. Tokyo: Azekura Shobō, 1973.

Trimberger, Ellen Kay. "State Power and Modes of Production: Implications of the Japanese Transition to Capitalism" in *The Insurgent Sociologist,* vol. 7 no. 2 (Spring 1977).

Tsuda, Hideo. *Nihon no rekishi 22. Tenpō kaikaku* (Japanese History 22, The Tenpō Reforms). Tokyo, Shōgakukan 1975.

Tsuji, Tatsuya. *Kyōhō Kaikaku no Kenkyū* (A Study of the Kyōhō Reforms). Tokyo: Sōbunsha, 1963.

Tsuyama shishi (The History of Tsuyama City). Vol. 1, *Prehistory and Antiquity* (Tsuyama City Office, 1972). Vol. 3, *Early Modern I, The Age of the Mori Fief*

(1973). Vol. 5, *Early Modern III, The Bakumatsu-Restoration Period* (1974). Vol. 6, *Modern I, Meiji* (1980).

Ueda Chiisagata shishi, yohen (The History of Ueda Chiisagata City: Supplement). Chiisagata Jihosha, 1923.

Ueda shishi (The History of Ueda City). Vol. 1 and 2. Edited by Fujisawa Naoe and Itō Denbei. Nagano City: Shinano Mainichi Shimbunsha, 1940, 1974.

Urry, John. *Reference Groups and the Theory of Revolution.* London and Boston: Routledge & Kegan Paul, 1973.

————. "Some Themes in the Analysis of the Anatomy of Contemporary Capitalist Societies." *Acta Sociologica: The Journal of the Scandinavian Sociological Association* 25, no. 4 (1980).

Vucinich, Wayne S., ed. *The Peasant in Nineteenth-Century Russia.* Stanford: Stanford University Press, 1968.

Wallerstein, Immanuel. *The Modern World System: Capitalist Agriculture and the Origins of the European World Economy in the Sixteenth Century.* New York: Academic Press, 1974.

Walthall, Anne. "Narratives of Peasant Uprisings in Japan." *Journal of Asian Studies* 42, no. 3 (May 1983).

Wood, Ellen Meiksins. "The Separation of the Economic and the Political in Capitalism." *New Left Review*, no. 127 (May–June 1981).

Yamada, Tadao. "Hōreki-Tenmeiki no bakusei no tenkai" (The Development of Bakufu Politics in the Hōreki and Tenmei Eras). In *Nihonshi 5, kinsei 2* (Japanese History 5, The Early Modern Era, vol. 2). Edited by Ōishi Shinzaburō. Tokyo: Yūhikaku Shinsho 560, 1978.

————. "Bakuhansei kokka to ikki" (The Bakuhan State and Peasant Risings). In *Ikki—ikki to kokka 5* (Uprising—Uprisings and the State, vol. 5). Tokyo: Tokyo Daigaku Shuppankai, 1981.

Yamanaka, Kiyotaka. "Hyakushō ikki no jidaisei to chiikisei" (The Periodization and Geographical Distribution of Peasant Risings). *Rekishi kōron* (Historical Forum), June 1978.

Yamazaki, Ryūzō. *Kinsei bukka shi kenkyū* (A Study of the History of Prices in the Early Modern Era). Tokyo: Hanawa Shobō, 1983.

Yasumaru, Yoshio. *Nihon no kindaika to minshū shisō* (Japan's Modernization and Popular Thought). Tokyo: Aoki Shoten, 1974.

————. "Konmintō no ishiki katei" (Developing the Thought of the Poor People's Party). *Shisō* (Thought), December 1984.

Yasumaru, Yoshio, et al., eds. *Nihon shisō taikei 58, minshū undō no shisō* (Compendium of Japanese Thought, vol. 58, The Thought of the People's Movements). Tokyo: Iwanami Shoten, 1970.

Yokochi, Jōji. "Ina-ken ni okeru nōmin tōsō no tenkai (1)" (The Development of Peasant Struggles in Ina Prefecture, Part I). *Shinano* 22, no. 6 (June 1970).

Yokoyama, Toshio. "*Gimin: hyakushō ikki no shidōshatachi*" (Exemplary Martyrs:

Leaders of Peasant Risings). Tokyo: Sanseido, 1973.

———. *Uedahan nōmin sōdōshi* (The History of Peasant Uprisings in Ueda Fief).
Ueda City: Ueda Chiisagata, Shiryō Kankōkai 1968. Revised and expanded version published under the same title. Heirindō Shoten, Ueda City: Nagano, 1981.

———. *Hyakushō ikki to gimin denshō* (Peasant Uprisings and Legends of
Exemplary Martyrs). Tokyo: Kyōikusha, Rekishi Shinsho 85, 1977.

Yubara chōshi (History of Yubara Town). Vols. 1 and 2. Edited by Taniguchi
Sumio and Morimoto Kiyoshi. Okayama: Ōba-gun, Yubara-machi, 1953,
1957.

Yura, Nissho. "Gōso nikki" (Record of the Violent Appeal) 1867. In *Bizen, Bitchū,
Mimasaka hyakushō ikki shiryō*. Vol. 3. Edited by Nagamitsu Norikazu. Tokyo:
Kokusho Kankōkai, 1978.

Index

Abe Masakiyo (daimyo), 130

Abe Masatomo (daimyo), xxxvi, 114, 119; disagrees with fief elders, 123, 124; appointed senior bakufu councillor, 126; settles with peasants, 124–26; returns to Fukuyama, 127, 129; and Kansei reforms in Fukuyama, 129–30

Abeno dōjimon, 115, 116, 119, 122

Abolition of fiefs and establishment of prefectures, 173, 226

Age of ikki and yonaoshi ends, 224

Agricultural servants: *nago* and *kerai,* xxx; bonded labor, 217

Aida (Ina or Chikuma) prefecture rising: 196, 201–03; troops and outcasts used in suppression of, 202

Akai Tadaakira (bakufu finance magistrate), 113

Alcohol: uses of, 144. *See* Mob drunkenness

Alexander II, 148. *See* Serfs

Alternate attendance system, 71, 91, 190; ended, 176

Alternatives to tax increases in Tsuyama, 29, 30

Amakusa Shirō Tokisada, 7

Amamiya Yuki (historian), 66, 69

Amida Nyorai, 99

Andō Motome (senior councillor), 119, 120

Andō Shōeki (physician): and agrarian communism, 138

Anger: displacement of, 81

Annual field inspection changed to fixed tribute, 64

Antagonistic unity of peasant-merchant existence, 24

Anti-Marxist scholarship and problem of poverty, xx, 230n 13

Anti-urban feelings of Ueda peasants, 65. *See* Ueda Hōreki rising

Asahi River, 3

Asanojō, xxxiii, 73, 75, 76, 93, 94, 95, 96, 98, 100. *See* Gimin and gimin legends

Asian peasant revolt, 190

Bakufu: moves toward uniform system of punishments, 109; and class struggle, 110; cotton monopoly, 110; strengthens centralizing powers, 110; recoinages, 110, 111; dependence on merchants, 111; mercantilist policies, 111; relief loans, 128; leadership in 1790s and 1800s, 132; currency reform of 1860, 151, 194; second anti-Chōshū campaign, 168
—edicts: May 1762, 95; September 1767, 96; encouraging informers (1770), 96

Bakuhan state, 109, 137, 217; and peasant production, xxv–xxx; construction of, xxvi; position of peasants in, xxix, xxx; and weakening equilibrium, 112; challenges to, 133; peasant demands against policies of, 139; new stages of crisis in, 149, 220; and imperialist pressure, 150; disaffections from, 159; becomes self-negating, 185; destruction of, 221, 222

Banking and relief warehouses, 131

Banks, courts, and police stations: first appearance of in modern form, 210–11

Battle of Osaka, 6
Behavior, deferential and manipulative, 94,
    244n 53
Belief in person and family as values, 146
Benevolence: appearance of, 133; as incite-
    ment to protest, 54
Bloch, Marc, 146
Blood-tie groups, xxx, 232n 25. *See also*
    Bonded labor
Bolshevik Revolution, 92
Bonded labor, 217
Bonten, religious symbolism of, 142
Borton, Hugh, xiii
Boshin civil war, 172
Bourgeois landownership rights, 173
Bravery and concept of feudal discrimina-
    tion, 100
Buddhism: medieval, xxviii; popular, 142
Buddhist and Shintō priests: role in Ueda
    rising, 93
Buddhist doctrine: hell, 82; view of life and
    death, 98–100
Buddhist temples and Shintō shrines as con-
    trol mechanisms of Bakuhan state, xxviii
Bureaucratic reform, 51
Bushū rising: discipline and solidarity in,
    169
Bushū yonaoshi rising (1866), 153, 168–70

Capitalism: rise of, 150; multiplicity of
    paths, 160
Capitalist business cycle: signs of, 224
Carr, E. H., 216
Cash charges in lieu of labor services, 93
Censorship, problem of, 115
Chichibu, Fuppu village, 213
Chichibu incident (1884), 211–14, 225
Chichibu peasant leaders, 211, 213
Chief inspectors (ōmetsuke), 114, 122
Chiisagata district, 57
Chikamatsu Monzaemon, 145
Chikuma River, 57, 58
Chōnin culture and samurai values, 144
Christianity: proscribed, 6, 7; and ruling-
    class solidarity, xxix, 231n 23
Class, xv; definition of, xvi
Class consciousness: and class struggle, xvii;
    and limits to, 139, 140
Classes, polar: samurai and peasants, xvi
Class exploitation: targeted in villages, 167
Classness: vs. statusness, xvii; increasing
    importance of, 103
Class polarization, 147; and religious re-
    vival, 154

Class relations: in Tokugawa society, xvi;
    in Fukuyama after 1787, 130, 131; inher-
    ent dynamism of, 216
Class struggle: in 1780s, 113; undermines
    feudal laws, 127, 128; reasons for lull in,
    132, 133; meaning of experience, 139; in
    villages and towns, 151; and transition to
    capitalism, 189
Class unity: rulers vs. ruled, 52
Cobb, R. C., 183
Coercive recruitment: meaning of, 74; am-
    biguity of, 214
Commander of foot soldiers, 76
Commercial profiteering: peasant punish-
    ment of, 187
Commodity economy in Ueda, 104. *See*
    Ueda fief
Commoner culture, growth of, 152
Communal solidarity: Russian and Japanese
    compared, 166, 167
Commune as leveling mechanism: mir vs.
    mura, 165
Community regeneration through property
    destruction, 147
Community warehouses (*shasō*) and poor-
    relief warehouses (*gisō*), 131, 132
Concessions and benevolence principle, 91
Conflict: vertical and horizontal, 75, 82;
    three levels of mobilization, 150, 151; ex-
    ternalization and internalization of, 167
Confucianism: teachings of, 120; and Tsu-
    yama fief officials, 180
"Congratulation rice" and new tax orders,
    121
Conscription, 149, 173, 257n 4
Continuities: between medieval and early
    modern Japan, 216; between feudal and
    capitalist Japan, 227–28
Conversion rate trickery, 69
Corruption, perceptions of, 111
Corvees, xxxi, 70, 71, 138, 141
Cotton, silk, tea, tobacco: and regional
    markets, 110
Council of State, 172; abolishes tribute re-
    ductions, 194, 203
Crimean War, 163
Crows, symbolic meaning of, 75
Cultural associations in Kantō plain, 222
Currency disorders, 151. *See* Shinshū
    risings

Daimyo, xxvi; way of life, 112; disagree-
    ments on eve of Kansei Reforms, 115;
    rule stabilized at end of 18th c., 132; re-
    sponse to crisis at end of 18th c., 221
"Dance-in" (*odorikomi*), 171

Death ritual, 49
Debased coins and devalued notes, 151. *See also* Shinshū risings
Deflation of 1880s, 210
"Deities in fashion," 153
Deity of renovation (yonaoshi daimyōjin), 145
Dependent consciousness and class structure, 80
De Ste. Croix, G. E. M., 69, 183
Dewa and Echigo provinces: mass protests in, 26
Discipline, communitarian and individualistic, 144
Dispersion of political power, and peasant struggles, 224–27
District headmen, deputies, and village headmen: in Tsuyama fief, 6, 14, 15, 16. *See also* Peasant officials
District tribute officers (*wariban*), 62, 63, 200
Disturbance (*sōdō*), xix. *See also* Unrest and disturbance
Division of labor, regional, 110
Document of guarantee (*ukesho*), 91
Documents: criteria for selection, xxxvi, xxxvii; fictional passages in, xxxvii; two types of for Fukuyama rising, 114–15; on Sanchū rising, 233*n* 1; on Ueda Hōreki rising, 239*n* 1; on Kaisei rising, 253*n* 1
Dominant ideology: and peasant virtues, 130; as source of tensions, 152
Domination: fusion of political and economic aspects of, xviii, 205
Dress during ikki, 76, 79, 116, 144, 169, 179, 183, 213

Echigo province, 26
Economic backwardness, 140
Economic crisis, manipulation of, 133
Economic equality and security, longing for, 154
Economic growth and Sanchū rising, 52
Economic history and development of political consciousness, 215, 216
Edict of debt cancelation, 34; and tokusei ikki, 247*n* 9
Edo: 7, 58, 80, 82, 83, 88, 97; yonaoshi riots of 1787 in, 112; Tenma demonstration moves toward, 141; favors Ōshio, 158; daimyo withdraw support from, 168; alternate attendance system discontinued, 190; loses power to rotate daimyo at will, 222
Ee jya nai ka (1867), xxxvii, 170–72, 252*n* 56; and moral permissiveness, 172

Endō Benzō, 115; in *Abeno dōjimon*, 119; as scapegoat, 120; repudiates fief debts, 120; increases tributes, 121; as peasant target, 124; sacrificed by Masatomo, 125; imprisoned, 126
Enterprise taxes (*unjōkin*), 22, 65, 70
Equal-field land system, 146
Equal land distribution, rumors of, 173
Evil-minister mechanism and bakuhan state, 42, 115, 116, 119, 120
Exemplary martyrs, 214. *See* Gimin and gimin legends
Exodus, desertion, or flight (*chōsan*), xix, xxi, xxii, 8. *See* Chōsan
Exploitation: and tribute, xv; definition of, xvii, xviii, xxxvii; in Tsuyama, 20–22, 23; existing level of, 30; feudal essence of, 52; high level of, 53; increasing resistance to, 137; under Meiji regime, 172–73; in Greek and Roman world, 242*n* 17. *See also* Tenant rents
Extra-economic coercion, xviii, 22. *See* Exploitation

Fact and value: close connection between, xvii
Famine relief measures and grain warehouses, 128
Fetishism, pre-Buddhist, 142
Feudal and capitalist hegemony, problem of, 133
Feudal benevolence and tribute discounts, 14
Feudal division of labor, breakdown of, 197
Feudalism, xvi, xviii; compared with capitalism, 30; two kinds of contradictions within, 105; daimyo no longer fundamental to, 200
Fief: xxv, xxvi; definition of, 4; aging process of, 105; and five-man groups, 130
Fiefs and prefectures, coexistence of, 196
Field-inspection officials, billeting of, 87
Five-family-group responsibility system, xxviii
Fixed tribute shifted to annual field inspection, 71
Food egalitarianism in French Revolution, 183. *See* Graffiti, Symbolic actions
Forced loans (*goyōkin*): levied broadly, 70
Forceful appeals (*gōso*) and riots (*bōdō*), xix, xxii, xxiii
Freedom and people's rights movement, 213, 227, 228
Freedom of trade, 220. *See* Trade
French peasants: right to land, 146
Fuchinobe Yoshihiro (Ashikaga retainer), 99

Fudai daimyo: at center of bakufu affairs, 113

Fujii Masao, historian, 129, 131, 247n 10

Fujiwara Tokihira, 99

Fukushima rising (1866), 169, 174

Fukuyama fief: location of, 114, 116, 117; tradition of peasant protest in, 116, 118; reforms in, 119, 120; intensifies exploitation, 121, 122; leading merchants in, 121; uncontrolled economy in, 120; countermeasures against peasants, 122

Fukuyama rising (1786–87): documentary evidence for, 114, 115; leadership described in *Abeno dōjimon*, 116; causes of, 118–22; peasant demands in, 118, 122, 124; peasant negotiating tactics, 124, 125; foray into Okayama fief during, 124, 125; Stage II of, 124; ending and results of, 126; significance of, 220–21. *See also* Osso

Funakoshi Ban'emon ("tax specialist"), 69

Fuon. See Unrest and disturbance

Fusion of tenancy and wage labor, 189

Gamblers: Kurōemon, 198, 199; urban poor labeled as, 206

Gimin and gimin legends: definition of, xxxiii; exploitation of past and repression, xxxiv; and psychological mythmaking, xxxiv; and Chichibu incident, xxxiv, xxxv, 214; and yonaoshi, xxxv; in Ueda, 67, 68, 99; reverse official judgments, 138; memory of, 139; rise and decline of, 221. *See* Tokuemon; Hanbei and Asanojō

Good-conduct certificates awarded to peasants, 129

Gōso. See Forceful appeals and riots

Graffiti and peasant humor, 81, 82, 90; and defiance, 90

Grain concealment, 138

Gravestones: of martyrs, 3, 50, 101

Gregorian calendar adopted, 226

Gundai in Ueda and Tsuyama: differences noted, 242n 25

Guns: use against peasants legalized, 96

Hachinohe fief, 145

Hanbei and Asanojō, xxxiii, 73, 76, 93, 94, 95, 96, 98, 99, 100, 101. *See* Gimin and gimin legends

Harootunian, Harry, 154

Hashimoto Chūbei, 157. *See* Osaka (Ōshio's) insurrection

Hayashi Motoi (historian), 95, 144

Hayashi school of neo-Confucianism, 128

Hayashi Tokuemon, 67. *See* Gimin and gimin legends

Heaven: concept of, 42; as justice, 43; and revenge, 43, 248n 11; 142, 187

"Heavenly domain" (*tenryō*), xxvi, 25

"Heaven's mandate" and "heaven's punishment," 156

Hegemony: acceptance of, 133; perpetuation of, 148; and structural tensions in, 152

Heian and Kamakura period, and ikki, 143. *See* Ikki

Hideyoshi's Sword Hunting Edict (1588), xxvii

Higuchi Yajirō (peasant leader): capture of, 43

Hinindomo (poor souls), 81; homeless poor people, 112; as precursors of industrial proletariat, 175. *See* Semiproletariat

Hirabayashi Shinshichi, 67. *See* Gimin and gimin legends

Hisamatsu Shume (senior councillor), 72, 76, 82, 87

Historiography: Japanese peasant risings described by Westerners, xiii, xiv, xv

Hōki (revolts), xxiii

"Holy water," 7

Honjō post station, 140, 170

Hōreki era: meaning of name, 68; in Ueda, 86

Hostages: Ueda peasants' demand for, 76

House-smashing: definition of, xix, xxi, xxii; as numerically dominant type of disturbance, 104; tools of, 169; in Ueda, 198, 199. *See* Uchikowashi

Human capital theory: criticism of premodern, 53

Ichimi dōshin, 143. *See* Solidarity bands

Ide Tamekichi (Chichibu peasant leader), 211

Ideological reindoctrination, 95, 138

Ieharu, Shogun, 110; death of, 113, 140

Iemitsu, Shogun, 6

Ieshige, Shogun, 110

Iida fief rising (1869), 196

Ikki: definition and stages of, xix; occurrence of by province, xxiii, xxiv; covert initiators and open organizers of, 73; dress during, 76, 79, 116, 144, 169, 179, 183, 213; and pre-feudal ideas, 143; meaning of, 143–44; traditional features of, 190

Ikuta Yorozu, 158

Illegal appeal (*osso*), xix

Illiteracy: in Russia and Japan, 163

Imperial court domains, 195, 196

Imperialism: and political mobilizations, 161, 162; and class struggle, 222, 223

Inada Masahiro (historian), 212, 214
Incendiarism: in Osaka, 157; in Ueda, 199; in Susaka, 206
Inconvertible gold notes, 195
Indebtedness, subsystems of, 217
Indemnity payments to samurai, 226
Industrialization from above: start of, 224
Infanticide, 110
Informers and spies, 109
Inheritance mechanism: Japan and Russia compared, 166
"Instructions to the People on Civil Administration," 129, 130. *See* Abe Masatomo
Itagaki Taisuke: politician as gimin figure, xxxv
Itakura Sado no kami (shogunal councillor), 83

Japanese peasants: status of, xxvii; disarmed, xxvii, 250n 18. *See also* entries beginning "Peasant"
Japan–U.S. Treaty of Commerce, 151
Joint-council system of rule, breakdown of, 82
Jōmen (fixed-period tribute assessment), 27, 28
Jōshū, Matsuida rice exchange: and exchange rate manipulation, 69
Jōshū province, 57
Justice and revenge, 143

Kabuki: theatrical techniques and ikki accounts, 77
Kaisei ichiranki: meaning of, 174
Kaisei rising (1866–67), 149; as combined ikki and yonaoshi, 175; causes of, 175–77; mobilization for, 177; leaders of, 177, 178; targets of, 177, 178; hinin in, 178, 179; relief rice distributed in, 180; clash at Ōhashi barrier gate, 180; Buddhist priests in, 181; Stages I and II of, 182, 183; peasant demands in, 182, 186, 190; punishments in, 182, 192; peasant opposition to military mobilization, 187; dual structure of, 187, 188; results of, 191, 192; typicality of, 223, 224
Kako river rising (Harima province), 156
Kamei Masao (historian), 10
Kamigō sericultural area and Shinshū risings, 204–05, 207
Kamishimo village merchants: and bakufu mine, 120; and silver loans, 121
Kamo district (Mikawa province): yonaoshi festival in, 142
Kandaka system, 59, 240n 6

Kannoshoko (Sugawara no Michizane), 99
Kansei Reforms: xxxvi, 127–29; prolong life of daimyo, 129
Katō Orihei, Chichibu peasant leader, 213, 214
Katō Sachū (town magistrate), 84; threatened by townspeople, 86, 87
Katsumata Shizuo (historian), 143
Katsura Kakuemon (district magistrate), 82; promoted to post of censor in Edo, 96; postmortem on Ueda Hōreki rising, 105, 106
Katsuyama and Miuchi (Toki) fiefs affected by protests, 181, 182
Keian Circular (*Keian ofuregaki*): filial piety and tax paying in, xxix
Kemi (annual direct field inspection), 27
Kerai, 4, 9, 23. *See* Bonded labor
Khozyain, 164
Kinki provinces, 152
Kobayashi Sōsuke, physician, 174
Kokudaka system, 59
Kolchin, Peter, 165
Komononari, 22
Komoro fief riot, 202
Korean delegation, 140
Koyama Kyūsuke, 67. *See* Gimin and gimin legends
Kubo Shimbei: 25, 27, 28, 42; and Kyōhō reforms in Tsuyama, 28; and 4 percent tax increase order, 29, 35; leads bureaucratic reforms, 217
Kurakake Torajirō (pro-emperor activist): role in suppressing Kaisei rising, 181, 182, 192; leads anti-Tokugawa group, 192
Kurashiki town: penetrated by protestors, 179, 181
Kurōemon (a leader of Ueda rising of 1869), 199, 200
Kuse incident, 31; and unsigned circulars, 35; official account of, and Shimpūken's perspective on, 37; contradictions in official account of, 38
Kusunoki Masashige (warrior hero), 32, 36
Kuzuregōshi, closing lines of, 87
Kyōhō era: xxxv, xxxvi; and Ueda "town peasant" tributes, 86
Kyōhō reforms, xxxv, 25–27, 185, 217
Kyōto imperial court, 150

Labor-shortage problem, 219
Ladurie, Emmanuel Le Roy, 183
Land entitlements: multiple and direct, 147
Land forfeitures: bakufu ban on (1722), 26; problem of, 184; withdrawal of ban on, 185; and permanent sale, 185

Landholding consciousness: in peasants,
  145–48
Landholding in Ueda: paucity of data on,
  103, 104
Landlordism: sanctioned by bakufu, 128,
  129; extends feudal control, 221
Landlord policy of early Tokugawa: memory of, as peasant weapon, 167
Landlords: and relief warehouses, 132; Rus-
  sian and Japanese compared, 148, 163,
  164; Honma family of Yamagata, 185;
  Tokuyama of Oba (Tsuyama), 186; Ya-
  buki of Katsunan (Tsuyama), 186; and al-
  liance with Meiji state, 227
Landlord-tenant relations, disguised, xxxv
Land settlement and conscription in Meiji,
  173, 226, 227, 257n 4, 258
Land transfers and bakuhan state, 184. See
  Bakuhan state
Latin America: start of U.S. military inter-
  vention in, 251n 27
Leaflets, 140, 141
Legal petition for mercy (shūso), xxi, xxii
Legal struggles, xix, 66, 153
Letter of certification (goshōmon), 79
Lewin, Moshe, 164
Liberal party, xxxv, 211, 212, 214, 227
Literary images and Ranpōki, 36
"Little tradition" of Japanese peasants,
  xxxiii
Local control in Tsuyama fief, 6
Lowly people (shitakatadomo), 123
Loyalty oaths: in Tsuyama, 47; in Ueda, 92
Lyons (France): and Chichibu district, 211

Martial arts: as landlord countermeasure,
  153
Marx, Karl, xvi, xvii, 102, 103, 184, 255n 3
Mass pilgrimage (okage mairi), xxviii, 171
Mass protests: contagious nature of, 85
Matsuda Yukitoshi (historian), 205
Matsudaira Asagorō: death of, 33; official
  mourning for, 35
Matsudaira (Iganokami) Tadayori: in Ueda,
  64, 66; hostile rumors about, 66; de-
  scribed in Sōdō jikki, 83
Matsudaira Naganori (daimyo): in Tsu-
  yama, 14; appointed lord of reduced
  Tsuyama, 216
Matsudaira retainer band in Ueda: size of,
  58
Matsudaira Sadanobu (bakufu senior coun-
  cillor), 113, 114; and Kansei reforms, 127
Matsudaira Tadachika (daimyo): and cen-
  tralization of power in Ueda, 59, 60; rural

policy of, 60; tax increases of, 60; administrative reforms of, 62
Matsudaira Tadazane: tribute income de-
  cline under, 62, 64; administrative reform
  of, 64
Matsudaira Taketomo (bakufu finance
  councillor), 110
Matsukura Katsuie, lord of Shimabara, 7
Matsushiro rising (1870), 196, 203–08;
  Ōtani Kōzō and destruction of fief's
  commercial firm, 204; peasant sanctions
  in castle town, 204, 207; targets of protest
  in, 204–05; participants in, 205–06
Meiji emperor, 170
Meiji government: frustrates peasant hopes,
  200; crushes dissent, 210
Meiji landlord system, 227
Meiji Restoration, 15; trends and episodes
  leading to, 149–73; periodization of, 150,
  151; and role of peasant risings in, 192,
  193; social change reflected in risings, 196
Merchant activities in Sanchū area villages:
  and debt cycle, 10
Merchant capitalists, 112
Merchant-peasant exchange relationship: de-
  terioration in, 11
Mercy as value and stratagem, 93
Message receivers: 31; and "message head-
  men," 40, 217
Methodology of study, 215
Michishige Tatsuo (historian), 114, 246n 2
Middle-strata peasants and semiproletarians:
  historical role of, 222, 223
Mikamo village: town-countryside conflict
  in, 46
Mikawa province, 171
Miki Jinzaemon and Yamada Bunpachi (in-
  tendants), 31, 40, 45, 47
Mikoku shimin ranpōki, xxxvii; characteristics
  of, 32, 33. See Documents
Minegishi Kentarō (historian), xxvii, xxix
Miyata Noboru, historian, 144
Mizunomi-byakushō, 4, 9, 23
Mizuno Tadakuni and Tenpō reforms, 159
Mob drunkenness, 187, 252n 56
Mobilization: of poor and middle-strata
  peasants, 162; by village units in Shinshū,
  209; of Aida peasants, 201. See Coercive
  recruitment
Modernization studies, xiv
Moral ceilings, concept of, 241n 17
Moral considerations: vs. market calcula-
  tions, 140; at the local level, 210
Moral economy, 149; end of, 209–14
Moral justice, peasant sense of, 186
Moral machinery of the state, xxviii, xxix

Mori family in Tsuyama, 216. *See* Tsuyama fief
Mori Naganori (daimyo), 15
Mori Nagatsugu (daimyo), 6, 7, 12
Mori Tadamasa (daimyo), 4, 5, 6
Morooka Kakei (gundai and senior councillor), 72, 76, 84, 87
Moore, Barrington, Jr., 92, 244*n* 47
Motohashi Mitsujirō (constable), 158
Mountain gods, 142
Musashi province, 140–42
Mutual financing associations (tanomo-shikō) and Fukuyama rising, 121

Nagamitsu Norikazu (historian), 32, 50, 174, 192, 253*n* 1, 253*n* 6
Nago, 4, 9, 23. *See* Bonded labor
Najita, Tetsuo, 158
Nakajima river beach execution ground, 98, 101
Nakamura Yazaemon ("tax specialist"), 71
Nakano Michiko (historian), 11, 13, 14, 25, 40
Nakano prefecture rising (1870), 196, 206–09
Nakasendō, 140, 141
Namba Munemori and kokujin or kuniza-murai, 4
"Naniwa jōnan inshi," 115; and author's preface to *Abeno dōjimon,* 119
Nanryō coin, or *nishu-gin,* 111
Natural disasters, 25, 28; drought of 1759–61, 71; fire and volcanic eruptions, 111; in Fukuyama, 121; of 1866, 129, 176, 177
Natural rights, 150
Negotiations, samurai purpose in, 44
Neo-Confucian ideology and thought control, xxix, 128; reemphasized, 152
New religions and self-renewal, 154
Nibu gold coins, 195
Nichiren Buddhism, 7
Nihonbashi and strategic post roads, 140
Nishihara incident, 31, 33–35; official vs. unofficial versions, 34–35
Nishihara warehouse: operation of, 35
Nishu-gin, or nanryō, coin, 111
Noncompliance: indirect forms of, 133
Norman, E. H., xiii, 251*n* 29, 252*n* 56
Numeri river beach execution ground, 49

Obedience: samurai cultivation of, 79
Ochiai Nobutaka (historian), 203
Ōdankōge, negotiations at, 39
Official ideology and exploitation, xxix
Official notary book of seals, 213

Ogami village (Urano district, Ueda), 66; signal fires in, 75
Ōhira band and Tenmei Fukuyama rising (1786–87), 116, 220, 221
Ōjōyōshū and Buddhism, 99
Okabe Kurobei (gundai and junior councillor), 72; and Hisamatsu and Morooka, 76, 87; as hero of ikki, 79; drinks with peasants, 80; and Hisamatsu in Edo, 82; formulates counterstrategy with Morooka, 84; issues notice to villages, 88; orders peasants to send representatives to castle, 90; reads nine-point document, 90; interrogates peasant leaders, 94, 95; death of, 101; compared with Alexander's dialogue with a pirate, 244*n* 52
Okuhikimai (office fees and relief rice), 22, 25
Ōmiya district office as Chichibu "revolutionary headquarters," 213
Ōmiya shrine drinking scene, 80
Ooms, Herman, 112
Opening of Japan, 161
Opium War, 159
Osaka, 112, 152; peasant lawsuit against cotton wholesalers in, 155; mint issues new gold notes, 195
Osaka (Ōshio's) insurrection: xxxvii, 149, 155–59, 222; Ōshio's summons, 156; Ōshio's followers, 157; Ōshio as martyr, 158
Ōtani Kōzō (silk merchant), and Matsushiro rising, 203
Otaniya Heibei (iron mine owner and merchant), 23, 236*n* 3
Outcasts: participation in Ueda rising, 93, 103; and unbridgeable gap with peasants, 103; compared with black-white cleavage in U.S. working class, 103, 245*n* 1; in Fukuyama rising, 124
Overtaxation and peasant production, 11

Pacifism: Japanese peasants' convention of, 250*n* 18
Paper-cord makers in Iida fief, 196
Past: peasant uses of, 104, 118, 200; incomplete transcendence of, 227–28
Pawned land: demand for return of, 26, 202; and servants and landless peasants, 104; tenancy, 130, 184, 185
Pawnshop financing system transformed, 210
Peasant achievements through struggle, 225, 226

Peasant beliefs: heaven's punishment, 52; Buddhist and Shintō gods, 52; village deities, 52, 142, 143
Peasant consciousness, xv, 142, 143
Peasant demands: and feudal ruling class, 137; old and new elements in Shinshū rising, 202
Peasant feelings of revenge and contempt, 94
Peasant martyrs: Tokuemon, Hanbei, Asa-nojō, Sakura Sōgorō, 138. See Gimin and gimin legends
Peasant-merchant relations in Tsuyama, 22–25
Peasant militia (nōhei): in Bushū rising, 170; in Kaisei rising, 181; in Shinshū risings, 209
Peasant mobilization: by five-family teams, 74; by village units, 209. See Coercive recruitment
Peasant motivation: elements in, 34, 36
Peasant officials: definition of, and as agents of repression, xxviii; recruitment and pre-rogatives of, xxxi. See District headmen, deputies, and village headmen; District tribute officers
Peasant protests: causes and types, xv, xix, xxi, xxii; refusal to celebrate New Year in Ueda, 89; significance of refusal to make demands, 190; traditions and legacies, 227–28
Peasants as ideologically creative beings vs. theory of "honorable peasants," 102
Peasants as negotiators, xxx, 124
Peasant self-exploitation, 132
Peasant unity: weakness of, 43, 44
Peasant virtues and dominant ideology, 130
"People's commanders": Tokuemon and Higuchi Yajirō, 36
Periodization of Tokugawa rule, xxxv, xxxvi
Perry Expedition, 160, 251n 27
Personal servant services, 71
Piven, Francis, and Cloward, Richard, 85, 192
Plebeian bloody-mindedness, image of, 209
Police bureaucrats and bailiffs, 155
Political consciousness of rulers and ruled, 139
Political repression: new bakufu measures of, 95
Politics of anger, 143
Polarization in Russia and Japan, 162–67
Pongee: defined, 243n 33
Poor peasants (people): religious activity of, xxxvii; militancy of, 89; concern for rents

and pawned items, 126; vs. upper-stratum peasants, 153; opposed to re-demptive killing, 157; new self-image of, 175; turn inward for salvation, 222
Poor people: progressive aspect of strug-gles, 147; and semiproletarians in Ma-tsushiro, 203
"Poor people's disturbance" (hinin sōdō), 174, 175
"Poor people's party," 211–13, 227
Poor relief as protection insurance, 131
Population registers, 137, 138
Poverty: and economic diversification, 53; in Ueda, 104; problem of, 111, 154; in Shinshū, 201. See Hinindomo; Semiprole-tariat
Power: interpenetrating networks of, xxv; dispersal of in bakuhan and Meiji states, 225
Precedent: changed into "right," 19
Prices: decline of rice price and Kyōhō re-forms, 26, 27; rise of commodity prices, 112; inflation, 151; traditional structures and commodity circulation routes dis-rupted, 168–69, 209, 224
Priests: in bakuhan state, xxviii; in Ueda Hōreki rising, 95; in Tenma disturbance, 141
Primitive capital accumulation, period of, 209–10, 228
Private landownership: peasant opposition to, 224
Production process, control over through appointment mechanism, 217
Pro-emperor activists, 150, 192. See Kura-kake Torajirō
Proletarians and capitalists: formation of, 210
"Proper way of government," 125
Property destruction as festival, 170
Property rights in land: stabilization of, xxvii
Protest: causes of, 51; humanity as incite-ment to, 54
Public authority (kōgi), xxx, 125; conscious-ness of, 147
Public bulletin boards, 95
Public relief assumed by rural elite, 221
Public workhouses and peasant poverty, 128
Punishment: manacles, 39; scenes of and their uses, 49; in Ueda, 92, 96; in Tenmei Fukuyama rising, 126; and law, 129; in Tenma disturbance, 141, 191, 192, 199
Purification religion (misogikyō) and Chi-chibu rebellion, 212

Ranpōki: and Nishihara incident, 34; and rebel leaders, 36, 46, 49. *See* "Shimpūken Chikuo"

Razobran: compared with uchikowashi, xix

Regeneration and renewal, peasant desire for, 147

Regional cultural associations, 153

Regional markets: growth of, 110, 218–19; specialization of, 152

Registered population: in Ueda castle town, 243*n* 16; in Ueda fief in 1868 and 1871, 256*n* 13

Religion, xxviii; role of after Shimbara revolt, 7; and mountain gods, 74, 142, 198, 200; slogans and symbols, 141, 142; and village poor, 153, 154; and mentality of Russian and Japanese peasants, 167. *See also* "Deities in fashion"; Heaven; *Ichimi dōshin*; Ikki; Priests

Rent collectors, hierarchy of, 185

Representatives of commercial capitalism as targets of attack, 191

Resistance: psychological obstacles to, 68

Revenge, 198

Revisionist current. *See* Historiography

Revolts (*hōki*), xxii, xxiii

Rice: loan system and exchange tickets, 24; discounts (jobiki), 64; categories and measurement of tribute, 68; tribute manipulation and its effects, 70; price discrepancy, 91

Rights: general and particular, xxxii, xxxiii; exercised unilaterally, 29; and ikki, 143; to land, 146, 186

Risings: and Tokugawa political economy, 30; in Meiji era, 172, 173

Role reversals, xxxviii, 183–84

Ruling-class morality: and promises to the people, 29; and big-merchant alliance, 111

Ruling-class obsessions, 12

Rural and urban movements, unity and disunity of, 138, 140–42

Rural districts on periphery of castle town districts, 191, 254*n* 8

Rural elite, mobilization of, 162

Rural hierarchies of control, xxx, xxxi

Rural-urban competition, 219

Russian peasant rebellion of 1905–07, 164

Russian peasants: and Pugachev rebellion, 163; serf status and redemption payments, 163; monarchism of, 164; denial of landlord ownership per se, 165; and differences from Japanese peasants, 163–67

Saburōemon and appeal of 1698, 18

Sakura Sōgorō, xxxv, 212. *See also* Gimin and gimin legends

Sakushū hinin sōdōki, 174, 175, 176, 179, 181, 253*n* 2

Samurai: defined, xvi; as military-administrative servants, xxx; as "rice thieves," 38; personnel retrenchment of, 50; fear of peasant casualties and of Edo, 78; class mission of, 79; rules of behavior, 79; obligations, 81; contempt for peasants, 83; factional disagreements among, 83; proper manner for killing of, 94; sympathy for peasants as germ of new self-consciousness, 106; punishment tactics of, 126; class morale raised, 128; demoralization of retainers, 152; matrimonial relations with peasants, 158; and Restoration process, 161, 162; splits within retainer bands, 219

Sanada daimyo, 59

Sanada Masayuki, 243*n* 16

Sanchū area: defined, 10, 38

Sanchū rising (1726–27): significance of, xxxvi, 217, 218; Stage I, 31–44; Stage III loyalty oaths, reindoctrination, and retrenchment, 32, 50; leaders of, 38; Stage I demands, 39–41; eastern and central districts in, 41, 42; ideology of struggle, 42, 43; Stage I results, 42, 44; Stage II demands, 44, 45; movement to convert rice tickets into rice, 45; new targets of attack, 45, 46; Shimpūken's account of final battle, 47, 48; samurai use of guns and cannon in, 48; Shimpūken's last lines on, 50; compared with Kaisei rising, 189–93. *See also* "Shimpūken Chikuo"

Sasaki Junnosuke, 147, 187, 188, 252*n* 55

Satsuma and Chōshū fiefs, 150

Scheiner, Irwin, xiv

Scott, James C., xxxv, 69

Seclusion policy: and Deshima, xxvi, xxvii, 127, 151

"Selfishness of small holders," 130

Semiproletariat: xxxviii, 149; and relief warehouses, 131; in follower capacity, 162; problem of, 188; defined, 189; in Ueda, 198

Sengoku Masaaki (daimyo), 59

Separation of soldiers and peasants (*heinō bunri*), xxvii

Serfs: emancipation of, 148, 163. *See* Russian peasants

Servant services, 91

Servility and manipulation, dialectic of, 81, 94, 123

Shakamuni, 98

Shanin, Teodor, 165
Shimabara revolt, 7, 141
Shimo Yoshida village (Chichibu), 213. See Chichibu incident
"Shimpūken Chikuo," 32, 36
Shingon and Zen temples celebrate mass, 50
Shinsaku (tenant): deposition of, 188
Shinshū risings, 149; causes of, 194–96; new demands in, 209; significance of, 224
Shinshū (Shinano) province, 57
Shintō deities, 142
Shōdo Island disrupted, 182
Shogun, xxvi, 170
Shugendō exorcists and religious reciters as riot leaders, 112
Shūso. See Legal petition for mercy
Signal fires and messengers in Ueda, 76. See Ueda Hōreki rising
Silk thread exports, 195
Smith, Thomas C., xiv
Social hierarchy, imagined reversal of, 139
Sōdō. See Unrest and disturbance
Sōdō jikki, 81, 93, 99, 101
Solidarity bands: and "holy water," 7; and ikki, 143, 200, 212
Spies, 47, 48
Starosta, 165, 166
State-village relationship, xxx–xxxiii
Status, xv; definition of, xvii; introduced in Tsuyama fief, 5–6; forged into weapon, 8; and peasant beliefs, 133; and division of labor, 140; breakdown of, 175; and hinindomo, 218; as instrument of class domination, 218; as ideology, 219
Status consciousness, 112, 218
Status discrimination, xxvii, xxviii, 5, 103
Subsistence right of poor people, 146
Sugi Hitoshi (historian), 153
Sumptuary regulations, 128, 130
Suppression of armed protests: and family intimidation, 43; and U.S. in Vietnam, 43. See Punishment
Susaka fief rising (1870), 196, 206–09; peasants demand indemnity payments, 206
Suzuki Sukenoshin (Lord Tadayori's adviser), 71, 83
Sword hunting, xxvii, 5
Symbolic actions: food metaphors, 81, 90; reversal of dominant teachings, 139

Taiheiki, 32, 36
Takano Hiroma (Matsushiro deputy councillor): changes price of tribute rice, 203
Tama river (Tama district), 153
Tanuma Okitsugu, 110–13, 119, 121, 220

Tashiro Eisuke, Chichibu peasant leader, 213, 214
Taxation in Ueda under Tokugawa peace, 68, 69
Tax reduction: peasant demands for, 68. See also Tribute
Temple bells, ringing of, 116, 122
Tenancy, tenant labor: as debt bondage, xxxviii; increase of, 111, 126, 152; and relief warehouses, 131; in Shinshū, 195; in Ueda, 197, 198
Tenant rent, 151; as "tribute," 185; and return of forfeited land, 188
Tenma disturbance (1764–65), 140–42; shifting of targets in, 141
Tenmei era: famine deaths, 111; urban riots and ikki in, 111, 112; political purges in, 123, 220
Tenpō era: famine and class struggle, 154; characteristics of ikki in, 155; reforms in, 159, 160
Tenryō, xxvi, 25
Terao Gorō (historian), 157
Thought control and depoliticalization, 138
Time as cyclical vs. dynamic change, 145
Tokuemon ("Amano Tokisada"), 36; recounts a rumor, 46; execution of, 48–50; last words of, 49, 50; equated with Kusunoki Masashige, 51; as gimin figure, 51, 54
Tokugawa: meaning of "peace," xxx; semantics of protest in, xxxviii; villages, 109; peasant culture in, 142, 143; class struggle tradition in, 146; monetary system abolished, 195
Tokugawa Ieyasu, xxvi, 6, 114
"Tools of house-smashing," 169
Torture of Hanbei and Asanojō, 94, 95
Totman, Conrad, 27
Town-countryside conflict in Ueda, 65, 66, 197
Town peasants, 86, 244n 35
Townsmen's demands in Ueda, 85, 86, 87. See also Ueda Hōreki rising
Toyama Shigeki, 241n 11
Toyotomi Hideyoshi, xxiii, xxvi
Trade: foreign merchants barred from interior, 160; "free trade," 160, 194, 223; multiple impact of on Japan, 161; as "internal" factor, 161; freedom of trade, 220
Traditional currency system, 249n 1
Trans-fief risings, 3; first countrywide wave of, 220
Tribute, rice tribute (nengu): definition of, xvii, xviii, xxix, 13; in Tsuyama, 20–25, 53; removal from district, 44; transport

costs, 69; levied on forest lands within temples, 93; in Fukuyama, 122; system reorganized, 221

Trimetallic currency system, 151

Tsar as deliverer and protector, 164

Tsarist land reform, consequences of, 163

Tsarist state vs. bakuhan state, 163

Tsuda Shigemichi and "upland products association," 24

Tsuyama and Ueda risings, comparison of, 97, 98

Tsuyama fief: geography, 3; rural class hierarchy, 4; cadastral survey and resurvey, 5, 8; administrative regions, districts, and officials, 6; economic development, 8; Mori support for full-status cultivators in, 9, 10; mountain forests and iron mining, 11; transfer of government to bakufu intendants, 12, 13, 14; tribute rates, 13, 14, 20–22; reduced jurisdiction of, 15; first peasant protest in, 15, 18, 19; iron mining as off-season employment in, 23; political crisis, 28, 29; rumors of confiscation in, 33; peasant suppression strategy, 47; Kyōhō reforms, 51; power weakened by bakufu, 52; reforms of 1860s, 175, 176; grain inspection system, 176; castle town in 1866, 179

Tsuyama rising: hierarchy of causes, 216–17. See Sanchū rising

Tutelary shrine as meeting place, 188

Uchikowashi: reflects changes in Tokugawa economy, xix, xx, 81, 104, 169, 198, 199. See also House-smashing; Razobran

Ueda and Tsuyama risings, comparison of, 97, 98

Ueda artisans, 66

Ueda castle town: population of, 79, 243n 16; disrupted by peasants, 84; use of commercial licenses, 85; absorption of villages and later decline, 85, 86; peasant representatives at, 87

Ueda fief: geography and origins, 57, 58; financial problems, 59; origin of village headmen in, 60; district tribute officers and district headmen, 62, 63; agricultural production and wholesale merchants, 65; legal struggles of 1750s, 66, 67; peasant struggles against rural officials, 82; avoidance of force, 89; fear of shogunal confiscation, 90; final concessions to peasants, 91; use of shogunal authority, 92; weaknesses of peasant movement in, 103; reliance on forced loans, 104; alliance with merchant capital, 104; sale of samurai

ranks, 105; silk thread manufacture in, 105, 197; tribute officers brought closer to castle in, 106

Ueda Hōreki rising (1761–63): causes, 70, 218; as protracted class struggle, 71; leaders of, 73, 76; role of outcasts, 75; stages, 75; mass appeal at castle gate, 76; peasant demands analyzed, 78, 79; targets of attack, 81; Ubugawa meeting, 81; Phase II, 81, 82; firing of rural officials, 83, 84; Matsudaira family, 84; fief rebuke of peasants, 89; Phase III, 89–92; peasant punishment of officials, 90; Matsudaira retainers' dilemma, 89, 90, 91; absence of revolutionary sentiment in, 92; carpenters', coopers', and outcasts' protest, 93; peasant leaders jailed, 93; priests' petition for mercy, 95; significance, 59, 218, 219; documents on, 239n 1

Uedajima kuzuregōshi, nature of, 293n 1

Ueda sōdō jikki, xxxvii, 239n 1

Ueda town officials, 243n 30

Ueda town peasants (machi byakushō), 86

Ueda townsmen protest loss of rural markets, 86

Ueda village headmen, divisions among, 70

Ueda yonaoshi rising of 1869: mobilization procedure, 198; targets of attack, 199; breakdown of discipline, 199; compared with Ueda Hōreki rising, 199, 200

Unequal treaties, 160, 161, 222, 223

Unregistered, homeless people: increase in numbers, 191. See Poor people; Poverty

Unrest and disturbance, xix, xxi, xxii

Upland products associations in Tsuyama, 23, 24

Urano district (Ueda), 198, 200

Urban "rice riots": as main form of urban disturbance from 1760s onward, 219

Vietnam: U.S. in, 43; revolts in, 190

Village associations: four types of, xxxi, xxxii; imposed and autonomous, xxxii, 221; Japanese and Russian compared, 166

Village autonomy issue: modern historians' myth, xxviii; 231n 20, 232n 30

Village community: as tool of state, xxv; as basis of landholding right, 146

Village couriers, 15

Violence: gōso, xix, 101; increasing level of, xxxiv; sparked by minor incident, 81

Wang Yang-ming (Ōyōmei), 155, 159

Wariban, 62, 63

World capitalist market system, 161; and Japan's integration into, 195

Yamadaya Daisuke: leads rising, 158
Yamagata Daini (loyalist scholar), 138
Yazawa Yorisada (Sanada retainer), 62
Yokohama, raw silk shipped through, 168
Yokoyama Toshio, xv, xx, xxiii, 69, 198

Yonaoshi: and yonaori, 144; meaning, 144–45; limitations of rhetoric, 147; "yonaoshi warfare" and Chichibu, 212; and yonarashi, 220
Yoshimune, Shogun, 25, 110, 127
Yoshiwara in Edo, 66
Yukishige village (Tsuyama), 177, 179

Zenkōji town, 204, 208